CONSTITUTIONAL
LAW *for the*
CRIMINAL JUSTICE
PROFESSIONAL

CONSTITUTIONAL LAW *for the* CRIMINAL JUSTICE PROFESSIONAL

Carl J. Franklin

CRC Press
Boca Raton   London   New York   Washington, D.C.

Contact Editor:	Becky McEldowney
Project Editor:	Christine Andreasen
Marketing Managers:	Barbara Glunn, Jane Lewis, Arline Massey, Jane Stark
Cover Design:	Dawn Boyd

Library of Congress Cataloging-in-Publication Data

Franklin, Carl J.
    Constitutional law for the criminal justice professional / by Carl
J. Franklin.
        p. cm.
    Includes index.
    ISBN 0-8493-1155-1 (alk. paper)
    1. Criminal justice, Administration of--United States.
2. Constitutional law--United States. 3. Criminal justice
personnel--United States--Handbooks, manuals, etc. I. Title.
KF390.P65F73   1999
342.73--dc21
                         98-51554
                           CIP

No claim to original U.S. Government works
International Standard Book Number 0-8493-1155-1
Library of Congress Card Number 98-51554
Printed in the United States of America 1 2 3 4 5 6 7 8 9 0
Printed on acid-free paper

Preface

The criminal justice system, like the society it serves, is more diverse today than at any other time in our country's history. Along with that diversity has come a continuing need to monitor and adjust the rules guiding the justice system and those who participate in it. The issues which arise under the Constitution are often the most divisive and far reaching of all legal questions that arise in the criminal justice system. With the stroke of a pen a single court consisting of only nine Justices can change the way an entire profession — in fact an entire society — treats a person accused of a criminal act.

The most dramatic changes in the system have occurred in the last 40 years. The great pendulum of social justice has swung from one extreme to the other in that time. The powers of the police have expanded and contracted with ever-changing rules of procedure adopted under the auspices of the constitutional amendments. New procedural requirements establish protocol for arrest and detention one year and then are attacked as overly restrictive the next. Keeping up with these changes is imperative if our law enforcement professionals are to be an effective deterrent against crime.

Written for the criminal justice professional, this book is a study of the most dramatic and significant areas in constitutional law. It is designed to be both an educational and reference tool providing a single source of information for professionals at all levels of the system. The concise commentary focuses on the precise issues that most affect today's criminal justice professional. As we move ahead in the twenty-first century it is important for those working in the criminal justice professions to understand and properly apply the fundamental principles of our Constitution.

About the Author

Carl J. Franklin is director of the Administration of Justice Department at Cloud County Community College, Concordia, Kansas. He holds a certificate in Police Science from Oklahoma State University, a Bachelor of Arts degree in Law Enforcement Administration from the University of Oklahoma, and a Juris Doctor degree from the University of Oklahoma College of Law. He also has completed advanced graduate study in criminology and criminal justice administration.

Active in criminal justice since the mid-1970s, Dr. Franklin has worked as a police dispatcher, police officer, detective, field supervisor, prosecutor, and professor. He has more than ten years experience as a police officer, and has worked for the University of Oklahoma Police Department (Norman), the Norman (Oklahoma) Police Department, and the Oklahoma City Police Department.

Dr. Franklin has written extensively on police procedure, constitutional law, police civil liability, and public administration. The author of two other books, he is a frequent contributor to several national journals on law and police procedure. His writing has received national recognition from the Nathan Burkan Writing Competition, the *Computer Law Journal,* and the American Society of Composers, Authors and Publishers.

Dr. Franklin is past recipient of the Presidential Award of Honor from the Oklahoma Reserve Law Officers Association and the Governor's Award for Academic Excellence.

Dedication

———————

for my parents

*To my father, who gave to me a love
of reading and a desire for knowledge.
The smartest man I know.
To my mother, for her belief and support.
When I said I can do it,
she said, "Yes, you can."*

Contents

Section Three: First Amendment — Religion and Expression

Section Four: Fourth Amendment — Search and Seizure

Chapter 14   Electronic Surveillance under the Fourth Amendment

Chapter 15   Enforcing the Fourth Amendment

Section Five: Fifth Amendment — Rights of Persons

Chapter 16   Indictment by Grand Jury

Chapter 17   Double Jeopardy

Chapter 18   Self-Incrimination

Chapter 19 Self-Incrimination:
From Voluntariness Standard to *Miranda*

Chapter 20 Due Process under the Fifth Amendment

Section Six: Sixth Amendment —
Rights of Accused in Criminal Prosecutions

Chapter 21 Speedy Public Trial

Chapter 22 Right to Trial by Impartial Jury

Chapter 23 Right of Notification and Confrontation

Section Seven: Eighth Amendment — Further Guarantees in Criminal Cases

Section Eight: Fourteenth Amendment —
Due Process and Equal Protection

Section One

Introduction to Constitutional Law

1 Why is the Constitution So Important?

I. FOUNDATIONS OF THE TERM "CONSTITUTION"

In today's society, we know the Constitution mandates certain conduct for police officers and criminal justice professionals. It is well established that the Constitution is the Supreme Law of the land, and no other statutory provision or court decision can exceed the power of the Constitution. What few of us stop to think about, however, is just why the Constitution is so important to our society and why it works so well.

To understand the Constitution and its application to a modern society, we must first understand the basics of government and society. From a historical standpoint, there have been governments for as long as there has been a known history. In fact, anthropologists have shown that men lived together in small groups long before recorded history. The earliest forms of government, i.e., the control of individual actions to fill a societal need, presumably developed even before the development of writing.

As our social groups expanded and interaction between groups became more common the complications of governance began to emerge. An evolving society meant that the means of governing must evolve as well. In many respects, the two go hand in hand, and without one you are not likely to have the other. Development of what we know as a constitution was far off, but early history indicates the concept was not unknown.

In its simplest form, the nature of any constitution serves two purposes. First, a constitution establishes a form of government and, where appropriate, dictates the means for change to that government. Second, a constitution sets forth specific rights that are extended to members of the society. This is true in the case of the U.S. Constitution. In the first part of the Constitution, the Articles, we see the establishment of the basic forms of government as well as provisions for operation and change. In the later sections of the document, the Amendments, we see the principles upon which our citizens retain rights against their government.

II. DEVELOPMENT OF THE TERM

In Roman and medieval times the word *constitutio*, of which "constitution" is a transliteration, referred to enactments, decrees, or regulations of a ruler or sovereign. In this sense, the word fits a broader definition in describing government mandates.

In Latin, *constituere* means "to cause to stand" or "to fix, set, or make" a thing. Historians suggest that the term was used to describe the acts of the Roman emperor and implied the idea of limited government insofar as they collectively defined the scope of state action. Rome was a republic controlled not solely by an emperor — although during various historical times the emperor held more power than at others — but also governed, in part, by a legislative body commonly known as the Senate.

Subsequently, "constitution" was superseded by the term "statute" as a means of referring to government edicts or laws. In this early sense, "constitution" was used synonymously with the terms "statute," "law," and "mandate" in the sense that constitution provided rules of action for the community.

In the seventeenth century, the word constitution entered political discourse as a term describing the structure of the federation or empire or the arrangement of governmental institutions. Although the term did not have the same meaning we commonly apply to it today, it did establish a representation of government somewhat analogous to the constitution of the human body — the term was used to describe the makeup and physical nature of the body politic.

By the late eighteenth century the term constitution was proposed as a translation of the Greek word *politeia*. This term was usually translated as "government," "regime," or "policy," and the expansion of the term signified a significant change in the way the term was applied. Where the word once was used in a general sense to describe all actions of the government, much like we use "statute" today, "constitution" began to change and to develop specific meaning throughout the eighteenth and nineteenth centuries.

Even the science of political study, today commonly known as political science, which derives from the work of Aristotle, did not require use of the word constitution. In fact, the word did not fully develop until its application in the unique new American form of government.

III. THE CONSTITUTION AS A PARADIGM

A form of American constitutionalism began in the seventeenth century as voluntary associations of settlers founded colonies under royal charters. The colonists wrote and adopted covenants, compacts, combinations, ordinances, and other instruments of mutual consent as the basis of local government. Through these documentary agreements settlers constituted themselves as a political community, defined their purposes, affirmed the principles of a way of life, specified the rights of citizens, and organized governmental institutions.

The imperial conflicts of the mid-eighteenth century provided Americans with a new understanding of what the constitution of a free state was and how it functioned to guarantee liberty. They rejected the idea that a constitution described the governmental order of the commonwealth. American critics of English policy argued that a constitution was a deliberately framed agreement among the people that imposed effective limits on government in order to protect community and individual liberty. If Parliament was a component of the English constitution and could change the fundamental law by its enactments, they concluded, then England did not have a real constitution. The important distinction was that, although a constitution conferred power, it was not the simple equivalent of a mandate to legislate or govern.

During the American Revolution, Americans wrote constitutions of liberty, the distinctive feature of which was their legal superiority to legislative enactments and other sources of ordinary law. In theory the individual constitutions were supreme to other state law, but in practice they rarely were applied in that manner. Over time, the constitutions, and specifically our federal Constitution, took on greater authority when popularly elected conventions wrote them and the people ratified them.

From the standpoint of a political mechanism, our Constitution holds three important principles. First, the Constitution establishes the basic principles of our government itself; that is, the Constitution creates a supreme federal government with precisely mandated and separate units of government. As we will see in the coming chapters, without these provisions there is little doubt that the new country would have splintered into at least 13 separate, not-so-powerful countries. Even today, there are those who maintain that without a constitution our country would simply fall apart.

Second, the Constitution establishes clear rights for the citizens. The rights, contained mostly in the first eight amendments, are supreme to any law created by Congress or any of the state legislatures. These immutable rights guarantee us, as citizens of a national body, fair treatment no matter where in the country we are. Although application of these principles is not always as consistent as might be expected, it is the Constitution that allows us to correct these mistakes when they do occur.

Third, the Constitution provides for us a means of change and evolution. It is true that we have a living constitution in the broadest sense of use. The Constitution itself provides for a means of change through action of the people and through interpretation of the Constitution by the judicial branch of the government. This ability, often seen as a part of the ever-important system of checks and balances, guarantees that we can adapt our Constitution to meet the needs of our society.

2 A Brief History of the U.S. Constitution

This introductory chapter details the struggle of the Founding Fathers to lay the groundwork for a great nation. The issues facing the country following the Revolutionary War were not much different from those we face today. By studying the history of the Constitution one becomes increasingly aware of the protections the document offers and the reasons these protections are so important in securing continued evolution of this country.

I. THE IDEA OF A CONSTITUTION

A. THE ENGLISH CHARTERS

> You give me credit to which I have no claim, in calling me 'the writer of the Constitution of the United States'...[i]t ought to be regarded as the work of many heads and many hands.

When James Madison wrote these words to a friend in 1834, he firmly admitted that many of the ideals brought forth in our Constitution were not new. As those who study history know, the concepts of liberty, democracy, and representative government can be traced back thousands of years to principles from across the globe. Representative forms of government evolved in the Middle East, Greece, China, and Africa at different times in history. In fact, the concept of a Bill of Rights was not even new in 1787 America. Many of the new states, former colonies of Britain, already had a constitution and possessed a Bill of Rights not unlike that found in the U.S. Constitution.

While representative forms of government evolved over the centuries throughout the world the roots of American freedom are most frequently traced to the history of England. From a constitutional perspective this requires an examination of English common law history beginning with the *Magna Carta* and its progeny. In the Magna Carta we see a written organic instrument exacted from a sovereign ruler by the bulk of the politically articulate community. For the first time, a group within the established system moved outside the system to create a binding set of rules for the ruler.

Much like our own Constitution, the Magna Carta was an instrument brought about by economic and political need. While historians provide different justifications for the reasons each side had in agreeing to the contents of the Magna Carta, the simple fact remains that the document resulted, in large part, from unrest among the subjects of the kingdom. In short, as England entered the second decade of the thirteenth century, political, social, and economic unrest created an environment where a king was forced by his subjects to surrender some of the sovereign power. These acts were the foundation of the stage upon which later American Revolution and a new constitution could be played out.

Two important concepts were taken from the Magna Carta to form our modern constitutional government. Chief among these is the requirement that a representative government include a legislative body. The British Parliament rose from the foundations of the Magna Carta and blazed a path for the later development of the American Congress.

Also of importance, from a constitutional standpoint, is the focus on individual liberty found in the Magna Carta. In particular, the federal Bill of Rights was based directly upon the great charters of English liberty, which began with the Magna Carta. Without these English developments, it is doubtful that the American colonists would have acted as they did in creating the new Constitution.

The Magna Carta represented a substantial change in English government. It moved the English society, primarily the barons and noblemen of the time, into a position of power never before held in English common law history. Yet, the Magna Carta, as an individual document, is not enough to explain the development of our own Constitution. To better understand the ideals that formed the early constitutional theories one must look at the other great English charters.

The second great charter of English liberty came in 1628 through the *Petition of Right*. While the Magna Carta is often considered an antecedent of the Constitution of the United States, the Petition of Right is often considered a predecessor of our Bill of Rights. One reason for this is the role that Sir Edward Coke, a primary force in the creation of the Petition of Right, played in the lives and studies of later American patriots. Patrick Henry, John Adams, and James Otis — to name a few — all studied Coke's writings and law career.

As a writer and judge, Coke tailored a doctrinal foundation for the constitutional movement of eighteenth-century America. His career was characterized by opposition to efforts by the Crown to place itself above the law. As one of the highest judges of the realm he used his judicial rulings to thwart the Crown's efforts to stand above the law. A common perception held by Coke was that all men were equal within the law, and many of his decisions from the bench reflected this philosophy.

Coke's actions from the bench were not well received by the monarchy. At times he was viewed as a traitor and as directly defiant to the crown. His work eventually led to his discharge as judge in 1616, and, at the age of 65, he appeared to be at the end of his public career.

In 1620 Coke's efforts were revived when he was elected to the House of Commons, a position made available by the creation of Parliament following adoption of the Magna Carta. In Parliament, Coke naturally gravitated toward the growing opposition to the Crown. His influence grew within Parliament, and he soon took a leadership role. As friction between the Crown and Parliament increased, Coke assumed a leading role in driving the conflict along legal lines; to this end his time on the bench served him well.

Some of the driving forces leading to the Petition of Right included the dismissal of the sitting Parliament and instillation of a new legislative body. Following Charles I's accession to the throne in 1625, the Stuart theory of monarchial prerogative was expanded. Attacks against personal liberty included a forced loan upon the free men of the realm, for which the Crown demanded repayment. Anyone who refused to pay was punished, and judges who refused to enforce the loan were dismissed from their positions.

Soldiers were also billeted with the people, forcing some to make room by moving out relatives or moving children into smaller quarters. The Petition of Right addressed such issues, and as we know from later American history similar complaints arose within the colonies. Such complaints led to specific provisions within our own Bill of Rights, such as the restrictions on housing of soldiers in private homes and the taking of property without just compensation.

Some of the worst infringements came when men were sent to prison by the command of the King and without bail or right of due process. The Petition of Right sought to limit such power over the English citizen, and again we see similar provisions in our own Constitution.

The Magna Carta and Petition of Right are certainly the two leading charters that influenced the Constitution and the Bill of Rights, but they were not the only English influences. Others include the *Agreement of the People* (1649), *A Healing Question* (1656) by Sir Henry Vane, and the English Bill of Rights (1689). The latter, also considered the third great charter of English liberty, has obvious influences on our own Bill of Rights.

By the late seventeenth century many English rights and liberties were being expanded to the English colonies. The colonists relied upon the tradition of English law as they developed their own grievances with the Crown. As we will see in coming sections, many of the concepts established in the great English charters were used in developing later colonial charters.

B. THE COLONIAL CHARTERS

Tracing the roots of our Constitution to the early developments in English liberty is only part of the story. Much of the work in laying a foundation for the Constitution was also done in the colonies. The British colonists embraced the strong tradition of individual liberties just as their ancestors before them had done.

As early as 1606 in the *First Charter of Virginia* we see the move toward protected liberty among the colonists. Although written more than a century before the American Revolution, the principles espoused in the early colonial charters would ultimately contribute to the Revolution itself. Of note is the fundamental principle that the colonists take with them all the rights and liberties of Englishmen.

As the First Charter of Virginia announced, the colonists are to "Have and enjoy all Liberties, Franchises, and Immunities…, to all Intents and Purposes, as if they had been abiding and born, within this our Realm of England." In this language we see the desire of the earliest colonists to protect the liberties they enjoy so that future generations born on American soil may enjoy them as well.

As the colonies were established in the New World many liberties and guarantees were sought from the Crown. Chief among the various charters granted to the colonies was the right of self-governance (in a limited fashion) through elected legislatures. Examples of this can be found in the *Charter of Massachusetts Bay*

(1629) and the *Charter of Maryland* (1632). Such charters created the second and third self-governing assemblies in the colonies, and set the pattern that prevailed until the Revolution itself.

Having established their claim to the rights of Englishmen the colonists next set about giving those rights specific content. They did this through legislative and related action by enacting statutes that sought to define the basic rights to which the colonists were entitled. These statutes were the direct American ancestors of the federal Bill of Rights. The more famous of these statutes were the *Massachusetts Body of Liberties* (1641) and the *Maryland Act for the Liberties of the People* (1639).

Other acts by the colonists sought further protection of liberties. Chief among these were the *Maryland Act Concerning Religion* (1649), the *Concessions and Agreements of West New Jersey* (1677), the *Pennsylvania Frame of Government* (1682), and the *New York Charter of Libertyes and Priviledges* (1701). Each of these documents, in its own way, established a claim to liberties and rights for the colonists. These documents built upon the earliest foundations for the protection of these liberties, and in their own way contributed to the later development of a national constitution.

II. AMERICANS AND THE REVOLUTION

Between 1754 and 1763 Great Britain and the American colonies fought against the French, and later the Spaniards, in a war commonly referred to as "The French and Indian War." Following the war Britain was left as sole holder of claims to all land east of the Mississippi River, outside of New Orleans, and from Canada to Florida. France maintained hold over lands in Canada, New Orleans, and the upper Mississippi valley. Spain retained lands in the west and southwestern part of the country.

Initially, the colonists found themselves firmly in a system based on strong traditions in law rather than monarchial tradition. Lord Coke and other early English leaders lay the foundation for an empire where all men, at least those who were white and landowners, were equal. This change in political and legal culture meant that for the colonists the promise following the war with France and Spain was full of hope.

The colonies quickly set about forming themselves into strong, independent states. The instrumentality of lawmaking and enforcement within the colonies were similar to those in England, and the colonial assemblies consciously adopted, as far as practical, the forms and procedures of the House of Commons and other British lawmaking institutions.

Not only were the inhabitants of the Empire bound together by similar, if not identical, systems of law and institutions of government, but the religious, ethical, intellectual, and social conceptions of the mother country were still largely those of the English-speaking colonials. The British people of both the Old and New World were by and large not only literate but also eager readers of weekly newspapers and pamphlets concerned with contemporary world developments. Likewise, Britons on both sides of the Atlantic studied the works of British theologians, philosophers, scientists, essayists, poets, novelists, and dramatists.

Social style and culture were also similar in the colonies and England. Fashion, architecture, home furnishing, and even etiquette remained substantially the same despite separation by a vast ocean. English practices exerted profound influence on the American colonies. While these commonalties produced a great degree of homogeneity within the Empire, there were, nevertheless, divergences that are equally important.

The colonies had one thing that England did not have: frontiers. Parts of the colonies remained wilderness and required hardy individualists to live there. Even along the settled Atlantic seaboard, where conditions of living were far less primitive, there were deviations from the refined institutions of England. Soon many colonists reveled in their pioneer outlook and spirit. Conformity to tradition began to lose its luster.

After 1763 the colonies grew more prosperous. Abundant natural resources and a growing population allowed the individual colonies to grow rapidly. Soon the population of the 13 colonies grew to around 2 million, including whites and blacks, and the frontiers began to expand westward. This growth, however, led to many internal problems, such as the ability to finance the local governments. Self-governance also became an important concern for the colonists.

In March of 1764 a series of resolutions providing for the raising of revenue in the colonies was presented to the British House of Commons. The fifteenth resolution called for the levying of "stamp duties." Although the measure was defeated, it was seen as a clear attempt to raise funds from the colonies for the purpose of supporting British troops kept there.

Such action by Parliament raised the issue of taxation without representation. In other words, the colonies were being asked to contribute through stamp taxation but were at the same time being denied a representative voice in the same body that was raising the tax. These concerns were not allayed, and by 1765 Parliament successfully imposed such taxation with the passage of the now infamous Stamp Act.

The British Stamp Act of 1765 greatly contributed to the colonial uprising, but it was not the only cause. In 1759 the Privy Council disallowed a Virginia legislative act and ordered the governor of the colony not to sign any bill passed by the legislature which had not been approved by the council. This infringement on the right of self-governance, along with similar acts, went a long way in arousing colonial dissatisfaction.

Another chief contributor to the Revolution was the general writ of assistance which empowered officers of the English customs service to break into and search colonial homes for alleged smuggled goods. The writs, issued without cause and upon no formal presentation of proof, allowed virtually unlimited rights of search and seizure against any home or business. Once issued, the writ remained in force throughout the lifetime of the sovereign and for six months thereafter. A writ, once issued, could be used almost unimpeded to search, without cause, one's home, business, or other property, and such authority lasted as long as the king remained alive.

Even more serious and far-reaching was the passage by Parliament, in April 1764, of the American Act of 1764. This act imposed new restrictions on colonial trade and levied new taxes in the colonies to support an enlarged British army in the colonies. To top it off, the colonists were not consulted about such action, and none of the former colonial officers who had served in the battle with France a few years earlier were even considered for the expanded positions. Colonists argued that it was unreasonable not to give them a share in determining the number, distribution, and kind of troops needed for their own protection.

Within the colonies a growing number of leaders found themselves in conflict with British policy and practice. Infringement on individual liberties had grown along with increased taxation. A failure of the British government to recognize the complaints of the colonies added to the problem, and soon many colonists found themselves opposed to continued British rule.

By the summer of 1776 a boiling point had been reached. The colonies joined together in their fight against the mother country. Independence was declared when attempts to redress grievances failed. The once independent colonies joined together in battle and the Revolutionary War began. By the time Lord Cornwallis surrendered at Yorktown in 1781, a new nation would be formed, and with it a need for a new government.

III. THE NEW GOVERNMENT

A. THE ARTICLES OF CONFEDERATION

At the time of the Revolution a form of federal government was created to manage the affairs of the newly joined 13 colonies. The Confederation Congress held its last session in 1781 and handed over the government of the 13 colonies to the new national government of the 13 states. The document that held the new country together was the Articles of Confederation.

From the beginning, the Articles of Confederation were doomed to failure if the new country was to have a strong central government, because many pre-Revolution leaders denied the need for an authority above the individual state legislatures. For many, the idea of "state sovereignty" was the key to the attainment of the goals of the Revolution. Since the primary motivators for the Revolution were self-governance, taxation only with representation, and increased economic opportunity, it was often argued that the only way to attain those goals was through individual state sovereignty.

Although many agreed, it was clear that at least a moderate national government was needed to meet certain requirements of the new nation. It was a given that the 13 colonies, and the new states that formed soon after the war, would need to band together for military strength and to prevent other nations from stepping in. However, the new federal government was decentralized and subservient to state rights, which often meant that the federal government had little, if any, power to manage the affairs of the new nation.

The Articles of Confederation placed few restraints upon the states. The controls that were in place tended to be of little consequence or required such qualifications that they were virtually ineffectual. There was no provision for a centralized government, no opportunity for veto of a state law (even when such law was contrary to the national welfare), and no power to enact uniform legislation. Similarly, the document contained no provision for the use of arms to subdue rebellious social groups within the states.

The Articles of Confederation established a new government, but it was one without much power. Even holding office within the new government was different from what we have today. Under the Articles of Confederation no one could be a member of Congress for more than three out of any six years. No one could be President of Congress for more than one year out of any three, ensuring no individual would be likely to acquire much power or prestige within the new government.

Such constraints were developed specifically to avoid giving power to a central government. The colonists had just won their independence from one strong central government and they were not ready to trade their new self-governance for the old way. To many in the new country the way to ensure a weak central government was to design it as such from the beginning. Few, however, would foresee the problems that such an act would have on the new country.

B. THE POST-WAR REBELLIONS

The problems of the new nation actually started before independence was won. In 1778 Alexander Hamilton, then a staff officer with General George Washington's army, expressed the widespread dissatisfaction with the new continental government. Hamilton complained that the delegates being sent to the new Congress were inferior men, and, as a result, "Congress is feeble, indecisive, and improvident." Others fighting in the Continental Army shared his frustration.

Complaints and dissatisfaction did not end with the war. The loosely organized central government faced a serious financial crisis. Continental banknotes — some issued using British denominations and others using the Spanish dollar — were received with varying degrees of contempt. For example, a Spanish dollar was considered to be worth eight shillings in New York, seven shillings in Pennsylvania, and only six shillings in upper New England. The same note, however, was worth an astounding 32 shillings in South Carolina. With such disparities, it was not long before most U.S. continental currency was virtually worthless, and the problems did not end there.

The national government had been formed under a loose set of rules and was designed to give power necessary to wage an effective campaign against Britain. With the war over, popular confidence in Congress waned, and the national government lost what little power it ever had to raise funds to pay its huge debts. Worthless paper money flooded the country, inflation spiraled upward, and the pitiful national government had little power to halt the plummeting economy.

Local governments heaped fuel on the fire by ordering stiff jail sentences for debtors. Farmers and merchants who had extended credit to the new government and its army now faced imprisonment and loss of their lands when they failed to pay their own debts. With little recourse against a government they had once trusted, many small farmers and businessmen lost all they had when the government failed to pay its own debt.

In order to raise needed funds for government operations some of the individual states began to impose import and export duties on farm products. New York aroused the anger of New Jersey and Connecticut when it passed such legislation. Pennsylvania added to the problem when it imposed stiff duties on imports from New Jersey that passed through the port of Philadelphia, a major trade route at that time.

In Pennsylvania and New Hampshire riots broke out in isolated areas. Lack of strong leadership among the groups prevented the outbreaks from spreading to the major cities, but this was not true across all the new states.

Expressions of discontent soon passed from mere strong words between state houses to violence. Massachusetts was a hotbed for violent rebellion, much as it was during the Revolution itself. Several armed bands of dissenters gathered in and around Concord, Cambridge, and Springfield. The groups threatened insurrection against both the state and federal authorities.

In the summer of 1786 an organized mob, led by Job Shattuck, gathered on the village green of Concord, Massachusetts. For several days the mob caroused through the central district of the town, while a Massachusetts militia troop gathered in Cambridge. The militia set out to disperse the angry mob and, upon its arrival in Concord many, including Shattuck, fled. Shattuck and a small group were trapped in the woods outside Groton where a fight ensued. Shattuck, among others, was injured in the battle.

Similar groups arose in other areas. In West Springfield a young rebel by the name of Luke Day gathered together a mob and began drilling in the town square. Day, who had been a brevet major in the Continental Army, made fiery speeches between drill sessions. Like many others of the time, Day called upon his fellow citizens to throw out the "rascals" who were running the government.

One of the more famous of the "mobbers" was Daniel Shays, who gathered and drilled a formidable force of about 1,000 men. The rebels' grievances included a poor economy, the imprisonment of small farmers for their debts, and court-ordered land forfeitures. Shays kept his force intact during the fall and winter of 1786 and even threatened to march on Boston.

Without a federally backed militia or army the governor of Massachusetts, James Bowdoin, formed a state militia financed in part by local merchants. At the same time Bowdoin asked the state legislature to hold an emergency session to authorize use of the militia to route out Shays' group. The legislature passed a law that allowed the confiscation of the "lands, goods, and chattels, of anyone who participated in a riotous assembly." The act also called for those convicted to be whipped at the public whipping post and imprisoned for a term of 6–12 months, with additional whippings at intervals during the time of imprisonment.

Shays was not intimidated by the legislation. The group soon took control of a number of courts and prevented them from operating. Local authorities, siding with the rebels, were reluctant to take action against Shays.

Soon Shays and his group gathered near Springfield. Shays had his group spread out to the east along the Boston Post Road, while rebels Luke Day and Eli Parsons each had 400 or 500 men from Berkshire County stationed across the river north of Springfield.

The Massachusetts militia was led by Major General William Shepherd. Initially Shepherd held his men at Springfield, but as events unfolded he soon moved in on the rebels. A confrontation between the rebels and the militia appeared likely to occur near the Post Road, a major route in and out of the Boston area.

There were few uniforms among the motley armies. Even General Shepherd's militia was made up mostly of farmers who had joined straight from their farms. According to reports of the day, the only identification of opposing forces were sprigs of hemlock in the hats of the rebels and strips of white paper worn by the Loyalists. To play it safe, travelers at the time often stuck both of these symbols in their three-cornered hats.

The fighting, known today as Shays' Rebellion, erupted on January 25, 1787, when Shays decided to attack the federal arsenal in Springfield. Tons of military equipment including gunpowder, shot, and several thousand muskets, were housed in the armory. General Shepherd was appalled when he saw the mobbers top the hill to face the militia. When Shepherd directed his gunners to fire a volley over the heads of the rebels, some hesitated, but only for a moment. The rebels were determined to overthrow the arsenal, and they continued the attack.

Shepherd ordered his cannons to fire point blank into the attacking mob. Four men were killed and the rest turned to run. Although he tried to rally his men, Shays found they had no desire to shed their own blood. Shays and the few remaining men who followed him joined with the group led by Eli Parsons, and the two leaders set about devising new strategy.

Government forces eventually overcame the rebellious groups around Springfield, and by January 29, 1787, the rebellion was broken. In a raging snowstorm, the militia covered 30 miles and surprised Shays' remaining mobbers at Petersham. The rebels surrendered without firing a shot. The rebellion was crushed and Shays' army swore allegiance to Massachusetts.

Although Shays' Rebellion was a military defeat, it brought attention to demands of local farmers and focused attention on the debate for change. Many argued that a national military would be more effective in defeating future rebellions. Likewise, supporters of a strong national government argued that such a government could provide better economic control.

This incident was cited by many as justification for abandoning the Articles of Confederation in favor of a stronger national government. One thing was clear, unless something was done to strengthen the national government there was little chance that the new country would remain united.

IV. THE EARLY CONVENTIONS

As Shays' Rebellion makes clear, the economy was a major driving force both before and after the American Revolution. Trade agreements between the states were continuing problems as well. Even George Washington faced financial difficulty following the Revolution.

Washington returned to his plantation, suffering from health problems related to rheumatism and other maladies and deep in debt. His plans to get the plantation operating efficiently so that he could erase the debts incurred during the war were stymied by the various trade agreements between the states. Despite his plans to spend the rest of his days as a country gentleman Washington found himself once again embroiled in public life.

In 1784 James Madison asked his old friend, Washington, to join with him in calling for a trade conference between Maryland and Virginia. Washington's influence increased the possibility of success in opening the Potomac River to free-flowing trade. The limited success of the conference led the delegates to consider broader opportunities for trade and the formation of a more effective federation.

With Washington's help, Madison soon moved to the forefront of the efforts to strengthen federal authority. Madison spoke eloquently at both the Virginia legislature and in public about giving full authority to Congress to regulate interstate commerce as well as foreign trade. Although his proposed legislation was defeated in the Virginia legislature, Madison successfully pushed to a vote a bill calling for a convention of all states to discuss "how far a uniform system in their commercial relations may be necessary to their common interest and their permanent harmony." After heated debate a call went out for a meeting of state delegations to be opened in Annapolis on the first Monday of September 1786.

From the beginning, the Annapolis Convention was mired in controversy. Initially all the states agreed to give Congress authority over commerce, but New York demanded a number of conditions that killed the plan before it could be put into operation. Among its demands, New York insisted that revenue collectors be kept under state control and that duties be paid in state, not federal, currencies.

Other states responded quickly. New Jersey and Connecticut immediately abolished duties to attract trade away from New York. This act did nothing more than heat up the commerce war between the states and drive a larger wedge between the states. By the time of the Annapolis Convention only 9 of 13 states had elected delegates, and on the first morning only a handful of men showed up.

New York sent only two delegates, Pennsylvania sent only one. After several days, only New Jersey, Delaware, and Virginia had complete delegations, and only Abraham Clark of New Jersey arrived with anything close to full authority to act on behalf of his state. Clark, an original signer of the Declaration of Independence, proposed another convention to "effectually provide for the exigencies of the union."

From a practical standpoint the convention at Annapolis did little more than lay a foundation for later work. A handful of men, who had utterly failed to organize a national convention, nevertheless formed a committee to persuade their state legislatures that their cause was so urgent that a second convention was needed. In a resolution and report drawn up by Alexander Hamilton, the time and place were set for Philadelphia on the second Monday in May 1787.

With the Philadelphia Convention more than six months away, the various leaders set to work immediately to make use of the time. The men who had met in Annapolis in 1786 not only worried about their own individual business ventures but also about the future of personal freedom under the new and revolutionary government they had established ten years earlier.

The states had joined together in a time of war under the Articles of Confederation, but they all knew the loosely secured country would not stand as it was. The fledgling U.S. had reached a crucial turning point where men would either advance the principles of self-government or go back in political history to the easy solution of a supreme rule in the form of a monarch. The Philadelphia Convention would prove to be the turning point.

V. THE PHILADELPHIA CONVENTION

A. Preparing for the Convention

James Madison has long been viewed as a major force in the development of our Constitution, and as he approached the Philadelphia Convention he was charged with enthusiasm. Madison convinced his own state, Virginia, to send a distinguished delegation. He also wrote his longtime friend George Washington a letter suggesting that the old General join them to lend credence to the delegation.

Washington was not immediately persuaded. He worried that the Philadelphia Convention would be no more fruitful than the Annapolis Convention. Washington also worried about lending his name to another failure.

Faced with the reality that Virginia's most prominent citizen would not serve as a delegate, Madison turned to a mutual friend, Governor Edmund Randolph. Randolph spoke with Washington, pointing out that it was the duty of all prominent Americans to seek solutions to the country's dilemma, and Washington agreed to attend.

Not surprisingly, after the announcement that Washington would be among the Virginia delegates, other states turned to their leading citizens to participate. By the time of the Philadelphia Convention several states included within their delegations many of their most prominent citizens, many of whom had signed the Declaration of Independence.

An interesting note to the Philadelphia Convention is the fact that the Continental Congress never actually acknowledged Hamilton's call for a convention. Congress did announce, however, that a general meeting of state delegations would be held at the same time and place as the Philadelphia Convention. This meeting, Congressional members stated, would be "for the sole...purpose of revising the Articles of Confederation." In reality, the meeting was an opportunity to gather the best from the new states together for the purpose of finding a better form of government.

B. The Beginning of the Convention

Ten years earlier the State House in Philadelphia had been the location of the signing of the Declaration of Independence, and once again the venerable site would see a historical document created. The cobbled streets still resounded to the clatter of horses' hooves and the rumble of cart and carriage wheels. Along the riverfront, noisy markets did a brisk trade in produce from the surrounding farms. Within view of Independence Hall were livery stables and blacksmith shops, bakeries, butchers, and a whole host of businesses. Although Philadelphia had not changed much since the revolutionary days, the events of the day changed the atmosphere.

Only a dozen delegates had managed to appear by the opening day of the Convention, Monday, May 14, 1787. Travel during this time was often arduous, and many delegates were elderly gentlemen who came by carriage over long distances. While many had not expected the opening day to see a full complement of delegates, those in attendance were dismayed that so few were on hand.

Among the delegates for the first day was the Virginia group, led by George Washington and James Madison. Pennsylvania, the home state of the Convention, naturally had all of its delegates in place. A few from other delegations were also in attendance, but there were not enough for a quorum. The first official business of the Constitutional Convention was to vote on an agreement to reconvene each morning until a quorum was assembled.

Two weeks passed before a quorum could be counted. On Tuesday, May 29, seven states were represented and the convention was ready to start. On that day the men gathered at the State House knew they were about to embark on a monumental task, and they set about their business with vigor.

Of interest to all who study the history of the Convention was the secrecy that was maintained during the Convention. Many felt that anything said within the Convention should stay within the Convention. This way, no man would be afraid to speak his mind freely and without fear of recourse by others. In fact, this idea went so far as to prompt the installation of heavy curtains over all the windows to block out noise from the streets and also prevent prying ears on the outside from hearing the voices of conventioneers. Although an early amendment to the new Constitution provides "freedom of the press," the early Convention went to extreme measures to keep leaks to the local press from occurring.

The various representatives came to the Convention as individual delegates representing their respective states. Each carried with him instructions to protect the interest of his state. Each maintained that interest even as he endeavored to create a stronger central government. As such, it is not surprising that many of the delegates worked within small groups comprised primarily of members from their own delegation.

As he had during the turbulent days leading to the signing of the Declaration of Independence, Dr. Benjamin Franklin took the role of revered senior delegate. Commentators from the Convention noted that he still had a sparkle in his eye and an irrepressible humor, and his wise counsel frequently cooled the volatile tempers that sometimes flared during the long debates of that hot summer.

George Washington also played an important leadership role in creating the new Constitution. One of the tallest men of his time, he towered above the others as a physical symbol of leadership. For many in attendance, Washington's presence alone lent importance to the proceedings.

When on May 29 it was agreed that the seven states represented constituted a quorum, Robert Morris, a wealthy shipping company owner from Pennsylvania, proposed that Washington be appointed President of the Convention. In reality, the nomination was a mere formality since it was a foregone conclusion among the delegates that Washington would preside. The vote to elect Washington as President of the Convention was unanimous.

While Thomas Jefferson had been the author of the first great American document, the Declaration of Independence, James Madison now emerged as the prime mover in the creation of the new Constitution. Madison had insisted upon holding the Convention, and once the formal business began it was his voice and quick pen that were most active in shaping the document.

Madison was only 36 years old when the Constitutional Convention met, yet his knowledge of historic governments, his vision, and keen insight shone as a constant beacon throughout the sessions. While the dignified Washington officially presided over the Convention, it was Madison's enthusiasm and logic that actually led the meetings day after day.

The delegates' first tasks, the election of a presiding officer and adoption of procedural rules, were quickly accomplished, and Edmund Randolph of Virginia was called upon to deliver the opening speech of the Convention. He began by reminding the delegates that the convention was "absolutely necessary in this difficult crisis to prevent America's downfall." He then asked a series of pointed questions designed to focus the delegates immediately on the issues at hand. Randolph's speech also focused the delegates on issues addressed neatly by the plan the Virginia delegates were to propose.

C. THE VIRGINIA PLAN

The Virginians, who had arrived in advance of most other delegations, met frequently in informal caucus and drafted a series of resolutions, largely the work of Madison, which were presented to the Convention on May 29. The Virginia Plan, as the resolutions were called, provided for a division of the central government into three departments: legislative, executive, and judicial. The legislature would be divided into two houses: the lower house, elected by popular vote of the people; and the upper house, elected by the lower house from delegates submitted by the state legislatures.

The Virginia Plan called for election of the executive leaders by the national legislature. The executive was ineligible for a second term, and, from a practical standpoint, the executive was to have much less power than the current executive has today.

The plan also called for the creation of a single Supreme Court with inferior courts as the legislature should deem necessary. The judicial branch was to determine issues of law and equity but not pass on the constitutionality of state laws. That power was reserved for the national legislature.

It was immediately apparent that the Virginia Plan called for sweeping changes to the central government. The changes in the structure and character of the federal government were so dramatic that they could scarcely be regarded as mere amendments to the Articles of Confederation. This is interesting since it appears the initial plan was merely to amend the Articles. Had the delegates stuck to this proposal, there is little doubt that the Constitution we know today would not have been created. The great historical importance of the Virginia Plan lies in the fact that the Constitution in its final form evolved from it, after many changes.

D. THE PINCKNEY PLAN

On May 29 Charles Pinckney of South Carolina submitted another plan to the Convention. Pinckney, who had been on Washington's staff during the Revolution, was only 29 at the time, but, like Madison, he did not allow his relative youth to interfere with his push for change.

The Pinckney Plan called for the establishment of supreme executive, legislative, and judicial branches. It also would establish two houses of the legislature: a "House of Delegates" to be chosen by the people of the several states and a "Senate" to be elected by the lower house.

Pinckney's plan differed from Madison's in that it called for three classes of senators, each with different times of service. As a given class of senators retired or left office the vacancies would be filled, thus assuring a continuity of service and avoiding a complete change in the legislative body in any given election.

Pinckney also suggested a method of overriding an executive veto of legislation by a two-thirds majority, at which point the bill in question would become law. He spelled out in detail the specific authority to be allotted to each branch of government and provided for amendment of the Constitution on approval of two-thirds of the state legislatures.

While Pinckney's plan contained many useful proposals it was not considered a leading candidate for adoption. Like the Virginia Plan, the Pinckney Plan was assigned on the first day to the Committee of the Whole. These two plans were the only plans introduced on that first day of the Convention, and discussion of the plans dominated the first day's work.

E. THE DEBATES

The Virginia Plan moved almost immediately to the forefront as a workable model. The Pinckney Plan also attracted much of the delegates' early attention, and a debate over the two plans filled the early days of the convention.

Debate among the parties as to the merits and weaknesses of each plan sometimes took on dramatic posture. At one point Pinckney sharply asked Governor Randolph if it was his intention to abolish state governments altogether.

"I meant by these general propositions merely to introduce the particular ones which explained the outlines of the system we had in view," Randolph replied noncommittally.

This did not satisfy the fiery Pinckney, who wanted a more specific answer. Fortunately, Pierce Butler of South Carolina interjected a soothing note by suggesting that no delegate had fully made up his mind and that each should give all participants a chance for full discussion of the issues.

Over the next several weeks various other proposals and plans were presented at the Convention. One of the central issues during the early days of the Convention focused on the powers of the state and federal government. The major division was between federalists (those desiring a strong federal government) and anti-federalists (those seeking to protect the independence and sovereignty of the individual states). The debate, however, was not just how much power would be divided between the two, but whether we should even have a federal or national government.

In the course of the debate over the question Governor Morris of Pennsylvania reminded the delegates that there was a great difference between the terms "federal" and "national" in regard to a supreme government. "The former," Morris explained, "is a mere compact, dependent upon the good faith of the parties; whereas the latter consists of a complete and *compulsive* operation." [Emphasis added]

A major component of the federal-state debate was the question of proportional representative authority. This question was pushed to the forefront of the debate by the delegates from Delaware, one of the smaller states. The second of the resolutions contained in the Virginia Plan called for "the rights of suffrage in the National Legislature to be proportioned to the quotas of contribution, or the number of free inhabitants." This meant that the number of representatives, and eventually the amount of power one state might hold in the national legislature, would be based on state size by measuring population. Under such a plan, those states that were smaller in physical size would also likely be smaller in population.

Madison argued that this last phrase should be removed, as it could clearly become the subject of endless debate between advocates and opponents of slavery. As the debate became more heated the Delaware delegates threatened to withdraw from the Convention if there were any change in the general rule of suffrage. For the small states the issue was not simply proportional representation, but one of equal power among the individual states themselves. With proportional representation the small states would be overwhelmed by the power seized by the larger states. If the assignment of delegates to any national legislature were based on population alone then the small states would always suffer.

Other issues that arose during the summer included the question of how a chief executive should be chosen. Debates focused on the power to be granted the chief executive and his role in running the country. Some wanted the office to actually be shared by more than one man while others saw the need for a single strong leader.

Debate also focused on issues surrounding the ability of an individual to serve in such an esteemed office. One question that arose was what could (or should) be done if, after a short period in office, it were discovered that the new executive of the country was incompetent or otherwise unworthy of the office. This issue was ultimately settled by agreement that the office should only be held for a limited period of time. Earlier debate had suggested that the office be an elected rather than appointed position, and the idea of running for the office fit well with the new proposition that it be held for a limited term.

One of the more interesting debates surrounding the position of president focused on the issue of pay for serving. Although his suggestions were not fully implemented, Benjamin Franklin gave us the idea that the president should receive no salary while in office. "There are two passions," Franklin began, "which have a powerful influence on the affairs of men. These are ambition and avarice; the love of power, and the love of money. Separately, each of these has great force in prompting men to action; but when united in view of the same object, they have in many minds the most violent effects."

The motion was seconded by Alexander Hamilton. In his record of the Convention, Madison wrote that Franklin's proposal "was treated with great respect, but rather for the author of it than from any apparent conviction of its expediency or practicability." At the time of the convention the eighty-one-year-old Franklin was "President of Pennsylvania," a post that he had held since returning from France after negotiating the final peace treaty with England.

Similar debates were held about other national offices concerning power, service, time in office, and pay. Some of the more hotly contested of these debates focused on the election of representatives to Congress and other government offices. Charles Pinckney and Elbridge Gerry led the fight against voting by the people. James

Wilson, George Mason, and James Madison were among those who argued power-fully for popular elections.

In one eloquent speech Madison defended the overall wisdom of the electorate. "In all cases," he began, "where a majority are united by a common interest or passion, the rights of the minority are in danger. What motives are to restrain them? A prudent regard to the maxim that honesty is the best policy, is found by experience to be as little regarded by bodies of men as by individuals. Respect for character is always diminished in proportion to the number among whom the blame or praise is to be divided."

Madison further explained that from a historical standpoint we know that the rich and poor as well "as the patricians and plebeians" alternately oppressed each other with equal unmercifulness. "The lesson we are to draw from the whole is, that where a majority are united by a common sentiment, and have an opportunity, the rights of the minor party become insecure."

On June 18 Alexander Hamilton read in the convention a sketch which he intended not as a plan to be acted upon but more as an indication of his own ideas and a suggestion for amendments he would propose to the Virginia Plan. Hamilton's suggestions called for a strong central government with a reduction in state power. In fact, under Hamilton's proposal, the states would be reduced essentially to provinces subservient to the federal government.

Although Hamilton's proposals never gained real popularity, it is important to note that other ideas were considered during the Convention. In fact, it was Hamilton himself, during final discussions of the proposed Constitution, who urged the Convention delegates to adopt the current Constitution even though it was far different from his own proposals. In his support for the final Constitution Hamilton said, "no man's ideas were more remote from the plan [the Constitution] than my own."

By July 16 a major break in the deadlock over representation came in the form of a resolution assigning a specific number of representatives to each state. The "Great Compromise," as it was called, further stated that, as the current situation of the states would undoubtedly change as to the number of inhabitants, the legislature of the United States would be authorized from time to time to apportion the number of representatives, provided that the representation would be proportioned to the amount of direct taxation.

Other issues soon began to be resolved in the various committees and debates of the convention. On Monday, September 17, Benjamin Franklin rose with a speech in his hand. He began to read it, but his voice failed, so he passed the paper over to James Wilson, who continued for him. Franklin echoed the sentiments of many when he stated that there were parts of the proposed Constitution of which he did not approve. He added, "the older I grow, the more I am apt to doubt my own judgment and to pay more respect to the judgment of others." He then urged all who dissented to join him in unanimous approval of the new Constitution.

Other leaders of the Convention rose in turn to give their support to the work of the Convention and urge all to join together in presenting the work to the various states for adoption; however, not all joined in the general acceptance of the document. Edmund Randolph, Elbridge Gerry, and others refused to sign.

Despite the chilling effect of these objections, delegates prepared to sign the document. George Washington was asked to hold all records of the proceedings, subject to further instructions from a new Congress if it should be formed under the Constitution. The Constitution was placed upon the table in front of Washington, and 42 of the 55 Framers were in their seats at this historic moment. Once again the richly paneled room in Independence Hall became the scene for the signing of a historic document.

The men in their frock coats, knee breeches, and buckled shoes came forward and inscribed their names, by state, on the last page under George Washington's signature. Only three refused to sign: Edmund Randolph, Elbridge Gerry, and George Mason.

As the last members affixed their signatures to the new Constitution Benjamin Franklin once again put the events into perspective. Referring to the picture of a rising sun painted on the back of the chair used by George Washington, president of the Constitutional Convention, Franklin said, "I have often, in the course of the session, and the vicissitude of my hopes and fears as to its issue, looked at that behind the President without being able to tell whether it was rising or setting; but now at length, I have the happiness to know that it is a rising, and not a setting sun."

VI. THE CAMPAIGN FOR RATIFICATION

The early work of creating a constitution was only half the battle in getting it put into place. Now the Framers moved to their next big challenges. They must now take the Constitution back to their respective states for consideration and ratification. Then, if the Constitution was ratified, they must find a way to implement the document and make it work.

Despite the difficulties of mass communication at the time, the framers made dramatic headway in getting the document to the people. Newspapers in Philadelphia and other cities printed the complete text by September 19, just two days after the Convention ended. On September 18 the Constitution was read to the Pennsylvania Assembly before the State House. A courier arrived in New York on September 20 to lay the document before the U.S. Congress.

German translations were available in Pennsylvania Dutch regions the same week. In these editions the Preamble began, "Wir das Volk." In English the Preamble reads "We the People."

By October 1, English, German, and other versions of the document were being circulated throughout America. According to newspaper accounts of the time, virtually every literate adult American had read the new Constitution by the end of October.

One of the early surprises in the ratification of the new Constitution was the fact that the first real support came from the old Congress. The new Constitution would, in effect, eradicate the old Congress and replace it with the new Constitutional Congress. On September 28, 1787, driven by the persuasive arguments of several of the framers who had returned to their legislative seats, Congress sent copies of the Constitution to each of the state legislatures with recommendations to ratify and adopt the new document.

Ratification by nine states was required to put the Constitution into effect, and at the outset it appeared there would be less difficulty than many had anticipated. Delaware was the first to ratify the Constitution when its legislature voted solidly to adopt it on December 7, 1787. Pennsylvania, New Jersey, Connecticut, and Georgia followed suit within a few weeks, and by January 1788 five states had ratified the Constitution.

This initial ratification by five states in rapid succession proved to be only an illusion that overall passage would occur quickly. Future ratification efforts were slowed by concerns raised by the anti-federalists. Where once it appeared that ratification would snowball quickly, the effort now seemed at a virtual halt. Bitter debate raged in several states, and the movement for ratification faltered.

The battle for ratification would last almost a year as rival efforts took their best rhetoric to the people. Leading the federalists (those most in favor of ratification) was Alexander Hamilton, who had been outvoted in his own delegation to the Convention just months before. Hamilton, along with Madison and others seeking ratification, wrote a series of papers urging adoption of the Constitution. Although Hamilton had been uncharacteristically silent during the Convention he now took a prominent role in seeking ratification.

In letters later given the title of *The Federalist Papers*, Hamilton poured forth some of the country's most potent arguments for ratification. Hamilton's skillful pen was sorely needed in New York, where two thirds of the members of the state legislature were opposed to the Constitution.

Stories from the period tell of politically aggressive tactics used by both sides in the ratification debates. Opposition members in Pennsylvania would effectively block the vote on ratification by staying away from the State House during the call for votes. Those in favor of ratification, however, used their own tactics to "encourage" the dissenters to vote. In several reports those who stayed away found themselves bodily dragged from their homes and forced to take their seats in the State House to ensure a quorum when a vote was called. The Constitution was approved in Pennsylvania by a vote of 46–23.

Hot debate on adoption erupted even in Virginia, home of James Madison and George Washington. From Mount Vernon, George Washington wrote to his longtime friend the Marquis de Lafayette, "The plot thickens fast. A few short weeks will determine the political fate of America."

To everyone's surprise Governor Edmund Randolph of Virginia agreed to support the Constitution even though he was one of only three who refused to sign it at the Convention. However, opposition, led by Patrick Henry, was equally powerful in Virginia. Henry, the fiery orator of the Revolution, now lent his talent to tirades against the new government. "The Constitution is a threat to liberty," Henry thundered during one of his speeches. "I would rather have a King, a House of Lords and Commons than the new government."

In the month since Delaware had first ratified the Constitution with a unanimous vote only four other states adopted the document. New Jersey and Georgia also had unanimous votes, but none of the other states came close. The ninth state to ratify the Constitution was also one of the closest votes. On June 21, 1788, more than six months after Delaware's unanimous vote, New Hampshire ratified the Constitution with a 57–47 vote.

It would be almost another three years before all 13 original states would vote to ratify the new Constitution. Rhode Island was the last to ratify the Constitution when it voted 34–32 on May 29, 1790. By that time, however, the new government had been firmly established. In fact, before all of the states ratified the Constitution others had already moved ahead with celebrations of the new government. Philadelphia, among others, selected the Fourth of July to honor the new Federal spirit.

With the new Constitution ratified in 1788 it was time to set in motion the machinery of the new government. Congress had taken the first step on July 2, 1788, by appointing a committee to implement provisions of the Constitution. By September of that year specific plans had been established to implement the plans for the new government. A presidential election was scheduled for March 4, 1789, and electors were chosen in the 11 states that had ratified the Constitution up to that point. Likewise, Congressional elections were held so that when the old Congress ceased to exist under the Articles of Confederation a new one would be ready to take its place.

VII. ADDING THE FIRST AMENDMENTS

Individual rights moved quickly to the forefront of the first Constitutional Congress' order of business. Once again James Madison assumed a leading role in the task at hand. Madison, who had been elected to the new Congress along with seven other original Framers, introduced a proposal for amendments to the new Constitution that would spell out a declaration of individual rights.

Under Article V of the Constitution, which provided a routine for amendment, the Congress moved rapidly to draft what is now known as the Bill of Rights. The original draft was in the form of a proposal with 12 amendments. The first two, which sought to clarify the proportional representation in Congress and the size and composition of the House of Representatives, fell by the wayside and were never approved by the states. The remaining ten amendments became law on December 15, 1791, after they were ratified by the requisite number of states.

Section Two

Article III — The Judiciary

Article Text

Section 1.

The judicial Power of the United States, shall be vested in one supreme Court, and in such inferior Courts as the Congress may from time to time ordain and establish. The Judges, both of the supreme and inferior Courts, shall hold their Offices during good Behaviour, and shall, at stated Times, receive for their Services, a Compensation, which shall not be diminished during their Continuance in Office.

Section 2.

The judicial Power shall extend to all Cases, in Law and Equity, arising under this Constitution, the Laws of the United States, and Treaties made, or which shall be made, under their Authority; — to all Cases affecting Ambassadors, other public ministers and Consuls; — to all Cases of admiralty and maritime Jurisdiction; — to Controversies to which the United States shall be a Party; — to Controversies between two or more States; — between a State and Citizens of another State; — between Citizens of different States; — between Citizens of the same State claiming Lands under Grants of different States, and between a State, or the Citizens thereof, and foreign States, Citizens or Subjects.

In all Cases affecting Ambassadors, other public Ministers and Consuls, and those in which a State shall be Party, the supreme Court shall have original Jurisdiction. In all the other Cases before mentioned, the supreme Court shall have appellate Jurisdiction, both as to Law and Fact, with such Exceptions, and under such Regulations as the Congress shall make. The Trial of all Crimes, except in Cases of Impeachment, shall be by Jury; and such Trial shall be held in the State where the said Crimes shall have been committed; but when not committed within any State, the Trial shall be at such Place or Places as the Congress may by Law have directed.

Section 3.

Treason against the United States, shall consist only in levying War against them, or in adhering to their Enemies, giving them Aid and Comfort. No Person shall be convicted of Treason unless on the Testimony of two Witnesses to the same overt Act, or on Confession in open Court. The Congress shall have Power to declare the Punishment of Treason, but no Attainder of Treason shall work Corruption of Blood, or Forfeiture except during the Life of the Person attainted.

3 Organization of the Courts

I. CREATING THE FEDERAL SYSTEM

During the Philadelphia Convention there was little, if any, debate on creation of the federal court system. It was clear that a judiciary was needed, but how much power and how broad a reach the federal courts were to have were rarely discussed. One issue that did arise was whether the federal court system was to consist of one high court at the apex of a federal judicial system or a high court exercising only appellate jurisdiction over state courts which would initially hear all but a select group of cases raising national issues.[1]

The Virginia Plan called for a "National judiciary [to] be established to consist of one or more supreme tribunals, and of inferior tribunals to be chosen by the National Legislature...." This plan was submitted to the Committee of the Whole for further review and amendment. As we saw in earlier chapters, Madison was a prominent figure in both the development of the Virginia Plan and as a member of the Committee of the Whole. His efforts helped shape the propositions that would later become Article III of the Constitution.

It was quickly and unanimously agreed that "a national judiciary be established" and that it "consist of One supreme tribunal, and of one or more inferior tribunals." Later arguments that state courts could adequately adjudicate all necessary matters soon led to the striking of the language calling for inferior courts.

Recognizing that such a provision would leave the federal government with nothing more than a superior court with appellate jurisdiction, Madison moved to authorize Congress "to appoint inferior tribunals," as necessary. Such language implied that Congress could, at its discretion, either designate the state courts to hear federal cases or create separate federal courts for the task.

The word "appoint" was initially adopted, but over the course of the Convention was changed into phrasing that suggests something of an obligation for Congress to establish inferior federal courts. The final language used the more emphatic term "shall" when designating the Supreme Court, and such emphasis carries over into Congressional power to create inferior courts. Thus, many have held that the issue of whether there would be any inferior courts was solved by substituting the stronger language. The question was no longer one of "should" such courts be created, but more of how many and with what authority.

Almost immediately after ratification of the Constitution planners set about building the foundation for our current court system. Today we enjoy a three-tiered system designed to meet the needs of a growing population and country. At the top of the federal system is the highest court in the U.S.: the Supreme Court. Below the Supreme Court are the circuit courts, which are intermediate appellate courts, and below the circuit courts are the courts commonly called "trial courts" or "district courts."

With few exceptions, all cases are begun in the lowest level of the courts, the district courts. These courts are established by Congressional act and serve every state in the Union. The first district court appeared in 1789. These courts are also called courts of "original jurisdiction" since it is here that an action originally begins.

Each state has at least one federal district court, and some states have more than one. Each district court is responsible for those cases filed within the boundaries of the court. For instance, one federal district court serves the state of Kansas. All cases filed in the federal court system arising in Kansas are filed in the U.S. District Court for the District of Kansas. Other states may have more than one district and more than one district court. As a general rule, the courts are established by need.

One should also note that some of these district courts may have different divisions. In Kansas, there are multiple divisions and judges within the district court. Although there is only one district court in Kansas, that court has offices, courtrooms, and judges serving in different cities. These include the state capital, Topeka; the state's largest city, Wichita; and one of the state's busiest cities, Kansas City. The court may also assign judges or other personnel to other cities as the need arises.

The intermediate courts likewise serve a geographical region. Instead of serving a single state or part of a state, however, the circuit courts serve a geographical region of the country. These courts often serve as an intermediate appellate court for multiple districts. There are currently 13 circuit courts serving the U.S. and its possessions.

All district courts fall within one of the 13 circuit courts. As in our example above, a case arising in the state of Kansas will be filed with the district court serving that district. Once the trial or other proceedings are completed, one or more parties in the lawsuit may wish to appeal the case. The first line of appeal is to the circuit court. For Kansas this means the appeal will be taken to the U.S. Court of Appeals for the Tenth Circuit. The main office and courthouse for the Tenth Circuit is in Denver, Colorado, but the court also has access to personnel and courtrooms in other cities within the circuit.

Should a party choose to appeal the decision of the circuit court then the case is taken to the U.S. Supreme Court; however, not all cases can be appealed to the Supreme Court. Congress has limited the cases that may be heard by the Supreme Court, and, as such, only those cases that have received permission to be heard, known as *certiorari*, may be fully prosecuted in the Supreme Court.

II. ONE SUPREME COURT

The Constitution mandates that there shall be one Supreme Court, and by specifying this the Framers established what is now known as the third branch of the government. The Constitution also creates a court which cannot be abolished by an act of either of the other two branches of the government. While Congress can create and dissolve the inferior courts virtually at will, it may not dissolve the Supreme Court as an entity. Congress may, however, alter the makeup of the court and affect its ultimate authority to hear cases.

The Framers of the Constitution left up to Congress decisions on the size and composition of the Supreme Court, the time and place for sitting, its internal organization — except for the reference to the Chief Justice in the impeachment provision — and other matters concerning the Court's operation. These details were addressed by Congress in the Judiciary Act of 1789,[2] one of the seminal statutes of the U.S.

Among other things, the Judiciary Act established the size and makeup of the original Court. The Court is headed by a single Justice known as the Chief Justice, appointed by the President with advise and consent of the Senate. Initially, the court also consisted of five Associate Justices[3] who were also appointed by the President with advise and consent of the Senate. The number of Justices was gradually increased until it reached a total of ten on March 3, 1863.[4]

Since the President has the duty of appointing the Justices of the Supreme Court it is not uncommon for the President to appoint Justices who share his political and social philosophy. This has raised some concern over the ability of a President to appoint only Justices who share his political or social view and ultimately his ability to shape the future decisions of the Court. This has led, on at least one occasion, to an effort by Congress to control the makeup of the Court.

During the Reconstruction period following the Civil War, Congress, as a means of controlling President Andrew Johnson, used its power to set the number of Justices. At the time there were ten Justices on the Supreme Court, all of whom were nearing retirement age or were in ill health. It appeared certain that Johnson would have ample opportunity to appoint new Justices and shape the direction the Court would take. In an effort to control Johnson, Congress chose to amend the Judiciary Act as each Justice would retire or otherwise leave the bench.

The number of Justices was reduced from ten to seven as vacancies occurred.[5] Although the number never actually fell below eight before the end of Johnson's term it was clear that Congress could use its power to control the Court and, in a way, affect a presidency. Thus, a President could not appoint Justices who shared his philosophies and Congress controlled, to some extent, the movement of the Court in the future. Had Johnson had an opportunity to appoint those new Justices it is likely some of the decisions would have been substantially different from what we have today.

Following Johnson's tenure in office Congress increased the number of Justices to nine.[6] Today the Court continues to work with nine Justices, one of whom serves as Chief Justice, and it appears unlikely that Congress will use its power again to reduce the number of Justices below nine.

It is worthwhile to note that at least once during the twentieth century both the President and Congress addressed the issue of raising the number of Justices on the Court in order to affect the decisions coming from the Court. In 1937 President Franklin D. Roosevelt sent to Congress a bill to change the composition of the federal judiciary. This bill, commonly called the "Court-Packing Bill," was Franklin Roosevelt's attempt to expand the membership of the Supreme Court so that he could nominate justices who would uphold his sweeping social and legal changes under the "New Deal."

As one may recall, Franklin Roosevelt instituted many programs that affected the country's social, political, and economic climate during the 1920s and 1930s.

The Supreme Court initially upheld many of these "New Deal" programs, but by 1937 the Court began striking down some of Franklin Roosevelt's programs.

Although the President could push the legislation through Congress there was no guarantee that the program would withstand the judicial scrutiny certain to follow. Franklin Roosevelt's plan in addressing this issue was to increase the number of Justices significantly. This would allow him to pack the court with his own appointees who would conceivably share his political philosophy.

Over the years there have been other proposals designed to alter the Court and the way it handles cases. One plan was to separate the Court and organize it into sections or divisions. Under such a plan there would no longer be one Supreme Court but actually a divided Court. Although no authoritative judicial decision has been given on whether such a scheme is plausible we do have a statement by then Chief Justice Hughes on the issue.

Justice Hughes wrote to Senator Wheeler in 1937, expressing doubts concerning the validity of any Congressional act to divide the Court. In part, the letter states that "the Constitution does not appear to authorize two or more Supreme Courts functioning in effect as separate courts."[7] The Congressional plan failed to achieve fruition, and there has not been a similar attempt since.

Along with the makeup of the Court it is clear that Congressional power extends to the ability to set the time and place of the Court's sessions. On at least one occasion Congress has used its power to change the terms of the Court so as to affect the Court's ability to take action. In 1801, in an effort to forestall a constitutional attack on the repeal of the Judiciary Act of 1801, Congress modified the Court's term so that it could not meet for a period of 14 months. Not since that time, however, has Congress made such a bold move.

It must be noted that while Congress retains a great deal of power on how and when the Court shall meet, it has absolutely no power over how the Court shall rule. Despite efforts to thwart certain rulings or to alter a particular chain of events leading to a decision, the simple fact is that the Court stands as a separate branch of our government. As such, the Supreme Court maintains its role as a powerful entity in our society. As we will see in the coming chapters, the decisions of the Supreme Court can substantially alter the paths our government and society take.

III. THE INFERIOR COURTS

A. Creation of the Courts

Along with addressing several issues surrounding the new Supreme Court, Congress also acted in the Judiciary Act of 1789 to create a set of inferior federal courts. Initially 13 district courts were created at the trial level of the court system in each of the 13 original states. Under the Act the courts were authorized to hold four sessions annually.[8]

Congress also created three "circuit courts" to handle appeals from the district courts. The circuit courts were intermediate level courts providing a buffer between the trial level and the higher Supreme Court. The Judiciary Act called for the intermediate courts to consist jointly of two Supreme Court Justices and one district judge from the district or districts being served.

The courts were designated as circuits since the Justices/judges were to appear in them at various times, which required the Justices to travel a "circuit" or specific route in order to hold session. For example, a Supreme Court Justice serving the northern districts of New York or Vermont would be on the road "riding the circuit" in order to provide service at the intermediate level. The circuit courts were to convene twice annually.[9]

From the outset the system had substantial operating faults. The most obvious was the burden imposed on the Justices who were required to travel thousands of miles each year to hold court. Weather and travel conditions often hampered or prevented Justices from reaching their appointed circuits on time, and it was not uncommon for the Justices to ride for weeks at a time in order to meet their appointed rounds.

Despite numerous efforts to change this system it continued, except for one brief period, until 1891.[10] At that time the system was modified to establish a circuit court system comprised of full-time judges serving exclusively in the appellate role.

B. ABOLITION OF COURTS

It is clear that the language of the Constitution allows Congress great latitude in creating the inferior federal courts. It is also implied that the Constitution authorizes Congress to abolish an inferior court as is necessary. An issue arises, however, when one considers that the language of the Constitution also authorizes a federal judge to hold tenure for life. As such, if Congress can abolish a court then what is to be done with the judge who holds life tenure when the system is contracted?

The first exercise of the Congressional power to abolish an inferior court occurred in a highly politicized situation in the first decades of our country's existence. The Judiciary Act of February 13, 1801[11] was passed in the closing weeks of the Adams administration. Under the act several new district courts were created along with three new circuit judgeships. As with many acts of Congress, however, the political turmoil of the day played a role in the act itself.

At the time, the act was passed at the end of Adams presidency, the Federalist party held power. Adams, a Federalist, quickly filled the positions with deserving party members. The incoming administration of Thomas Jefferson, however, did not relish the actions of the outgoing president. Upon assuming the office the Jeffersonians immediately set in motion plans to repeal the act. Jefferson's plan was carried forth in the first few weeks of his administration and the newly created judicial positions suddenly were abolished.[12]

The new judicial act made no provision for the now displaced judges. One theory held by the Jeffersonians was that if there were no courts there could be no judges to sit on them. The validity of Jefferson's actions in repealing the act was attacked in *Stuart v. Laird*.[13]

The case arose following the entry of judgment against a defendant in the trial court. The court of original jurisdiction was the U.S. District Court for the middle circuit, in the Virginia district, and the action was instituted in that court in January 1801. The issues presented were stated by the Court as follows:

The middle circuit court in the Virginia district was established by the judiciary act of 1789, and continued until the 13th of February 1801, when an act was passed, entitled "an act to provide for the more convenient organization of the courts of the United States."[14]

Under the new act all cases pending in the middle circuit court of Virginia were transferred to other circuit courts. The case in the middle circuit court went from that court in February 1801 to the newly created court established by the Judiciary Act of 1801. Afterward, upon the repeal of that law, the case was to return to the court in which it was originally commenced.

In the case before the Court, however, certain proceedings had commenced in the new court "which were brought up with the record, and to which the exceptions were taken by the defendant...."

The exceptions before the Court were: "1. That congress could not transfer causes from one circuit court to another; and therefore all the proceedings in the court established by the act of February 13, 1801, were void. 2. That the justices of the supreme court of the United States could not by an act of congress be assigned to hold circuit courts."[15]

The Supreme Court recognized the actions of Congress and quickly set about clarifying the power. In part the Court held that "Congress have (sic) constitutional authority to establish from time to time such inferior tribunals as they may think proper, and to transfer a cause from one such tribunal to another. In this last particular, there are no words in the constitution to prohibit or restrain the exercise of legislative power."[16]

Not until 1913 did Congress again utilize its power to abolish a federal court. This time, however, Congress abolished not a district court but a court originally established to hear specialized cases. Such courts, often designated courts of limited jurisdiction or "special courts," are limited in the type of cases they may hear. In this instance, the court was the Commerce Court. We will examine similar courts in coming sections as we further explore the creation and role of the inferior courts.

C. COMPENSATION OF JUDGES

Along with the power to establish the inferior courts Congress also has the power to establish the compensation received by the judges. The Compensation Clause of Article III has its roots in the longstanding Anglo-American tradition of an independent Judiciary. A Judiciary free from control by the Executive and the Legislature is essential if there is a right to have claims decided by judges "who are free from potential domination by other branches of government."[17]

Following this tradition it has been held that once a salary figure has gone into effect, Congress may not reduce it or rescind any part of an increase. That does not mean, however, that prior to the date of its effectiveness Congress may not repeal a promised increase. In other words, Congress has the authority to provide for an increase in judicial salary, but Congress may not take it away unless it does so before the date the act authorizing the increase goes into effect.

IV. COURTS OF SPECIALIZED JURISDICTION

The federal judiciary is traditionally viewed as a three-tiered system with the Supreme Court at the top, the intermediate appellate (circuit) courts in the middle, and the district (trial) courts on the lower level; however, since Congress has the power "to ordain and establish" all inferior courts as it deems necessary, we occasionally see the creation of courts under both Article I and Article III to exercise a specialized jurisdiction. These courts are often called "Courts of Specialized Jurisdiction."

From a technical standpoint one might say that all the federal courts are courts of limited jurisdiction. Because Congress must create the court and authorize its jurisdiction over a particular subject matter we may say that the court is limited in its authority. For the Court of Specialized Jurisdiction, however, this limitation is even more encompassing than for the other inferior courts of the federal system.

One example of such a court was the Commerce Court created by the Mann-Elkins Act of 1910.[18] This court was given exclusive jurisdiction to enforce orders of the Interstate Commerce Commission except those involving money penalties and criminal punishment. The court had the power to hear cases brought to enjoin, annul, or set aside orders of the Commerce Commission and to prevent unjust discriminations. The court operated for less than three years and was abolished in 1913.

A similarly created and short-lived court was the Emergency Court of Appeals organized by the Emergency Price Control Act of January 30, 1942.[19] The statute creating the court authorized the Chief Justice to select three or more judges from the judges of the U.S. district courts and circuit courts of appeal. The Court was established during World War II to oversee appeals or protests of actions by the "Price Administrator." The Emergency Court of Appeals had exclusive jurisdiction to set aside regulations, orders, or price schedules, in whole or in part, or to remand the proceeding for other action.

Other specialized courts are the Court of Appeals for the Federal Circuit. Created in 1982,[20] this court has exclusive jurisdiction to hear appeals from the U.S. Court of Federal Claims, the Federal Merit System Protection Board, the Court of International Trade, the Patent Office, and various contract and tort cases.

Even greater specialization is provided by the special court created by the Ethics in Government Act.[21] This court is charged, upon the request of the Attorney General, with appointing an independent counsel to investigate and prosecute charges of illegality in the Executive Branch. The court also has certain supervisory powers over the independent counsel.

V. BANKRUPTCY COURTS

One of the best known of the courts with specialized jurisdiction is the bankruptcy court. Beginning with the first judiciary act Congress has struggled with the ever-broadening issues of bankruptcy and the power of the bankruptcy courts. In the twentieth century we have seen important changes in this court and its jurisdiction.

Beginning in 1978 the modern scheme of bankruptcy courts was established by Congress. The courts, now an "adjunct" of the district courts, are composed of judges vested with practically all the judicial power of the U.S. Bankruptcy judges serve 14-year terms, subject to removal for cause by the judicial councils of the circuits, and may be appointed for consecutive terms. The judges' salaries are also subject to statutory change.[22]

The bankruptcy courts were given jurisdiction over all civil proceedings arising under the bankruptcy code or arising in or related to bankruptcy cases. Over the years the power of the court has been challenged, but Congress has continued to mandate adjudication of bankruptcy-related issues in these courts of limited jurisdiction.

ENDNOTES

1. The most complete account of the Convention's consideration of the judiciary is J. Goebel, *Antecedents and Beginnings to 1801, History of the Supreme Court of the United States,* Vol. 1 (New York: 1971), ch. 5.
2. Act of September 24, 1789, 1 Stat. 73.
3. Act of September 24, 1789, 1 Stat. 73, §1.
4. 12 Stat. 794, §1.
5. Act of July 23, 1866, 14 Stat. 209, §1.
6. Act of April 10, 1869, 16 Stat. 44.
7. Hearings before the Senate Judiciary Committee on S. 1392, Reorganization of the Judiciary, 75th Congress, 1st sess. (1937), pt. 3, 491.
8. Act of September 24, 1789, 1 Stat. 73, §§2–3.
9. *Id.,* 74, §§4–5.
10. Act of March 3, 1891, 26 Stat. 826. The temporary relief came in the Act of February 13, 1801, 2 Stat. 89, which was repealed by the Act of March 8, 1802, 2 Stat. 132.
11. Act of February 13, 1801, 2 Stat. 89.
12. Act of March 8, 1802, 2 Stat. 132.
13. 5 U.S. (1 Cr.) 299 (1803).
14. 1 Story's L. U.S. 797.
15. *Id.* at 307.
16. *Id.* at 309.
17. United States v. Will, 449 U.S. 200, 217–218 (1980).
18. 36 Stat. 539.
19. 56 Stat. 23, §§31–33.
20. By the Federal Courts Improvement Act of 1982, P. L. 97-164, 96 Stat. 37, 28 U.S.C. §1295. Among other things, this Court assumed the appellate jurisdiction of the Court of Claims and the Court of Customs and Patent Appeals.
21. Ethics in Government Act, Title VI, P. L. 95-521, 92 Stat. 1867, as amended, 28 U.S.C. §§591–599.
22. Bankruptcy Act of 1978, P.L. 95-598, 92 Stat. 2549, codified in titles 11, 28. The bankruptcy courts were made "adjuncts" of the district courts by Sec. 201(a), 28 U.S.C. §151(a). For citation to the debate with respect to Article III vs. Article I status for these courts, see Northern Pipeline Const. Co. v. Marathon Pipe Line Co., 458 U.S. 50, 61 n.12 (1982) (plurality opinion).

4 Judicial Power

I. CHARACTERISTICS AND ATTRIBUTES
OF JUDICIAL POWER

As we discussed in earlier sections of this book, our government is designed to work effectively by allocating power to three distinct branches of the government. The Constitution allocates and authorizes that power to the Executive, Legislative, and Judicial branches. But just how much power do the courts have under the Constitution? In the following sections we will explore this issue. We begin by defining the characteristics and attributes of judicial power.

Judicial power is the power of a court to decide and pronounce a judgment and carry it into effect between persons and parties who bring a case before it for decision. It is "the right to determine actual controversies arising between diverse litigants, duly instituted in courts of proper jurisdiction."[1]

Many choose to use the terms "judicial power" and "jurisdiction" interchangeably. Depending on the context within which they are used, this may be acceptable, but one must not confuse the two as distinct legal theories. Broadly defined, jurisdiction is the power to hear and determine the subject matter in controversy between parties to a suit.[2] It has also been defined as the "power to entertain the suit, consider the merits and render a binding decision thereon."[3] Jurisdiction is the authority of a court to exercise judicial power in a specific case and is, of course, a prerequisite to the exercise of judicial power.

Where we define jurisdiction as the authority under which a court may exercise its judicial power, we then define judicial power as the authority of the court to act in a given controversy. In other words, it is jurisdiction that gives a court the authority to act over a case brought before it, but it is judicial power that gives the court the authority to perform the various acts necessary to conclude the particular case.[4]

Examples of judicial power include the general power to decide cases and may also include the ancillary powers of courts to punish for contempt of their authority.[5] Judicial power also includes the ability to issue writs in aid of jurisdiction when authorized by statute[6] and to make rules governing their process in the absence of statutory authorizations or prohibitions.[7] A court's ability to order its own process so as to prevent abuse, oppression, and injustice and to protect its own jurisdiction is another form of judicial power.[8] In today's courts judicial power allows the courts to appoint masters in chancery, referees, auditors, and other investigators,[9] as well as to admit and disbar attorneys practicing before the court.[10]

As we move forward in the study of constitutional law, it is important to remember that without jurisdiction a court may not exercise even the judicial power it has. Consider this simple example. Would you file a claim for violation of your constitutional rights in a probate court? Probably not, and in this instance the example illustrates that by choosing the court with the proper jurisdiction, the authority to act with regard to that type of case, you have chosen a court with both jurisdiction and judicial power.

II. "SHALL BE VESTED"

As we examine Article III of the Constitution, we concentrate on the creation of the federal judiciary and the allocation of power to that system. Nowhere else is the distinction between judicial power and jurisdiction more important than when examining the allocation of power to the courts. In Section 1 of Article III we see that through the phrase "shall be vested" the Constitution gives judicial power to the Supreme Court and the inferior federal courts created by Congress.

The most prominent distinction is that while the Constitution vests all the judicial power of the U.S. in these courts it does not vest with them all the jurisdiction that could be granted. Except for the original jurisdiction of the Supreme Court, which flows directly from the Constitution, two prerequisites to jurisdiction must be present: first, the Constitution must have given the courts the capacity to receive it,[11] and, second, an act of Congress must have conferred it.[12]

In this sense we can see that the federal courts are of limited jurisdiction, that is, these courts can hear only those cases designated as proper by Congress. While they may have the broad judicial powers granted under the Constitution they do not automatically have the jurisdiction necessary to hear certain cases; thus, a federal court, without specific grant from Congress, may not hear a case which is otherwise proper in a state court. One example of this is divorce. Unless Congress grants to the federal courts the authority (jurisdiction) to hear a divorce case, regardless of how much judicial power the federal court has, it may not hear a divorce case.

The fact that federal courts are of limited jurisdiction means that litigants in them must establish affirmatively that jurisdiction exists and may not confer nonexistent jurisdiction by consent or conduct.[13] This means that, for a person to file a suit in the federal court, the court must first have the jurisdiction to hear such a case. Even if the parties to the lawsuit agree that they wish the federal court to hear a case, it cannot be filed in that court unless the court has been given authority by Congress.

A. GETTING INTO FEDERAL COURT

Congress, in granting jurisdiction to the federal courts, established a simple scheme for allowing parties access to the federal courts. Parties may file a lawsuit in a federal court under one of two possible alternatives. The first is commonly known as *federal question jurisdiction*, and the second is called *diversity jurisdiction*.

For a litigant to file a lawsuit in federal court under *federal question jurisdiction* the controversy must have arisen under federal law. In the broad sense of the term this means that the lawsuit must involve a law either created by Congress or arising from the Constitution. Even though an action may be governed by a state law the lawsuit cannot be filed in the federal court unless it also arises under federal law.

For those instances in which litigants wish to file a case in federal court but do not have a controversy that arises under federal law Congress has established the ability to file through *diversity of citizenship*. Under this standard the courts will not look at the legal issue being pursued. In other words, the case does not have to arise under federal law; instead, the case may arise under state law. To get into the federal court, however, the litigants must meet two narrow criteria.

First, all the litigants in opposition must be from different states. This is commonly called diversity of citizenship. In a lawsuit with two parties (one plaintiff and one defendant) diversity of citizenship is easy to measure. If the plaintiff is from a different state than the defendant then the parties have met the first leg of diversity of citizenship. It becomes more complicated, however, in lawsuits with multiple parties on one or more sides of the lawsuit. For example, if you have three plaintiffs seeking judgment against a single defendant then all three plaintiffs must be from different states than the defendant.

Where this issue may be complicated is when we confuse the requirement for parties in opposition with all parties. The requirement is that all parties who oppose each other must be from different states. In this sense, we may have three plaintiffs and only one defendant. No plaintiff may be from the same state as the defendant, but that does not mean each plaintiff must also be from a different state. Parties on the same side of a lawsuit, all plaintiffs or all defendants, may be from the same state, but they cannot be from the same state as any opposing party.

The second leg for applying this standard is known as *amount in controversy*. In order to limit access to the federal courts, Congress has established that along with a diversity in citizenship the litigants must have an amount in controversy that exceeds $50,000. Lawsuits that have complete diversity of citizenship cannot be filed in federal court unless the amount in controversy also exceeds the statutory amount.

Part of the purpose for restricting access to the federal courts is to allow the state courts to retain authority over controversies arising in their jurisdiction. Most will agree that the state courts handle the majority of controversies arising within our society. When the Constitution was constructed there was a concerted effort to retain as much authority at the state level as is proper to allow our government to work. From a judicial standpoint this is clear when one considers that more controversies are decided in state court than in federal court. That does not mean that the federal courts do not play an important role in our judicial scheme, but it does mean that their role is limited.

B. Choosing between State and Federal Court

In some instances a single act may result in the ability to file a lawsuit in two different courts. For example, if a police officer stops a citizen without probable cause and then physically strikes the citizen, again without cause, the police officer may face both civil and criminal liability. Staying with the civil liability issue for a moment, the citizen may seek a redress of grievances in either the state court or the federal court. In this instance the citizen, who becomes the plaintiff, would have a violation of the Constitution — improper seizure — as well as a civil claim for battery under state tort law.

When faced with such a case the plaintiff may file the lawsuit in either state or federal court. Both court systems have an ability to hear and decide questions under the Constitution. But what about the state law question for battery? Is the plaintiff restricted to just state court because of the state law violation?

Because many such lawsuits will combine both state law and federal law claims our system allows the interchange of claims within the courts. As stated, the plaintiff may file the suit in the state court because that court has jurisdiction over the state law claims and also over constitutional claims. These are inherent powers.

The federal court, on the other hand, does not have an inherent power to hear state law claims. One must remember that the federal courts are restricted to only those cases over which Congress has given them power. But, because the lawsuit does involve a federal question arising from the Constitution, there is a way for the federal court to hear both claims at once. This is known as *pendant jurisdiction.*

Pendant jurisdiction was created by Congress to give the federal courts an ability to hear both state law and federal claims when they are in the same lawsuit. The principle is simple. Because the federal law question (or even diversity issue) is allowed in court, it is logical — and judicially economical — to hear all controversies arising together at the same time. Without pendant jurisdiction a litigant with both state and federal claims would be forced either to use the state courts alone or to split his or her claims between state and federal courts.

How, then, does a litigant choose in which court the claim should be filed? There are no magic guidelines, but there are some general rules attorneys use when confronted with this question. One of the first issues when choosing the court is the court's overall competency with the issues. It is clear that a state court will be more capable of handling cases involving state law claims, but does that mean they are incompetent when it comes to constitutional issues? Definitely not; in fact, many state law judges are very capable of handling such controversies. A state court, however, may not handle many cases of that nature, and the litigants may choose instead to seek redress before the federal courts.

Likewise, the ability to move the case along in a timely fashion may be important to litigants. The state courts handle many more cases a year than do the federal courts. In some jurisdictions the number of cases handled by a state law judge exceeds 2,000 per year, while the federal judge's counterpart may handle only 200 per year. Of course, there are differences in case types; yet, the fact remains that a court packed with 2,000 small cases will have less time to hear a case with complicated constitutional issues.

From the criminal justice standpoint, however, the majority of these decisions are made by prosecutors who are seeking to enforce state law and, as such, the state law questions will be filed in the state courts. Constitutional questions arise in these cases all the time, and the state law judges are more than competent to handle them. As we will see in the coming chapters, however, some of these issues make their way not only through the state courts but also into the federal system. Ultimately, all questions of a constitutional nature can end up in the federal system, and the highest authority on any constitutional issue is always the U.S. Supreme Court.

III. THE POWER OF CONTEMPT

A court has broad-reaching powers to rule on a given controversy, but does a court have the power to enforce its own orders? The broad answer is, yes, the court has such power. One means for enforcing such orders and judgments is through contempt proceedings. In this section we will examine the power of the court through contempt.

The summary power of U.S. courts to punish contempt of their authority has its origin in the law and practice of England, where disobedience of court orders was regarded as contempt of the monarch. By the latter part of the eighteenth century, summary power to punish was extended to all contempt whether committed in or out of court.

In the U.S., the Judiciary Act of 1789[14] conferred power on all U.S. courts "to punish by fine or imprisonment, at the discretion of said courts, all contempt of authority in any cause or hearing before the same." This broad power was later curtailed by the Act of 1831. The new statutory scheme limited the power of the federal courts to punish contempt to misbehavior in the presence of the courts, "or so near thereto as to obstruct the administration of justice," to the misbehavior of officers of courts in their official capacity, and to disobedience or resistance to any lawful writ, process or order of the court.[15]

While contempt power may be inherent, it is not unlimited. In *Spallone v. United States*[16] the Supreme Court overturned a lower court's use of the power of contempt to force a city council to pass a measure designed to remedy housing discrimination. Although the Court did not limit the lower court's judgment on the consent decree, it did limit the court's ability to use contempt to compel legislative action by the city counsel. The proper remedy, the Court indicated, was to proceed first with contempt sanctions against the city, and only if that course failed should it proceed against the council members individually.

IV. SANCTIONS OTHER THAN CONTEMPT

Long recognized by the courts as inherent powers are those authorities that are necessary to the administration of the judicial system itself. Courts, as an independent and coequal branch of government, once they are created and their jurisdiction established, have the authority to do what courts have traditionally done to accomplish their assigned tasks.[17]

One such method is the imposition of monetary sanctions against a litigant and the litigant's attorney for bad-faith litigation. To this end the courts have used their power to regulate conduct in a lawsuit as well as in the court itself, and all federal courts follow a strict set of rules for such conduct.[18]

Courts also have the power to regulate conduct during trial or pretrial phases. Not only may a court use monetary sanctions as a means of exercising its judicial power but it may also take internal actions. For instance, failure to comply with the court's rules governing discovery or pleadings may subject a party to restrictive orders on presentation of evidence or witness.[19] Likewise, a party may find its suit dismissed by the court when it fails to follow the rules of the court to comply with prior orders.

V. POWER TO ISSUE WRITS: THE ACT OF 1789

Relying on the "necessary and proper clause" of Article III, Congress has assumed its power to establish inferior courts, its power to regulate the jurisdiction of federal courts, and the power to regulate the issuance of writs.[20] Section 13 of the Judiciary Act of 1789 authorized the circuit courts to issue writs of prohibition to the district courts and the Supreme Court to issue such writs to the circuit courts. The Supreme Court was also empowered to issue writs of mandamus "in cases warranted by the principles and usage of law, to any courts appointed, or persons holding office, under the authority of the United States."[21]

Section 14 of the Judiciary Act provided that all U.S. courts should "have power to issue writs of scire facias, habeas corpus, and all other writs not specially provided for by statute, which may be necessary for the exercise of their respective jurisdiction, and agreeable to the principles and usages of law." Although the Act of 1789 left the power over writs subject largely to the common law, it is significant as a reflection of the belief, in which the courts have on the whole concurred, that an act of Congress is necessary to confer judicial power to issue writs.[22]

Whether Article III itself is an independent source of the power of federal courts to fashion equitable remedies for constitutional violations or whether such remedies must fit within congressionally authorized writs or procedures is often left fully unexplored. It is not that the issue has not arisen previously, but that the issue has not been fully addressed, in part because the cases raising the issue are often decided on other grounds, which leaves the Court free to ignore the larger issue.

VI. HABEAS CORPUS: CONGRESSIONAL
AND JUDICIAL CONTROL

The Constitution specifically authorizes the Writ of Habeas Corpus,[23] and the power is vested in the federal courts. In this section we will explore the broader question of whether there is any limitation on such judicial power.

Since at least the earliest part of the nineteenth century the courts have held that "the power to award the writ by any of the courts of the United States, must be given by written law."[24] In the case of *Ex parte Bollman*, Chief Justice Marshall wrote that while the writ is specifically stated in the Constitution it is not an automatic power. Having determined that a statute was necessary before the federal courts had power to issue writs of habeas corpus, Chief Justice Marshall pointed to Section 14 of the Judiciary Act of 1789 as containing the necessary authority.

As the Chief Justice read it, the authorization was limited to persons imprisoned under federal authority, and it was not until 1867, with two small exceptions,[25] that legislation specifically empowered federal courts to inquire into the imprisonment of persons under state authority.[26] Pursuant to this authorization, the Court expanded the use of the writ into a major instrument to reform procedural criminal law in federal and state jurisdictions.

VII. HABEAS CORPUS: THE PROCESS OF THE WRIT

A court may only exercise its judicial power under habeas corpus after a petition for such writ is filed by or on behalf of a person in "custody." One should note that the term "custody" has been expanded recently so that it is no longer restricted to actual physical detention in jail or prison.[27]

Petitioners seeking federal relief through a habeas action must first exhaust their state remedies, a limitation long settled in the case law and codified in 1948.[28] In this sense, it is only required that prisoners once present their claims in state court, either on appeal or collateral attack. They need not return time and again to raise their issues before coming to federal court.

It must also be noted that habeas corpus is not a substitute for an appeal.[29] It is not a method to test ordinary procedural errors at trial or violations of state law but a means only to challenge alleged errors, which, if established, would render the entire detention unlawful under federal law.[30]

Once the petition has been presented, the court holds a hearing on the issues raised. If, after appropriate proceedings, the court finds reasonable grounds for habeas, it must grant it. Ordinarily the court orders the government to release the prisoner unless the prisoner is retried within a certain period.

ENDNOTES

1. Muskrat v. United States, 219 U.S. 346, 361 (1911).
2. United States v. Arrendondo, 31 U.S. (6 Pet.) 691 (1832).
3. General Investment Co. v. New York Central R. Co., 271 U.S. 228, 230 (1926).
4. William v. United States, 289 U.S. 553, 566 (1933); Yakus v. United States, 321 U.S. 414, 467–468 (1944) (Justice Rutledge dissenting).
5. Michaelson v. United States, 266 U.S. 42 (1924).
6. McIntire v. Wood, 11 U.S. (7 Cr.) 504 (1813); Ex parte Bollman, 8 U.S. (4 Cr.) 75 (1807).
7. Wayman v. Southard, 23 U.S. (10 Wheat.) 1 (1825).
8. Gumble v. Pitkin, 124 U.S. 131 (1888).
9. Ex parte Peterson, 253 U.S. 300 (1920).
10. Ex parte Garland, 4 Wall. (71 U.S.) 333, 378 (1867).
11. Marbury v. Madison, 5 U.S. (1 Cr.) 137 (1803).
12. The Mayor v. Cooper, 73 U.S. (6 Wall.) 247, 252 (1868); Cary v. Curtis, 44 U.S. (3 How.) 236 (1845); Sheldon v. Sill, 49 U.S. (8 How.) 441 (1850); United States v. Hudson & Goodwin, 11 U.S. (7 Cr.) 32, 33 (1812); Kline v. Burke Construction Co., 260 U.S. 226 (1922); Eisentrager v. Forrestal, 174 F. 2d 961, 965–966 (D.C.Cir. 1949), revd. on other grounds sub nom, Johnson v. Eisentrager, 339 U.S. 763 (1950); Battaglia v. General Motors Corp., 169 F.2d 254, 257 (2d Cir.), cert. den., 335 U.S. 887 (1948); Petersen v. Clark, 285 F. Supp. 700. 703 n. 5 (D.N.D. Calif. 1968); Murray v. Vaughn, 300 F. Supp. 688, 694–695 (D.R.I. 1969).
13. Turner v. Bank of North America, 4 U.S. (4 Dall.) 8 (1799); Bingham v. Cabot, 3 U.S. (3 Dall.) 382 (1798); Jackson v. Ashton, 33 U.S. (8 Pet.) 148 (1834); Mitchell v. Maurer, 293 U.S. 237 (1934).
14. §17165.

15. 18 U.S.C. §401.
16. 493 U.S. 265 (1990).
17. See Anderson v. Dunn, 19 U.S. (6 Wheat.) 204, 227 (1821); Ex parte Robinson, 86 U.S. (19 Wall.) 505, 510 (1874); Link v. Wabash R. Co., 370 U.S. 626, 630–631 (1962); Chambers v. NASCO, Inc., 501 U.S. 32, 43–46 (1991); and *id.*, 58 (Justice Scalia dissenting), 60, 62–67 (Justice Kennedy dissenting).
18. See Rule 11, Federal Rules of Civil Procedure.
19. See Rule 37, Federal Rules of Civil Procedure.
20. 1 Stat. 73, §81.
21. *Id.*, §§81–82.
22. Pennsylvania Bureau of Correction v. United States Marshals Service, 474 U.S. 34 (1985) (holding that a federal district court lacked authority to order U.S. marshals to transport state prisoners, such authority not being granted by the relevant statutes).
23. Art. I, Sec. 9, Cl. 2.
24. Ex parte Bollman, 8 U.S. (4 Cr.) 75 (1807).
25. Act of March 2, 1833, §7, 4 Stat. 634 (federal officials imprisoned for enforcing federal law); Act of August 29, 1842, 5 Stat. 539 (foreign nationals detained by a State in violation of a treaty). See also Bankruptcy Act of April 4, 1800, §38, 2 Stat. 19, 32 (habeas corpus for imprisoned debtor discharged in bankruptcy), repealed by Act of December 19, 1803, 2 Stat. 248.
26. Act of February 5, 1867, 14 Stat. 385, conveyed power to federal courts "to grant writs of habeas corpus in all cases where any person may be restrained of his or her liberty in violation of the constitution, or of any treaty or law of the United States...." On the law with respect to state prisoners prior to this statute, see Ex parte Dorr, 44 U.S. (3 How.) 103 (1845); cf. Elkison v. Deliesseline, 8. Fed. Cas. 493 (No. 4366) (C.C.D.S.C. 1823) (Justice Johnson); Ex parte Cabrera, 4 Fed. Cas. 964 (No. 2278) (C.C.D.Pa. 1805) (Justice Washington).
27. 28 U.S.C. §§2241(c), 2254(a).
28. 28 U.S.C. §2254(b). See Preiser v. Rodriguez, 411 U.S. 475, 490–497 (1973), and *id.* 500, 512–524 (Justice Brennan dissenting); Rose v. Lundy, 455 U.S. 509, 515–521 (1982).
29. Glasgow v. Moyer, 225 U.S. 420, 428 (1912); Riddle v. Dyche, 262 U.S. 333, 335 (1923); Eagles v. United States *ex rel.* Samuels, 329 U.S. 304, 311 (1946). But compare Brown v. Allen, 344 U.S. 443, 558–560 (1953) (Justice Frankfurter dissenting in part).
30. Estelle v. McGuire, 112 S.Ct. 475 (1991); Lewis v. Jeffers, 497 U.S. 764, 780 (1990); Pulley v. Harris, 465 U.S. 37, 41–42 (1984).

5 Judicial Review

I. THE ESTABLISHMENT OF JUDICIAL REVIEW

In its broadest definition *judicial review* is the power of the courts to review all actions of the government including legislative acts, executive actions, and even judicial decisions. Surprisingly, while this is the broadest of the judiciary's powers, it is not specifically established through the Constitution. As such, it is no surprise that the power of judicial review has often been the most challenged of all judicial powers.

The most celebrated and most cited case dealing with this issue is *Marbury v. Madison*.[1] In this case the Supreme Court used its power to strike down an act of Congress as inconsistent with the Constitution. In so doing the Court firmly established that the acts of Congress would be subject to review, when properly challenged, by the Supreme Court and by the lower federal courts.

One should note that while the concept was firmly established in this early case the theory of judicial review did not spring full-blown from the brain of Chief Justice Marshall. The concept had long been utilized in a much more limited form by Privy Council review of colonial legislation and its validity under the colonial charters.[2] Several instances of state court invalidation of state legislation were known to the Framers as inconsistent with state constitutions.

It is also worth noting that the issue of judicial review — the ability of the judiciary to review and decide what falls within the Constitution — was discussed during the Philadelphia Convention. Many of the notes and writings from that time show that most of those in attendance supported the concept. In fact, Madison wrote that many at the Convention assumed and welcomed the notion of court review of the constitutionality of legislation.

At the Virginia Convention, John Marshall observed if Congress "were to make a law not warranted by any of the powers enumerated, it would be considered by the judge as an infringement of the Constitution which they are to guard..." Marshall also told the delegates that, if such law were made, the Court would have little choice but to void it. This is in fact what he did when, as Chief Justice, the case of *Marbury v. Madison* came before his court.

Prior to *Marbury* the Justices seemed very generally to assume judicial review existed. In enacting the Judiciary Act of 1789, Congress explicitly made provision for the exercise of the power. Questions of constitutionality and of judicial review were prominent in other debates. Although judicial review is consistent with several provisions of the Constitution, and the argument for its existence may be derived from these provisions, they do not compel the conclusion that the Framers intended judicial review or that it must exist. To firmly establish the principle, one must dig more deeply. We begin with a more detailed analysis of that famous case.

A. MARBURY V. MADISON

Chief Justice Marshall's argument for judicial review of congressional acts in *Marbury v. Madison* was largely anticipated by Hamilton.[3] For example, Hamilton wrote:

> The interpretation of the laws is the proper and peculiar province of the courts. A constitution, is, in fact, and must be regarded by the judges, as a fundamental law. It therefore belongs to them to ascertain its meaning, as well as the meaning of any particular act proceeding from the legislative body. If there should happen to be an irreconcilable variance between two, that which has the superior obligation and validity ought, of course, to be preferred; or, in other words, the constitution ought to be preferred to the statute, the intention of the people to the intention of their agents.[4]

At the time of the change of administration from Adams to Jefferson, several commissions of appointment to office that had been signed but not delivered were withheld on Jefferson's express instruction. William Marbury sought to compel the delivery of his commission by seeking a writ of mandamus in the Supreme Court in the exercise of its original jurisdiction against Secretary of State Madison. Jurisdiction was based on Section 13 of the Judiciary Act of 1789, which Marbury, and ultimately the Supreme Court, interpreted as authorizing the Court to issue writs of mandamus in suits in its original jurisdiction.

Despite deciding all other issues in Marbury's favor, the Chief Justice concluded that the Section 13 authorization was an attempt by Congress to expand the Court's original jurisdiction beyond the constitutional prescription and was therefore void.[5] Marshall wrote: "The question, whether an act, repugnant to the constitution, can become the law of the land, is a question deeply interesting to the United States." In his discussion of these issues he added, "but, happily, not of an intricacy proportioned to its interest."[6]

Marshall went on to explain that because the Constitution is "a superior paramount law," it is unchangeable by ordinary legislative means and "a legislative act contrary to the constitution is not law."[7] "If an act of the legislature, repugnant to the constitution, is void, does it notwithstanding its invalidity, bind the courts, and oblige them to give it effect?" The answer, thought the Chief Justice, was obvious. "It is emphatically the province and duty of the judicial department to say what the law is.... If two laws conflict with each other, the courts must decide on the operation of each."[8]

In his decision Marshall addressed the question of what a court was to do if it found a law written by the legislative body contradicted or contravened the Constitution itself. "If, then, the courts are to regard the constitution, and the constitution is superior to any ordinary act of the legislature, the constitution, and not such ordinary act, must govern the case to which they both apply."[9] To declare otherwise, Chief Justice Marshall said, would be to permit a legislative body to pass at pleasure the limits imposed on its powers by the Constitution.

Having so firmly established the power of judicial review it was now left for the courts and Congress to fashion any limitations such review may have. This began, not surprisingly, in *Marbury* when the Chief Justice addressed other clauses of the Constitution and their mandates to the courts.

The decision in *Marbury v. Madison* has never been disturbed, although it has been criticized and opposed throughout our history. Judicial review not only carried the day in the federal courts, but from its announcement, judicial review by state courts of local legislation under local constitutions made rapid progress and was securely established in all states by 1850.

B. JUDICIAL REVIEW AND NATIONAL SUPREMACY

One of the areas where judicial review is most notable is in the role of the federal courts in reviewing the acts of the individual state legislatures. It has long been held that review of state acts under federal constitutional standards is soundly based in the supremacy clause of the federal Constitution. Simply stated, since the Constitution, and constitutional laws arising therefrom, are the supreme law of the land, then all other laws, including those created by state legislatures, would be subject to its demands.

This concept has been challenged over the centuries. Virginia launched an early and effective attack when it provided a states' rights challenge to a broad reading of the supremacy clause and to the validity of Section 25 of the Judiciary Act. In *Martin v. Hunter's Lessee*[10] and in *Cohens v. Virginia*[11] it was argued that while the courts of Virginia were constitutionally obliged to prefer "the supreme law of the land" — as set out in the supremacy clause — over conflicting state constitutional provisions and laws, it was only by their own interpretation of the supreme law that they as courts of a sovereign State were bound.

Virginia also contended that cases at hand did not "arise" under the Constitution unless they were brought in the first instance by someone claiming such a right. This argument was extended by inferring that since no such right was claimed then "the judicial power of the United States" did not extend.

Chief Justice Marshall answered: "A case in law or equity consists of the right of the one party, as well as of the other, and may truly be said to arise under the Constitution or a law of the United States, whenever its correct decision depends upon the construction of either."[12] Passing on to the power of the Supreme Court to review such decisions of the state courts, Chief Justice Marshall said:

> Let the nature and objects of our Union be considered: let the great fundamental principles on which the fabric stands, be examined: and we think, the result must be, that there is nothing so extravagantly absurd, in giving to the Court of the nation the power of revising the decisions of local tribunals, on questions which affect the nation, as to require that words which import this power should be restricted by a forced construction.[13]

II. LIMITATIONS ON THE EXERCISE OF JUDICIAL REVIEW

A. CONSTITUTIONAL INTERPRETATION

It is clear that in our system we rely on a constitution that is binding on the government. Legislators propose and pass laws, the executive branch is charged with enforcing those laws, and the judicial branch is given the power to interpret and measure the law. Two of these three branches have at the heart of their operation elected officials who are technically still answerable to the electorate. The judicial branch, by constitutional mandate, is not so answerable. Since the primary actors are appointed for life within the judiciary, they are not subject to the whim of the electorate.

To many this difference between the elected branches and the judiciary raises a legitimate question related to judicial review. The question is one of legitimacy as to the ability of an unelected official to interpret the actions of the elected official. Simply stated, for some this issue eviscerates the idea of a republican or democratic system. Thus, whenever constitutional interpretation becomes controversial we often see massive movements to limit or thwart the ability of the courts to exercise judicial review.

In studying and understanding these issues many scholars suggest that there are in fact six distinct forms of constitutional argument or construction that may be used by courts or others in deciding a constitutional issue. These are (1) historical; (2) textual; (3) structural; (4) doctrinal; (5) ethical; and (6) prudential.

The historical argument is largely, though not exclusively, associated with the theory of original intent or original understanding. In this sense the Court limits interpretation to an attempt to discern the original meaning of the words being construed as that meaning is revealed in the intentions of those who created the law or the constitutional provision in question.

The textual argument, closely associated in many ways to the doctrine of original intent, concerns whether the judiciary is bound by the text of the Constitution and the intentions revealed by that language or whether it may go beyond the four corners of the constitutional document to ascertain the meaning. While the principle appears simple on the surface it is the application of the principle itself that creates the most controversy. From a textual standpoint, issues remain regarding awkward construction of the document, especially when compared to our modern language, and the proper interpretation of those words. In essence, by using a structural argument, one seeks to infer structural rules from the relationships that the Constitution mandates.

The remaining three modes sound in reasoning not necessarily tied to original intent, text, or structure, although they may have some such relationship. Doctrinal arguments proceed from the application of precedents and of specific doctrines within our society. For example, in weighing the issue of slavery some have suggested the Justices used a doctrinal argument in deciding cases that ultimately allowed continuation of the Jim Crow laws.

Prudential arguments seek to balance the costs and benefits of a particular rule. These types of arguments are seen in many criminal justice cases because there is always a need to balance the costs and benefits of the right being examined. For instance, when measuring the right of a citizen to be free from search or seizure while in his or her automobile, one can see the prudential argument applied to justify exceptions to the Fourth Amendment.

Ethical arguments derive rules from those moral commitments of the American ethos that are reflected in the Constitution. These arguments are most clearly seen in cases involving civil rights and related topics. Although scholarly writing presents a wide range of opinions, the scope of the actual political-judicial debate is much narrower. Rare is the judge who will proclaim a devotion to ethical guidelines, such as, for example, natural-law precepts.

The application of these particular methods ranges from those adherents of strict construction and original intent to those with loose construction and adaptation of text to modern-day conditions. It is, however, with regard to more general rules of prudence and self-restraint that one usually finds the enunciation of, and application of limitations on, the exercise of constitutional judicial review.

B. The Doctrine of "Strict Necessity"

The Court has declared repeatedly that it will decide constitutional issues only if strict necessity compels it to do so. This means that constitutional questions will not be decided in broader terms than are required by the precise state of facts to which the ruling is to be applied. It also means that if the case presents itself in a manner that allows a decision to be made on other grounds then the Court will take the alternative route.

The primary reason the Court will not address a constitutional issue first is also the simplest reason. Because the Constitution plays such an immense role in our country's unique character it is often considered foolhardy to rush to judgment on the provisions of the document. In other words, if we were to simply decide all constitutional issues out of hand we would quickly risk creating decisions with too narrow or even too broad a holding. The ramifications of such quick action, and the problems that would erupt while the "mistake" is being corrected, would be devastating.

One must remember that the development of our modern constitutional form of government is not necessarily unique in theory; however, it is unique in how well it works. Other countries have tried to establish a constitution much like ours, but their rush to interpret and establish fine lines of guidance as to the meaning of all parts of that constitution often has led to an unworkable document. For that reason, our highest court chose instead — some would suggest brilliantly — to avoid the narrow confines of the Constitution and instead focus on other solutions to problems that might arise.

Obviously, not all constitutional issues can be avoided. If that were so, there would be no need for a book of this nature. For that reason, one must try to understand fully the intricacies and pitfalls associated with constitutional law.

C. Presumption of Constitutionality

Somewhat related to the doctrine of strict necessity is the principle that a particular act will be presumed to be constitutional. "It is but a decent respect to the wisdom, integrity, and patriotism of the legislative body, by which any law is passed," wrote Justice Bushrod Washington, "to presume in favor of its validity, until its violation of the Constitution is proved beyond a reasonable doubt."[14]

A corollary of this maxim is that if the constitutional question turns upon specific circumstances and not the broader constitutional question then the courts will presume the existence of a state of facts which would justify the legislation that is challenged.[15] A part of the reason for such action is similar to the doctrine of strict necessity, i.e., a rush to judgment to find something unconstitutional can often have broader repercussions than continuation of the act under attack.

D. *STARE DECISIS* IN CONSTITUTIONAL LAW

The term *stare decisis* comes from the Latin meaning "to stand by a thing decided." In the law this is commonly known as "following precedent," the practice of deciding cases based on those decisions made in past similar controversies. From a practical standpoint, courts are slow — and reluctant — to interfere with principles announced in prior cases, and modern courts often uphold older decisions even when the current judge may have decided the past case differently.

Adherence to precedent ordinarily limits and shapes the approach of courts in deciding a presented question.

> Stare decisis is usually the wise policy, because in most matters it is more important that the applicable rule of law be settled than that it be settled right.... This is commonly true even where the error is a matter of serious concern, provided correction can be had by legislation. But in cases involving the Federal Constitution, where correction through legislative action is practically impossible, this Court has often overruled its earlier decisions. The Court bows to the lessons of experience and the force of better reasoning, recognizing that the process of trial and error so fruitful in the physical sciences, is appropriate also in the judicial function.[16]

Stare decisis is a principle of policy, not a mechanical formula of adherence to the latest decision "however recent and questionable, when such adherence involves collision with a prior doctrine more embracing in its scope, intrinsically sounder, and verified by experience."[17]

The application of *stare decisis* from a constitutional standpoint is somewhat schizophrenic. Current justices may consider a past decision fundamental error, and a strict adherence to *stare decisis* would be "a century of error."[18] There appears to be an obligation on each new Court to apply the principle when appropriate but set it aside when the needs of society so demand.

ENDNOTES

1. 5 U.S. (1 Cr.) 137 (1803).
2. For more information on the early charters and the acts of the Privy Council, see Chapter 2.
3. The Federalist, Nos. 78 and 81.
4. *Id.*, No. 78, at 525.
5. Marbury v. Madison, 5 U.S. (1 Cr.) 137, 173–180 (1803).
6. *Id.*, 1 Cr. (5 U.S.), 176.
7. *Id.*, 176–177.
8. *Id.*, 177–178.
9. *Id.*
10. 14 U.S. (1 Wheat.) 304 (1816).
11. 19 U.S. (6 Wheat.) 264 (1821).
12. 14 U.S. (1 Wheat.) 304 at 379 (1816).
13. *Id.*, 422–423.
14. Ogden v. Saunders, 25 U.S. (12 Wheat.) 213, 270 (1827).

15. See Munn v. Illinois, 94 U.S. 113, 132 (1877); Lindsley v. Natural Carbonic Gas Co., 220 U.S. 61, 78–79 (1911); Metropolitan Cas. Ins. Co. v. Brownell, 294 U.S. 580, 584 (1935).
16. Burnet v. Coronado Oil & Gas Co., 285 U.S. 393, 406–408 (1932).
17. Helvering v. Hallock, 309 U.S. 106, 110 (1940).
18. Pollock v. Farmers' Loan & Trust Co., 157 U.S. 429, 574–579 (1895).

Section Three

First Amendment — Religion and Expression

Amendment Text

Congress shall make no law respecting an establishment of religion, or prohibiting the free exercise thereof; or abridging the freedom of speech, or of the press; or the right of the people peaceably to assemble, and to petition the Government for a redress of grievances.

6 Religion: An Overview

I. INTRODUCTION

The First Amendment, much like the Fourth and Fifth Amendments, provides some of the strongest protections for individual freedom within the Constitution. More citizens know they have more protections under the First, Fourth, and Fifth Amendments than under any of the other amendments combined. Unfortunately, most citizens do not fully understand these protections, short of knowing cursory titles such as "Freedom of Speech" or "Freedom of Religion."

Among the better known provisions of the First Amendment are the protections to religious belief and freedom of speech. The First Amendment contains other protections to liberty as well, and in coming chapters we will explore those precious rights. In this chapter we will focus on a right not often encountered by police but which may be one of the most devastating when confronted.

As most students of American history know, it was a freedom to worship as one chose that drove many early immigrants to this country. As Europe crawled out of the dark days of the Middle Ages many oppressive religious practices were firmly in control of social, political, and economic conditions of the time. As people began to change the way they saw themselves and their government many chose to flee the oppressive religious governments of Europe to seek relative freedom in the New World.

One of the primary questions we face today when dealing with religious practice and freedom of religion concerns what is religion and what shall be protected. As we will see in the coming sections this question is not always easy to answer, and the answers have not always been the right ones. For the criminal justice professional this means it is likely that, at some point, there will be a confrontation between the alleged freedom of worship and the power of government. For that reason we include this section in this book.

A. EARLY WORK BY THE FOUNDERS

Any study of American history shows religious freedom at the heart of early colonization. Narratives from American history such as the story of the Pilgrims or the persecution of the Quakers impress upon us the importance of religious freedom in the early development of this country. As many citizens of England and other European countries left their homes to find religious freedom in the New World the need to protect those freedoms increased.

Chief among the concerns faced by the colonists was a strong desire to avoid government-sanctioned churches. Freedom to worship as one chose lay at the heart of this endeavor, and many were prepared to face the hardships of an unknown wilderness rather than succumb to the will of their mother countries.

Two men stand above all others as leaders in shaping both the Constitution and the first ten amendments. Thomas Jefferson and James Madison were especially active in the area of religious issues even before the American Revolution. Jefferson was the earlier innovator in the movement toward freedom of religion. Historians have long noted his support of various religious groups in and around his home. Likewise, Madison's views on religion surfaced very early in his political and public work.

Madison is noted for his involvement in a legislative struggle in the Virginia legislature during the 1784–1785 sessions. A tax was proposed to support teachers of religion in the state, and Madison led the group that opposed the bill. During the course of this effort Madison drafted his now famous work "Memorial and Remonstrance against Religious Assessments," which set forth many of the arguments against public-supported religion that we find were used successfully in shaping the First Amendment.

Madison and Jefferson joined forces later in opposing other acts designed to involve government and religion. Jefferson proposed an act known as the "Bill for Religious Liberty," and Madison was a major force in its support. Both men worked to advance the proposition that government support for any religion is wrong. By the time of the Convention in 1787 Madison, Jefferson, and others held strong opinions on the involvement of government in either sanctioning or opposing religion of any kind, and these men became deeply involved in the work to shape what is today the First Amendment.

B. Shaping an Amendment

From a historical standpoint, Madison's original proposal for a Bill of Rights provision concerning religion read:

> The civil rights of none shall be abridged on account of religious belief or worship, nor shall any national religion be established, nor shall the full and equal rights of conscience be in any manner, or on any pretence, infringed.[1]

The proposal was amended in committee to read: "No religion shall be established by law, nor shall the equal rights of conscience be infringed." After further debate, Madison suggested that the word "national" be inserted before the word "religion" as a means for "point[ing] the amendment directly to the object it was intended to prevent."[2] This early work demonstrated the desire of the Framers and early legislators to form a clause that thwarted the government in any effort to either establish or restrict religion.

In the House, debate focused on the language and overall intent of the amendment. A major issue focused on the extent the amendment would restrict state and government interaction. By August 20, 1789, on motion of Fisher Ames, the language of the clause was again amended.[3]

The Senate also made changes to the proposed amendment and finally adopted an amendment that read: "Congress shall make no law establishing articles of faith, or a mode of worship, or prohibiting the free exercise of religion,…"[4] Obviously, the two houses attacked the issue differently, and the proposals were sent to a joint conference committee to work out the details.

The conference committee, chaired by Madison, worked to blend the two proposals. During debate, Madison told his fellow members that "he apprehended the meaning of the words to be, that Congress should not establish a religion, and enforce the legal observation of it by law, nor compel men to worship God in any Manner contrary to their conscience."[5] It is clear that Madison's conception of "establishment" was quite broad. Government intervention was to be strictly controlled so as to avoid any hint of either establishment or hindrance of religious belief. Eventually a joint amendment was submitted that included the less definite "respecting" phraseology.[6]

Wording of the amendment was contested in Congress, and the application of the amendment causes controversy even today. Aside from the cases we will study in the coming sections, we do have some guidelines as to the intent of the Framers in drafting the amendment.

In 1802, President Jefferson wrote a letter to a group of Baptists in Danbury, Connecticut, in which he declared that it was the purpose of the First Amendment to build "a wall of separation between Church and State." This statement has become a mainstay of First Amendment belief. In *Reynolds v. United States*[7] Chief Justice Waite characterized this phrase as "almost an authoritative declaration of the scope and effect of the amendment."

C. EARLY CHALLENGES TO THE AMENDMENT

Some of the earliest challenges to the First Amendment came not through the courts but through legislative acts. One such act called for the granting of lands near Salem, Mississippi, and a part of the bill provided that certain parcels of land be reserved for a Baptist church. Such legislative action was seen as an extraordinary effort to ensure that land be available for a specific church.

In vetoing the bill President Madison explained that the bill "comprises a principle and precedent for the appropriation of funds of the United States for the use and support of religious societies, contrary to the article of the Constitution which declares that 'Congress shall make no law respecting a religious establishment.'"[8] When called upon, Madison effectively put into practice those ideals he so eloquently brought forth in the new amendment.

II. "ESTABLISHMENT OF RELIGION"

As we have already seen, one of the earliest and most difficult First Amendment issues focused on the establishment of a religion by the government. In understanding this area one must remember that the establishment of a state-sanctioned religion was a pivotal part of European politics through the Middle Ages and into the Age of Exploration. Christianity had grown in popularity throughout Europe, and many monarchs of this time blended both religion and government easily.

Protestants and monarchs alike shaped the religions of Europe. By the mid-seventeenth century much of Europe was ruled by monarchs who incorporated their various religions into their rule. England was not alone in having a government-sanctioned church, but the Church of England was one of the more powerful at that time. As such, it is little wonder that the early efforts at separating church and state focused so much on the idea of restricting government's ability to sanction or develop a particular religion. "[F]or the men who wrote the Religion Clauses of the First Amendment the 'establishment' of a religion connoted sponsorship, financial support, and active involvement of the sovereign in religious activity."[9] With this in mind we will begin our examination of the establishment of religion by looking at the financial support of religion.

A. FINANCIAL ASSISTANCE TO CHURCH-RELATED INSTITUTIONS

The first opportunity to rule on the validity of governmental financial assistance to a religiously affiliated institution occurred in 1899.[10] The assistance in question in this case was a federal grant for the construction of a hospital owned and operated by a Roman Catholic order. Although the Court had opportunity to establish some standard for constitutional interpretation, it followed the doctrine of strict necessity as discussed in the section on Article III and chose an alternative means for deciding the case rather than a strict constitutional interpretation. The Court viewed the hospital as a secular institution so chartered by Congress and not as a religious or sectarian body, and, in so doing, the Court avoided the constitutional issue.

The Court did not take such a view in a later case. In *Everson v. Board of Education*[11] the Court examined questions raised as to the right of local authorities to provide free transportation for children attending parochial schools. In pertinent part the Court said:

> The "establishment of religion" clause of the First Amendment means at least this: Neither a state nor the Federal Government can set up a church. Neither can pass laws which aid one religion, aid all religions, or prefer one religion over another. Neither can force nor influence a person to go to or to remain away from church against his will or force him to profess a belief or disbelief in any religion. No person can be punished for entertaining or professing religious beliefs or disbeliefs, for church attendance or non-attendance. No tax in any amount, large or small, can be levied to support any religious activities or institutions, whatever they may be called, or whatever form they may adopt to teach or practice religion. Neither a state nor the Federal Government can, openly or secretly, participate in the affairs of any religious organizations or groups and vice versa. In the words of Jefferson, the clause against establishment of religion by law was intended to erect a wall of separation between church and State.

While this language certainly appears to set forth some clear standards it is important to note that the Court ultimately upheld the local provision for school transportation. In other words, while the Court set forth such a standard separating church and state, the majority of the Court also found that the particular practices in this instance were not violative of such standards.

In *Everson* the Court recognized that the local acts approached the verge of the state's constitutional power. As Justice Black elucidated, however, the transportation was a form of "public welfare legislation" which was being extended "to all its citizens without regard to their religious belief."[12]

"It is undoubtedly true that children are helped to get to church schools. There is even a possibility that some of the children might not be sent to the church schools if the parents were compelled to pay their children's bus fares out of their own pockets when transportation to a public school would have been paid for by the State."[13] Because the transportation benefited the child, as did police protection at crossings, fire protection, connections for sewage disposal, public highways and sidewalks, the Court found that the service was proper.

The *Everson* case is best known for creating what has been labeled the "child benefit" theory. It was also in *Everson* that the Court, without much discussion of the matter, held that the Establishment Clause applied to the states through the Fourteenth Amendment and limited both national and state governments equally.[14] The issue is discussed at some length by Justice Brennan in *Abington School Dist. v. Schempp*.[15]

In 1968 the Court again relied on the "child benefit" theory to sustain state loans of textbooks to parochial school students.[16] The Court determined that the purpose of the loans was the "furtherance of the educational opportunities available to the young," while the effect was hardly less secular:

> The law merely makes available to all children the benefits of a general program to lend school books free of charge. Books are furnished at the request of the pupil and ownership remains, at least technically, in the State. Thus no funds or books are furnished to parochial schools, and the financial benefit is to parents and children, not to schools. Perhaps free books make it more likely that some children choose to attend a sectarian school, but that was true of the state-paid bus fares in Everson and does not alone demonstrate an unconstitutional degree of support for a religious institution.[17]

One should not conclude from these cases, however, that all financial actions of the government that support, in some way, a religion or its subsidiaries are constitutional. Over the years the number of cases addressing these issues has multiplied. Through the 1970s, at least, the Court took a more restrictive approach. While the "child benefit" theory remained a mainstay for supporting such action there were many other cases which were found violative of the constitutional provisions.

During the most recent decade Supreme Court decisions show a somewhat more accommodating approach by permitting public assistance if the religious missions of the recipient schools may be only marginally served. In these cases the directness of aid to the schools is drawn out by independent decisions of parents who receive the aid initially. The Court has allowed greater discretion when colleges affiliated with religious institutions are aided. Moreover, the opinions reveal a deep division among the Justices over the application of other standards.

For our purposes we should note that a secular purpose is the first requirement to sustain the validity of legislation touching upon religion. While there has been some debate on the exact standard to apply, most will agree that this issue must be involved in all tests. The Justices display little disagreement with this standard.

The Court has also held that there are adequate legitimate, nonsectarian bases for legislation to assist nonpublic, religious schools. Such needs include preservation of a healthy and safe educational environment for all school children, promotion of pluralism and diversity among public and nonpublic schools, and prevention of overburdening of the public school system that would accompany the financial failure of private schools.

In providing assistance, government must avoid aiding the religious mission of such schools directly or indirectly. For example, funds may not be given to a sectarian institution without restrictions that would prevent their use for such purposes as defraying the costs of building or maintaining chapels or classrooms in which religion is taught.[18] Likewise, loans of substantial amounts of purely secular educational materials to sectarian schools can also result in impermissible advancement of sectarian activity where secular and sectarian education are inextricably intertwined.[19] The extent to which the religious mission of the entity is inextricably intertwined with the secular mission and the size of the assistance furnished are factors for the reviewing court to consider.

B. GOVERNMENT ENCOURAGEMENT OF RELIGION IN PUBLIC SCHOOLS

Another area where the government has been restricted is in the encouragement of religion in the public schools. The first of the many issues surrounding this area, commonly known as "release time," deals with the establishment of a period during which pupils in public schools are to be allowed, upon parental request, to receive religious instruction.

In measuring such programs the Court often has focused on the message being taught in the proposed class as well as the circumstances surrounding the release time. In one case where such action was struck down the Court evaluated a program that allowed release time to students who would attend separate religious classes.[20] In *Illinois ex rel. McCollum v. Board of Education* the school established a separate class wherein students who volunteered were taught by outside instructors representing a religious conglomerate. Attendance reports were kept and reported to the school authorities in the same way as for other classes, and pupils not attending the religious instruction classes were required to continue their regular studies.

In addressing the scheme the Court said:

> The operation of the State's compulsory education system thus assists and is integrated with the program of religious instruction carried on by separate religious sects. Pupils compelled by law to go to school for secular education are released in part from their legal duty upon the condition that they attend the religious classes. This is beyond all question a utilization of the tax-established and tax-supported public school system to aid religious groups to spread their faith. And it falls squarely under the ban of the First Amendment....[21]

Four years later, the Court upheld a different release-time program in a case known as *Zorach v. Clauson*.[22] In this case the school released pupils during regular hours and upon written request of the parents, so that the students might leave the school building and go to religious centers for religious instruction or devotional exercises. The churches reported to the schools the names of children released from the public schools who did not report for religious instruction. Children not released remained in the classrooms for regular studies.

The Court found the differences between this program and the program struck down in *McCollum* to be constitutionally significant. The Court noted that in *McCollum* "the classrooms were used for religious instruction and force of the public school was used to promote that instruction." In *Zorach*, however, the Court noted that no religious instruction was conducted on the school grounds and "the public schools do no more than accommodate their [student's] schedules."[23]

In supporting this decision Justice Douglas wrote: "We are a religious people whose institutions presuppose a Supreme Being." He added:

> When the state encourages religious instruction or cooperates with religious authorities by adjusting the schedule of public events to sectarian needs, it follows the best of our traditions. For it then respects the religious nature of our people and accommodates the public service to their spiritual needs. To hold that it may not would be to find in the Constitution a requirement that the government show a callous indifference to religious groups. That would be preferring those who believe in no religion over those who do believe.[24]

Another area that has received a great deal of attention is the use of prayer and Bible reading in the schools. Over the years the Court has meandered through these cases, establishing first a doctrine against prayer and then a lesser restriction allowing prayer under certain conditions. For the student of constitutional law, however, the decisions rarely set a bright line test for when prayer may be allowed. One may find some semblance of order by looking at the various cases and their holdings as a whole rather than as individual cases.

The first issue in this area has to do with a requirement that a student (or other) participate in the prayer. One of the early cases dealing with this issue arose in New York where a local school, upon the recommendation of the state board, required each class to begin the school day by reading aloud a prayer in the presence of the teacher. In addressing this requirement the Court said:

> We think that by using its public school system to encourage recitation of the Regents' prayer, the State of New York had adopted a practice wholly inconsistent with the Establishment Clause. There can, of course, be no doubt that New York's program of daily classroom invocation of God's blessings as prescribed in the Regents' prayer is a religious activity.... [W]e think that the constitutional prohibition against laws respecting an establishment of religion must at least mean that in this country it is no part of the business of government to compose official prayers for any group of the American people to recite as a part of a religious program carried on by government.[25]

Following the prayer decision were two cases in which parents and their school-age children challenged the validity under the Establishment Clause of requirements that each school day begin with readings of selections from the Bible. The Court found that scripture reading, like prayers, was a religious exercise: "Given that finding the exercises and the law requiring them are in violation of the Establishment Clause."[26]

Rejected argument by the state included claims that the object of the programs was the promotion of secular purposes, such as the expounding of moral values, the contradiction of the materialistic trends of the times, the perpetuation of traditional institutions, and the teaching of literature.[27] Although the "place of religion in our society is an exalted one," the Establishment Clause, the Court continued, prescribed that in "the relationship between man and religion," the State must be "firmly committed to a position of neutrality."[28]

The school prayer decisions served as precedent for the Court's holding in *Lee v. Weisman*[29] that a school-sponsored invocation at a high school commencement violated the Establishment Clause. The Court rebuffed the practice, finding "[t]he government involvement with religious activity in this case [to be] pervasive, to the point of creating a state-sponsored and state-directed religious exercise in a public school."

State officials not only determined that an invocation and benediction should be given but also selected the religious participant and provided him with guidelines for the content of nonsectarian prayers. The Court, in an opinion by Justice Kennedy, viewed this state participation as coercive in the elementary and secondary school setting. The state "in effect required participation in a religious exercise," since the option of not attending "one of life's most significant occasions" was no real choice. "At a minimum," the Court concluded, the Establishment Clause "guarantees that government may not coerce anyone to support or participate in religion or its exercise."

In other cases the issue of access to the schools by religious organizations also has been addressed. The Court has found that while government may not promote religion through its educational facilities, it also may not bar student religious groups from meeting on public school property if it makes those facilities available to nonreligious student groups. These principles apply to public secondary schools as well as to institutions of higher learning.[30] In 1990 the Court upheld application of the Equal Access Act to prevent a secondary school from denying access to school premises to a student religious club while granting access to such other "non-curriculum"-related student groups as a scuba diving club, a chess club, and a service club.[31]

III. DEVELOPMENT OF OTHER LEGAL STANDARDS

Emphasis on a separation of church and state was not always a popular belief. One must remember that while the early colonies were populated with people fleeing religious persecution or restrictions in Europe there was a different state of mind in the New World. Christianity, in its many forms, was the dominant religion of the era, and many felt that God, as they worshipped, should be a part of our country and its government.

Over many decades the courts began to emphasize neutrality and voluntarism as the standard of restraint on governmental action when dealing with religion. Where a wall was built between religion and government during Jefferson's time, later courts found that such restraint may be violative of the provisions of the amendment. The issue, in many of the earliest cases, was not always one of separation but rather one of appropriate involvement. In this sense, we see in many of the earlier cases a tendency to overlook government involvement as long as the involvement did not infringe on some other competing right.

Toward the middle of the twentieth century we begin to see a change in this attitude. By 1968 the Court looked not to building a wall between government and religion but instead to finding a neutral ground on which both might operate. The concept of neutrality itself, however, is "a coat of many colors."[32] Three standards that could be stated in objective fashion emerged as tests of Establishment Clause validity.

The first two standards were part of the same formulation, as set forth in *Abington School District v. Schempp*.[33]

> The test may be stated as follows: what are the purpose and the primary effect of the enactment? If either is the advancement or inhibition of religion then the enactment exceeds the scope of legislative power as circumscribed by the Constitution. That is to say that to withstand the strictures of the Establishment Clause there must be a secular legislative purpose and a primary effect that neither advances nor inhibits religion.

As one may recall, the *Schempp* case dealt with issues of religion through the public schools. In evaluating this case one can clearly see that the first two standards are: (1) what is the purpose of the legislative act, and (2) what is the primary effect. If either the purpose or the effect serves to advance or inhibit religion the law violates the Constitution.

The third test focuses on government involvement with the religion or religious purpose. The test centers on whether the governmental program results in:

> ...an excessive government entanglement with religion. The test is inescapably one of degree... [T]he questions are whether the involvement is excessive, and whether it is a continuing one calling for official and continuing surveillance leading to an impermissible degree of entanglement.[34]

In 1971 these three tests were combined and restated in Chief Justice Burger's opinion for the Court in *Lemon v. Kurtzman*.[35]

While this standard still appears to apply today, on occasion the Court has deviated. In many instances this is because the test is difficult to apply. In such instances the Court has stated that the tests provide "helpful signposts,"[36] and are at best "guidelines" rather than a "constitutional caliper." The Court has also indicated that the test must be used to consider "the cumulative criteria developed over many years and applying to a wide range of governmental action." Inevitably, "no 'bright line' guidance is afforded."[37]

The tests have also come under direct attack by some Justices.[38] In two instances the tests have not been applied at all by the Court.[39] While continued application is uncertain, the *Lemon* tests have nonetheless served for 20 years as the standard measure of Establishment Clause validity, and they explain most of the Court's decisions in the area.

IV. GOVERNMENT NEUTRALITY
IN RELIGIOUS DISPUTES

Recognizing that our country was founded by men with quite different views on religion, one can easily see why there is a need for government neutrality on the issue of religion. At the heart of any debate on religion is the issue of which method is correct when worshipping or seeking religious experiences. Where people are free to worship as they wish there is often a dispute as to the correct religious belief or formulation for salvation. Just as groups in Europe split over religious interpretation and practice so too did groups in the colonies.

Differences developed within churches even within the same broad spectrum of religious belief. Likewise, differences and divisions developed between a local church and the general church above it. In many instances such divisions led to a secession of members from one or the other of the groups. Similarly, deep divisions in theology often led to the expulsion of one or more members of a given church. Entire factions of a local, regional, or even national church often found themselves divided.

Whenever people found the need to divide their church a dispute tended to arise as to who would maintain control of the property of the church. Such disputes often ended up in a local court where a magistrate or judge would be called upon to settle the dispute. Even today, our judicial branch finds itself in the middle of such disputes.

The courts soon established the principle that both religion clauses of the Constitution prevent governmental inquiry into religious doctrine to settle disputes within or among churches. In other words, if a church divided over religious philosophy or practice, it would be inappropriate, under the Constitution, for the courts to use the religious mandates of the same church to settle the dispute. Likewise, since no national religion could be established, the courts would be unable to look to a mandated religious belief in order to find a religious answer.

In these instances the courts chose, instead, to look to the decision-making body within the church when solving the intra-church dispute. In effect, the courts looked to the rule-making and decision-making bodies of the church itself in an effort to settle the disputes arising from the split.

The rule of neutrality was applied in a constitutional fashion in *Kedroff v. St. Nicholas Cathedral*.[40] In this case several North American branches of the Russian Orthodox Church declared their independence from the general church. A state statute was passed recognizing these new entities as separate from the original church, and the Court found such statute to be unconstitutional.

In making its decision the Supreme Court looked to the case of *Watson v. Jones*.[41] *Watson* did not explicitly rely on the First Amendment in settling another dispute but instead used common-law grounds in a diversity action to imply neutrality. Now the Supreme Court held that while *Watson* had not used First Amendment principles, per se, the decision "radiates...a spirit of freedom for religious organizations, and independence from secular control or manipulation — in short, power to decide for themselves, free from state interference, matters of church government as well as those of faith and doctrine."[42]

The Court further held that the power of civil courts to resolve church property disputes should be severely limited. To permit resolution of doctrinal disputes in court was to jeopardize First Amendment values. What a court must do, it was held, is to look at the church rules themselves to determine, first, if the church is a hierarchical one that reposes determination of ecclesiastical issues in a certain body.[43] In other words, does the church's own decision-making body have an ability to decide the issues? If the church is a congregational one — thus having a prescribing action by a majority vote — then the determination by such a body will prevail.[44]

In instances where such a body is absent, a court confronted with a church property dispute could apply "neutral principles of law, developed for use in all property disputes." In these instances the court would apply the law under which any property dispute would fall. As long as such action does not require resolution of doctrinal issues[45] the court is to treat the case just as if it were a dispute between two private parties.

In a later case the Court elaborated on this principle. Where the dispute focuses on property division alone the courts may be free to apply secular law. Where such disputes involve matters of internal church government, such as the power to reorganize the dioceses of a hierarchical church, then a court must turn back to the church for determination of such issues. In other words, where the dispute is "at the core of ecclesiastical affairs" a court cannot interpret the church constitution (or other articles of faith) to make an independent determination of the power but must defer to the interpretation of the body authorized to decide.[46]

In *Jones v. Wolf*,[47] however, a divided Court, while formally adhering to these principles, appeared to depart in substance from their application. In this case a split developed in a local church with a majority of the members seeking control of the church property. The church was a member of a hierarchical church (meaning there was a higher decision-making body than the local church), and the majority voted to withdraw from the general church. In response to the proposed split the proper authority of the general church determined that the minority constituted the "true congregation" of the local church and awarded it authority over the property of the church.

The state court applied "neutral principles" of property law by examining the deeds to the church property, state statutes, and provisions of the general church's constitution concerning ownership and control of church property. The trial court then determined that no language of trust was evident in these documents granting ownership or control to the general church. As such, the trial court found, the property belonged to the local congregation.[48]

The Supreme Court ignored that the heart of the dispute was not over property ownership but over ecclesiastical matters. In the majority opinion the Court held that the First Amendment did not prevent the state court from applying a presumption of majority rule to award control to the majority of the local congregation. As long as the general church had an opportunity to defeat such a finding by showing that ownership was controlled by some means other than state statute, such as the general church charter, the trial court's ruling would stand.[49]

The dissent argued against such a finding. By limiting the issue to property ownership alone the Court was able to ignore the central issue that had split the church in the first place. To permit a court to narrowly view only the church documents relating to property ownership permitted the ignoring of the fact that the dispute was over ecclesiastical matters and that the general church had decided which faction of the congregation was the local church.[50]

V. SUNDAY CLOSING LAWS

One area concerning religion and the Constitution in which police and the criminal justice system have often been involved is the so-called Sunday Closing Laws. Sunday Closing Laws go far back into American history. They were brought to the colonies with a background of English legislation dating to the thirteenth century. In 1237, Henry III forbade the frequenting of markets on Sunday. In 1354 Edward III banned the Sunday showing of wool at the staple. By 1409 even the playing of "unlawful games" was banned by Henry IV.

In 1444 Henry VI banned Sunday fairs, but only those fairs held in churchyards. With this distinction, the king made unlawful all fairs, markets, and showings of goods or merchandise on Sunday. Edward VI also disallowed Sunday physical labor with several mid-sixteenth century injunctions, including bans on Sunday sports and amusement. Charles I placed similar restrictions on sports in 1625.

Similar laws were put into place in the colonies. For example, one law from 1677 provided, in part:

> For the better observation and keeping holy the Lord's day, commonly called Sunday: be it enacted…that all the laws enacted and in force concerning the observation of the day, and repairing to the church thereon, be carefully put in execution; and that all and every person and persons whatsoever shall upon every Lord's day apply themselves to the observation of the same, by exercising themselves thereon in the duties of piety and true religion, publicly and privately; and that no tradesman, artificer, workman, laborer, or other person whatsoever, shall do or exercise any worldly labor or business or work of their ordinary callings upon the Lord's day, or any part thereof (works of necessity and charity only excepted);…and that no person or persons whatsoever shall publicly cry, show forth, or expose for sale any wares, merchandise, fruit, herbs, goods, or chattels, whatsoever, upon the Lord's day, or any part thereof…."[51]

Observation of the above language, and of that of the prior mandates, clearly reveals that the English Sunday legislation was in aid of the established church within England. Such restrictions, however, were not limited simply to the colonies and England. By the time of the Revolution the American colonies had their share of Sunday Closing Laws as well.

The American colonial Sunday restrictions arose soon after settlement. Starting in 1650, the Plymouth Colony proscribed "servile work, unnecessary travelling, sports, and the sale of alcoholic beverages on the Lord's day" and enacted laws concerning church attendance. The Massachusetts Bay Colony and the Connecticut and New Haven Colonies enacted similar prohibitions, some even earlier in the seventeenth century.

The religious orientation of the colonial statutes was also apparent. For example, a 1629 Massachusetts Bay instruction began, "And to the end the Sabbath may be celebrated in a religious manner...." Similarly, a 1653 enactment spoke of Sunday activities "which things tend much to the dishonor of God, the reproach of religion, and the profanation of his holy Sabbath, the sanctification whereof is sometimes put for all duties immediately respecting the service of God...."

These laws persisted after the Revolution and, at about the time of the adoption of the First Amendment, each colony had laws of some sort restricting Sunday labor.[52] By the latter part of the seventeenth century and certainly into the eighteenth century, we begin to see a change in justification for such laws. Despite the strongly religious origin of these laws, beginning before the eighteenth century, many non-religious arguments for Sunday closing began to be heard more distinctly, and the statutes began to lose some of their totally religious flavor. One respected supporter, Judge Blackstone, wrote:

> [T]he keeping one day in the seven holy, as a time of relaxation and refreshment as well as for public worship, is of admirable service to a state considered merely as a civil institution. It humanizes, by the help of conversation and society, the manners of the lower classes; which would otherwise degenerate into a sordid ferocity and savage selfishness of spirit; it enables the industrious workman to pursue his occupation in the ensuing week with health and cheerfulness.

Clearly, such well-meaning efforts moved the focus from a day for worship to a day of rest, but in essence merely mask the real intention of the law. Similar justifications are seen throughout the colonies. The New York law of 1788 omitted the term "Lord's day" and substituted "the first day of the week commonly called Sunday."[53]

More recently, further secular justifications have been advanced for making Sunday a day of rest, a day when people may recover from the labors of the week just passed and physically and mentally prepare for the workweek to come. In England, during the First World War, a committee investigating the health conditions of munitions workers reported that "if the maximum output is to be secured and maintained for any length of time, a weekly period of rest must be allowed.... On economic and social grounds alike this weekly period of rest is best provided on Sunday."[54] The proponents of Sunday closing legislation are no longer exclusively representatives of religious interests. In New Jersey Sunday legislation was supported by labor groups and trade associations.[55]

Throughout the years, state legislatures have modified, deleted from, and added to their Sunday statutes. As evidenced by the New Jersey laws mentioned above, changes are commonplace. Almost every state presently has some type of Sunday regulation restricting business or activity in some fashion. Some states enforce their Sunday legislation through their labor departments while others rely on commerce or other departments. Today, Sunday laws have evolved from the wholly religious sanctions that originally were enacted 500 years ago to more esoteric laws designed to provide specific restrictions on business types.

   Moreover, litigation over Sunday Closing Laws is not novel. Scores of cases in
the state appellate courts relate to sundry phases of Sunday enactment.[56] Religious
objections have been raised there on numerous occasions but sustained only once,
in *Ex parte Newman*,[57] a decision overruled three years later, in *Ex parte Andrews*.[58]
A substantial number of cases bearing on state Sunday legislation to some degree
have reached the Supreme Court as well.[59]

   The laws generally require the observance of the Christian Sabbath as a day of
rest, although in recent years they have tended to become honeycombed with excep-
tions. The Supreme Court rejected an Establishment Clause challenge to Sunday
Closing Laws in *McGowan v. Maryland*.[60] Similar decisions on the Establishment
Clause question have been addressed in *Two Guys from Harrison-Allentown v.
McGinley*,[61] *Braunfeld v. Brown*,[62] and *Gallagher v. Crown Kosher Super Market*.[63]

   The Court acknowledged that historically the laws had a religious motivation
and were designed to effectuate concepts of Christian theology, however, "[i]n light
of the evolution of our Sunday Closing Laws through the centuries, and of their
more or less recent emphasis upon secular considerations, it is not difficult to discern
that as presently written and administered, most of them, at least, are of a secular
rather than of a religious character, and that presently they bear no relationship to
establishment of religion...."[64]

   In addressing challenges to Sunday Closing Laws the Court has acknowledged
that the original purposes for the law may very well have been to meet a religious
need.[65] As the Court said in *McGowan*:

> [T]he fact that this [prescribed day of rest] is Sunday, a day of particular significance
> for the dominant Christian sects, does not bar the State from achieving its secular
> goals. To say that the States cannot prescribe Sunday as a day of rest for these purposes
> solely because centuries ago such laws had their genesis in religion would give a
> constitutional interpretation of hostility to the public welfare rather than one of mere
> separation of church and State.[66]

   The choice of Sunday as the day of rest, while originally religious, now reflected
simple legislative inertia or recognition that Sunday was a traditional day for the
choice. Valid secular reasons existed for not simply requiring one day of rest but
instead leaving it to each individual to choose the day, for reasons of ease of
enforcement and ensuring a common day in the community for rest and leisure.

   The Court has also addressed the issue as it arose in other fashions. For instance,
a state statute mandating that employers honor the Sabbath day of the employee's
choice was held invalid when the Court ruled that the statute promoted religious
purposes.[67]

   For the police officer or other criminal justice professional there is a recognition
that Sunday Closing Laws, in and of themselves, are not necessarily invalid. Where
such laws establish or restrict religious purpose, however, they may be held invalid.
As such, a police officer called upon to enforce statutes with such religious overtones
must recognize the implications of such action.

VI. FREE EXERCISE OF RELIGION

Another area where law enforcement officers may be called upon and which involves constitutionally protected freedoms is the free exercise of religion. "The Free Exercise Clause...withdraws from legislative power, state and federal, the exertion of any restraint on the free exercise of religion. Its purpose is to secure religious liberty in the individual by prohibiting any invasions by civil authority."[68]

The constitutional protection bars governmental regulation of religious beliefs and prohibits misuse of secular governmental programs "to impede the observance of one or all religions or...to discriminate invidiously between religions...even though the burden may be characterized as being only indirect."[69] In this sense, the Constitution protects the individual's right to worship as he/she sees fit. The government cannot take action to restrict that right, but there are some limitations.

Freedom of conscience is the basis of the Free Exercise Clause, and government may not penalize or discriminate against an individual or a group of individuals because of their religious views. The government also may not compel persons to affirm particular beliefs.[70]

Interpretation is complicated, however, by the fact that exercise of religion usually entails ritual or other practices that constitute "conduct" rather than pure "belief." When it comes to protecting conduct as free exercise, the Court has been inconsistent.

Academics as well as the justices grapple with the extent to which religious practices as well as beliefs are protected by the Free Exercise Clause. For contrasting academic views of the origins and purposes of the Free Exercise Clause, compare McConnell, *The Origins and Historical Understanding of Free Exercise of Religion*[71] (concluding that constitutionally compelled exemptions from generally applicable laws are consistent with the clause's origins in religious pluralism), with Marshall, *The Case Against the Constitutionally Compelled Free Exercise Exemption*[72] (arguing that such exemptions establish an invalid preference for religious beliefs over nonreligious beliefs).

It has long been held that the Free Exercise Clause does not necessarily prevent government from requiring or forbidding the performance of some act merely because religious beliefs underlie the conduct in question.[73] What has changed over the years is the Court's willingness to hold that some religiously motivated conduct is protected from generally applicable prohibitions.

The relationship between the Free Exercise Clause and the Establishment Clause varies with the expansiveness of interpretation of the two clauses. In a general sense both clauses proscribe governmental involvement with and interference in religious matters, but there is possible tension between a requirement of governmental neutrality derived from the Establishment Clause and a free-exercise–derived requirement that government accommodate some religious practices. For instance, the Court has struggled "to find a neutral course between the two Religion Clauses, both of which are cast in absolute terms, and either of which, if expanded to a logical extreme, would tend to clash with the other."[74]

So far, the Court has harmonized interpretation by denying that free-exercise–mandated accommodations create Establishment violations, and also by upholding some legislative accommodations not mandated by free exercise requirements. This Court has long recognized that government may (and sometimes must) accommodate religious practices and that it may do so without violating the Establishment Clause.[75] In holding that a state could not deny unemployment benefits to Sabbatarians who refused Saturday work, for example, the Court denied that it was "fostering an 'establishment'" of any religious practice over others. The Court held that "the extension of unemployment benefits to Sabbatarians in common with Sunday worshippers reflects nothing more than the governmental obligation of neutrality in the face of religious differences, and does not represent that involvement of religious with secular institutions which it is the object of the Establishment Clause to forestall."[76]

Legislation granting religious exemptions not held to have been required by the Free Exercise Clause have also been upheld against Establishment Clause challenge. For example, in *Walz v. Tax Comm'n*,[77] the Court upheld property tax exemptions for religious organizations. Likewise, in *Corporation of the Presiding Bishop v. Amos*, the Court upheld Civil Rights Act exemptions allowing religious institutions to restrict hiring to members of the religious group.[78] In other cases the Court interpreted conscientious objection in such a manner as to allow exemption from military service.[79]

While it is possible for legislation to provide protections it is also possible for legislation to go too far in promoting free exercise. For instance, in New York officials argued that a law providing for tuition reimbursement grants to parents of parochial school children was designed to promote free exercise by enabling low-income parents to send children to church schools. The Court held that such an act violates the Establishment Clause despite New York State's argument in favor of the program.[80] Likewise, Texas officials argued that a state sales tax exemption for religious publications did not violate the Establishment Clause; however, the Court disagreed in a plurality opinion and struck down the act.[81]

A. The Belief-Conduct Distinction

While the Court has consistently affirmed that the Free Exercise Clause protects religious beliefs, protection for religiously motivated conduct has waxed and waned over the years. The Free Exercise Clause "embraces two concepts — freedom to believe and freedom to act."[82] The Court has consistently held that the first is absolute in that all have the right to believe as they choose; however, according to the Court, "in the nature of things, the second cannot be."[83]

In *Reynolds v. United States*, its first free exercise case involving the power of government to prohibit polygamy, the Court invoked a hard distinction between the two, saying that although laws "cannot interfere with mere religious beliefs and opinions, they may with practices."[84] In *Reynolds* the Court struck down a religious belief by members of the Church of Jesus Christ of Latter-day Saints (the Mormons) allowing multiple marriages under church authority. In this case the leader of the church, Joseph Smith, told his followers that God had commanded him to reinstate the practice of multiple marriages, as seen in the Old Testament.

For many, *Reynolds* involved more a political question than a religious one, in that the Mormons had already been driven from Missouri west to the Utah territory. The Court wrote that "Crime is not the less odious because sanctioned by what any particular sect may designate as 'religion'..." and in so doing struck down for the Mormons what God had commanded of them to be right. While laws could not infringe on their right to believe in such practices, the Court found that it, in fact, could restrict them from acting on the belief.[85]

The rule thus propounded protected only belief, inasmuch as religiously motivated action was to be subjected to the police power of the state to the same extent as would similar action springing from other motives. The *Reynolds* no-protection rule was applied in a number of cases,[86] but later cases established that religiously grounded conduct is not always outside the protection of the Free Exercise Clause.[87]

The Court eventually began to balance the secular interest asserted by the government against the claim of religious liberty asserted by the person affected; only if the governmental interest was "compelling" and if no alternative forms of regulation would serve that interest was the claimant required to yield.[88] While freedom to engage in religious practices was not absolute, it was entitled to considerable protection once the Court worked out certain principles.

Recent cases evidence a narrowing of application of the compelling interest test, and a corresponding constriction on the freedom to engage in religiously motivated conduct. First, the Court purported to apply strict scrutiny, but nevertheless upheld the governmental action. Next, the Court held that the test is inappropriate in the contexts of military and prison discipline.[89] Then, more importantly, the Court ruled in *Employment Division v. Smith* that "if prohibiting the exercise of religion...is not the object...but merely the incidental effect of a generally applicable and otherwise valid provision, the First Amendment has not been offended."[90]

In the *Smith* case the state took action against an employee who was using "peyote" as part of an Native American religious ceremony. That individual was denied unemployment benefits following the criminal penalties imposed for the use of the controlled drug. Although the defendant argued that the use of peyote was done in furtherance of a religious belief the Court held that it was not unconstitutional for the state to restrict such activity.

Based on the *Smith* ruling it would appear that the Free Exercise Clause does not prohibit a state from applying generally applicable criminal penalties to use of peyote in a religious ceremony or from denying unemployment benefits to persons dismissed from their jobs because of religious ceremonial use of peyote. Accommodation of such religious practices must be found in "the political process," the Court noted; statutory religious-practice exceptions are permissible but not "constitutionally required."[91] The result is tantamount to a return to the *Reynolds* belief-conduct distinction found in the Mormon cases.

B. Government Restrictions on Conduct

Over the years there have been some rather disturbing cases of government interference with otherwise reasonable personal conduct for religious reasons. Probably some of the more famous of these actions have come from two of the more controversial

American religions. In the nineteenth century both states and the federal government moved rapidly to act against members of the Church of Jesus Christ of Latter-day Saints, better known as Mormons, for their practice of polygamy. Later, acting against the Jehovah's Witnesses, many states and the federal government sought to restrict that church's methods of proselytizing.

In the Mormon cases many of the states where members of the church resided had laws preventing a man from marrying two women; however, the leader of the church, Joseph Smith, told his congregation that God had commanded him to take a second wife, and that it was a "covenant" with God that would allow him to enter into Heaven.[92]

Although polygamy had been practiced for much of history in many parts of the world, to do so in "enlightened" America in the nineteenth century was viewed by most as incomprehensible and unacceptable, making it the Mormons' most controversial and least understood practice. The presence of large numbers of Mormons in some of the territories made convictions for bigamy difficult to obtain, and in 1882 Congress enacted a statute that barred "bigamists," "polygamists," and "any person cohabiting with more than one woman" from voting or serving on juries. The Court sustained the law, even as applied to persons entering the state prior to enactment of the original law prohibiting bigamy and to persons for whom the statute of limitations had run.[93]

The government's action against the Mormons did not stop with merely creating a law prohibiting their religious acts. Law enforcement officers of all types spread through the territories to find those church members who would not comply. While relatively few of the overall church membership participated in this practice, the lack of wholehearted acceptance and practice was not enough to slow down the government in its persecution of this "dastardly act."

What makes the Mormon cases so interesting is the fact that many within the church itself questioned the new commandment. Likewise, the taking of a second or subsequent wife was not something the Mormons held to be trivial. A man could not take a wife merely because he decided to do so. There is evidence that not all men seeking a second wife were granted the right under church law. The man had to be "righteous" above all else and had to prove himself worthy in other respects. To the Mormons, the act of taking a second wife was anything but carnal lust. It was a religious covenant with God and not one they held without some awe and respect.

Because of the Mormon practice the Supreme Court, for the first time, was asked to interpret the "free exercise" language of the First Amendment. In *Reynolds v. United States*[94] the Court held that the suppression of plural marriages was allowed even under the First Amendment.

George Reynolds, an English immigrant to Utah and private secretary to Brigham Young, was the husband of two wives. In March 1875 he was found guilty of violating the anti-bigamy provision of the Morrill Act. The conviction was overturned by the Utah Supreme Court on procedural grounds,[95] but on retrial Reynolds was again convicted and sentenced to two years in prison and a $500 fine.

In applying the First Amendment's Free Exercise Clause, Chief Justice Morrison R. Waite concluded that "Congress was deprived of all legislative power over mere opinion, but was left free to reach actions which were in violation of social duties or subversive of good order."[96] This distinction between protected religious belief and unprotected religious actions was followed for several decades, and this specific holding regarding plural marriage is still the law. Since 1940, however, the Court has said that religious conduct also may fall within the free exercise guarantee.[97]

As a historical note, the enforcement of the law eventually led the government to revoke the "charter" of the Mormon Church, thereby effectively taking away its status as a recognized religion. Plans were made to seize all of the church's property as a means of preventing its members from practicing this particular religious belief. The Court later sustained the revocation of the charter of the Mormon Church and confiscation of all church property not actually used for religious worship or for burial purposes was begun.[98]

Religious conduct has also been restricted when dealing with other controversial groups. As noted, the acts of members of the Jehovah's Witnesses have been subjected to government legislation and prosecution. Three Jehovah's Witnesses were convicted under a statute that forbade the unlicensed soliciting of funds for religious or charitable purposes and also under a general charge of breach of the peace.[99] The solicitation count was voided as an infringement on religion because the issuing officer was authorized to inquire whether the applicant did have a religious cause and to decline a license if, in his view, the cause was not religious. The Court held that such power amounted to a previous restraint upon the exercise of religion and was invalid.

Over the years, in a series of conflicting cases, the Court has granted and then withdrawn what would appear to be protections for practices of religion. For instance, the distribution of literature by members of a religious group has been held to be proper in some cases and improper in other cases.[100] Likewise, the Court has used child labor laws to restrict the activities of one group when using "child preachers" but has allowed such activity in other cases.[101]

The Court gradually abandoned its strict belief-conduct distinction and developed a balancing test to determine when a uniform, nondiscriminatory requirement by government mandating action or non-action by citizens must allow exceptions for citizens whose religious scruples forbid compliance. Then, in 1990, the Court reversed direction in *Employment Division v. Smith*,[102] confining application of the "compelling interest" test to a narrow category of cases.

The Court has also narrowly tailored exceptions to other matters affecting religious conduct. For instance, the government cannot compel a person to take an oath if the person's religion prevents him or her from swearing such oath.[103] Likewise, the government can compel participation in certain activities with religious overtones. The government cannot completely restrict one from exercising certain noninvasive religious acts even when such acts are in a public forum.[104]

ENDNOTES

1. 1 Annals of Congress 434 (June 8, 1789).
2. *Id.*
3. 1 Annals of Congress 766.
4. Senate Journal of September 9, 1789.
5. 1 Annals of Congress 730 (August 15, 1789).

6. 1 Annals of Congress 913 (September 24, 1789).
7. 98 U.S. 145 (1879).
8. The Writings of James Madison (G. Hunt. ed.) 132–33 (1904).
9. Walz v. Tax Comm'n, 397 U.S. 664, 668 (1970).
10. Bradfield v. Roberts, 175 U.S. 291 (1899).
11. Everson v. Board of Education, 330 U.S. 15, 16 (1947).
12. *Id.* at 16.
13. *Id.* at 17.
14. *Id.* at 8, 13, 14–16.
15. 374 U.S. 203 (1963).
16. Board of Education v. Allen, 392 U.S. 236 (1968).
17. *Id.* at 243–244.
18. Committee for Public Educ. & Religious Liberty v. Nyquist, 413 U.S. 756 (1973).
19. Meek v. Pittenger, 421 U.S. 349 (1975).
20. Illinois *ex rel.* McCollum v. Board of Education, 333 U.S. 203 (1948).
21. *Id.* at 210.
22. Zorach v. Clauson, 343 U.S. 306 (1952). Justices Black, Frankfurter, and Jackson dissented. *Id.* at 315, 320, 323.
23. *Id.* at 315.
24. *Id.* at 313–14.
25. Engel v. Vitale, 370 U.S. 421, 425 (1962).
26. Abington School District v. Schempp, 374 U.S. 203 (1963).
27. *Id.* at 223.
28. *Id.* at 225.
29. 112 S. Ct. 2649 (1992).
30. Widmar v. Vincent, 454 U.S. 263 (1981).
31. Westside Community Bd. of Educ. v. Mergens, 496 U.S. 226 (1990).
32. Board of Education v. Allen, 392 U.S. 236, 249 (1968) (Justice Harlan concurring).
33. 374 U.S. 203, 222 (1963).
34. Walz v. Tax Comm'n, 397 U.S. 664, 675 (1970).
35. 403 U.S. 602 (1971).
36. Hunt v. McNair, 413 U.S. 734 at 741 (1973).
37. Tilton v. Richardson, 403 U.S. 672 (1971). See also Committee for Public Educ. & Religious Liberty v. Nyquist, 413 U.S. 756 (1973); Committee for Public Educ. & Religious Liberty v. Regan, 444 U.S. 646 (1980).
38. See, e.g., Edwards v. Aguillard, 482 U.S. 578 (1987) (Justice Scalia, joined by Chief Justice Rehnquist, dissenting) (advocating abandonment of the "purpose" test); Wallace v. Jaffree, 472 U.S. 38 (1985) (Justice Rehnquist dissenting); Aguilar v. Felton, 473 U.S. 402 (1985) (Justice O'Connor dissenting).
39. See Marsh v. Chambers, 463 U.S. 783 (1983) (upholding legislative prayers on the basis of historical practice); Lee v. Weisman, 112 S. Ct. 2649, 2655 (1992) (rejecting a request to reconsider Lemon because the practice of invocations at public high school graduations was invalid under established school prayer precedents).
40. 344 U.S. 94 (1952).
41. 80 U.S. 679 (1872).
42. *Id.* at 116.
43. *Id.*
44. Presbyterian Church v. Hull Memorial Presbyterian Church, 393 U.S. 440, 450–51 (1969); Maryland and Virginia Eldership of the Churches of God v. Church of God at Sharpsburg, 396 U.S. 367 (1970).

45. Presbyterian Church v. Hull Memorial Presbyterian Church, 393 U.S. 440, 450–51 (1969); Maryland and Virginia Eldership of the Churches of God v. Church of God at Sharpsburg, 396 U.S. 367 (1970).
46. The Serbian Eastern Orthodox Diocese v. Dionisije Milivojevich, 426 U.S. 697 (1976). See also Gonzalez v. Archbishop, 280 U.S. 1 (1929).
47. 443 U.S. 595 (1979).
48. *Id.* at 602–06.
49. *Id.* at 606–10.
50. *Id.* at 610.
51. McGowan v. Maryland, 366 U.S. 420, 433 (1961).
52. See note, 73 Harv. L. Rev. 729–730, 739–740.
53. 2 Laws of N. Y. 1785–1788, 680.
54. Ministry of Munitions, Health of Munition Workers Committee, Report on Sunday Labour, Memorandum No. 1 (1915), 5.
55. Note, 73 Harv. L. Rev. 730–731.
56. See cases collected at 50 Am. Jur. 802 *et seq.*; 24 A. L. R. 2d 813 *et seq.*; 57 A. L. R. 2d 975 *et seq.*
57. 9 Cal. 502 (1858).
58. 18 Cal. 678.
59. See Soon Hing v. Crowley, 113 U.S. 703; Hennington v. Georgia, 163 U.S. 299.
60. 366 U.S. 420 (1961).
61. 366 U.S. 582 (1961).
62. 366 U.S. 59 (1961).
63. 366 U.S. 617 (1961).
64. McGowan v. Maryland, 366 U.S. 420 (1961).
65. *Id.*
66. *Id.* at 445.
67. Estate of Thornton v. Caldor, Inc., 472 U.S. 703 (1985).
68. Abington School District v. Schempp, 374 U.S. 203 at 223 (1963).
69. Braunfeld v. Brown, 366 U.S. 599 (1961).
70. Sherbert v. Verner, 374 U.S. 398 (1963); Torcaso v. Watkins, 367 U.S. 488 (1961).
71. 103 Harv. L. Rev. 1410 (1990).
72. 40 Case W. Res. L. Rev. 357 (1989–90).
73. See, e.g., Reynolds v. United States, 98 U.S. 145 (1879); Jacobson v. Massachusetts, 197 U.S. 11 (1905); Prince v. Massachusetts, 321 U.S. 158 (1944); Braunfeld v. Brown, 366 U.S. 599 (1961); Employment Division v. Smith, 494 U.S. 872 (1990).
74. Walz v. Tax Comm'n, 397 U.S. 668 (1970).
75. Hobbie v. Unemployment Appeals Comm'n, 480 U.S. 136 (1987).
76. Sherbert v. Verner, 374 U.S. 398 (1963).
77. 397 U.S. 664 (1970).
78. 483 U.S. 327 (1987).
79. Gillette v. United States, 401 U.S. 437 (1971).
80. Committee for Pub. Educ. & Religious Liberty v. Nyquist, 413 U.S. 756 (1973).
81. Texas Monthly, Inc. v. Bullock, 489 U.S. 1 (1989).
82. Cantwell v. Connecticut, 310 U.S. 296 (1940).
83. *Id.*
84. Reynolds v. United States, 98 U.S. 145 (1878).
85. It should be noted that the church leaders later revoked the commandment in compliance with the law.

86. Jacobson v. Massachusetts, 197 U.S. 11 (1905) (compulsory vaccination); Prince v. Massachusetts 321 U.S. 158 (1944) (child labor); Cleveland v. United States, 329 U.S. 14 (1946) (polygamy).
87. Sherbert v. Verner, 374 U.S. 398 (1963); Wisconsin v. Yoder, 406 U.S. 205 (1972); cf. Braunfeld v. Brown, 366 U.S. 599 (1961): "[I]f the State regulates conduct by enacting a general law within its power, the purpose and effect of which is to advance the State's secular goals, the statute is valid despite its indirect burden on religious observance unless the State may accomplish its purpose by means which do not impose such a burden."
88. Sherbert v. Verner, 374 U.S. 398 at 406–09 (1963). In Wisconsin v. Yoder, 406 U.S. 205 (1972), the Court recognized compelling state interests in provision of public education, but found insufficient evidence that those interests (preparing children for citizenship and for self-reliance) would be furthered by requiring Amish children to attend public schools beyond the eighth grade. Instead, the evidence showed that the Amish system of vocational education prepared their children for life in their self-sufficient communities.
89. Goldman v. Weinberger, 475 U.S. 503 (1986); O'Lone v. Estate of Shabazz, 482 U.S. 342 (1987).
90. 494 U.S. 872 (1990).
91. Id. at 890.
92. The Church of Jesus Christ of Latter-day Saints, Doctrine and Covenants, Section 132.
93. Murphy v. Ramsey, 114 U.S. 14 (1885).
94. 98 U.S. 145 (1879).
95. United States v. Reynolds, 1 Utah 226 (1875).
96. 98 U.S. 164.
97. Cantwell v. Connecticut, 310 U.S. 296 (1940).
98. The Late Corporation of the Church of Jesus Christ of Latter-day Saints v. United States, 136 U.S. 1(1890).
99. For a detailed discussion of these types of cases see Niemotko v. Maryland, 240 U.S. 268 (1951).
100. Jones v. Opelika, 319 U.S. 103 (1943); Murdock v. Pennsylvania, 319 U.S. 105 (1943). See also Follett v. McCormick, 321 U.S. 573 (1944) (invalidating a flat licensing fee for booksellers). Murdock and Follett were distinguished in Jimmy Swaggart Ministries v. California Bd. of Equalization, 493 U.S. 378, 389 (1990) as applying "only where a flat license fee operates as a prior restraint"; upheld in Swaggart was application of a general sales and use tax to sales of religious publications.
101. Prince v. Massachusetts, 321 U.S. 158 (1944).
102. 494 U.S. 872 (1990).
103. Torcaso v. Watkins, 367 U.S. 488, 494 (1961).
104. McDaniel v. Paty, 435 U.S. 618 (1978); Goldman v. Weinberger, 475 U.S. 503, 507 (1986).

7 Freedom of Expression: Speech and Press

I. INTRODUCTION

As with many of the First Amendment issues we have examined thus far, those associated with freedom of speech and press touch law enforcement in its role as enforcer within society. Congress or another law-making body may deem to suppress speech or press by the introduction of new bills, but it is the law enforcement branch of government that most often confronts these issues on a daily level as it sets about enforcing the laws created by our legislative branch.

In this section we will examine the relationship between the criminal justice system and the protections under the First Amendment. We begin by examining the history and development of these important rights.

A. ADOPTION AND THE COMMON LAW BACKGROUND

As we have seen in previous sections, much of the work associated with the development of the Constitution and the Bill of Rights, as well as the First Amendment protections of speech and press, was done by Madison and those groups with which he was involved.

Madison's version of the speech and press clauses, introduced in the House of Representatives on June 8, 1789, provided:

> The people shall not be deprived or abridged of their right to speak, to write, or to publish their sentiments; and the freedom of the press, as one of the great bulwarks of liberty, shall be inviolable.[1]

Although this initial language was passed by the House it was later defeated in the Senate.[2] A committee appointed to reach an agreement on language acceptable to both House and Senate rewrote the language and added from other provisions of Madison's draft to make it read:

> The freedom of speech and of the press, and the right of the people peaceably to assemble and consult for their common good, and to apply to the Government for redress of grievances, shall not be infringed.[3]

Subsequently, the religion, speech, and press clauses were combined by the Senate, and the final language was agreed upon in conference.[4]

The intent of the Framers was to construct an amendment that set forth simple principles of protection for speech and press. Madison warned against dangers that would arise "from discussing and proposing abstract propositions."[5] He further suggested that "if we confine ourselves to an enumeration of simple, acknowledged principles, the ratification will meet with but little difficulty."[6]

Commentators have often likened the protections of the First Amendment to the common law principles of the English system. These views, as expressed by Blackstone, hold that:

> The liberty of the press is indeed essential to the nature of a free state; but this consists in laying no previous restraints upon publications, and not in freedom from censure for criminal matter when published. Every freeman has an undoubted right to lay what sentiments he pleases before the public; to forbid this, is to destroy the freedom of the press: but if he publishes what is improper, mischievous, or illegal, he must take the consequences of his own temerity.[7]

The common law principle held that the press should not be subject to licensure, that is, that the press or the individual's sentiments, should not be limited by requiring one to gain license from a government arbiter. To subject the press to such restrictive power was to subject all freedom of sentiment to the prejudices of one man, and make him the arbitrary and infallible judge of all controverted points.[8]

One must recognize that prior to the American Revolution there were many who felt the need for constraints on both press and individual freedom of expression. For many, Madison's position on a free press and free speech was considered libertarian. The First Amendment operates not only to bar prior restraints on expression but also to prevent subsequent punishment against all but a narrow range of expression. Even the Common Law, of which many of the day were familiar, left some control on speech and press.

There seems little doubt that Jefferson strongly contemplated the Common Law theories as set forth by Blackstone.[9] Writing to Madison in 1788, Jefferson said: "A declaration that the federal government will never restrain the presses from printing anything they please, will not take away the liability of the printers for false facts printed."[10] Commenting a year later to Madison on his proposed amendment, Jefferson suggested that the free speech–free press clause might read something like: "The people shall not be deprived or abridged of their right to speak, to write or otherwise to publish anything but false facts affecting injuriously the life, liberty, property, or reputation of others or affecting the peace of the confederacy with foreign nations."[11]

By the end of the eighteenth century we began to see challenges to the freedoms enjoyed by the press. One act by Congress punished anyone who would "write, print, utter or publish...any false, scandalous and malicious writing or writings against the government of the United States, or either house of the Congress of the United States, or the President of the United States, with intent to defame the said government, or either house of the said Congress, or the said President, or to bring them, or either of them, into contempt or disrepute."[12] Such actions often grew from political turmoil or confrontation. Such was the case in both Jefferson's counterattack on the Sedition Act[13] and the use of the act by the Adams administration to prosecute its political opponents.[14]

Only since the beginning of this century have we seen the full protections of the amendment come to light.

In 1907, Justice Holmes observed that:

[T]he main purpose of such constitutional provisions is "to prevent all such previous restraints upon publications as had been practiced by other governments," and they do not prevent the subsequent punishment of such as may be deemed contrary to the public welfare.... The preliminary freedom extends as well to the false as to the true; the subsequent punishment may extend as well to the true as to the false. This was the law of criminal libel apart from statute in most cases, if not in all.[15]

But Justice Holmes also observed, "[t]here is no constitutional right to have all general propositions of law once adopted remain unchanged."[16]

In *Schenck v. United States*[17] the defendant was convicted for violating the Espionage Act. The defendant had circulated leaflets intended to cause insubordination in the military service and unrest among the soldiers. Although the Court ultimately upheld the conviction, Justice Holmes suggested that act created First Amendment restraints on subsequent punishment as well as prior restraint.

It well may be that the prohibition of laws abridging the freedom of speech is not confined to previous restraints although to prevent them may have been the main purpose.... We admit that in many places and in ordinary times the defendants in saying all that was said in the circular would have been within their constitutional rights. But the character of every act depends upon the circumstances in which it is done. The most stringent protection of free speech would not protect a man in falsely shouting fire in a theater and causing a panic.... The question in every case is whether the words used are used in such a nature as to create a clear and present danger that they will bring about the substantive evils that Congress has a right to prevent.[18]

During the first quarter of the twentieth century the Court continued to uphold statutes that placed restraints on freedom of speech.[19] Justices Holmes and Brandeis were often the only dissenting members, and they argued that the majority held a false assumption when it held that the Fourteenth Amendment allowed states to suppress speech and press. By 1925, however, Holmes and Brandeis were no longer a dissenting minority when it came to protecting freedom of speech or press.

In *Fiske v. Kansas*[20] the Court sustained a First Amendment-type claim in a state case, and in *Stromberg v. California*[21] a state law was voided on grounds of its interference with free speech. Other cases soon followed.[22]

State common law was also voided when the Court, in an opinion by Justice Black, used the First Amendment to enlarge protections for speech, press, and religion beyond those enjoyed under English common law.[23] Development over the years since then has been uneven, but by 1964 the Court could say with unanimity:

[W]e consider this case against the background of a profound national commitment to the principle that debate on public issues should be uninhibited, robust, and wide-open, and that it may well include vehement, caustic and sometimes unpleasantly sharp attacks on government and public officials.[24]

By 1969 the Court had fashioned the principles of free speech and press to forbid the states from limiting speech or press except where such freedom is directed to inciting or producing imminent lawless action.[25] In the following section we will examine the application of these principles in our modern era.

B. Is There a Difference between Speech and Press?

An early question addressed in studying the application of First Amendment freedoms is whether there is a difference between the Freedom of Speech and Freedom of Press within the Constitution. For example, there has been much debate as to whether the "institutional press" may assert or be entitled to greater freedom from governmental regulations or restrictions than are nonpress individuals, groups, or associations.

Today, our modern media, in all of its current incarnations, enjoys freedom to report on wide-ranging topics that fall under the umbrella of journalism. Newspapers, magazines, television, radio, and even Internet "news" reports vary in style and methodology. Few would disagree, however, that there is substantive difference between the so-called "tabloid news" and the more traditional sources. Do both deserve the same protections? Should either or both be afforded a higher level of protection than that given an individual?

Justice Stewart has argued: "That the First Amendment speaks separately of freedom of speech and freedom of the press is no constitutional accident, but an acknowledgment of the critical role played by the press in American society. The Constitution requires sensitivity to that role, and to the special needs of the press in performing it effectively."[26]

One might interpret such language to mean the press enjoys a higher level of freedom than do others within our society. On the other hand, there are those who join Chief Justice Burger when he wrote: "The Court has not yet squarely resolved whether the Press Clause confers upon the 'institutional press' any freedom from government restraint not enjoyed by all others."[27]

One area that does appear to be clearly delineated is that the press clause does not confer upon the press the power to compel government to furnish information or to give the press access to information that the public generally does not have.[28] In many respects the press is also not entitled to treatment different in kind from the treatment to which any other member of the public may be subjected.[29]

It does, however, seem clear that to some extent the press, because of the role it plays in keeping the public informed and in the dissemination of news and information, is entitled to particular if not special deference to which others are not similarly entitled. For instance, several concurring opinions in *Richmond Newspapers v. Virginia*[30] imply recognition of some right of the press to gather information that apparently may not be wholly inhibited by nondiscriminatory constraints. The Court has also suggested that the press is protected in order to promote and to protect the exercise of free speech in the society, including the receipt of information by the people.[31]

The more interesting issues in dealing with a higher level of protection for the press are found in cases arising under First Amendment protections for good faith defamation.[32] In these instances the press is protected when it publishes material that was defamatory to the plaintiff. Although the material may be false and certainly may be damaging to reputation, the press is granted a limited degree of immunity unless the plaintiff can show malicious intent or a reckless disregard for the truth.

II. THE DOCTRINE OF PRIOR RESTRAINT

"[L]iberty of the press, historically considered and taken up by the Federal Constitution, has meant, principally although not exclusively, immunity from previous restraints or censorship."[33] This quote, from a 1931 Supreme Court case, sets the stage for our discussion on prior restraint.

We can sum up the modern view of prior restraint with two quotes from relatively recent cases. "Any system of prior restraints of expression comes to this Court bearing a heavy presumption against its constitutional validity."[34] Government "thus carries a heavy burden of showing justification for the imposition of such a restraint."[35]

Under the English licensing system, which expired in 1695, all printing presses and printers were licensed, and nothing could be published without prior approval of the state or church authorities. The great struggle for liberty of the press was for the right to publish without a license that which, for a long time, could be published only with a license.[36]

The U.S. Supreme Court's first encounter with a law imposing a prior restraint came in *Near v. Minnesota ex rel. Olson*,[37] in which a 5–4 majority voided a law authorizing the permanent enjoining of future violations by any newspaper or periodical once found to have published or circulated an "obscene, lewd and lascivious" or a "malicious, scandalous and defamatory" issue.

An injunction was issued after the newspaper in question printed a series of articles tying local officials to gangsters. While the dissenters maintained that the injunction constituted no prior restraint, inasmuch as that doctrine applied to prohibitions of publication without advance approval of an executive official,[38] the majority deemed the difference of no consequence, since in order to avoid a contempt citation the newspaper would have to clear future publications in advance with the judge.[39]

Liberty of the press to scrutinize closely the conduct of public affairs was essential, said Chief Justice Hughes for the Court.

> [T]he administration of government has become more complex, the opportunities for malfeasance and corruption have multiplied, crime has grown to most serious proportions, and the danger of its protection by unfaithful officials and of the impairment of the fundamental security of life and property by criminal alliances and official neglect, emphasizes the primary need of a vigilant and courageous press, especially in great cities. The fact that the liberty of the press may be abused by miscreant purveyors of scandal does not make any the less necessary the immunity of the press from previous restraint in dealing with official misconduct. Subsequent punishment for such abuses as may exist is the appropriate remedy, consistent with constitutional privilege.[40]

The Court did not undertake to explore the kinds of restrictions to which the term "prior restraint" would apply or do more than assert that only in "exceptional circumstances" would prior restraint be permissible.[41] Subsequent cases did not substantially illuminate the murky interior of the doctrine. The doctrine of prior restraint was called upon by the Court as it struck down a series of loosely drawn statutes and ordinances requiring licenses to hold meetings and parades and to distribute literature, with uncontrolled discretion of the licensor whether or not to issue them, and as it voided other restrictions on First Amendment rights.[42]

From this series of cases the Court established a clear doctrine on licensing. The current system of permits may be constitutionally valid as long as the discretion of the issuing official was limited to questions of times, places, and manners.[43] In other words, a statute or ordinance may place restraints on speech as long as the licensing requirements focus on time, place, or manner of the speech and not the content of the speech.

III. INJUNCTIONS AND THE PRESS IN FAIR TRIAL CASES

Another instance where the criminal justice system confronts the protections of speech and press comes from the right to a "fair trial." In the past, states have relied upon such tactics as injunctive relief to bar press coverage of notable trials. Confronting the claim of a conflict between free press and fair trial guarantees, the Court typically sets aside any state court injunction barring the publication of information that might prejudice the subsequent trial of a criminal defendant.[44]

Although agreed on result, the Justices were divided with respect to whether "gag orders" were ever permissible and, if so, what the standards for imposing them were. The opinion of the Court utilized the Learned Hand formulation of the "clear and present danger" test.[45] This test considers three key factors when deciding on the imposition of a restraint upon press reporters, to wit:

(a) the nature and extent of pretrial news coverage;
(b) whether other measures were likely to mitigate the harm; and
(c) how effectively a restraining order would operate to prevent the threatened danger.[46]

It is easy to see that anyone seeking a restraining order against the press would have a heavy burden in justifying the need. In essence, the burden requires one to show that without a prior restraint, in this instance a restraining order against the press, the defendant would be denied a fair trial.

The extremely narrow exceptions under which prior restraints might be permissible relate to probable national harm resulting from publication. In such an instance the government or other moving party must show that without the restraint some likely harm would occur. As with the gag orders against the press discussed above, the moving party would carry a heavy burden in providing such proof.

While these rulings do not foreclose the possibility of "gag orders" against the press, they do lessen the number to be expected. These rulings also shift the focus to other alternatives for protecting trial rights. One such alternative is the banning of communication with the press on trial issues by prosecution and defense attorneys, police officials, and court officers. This, of course, also raises First Amendment issues.[47]

On a different level are orders restraining the press as a party to litigation. In this instance, the press stands no differently before the court than any other party to a lawsuit. A judge holds the power to issue a gag order against the parties, and the press is no different. Such gag orders have been used effectively to prevent the press from disseminating information obtained through pretrial discovery. As the Court noted in *Seattle Times Co. v. Rhinehart*,[48] such orders protecting parties from abuses of discovery require "no heightened First Amendment scrutiny."[49]

IV. OBSCENITY AND PRIOR RESTRAINT

Only in the obscenity area has there emerged a substantial consideration of the doctrine of prior restraint. In many instances the doctrine may be based upon the proposition that obscenity is not a protected form of expression. As such, the states — and municipalities within them — have an ability to use their police powers to establish and enforce strict ordinances designed to curb or limit access to pornographic material.

In one such case, the Court upheld a state statute which, while it embodied some features of prior restraint, was seen as having little more restraining effect than an ordinary criminal statute.[50] In the case the Court noted that the law's penalties applied only after publication and as such were not an intolerable matter of prior restraint.

In other cases the Court has not been so supportive of such restraint. In *Times Film Corp. v. City of Chicago*[51] a divided Court specifically affirmed that, at least in the case of motion pictures, the First Amendment did not proscribe a licensing system under which a board of censors could refuse to license for public exhibition films it found to be obscene.

On the other hand, the Court has upheld schemes that provided prior restraint by restricting the location of a movie theater. In *Young v. American Mini Theatres*[52] the Court upheld a zoning ordinance prescribing distances adult theaters may be located from residential areas and found that such an ordinance is not an impermissible prior restraint.

Books and periodicals may also be subjected to some forms of prior restraint,[53] but the thrust of the Court's opinions in this area with regard to all forms of communication has been to establish strict standards of procedural protections to ensure that the censoring agency bears the burden of proof on obscenity. The Court has also held that only a judicial order can restrain exhibition and that a prompt final judicial decision is assured before permanent action may be had.[54]

V. SUBSEQUENT PUNISHMENT: "CLEAR AND PRESENT DANGER" AND OTHER TESTS

In the earlier sections we focused on the issue of "prior restraint," that is, the ability of the government to prevent certain expressions by speech or press before they happen. We now turn to the issues raised when a person is punished after the fact for expressions through speech or press. This is commonly referred to as "subsequent punishment."

As freedom of expression, through speech or press, evolved, the focus very early on appears to have fallen on the principle that a rule of law permitting criminal or civil liability to be imposed upon those who speak or write on public issues would lead to self-censorship. This sentiment is echoed in the now famous Supreme Court decision in *New York Times Co. v. Sullivan*,[55] to wit:

> Under such a rule, would-be critics of official conduct may be deterred from voicing their criticism, even though it is believed to be true and even though it is in fact true, because of doubt whether it can be proved in court or fear of the expense of having to do so.... The rule thus dampens the vigor and limits the variety of public debate.[56]

While it may be argued that the fixing of a standard is necessary there is the larger question of just what standard would be most effective. For many the issue is what degree of evil is substantial enough to justify resort to abridgment of speech and press and assembly as a means of protection. Similarly, the issue arises as to how clear the harmful act must be to justify action by prior restraint of subsequent punishment. One must also determine just how imminent and likely the danger is.[57]

That standard for addressing these issues has fluctuated over a period of some 50 years, and it cannot be asserted with a great degree of confidence. While the Court has yet to settle on any firm standard or set of standards it does appear that the prior cases do give some instruction on what will or will not be allowed. With this in mind we now turn to the more applicable of the tests: clear and present danger.

A. "CLEAR AND PRESENT DANGER"

It is agreed that certain expressions, both oral and written, may incite, urge, counsel, advocate, or importune the commission of criminal conduct. Other expressions, such as picketing, demonstrating, and engaging in certain forms of "symbolic" action may either counsel the commission of criminal conduct or itself constitute criminal conduct. As such, it becomes necessary to determine when expressions may be a link or contributor to criminal conduct and as such should be subject to punishment and restraint.

At first, the Court seemed disposed in the few cases reaching it to rule that if the conduct could be made criminal, the advocacy of or promotion of the conduct could be made criminal.[58] Then, in *Schenck v. United States*,[59] Justice Holmes formulated the "clear and present danger" test which has since been the starting point of argument.

As you should recall from the earlier section, in *Schenck* the defendant was accused of handing out disruptive pamphlets. The defendant had been convicted of seeking to disrupt recruitment of military personnel in the years surrounding World War I. According to Justice Holmes, "The question in every case is whether the words used are used in such circumstances and are of such a nature as to create a clear and present danger that they will bring about the substantive evils that Congress has a right to prevent. It is a question of proximity and degree."[60]

The convictions were unanimously affirmed. One week later, the Court again unanimously affirmed convictions under the same act with Justice Holmes stating:

> [W]e think it necessary to add to what has been said in Schenck v. United States ... only that the First Amendment while prohibiting legislation against free speech as such cannot have been, and obviously was not, intended to give immunity for every possible

use of language. We venture to believe that neither Hamilton nor Madison, nor any other competent person then or later, ever supposed that to make criminal the counseling of a murder within the jurisdiction of Congress would be an unconstitutional interference with free speech.[61]

While Justice Holmes set the tone with the majority opinion in earlier cases he added to the debate when he and Justice Brandeis dissented in other cases. In *Abrams v. United States*[62] Justices Holmes and Brandeis dissented upon affirmance of the convictions of several alien anarchists who had printed leaflets seeking to encourage discontent with U.S. participation in World War I. The majority simply referred to *Schenck* and *Frohwerk* to rebut the First Amendment argument, but the dissenters maintained that the Government had made no showing of a clear and present danger. Thus, by dissenting, Holmes and Brandeis upheld the ideal that in fact a "clear and present" danger must be shown, and that in these cases the burden had not been met.

In another affirmance of a conviction the majority simply said that "[t]he tendency of the articles and their efficacy were enough for the offense," when dealing with similar acts. Again, Holmes and Brandeis dissented in similar fashion.[63]

In *Gitlow v. New York*[64] the Court affirmed a conviction for distributing a manifesto in violation of a law making it criminal to advocate, advise, or teach the duty, necessity, or propriety of overthrowing organized government by force or violence. In reviewing the case it appears that the Court affirmed in the absence of any evidence regarding the effect of the distribution and in the absence of any contention that it created any immediate threat to the security of the State. In so doing, the Court discarded Holmes' test. The Court wrote:

> It is clear that the question in such cases [as this] is entirely different from that involved in those cases where the statute merely prohibits certain acts involving the danger of substantive evil, without any reference to language itself, and it is sought to apply its provisions to language used by the defendant for the purpose of bringing about the prohibited results.... In such cases it has been held that the general provisions of the statute may be constitutionally applied to the specific utterance of the defendant if its natural tendency and probable effect was to bring about the substantive evil which the legislative body might prevent.... [T]he general statement in the Schenck Case...was manifestly intended...to apply only in cases of this class, and has no application to those like the present, where the legislative body itself has previously determined the danger of substantive evil arising from utterances of a specified character.[65]

Thus, a state legislative determination "that utterances advocating the overthrow of organized government by force, violence, and unlawful means, are so inimical to the general welfare, and involve such danger of substantive evil that they may be penalized in the exercise of its police power" was almost conclusive on the Court.

Justice Holmes dissented, stating, in part:

> If what I think the correct test is applied, it is manifest that there was no present danger of an attempt to overthrow the government by force on the part of the admittedly small minority who share the defendant's views. It is said that this manifesto was more than a theory, that it was an incitement. Every idea is an incitement. It

offers itself for belief, and, if believed, is acted on unless some other belief outweighs it, or some failure of energy stifles the movement at its birth. The only difference between the expression of an opinion and an incitement in the narrower sense is the speaker's enthusiasm for the result. Eloquence may set fire to reason. But whatever may be thought of the redundant discourse before us, it had no chance of starting a present conflagration. If, in the long run, the beliefs expressed in proletarian dictatorship are destined to be accepted by the dominant forces of the community, the only meaning of free speech is that they would be given their chance and have their way.[66]

It is not clear what test, if any, the majority would have utilized, although the "bad tendency" test has usually been associated with the case. In *Whitney v. California*[67] the Court affirmed a conviction under a criminal syndicalism statute based on defendant's association with and membership in an organization which advocated the commission of illegal acts, finding again that the determination of a legislature that such advocacy involves "such danger to the public peace and the security of the State" was entitled to almost conclusive weight.

In a technical concurrence which was in fact a dissent from the opinion of the Court, Justice Brandeis restated the "clear and present danger" test when he wrote:

[E]ven advocacy of violation [of the law]…is not a justification for denying free speech where the advocacy falls short of incitement and there is nothing to indicate that the advocacy would be immediately acted on…. In order to support a finding of clear and present danger it must be shown either that immediate serious violence was to be expected or was advocated, or that the past conduct furnished reason to believe that such advocacy was then contemplated.[68]

B. The Adoption of "Clear and Present Danger"

While it may be said that a standard had been set by adopting "clear and present danger" it is also clear that the court did not apply it evenly from case to case. For example, in *Fiske v. Kansas*[69] the Court held that a criminal syndicalism law had been invalidly applied when it overturned a conviction under a state statute. In *Fiske* the defendant was convicted in the District Court of Rice County, Kansas, after he distributed materials supportive of certain unions.

The information charging the defendant stated:

[T]hat the defendant did "by word of mouth and by publicly displaying and circulating certain books and pamphlets and written and printed matter, advocate, affirmatively suggest and teach the duty, necessity, propriety and expediency of crime, criminal syndicalism, and sabotage by…knowingly and feloniously persuading, inducing and securing" certain persons "to sign an application for membership in…and by issuing to" them "membership cards" in a certain Workers' Industrial Union, 'a branch of and component part of the Industrial Workers of the World organization, said defendant then and there knowing that said organization unlawfully teaches, advocates and affirmatively suggests: "That the working class and the employing class have nothing in common, and that there can be no peace so long as hunger and want are found among millions of working people and the few who make up the employing class have all the good things of life." And that "Between these two classes a struggle must go on until the workers of the World organize as a class, take possession of the earth and the machinery of production and abolish the wage system." And that: "Instead of the conservative motto, 'A fair day's wages for a fair day's work,' we must inscribe on our banner the revolutionary watchword, 'Abolition of the wage system.'" By organizing industrially we are forming the structure of the new society within the shell of the old.

The Court held it was improper to convict someone where the only evidence against the person was the "class struggle" language of the constitution of the organization to which he or she belonged.[70]

In *De Jonge v. Oregon*[71] the Court applied what might be labeled as an "incitement" test when it overturned a conviction under a criminal syndicalism statute. In this case the defendant had attended a meeting held under the auspices of an "organization which was said to advocate violence as a political method." The meeting, in fact, had been conducted in an orderly fashion and no violence was advocated during it.

The "clear and present danger" test appears to be used once again in *Herndon v. Lowry*,[72] where the Court narrowly rejected the contention that the standard of guilt could be made the "dangerous tendency" of one's words. The Court indicated that the power of a State to abridge speech "even of utterances of a defined character must find its justification in a reasonable apprehension of danger to organized government."[73]

Finally, in *Thornhill v. Alabama*[74] a state anti-pickcting law was invalidatcd because "no clear and present danger of destruction of life or property, or invasion of the right of privacy, or breach of the peace can be thought to be inherent in the activities of every person who approaches the premises of an employer and publicizes the facts of a labor dispute involving the latter."

One of the more controversial cases faced by the Court in applying clear and present danger occurred in *Terminiello v. City of Chicago*.[75] The trial judge had instructed the jury that a breach of the peace could be committed by speech that "stirs the public to anger, invites dispute, brings about a condition of unrest, or creates a disturbance."

Justice Douglas wrote the majority opinion and stated:

A function of free speech under our system of government is to invite dispute. It may indeed best serve its high purpose when it induces a condition of unrest, creates dissatisfaction with conditions as they are, or even stirs people to anger. Speech is often provocative and challenging. It may strike at prejudices and preconceptions and have profound unsettling effects as it presses for acceptance of an idea. That is why freedom of speech, though not absolute, . . . is nevertheless protected against censorship or punishment, unless shown likely to produce a clear and present danger of a serious substantive evil that rises far above public inconvenience, annoyance, or unrest."[76]

C. "CLEAR AND PRESENT DANGER" REVISED: THE *DENNIS* CASE

Over the years the "clear and present danger" case has seen acceptance and rejection by the Court. It eventually was revived to its relative strength through the now famous case of *Dennis v. United States*,[77] in which the Court sustained the constitutionality of a federal act that proscribed advocacy of the overthrow by force and violence of the U.S. government.

The importance of the *Dennis* case is in the rewriting of the "clear and present danger" test. For a plurality of four, Chief Justice Vinson acknowledged that the Court had in past years relied on the Holmes-Brandeis formulation of clear and present danger without actually overruling the older cases that had rejected the test. The Justices contended that while clear and present danger was the proper constitutional test the "shorthand phrase should [not] be crystallized into a rigid rule to be applied inflexibly without regard to the circumstances of each case."

The application of the rule, the Court held, was an important consideration and was always relative to the concept or speech being limited. Many of the cases in which it had been used to reverse convictions had turned "on the fact that the interest which the State was attempting to protect was itself too insubstantial to warrant restriction of speech."[78]

The Court stated that "[o]verthrow of the Government by force and violence is certainly a substantial enough interest for the Government to limit speech." And in combating that threat, the government need not wait to act until the blow is about to be executed and the plans are set for action. "If Government is aware that a group aiming at its overthrow is attempting to indoctrinate its members and to commit them to a course whereby they will strike when the leaders feel the circumstances permit, action by the Government is required."[79]

In upholding the conviction of Dennis the Court in effect cleared the ground for the government to restrict speech when it comes to certain acts. Certainly acts of sedition or violent overthrow are within the exceptions to First Amendment protections. Later courts, however, have struggled with the application of the "clear and present danger" test, and a more pragmatic approach has evolved.

D. BALANCING THE SPEECH AND THE RESTRICTION

The "clear and present danger" test virtually disappeared from the Court's language over the next 20 years. Its replacement for part of this period was the much disputed "balancing" test, which appeared the year prior to *Dennis* in *American Communications Ass'n v. Douds*.[80]

The *Douds* case addressed issues raised when the National Labor Relations Board required labor union officers to file an annual oath disclaiming membership in the Communist Party. The Court, led by Chief Justice Vinson, rejected reliance on the "clear and present danger" test when it stated:

> Government's interest here is not in preventing the dissemination of Communist doctrine or the holding of particular beliefs because it is feared that unlawful action will result therefrom if free speech is practiced. Its interest is in protecting the free flow of commerce from what Congress considers to be substantial evils of conduct that are not the products of speech at all. Section 9(h), in other words, does not interfere with speech because Congress fears the consequences of speech; it regulates harmful conduct which Congress has determined is carried on by persons who may be identified by their political affiliations and beliefs. The Board does not contend that political strikes...are the present or impending products of advocacy of the

doctrines of Communism or the expression of belief in overthrow of the Government by force. On the contrary, it points out that such strikes are called by persons who, so Congress has found, have the will and power to do so without advocacy.[81]

The Court held that the true test must be one of balancing of interests. "When particular conduct is regulated in the interest of public order, and the regulation results in an indirect, conditional, partial abridgement of speech, the duty of the courts is to determine which of these two conflicting interests demands the greater protection under the particular circumstances presented."

Thereafter, during the 1950s and the early 1960s, the Court utilized the balancing test. In the leading case on balancing, *Konigsberg v. State Bar of California*,[82] the Court upheld the refusal of the State to certify an applicant for admission to the bar. Required to satisfy the Committee of Bar Examiners that he was of "good moral character," Konigsberg testified that he did not believe in the violent overthrow of the government and that he had never knowingly been a member of any organization that advocated such action. He also declined to answer any question pertaining to membership in the Communist Party.

In writing the opinion for the Court, Justice Harlan began by asserting that freedom of speech and association were not absolutes but were subject to various limitations. Among the limitations, "general regulatory statutes, not intended to control the content of speech but incidentally limiting its unfettered exercise, have not been regarded as the type of law the First or Fourteenth Amendment forbade Congress or the States to pass, when they have been found justified by subordinating valid governmental interests, a prerequisite to constitutionality which has necessarily involved a weighing of the governmental interest involved."[83]

E. OTHER TESTS AND STANDARDS

In addition to the foregoing tests, the Court has developed certain standards that are exclusively or primarily applicable in First Amendment litigation. Some of these, such as the doctrines prevalent in the libel and obscenity areas, are very specialized, but others are not. One such test is known as the "vagueness" standard.

Vagueness is a due process issue which can be brought into any criminal and many civil statutes. The vagueness doctrine generally requires that a statute be precise enough to give fair warning to actors that contemplated conduct is criminal, and to provide adequate standards to enforcement agencies, factfinders, and reviewing courts.[84]

Vagueness has been the basis for voiding numerous laws such as the requirement for loyalty oaths,[85] obscenity,[86] and restrictions on public demonstrations.[87] It is usually combined with the overbreadth doctrine, which focuses on the need for precision in drafting a statute that may affect First Amendment rights, and is the foundation for attacking a statute as being overbroad. Generally such statutes will be struck down as facially invalid.

Similarly, and closely related at least to the overbreadth doctrine, the Court has insisted that when the government seeks to carry out a permissible goal and it has available a variety of effective means to the given end, it must choose the measure that least interferes with rights of expression.[88]

F. The Present Test

The creation of one clear test that can be applied to all freedom of expression cases is not feasible. Speech today is too complicated to create such a standard, and this means that there is no clear test for all situations.

For certain forms of expression for which protection is claimed, the Court engages in "definitional balancing" to determine that those forms are outside the range of protection. As an example, obscenity,[89] by definition, is outside the coverage of the First Amendment as are "fighting words."[90] The Court must, of course, decide in each instance whether the questioned expression, by definition, falls within one of these categories or another category.[91]

Balancing enables the Court to determine whether certain covered speech is entitled to protection in the particular context in which the question arises. Utilization of vagueness, overbreadth, and less intrusive means may very well operate to reduce the occasions when questions of protection must be answered squarely on the merits. In this sense, what is observable is the re-emergence, at least in a tentative fashion, of something like the "clear and present danger" standard in advocacy cases and the application of other standards where they are required.

ENDNOTES

1. 1 Annals of Congress 434 (1789).
2. 1 Annals of Congress 957 (1789).
3. *Id.* at 731 (August 15, 1789).
4. *Id.* at 1153 (1789).
5. 1 Annals of Congress 731–49 (August 15, 1789).
6. *Id.* at 738.
7. 4 W. Blackstone's Commentaries on the Laws of England 151–52 (T. Cooley 2d rev. ed. 1872).
8. *Id.*
9. *Id.* at footnote 7.
10. 13 Papers of Thomas Jefferson 442 (J. Boyd ed. 1955).
11. 15 Papers of Thomas Jefferson 367 (J. Boyd ed. 1955).
12. Ch. 74, 1 Stat. 596 (1798).
13. The Act, Ch. 74, 1 Stat. 596 (1798).
14. *Id.* at 159 *et seq.*
15. Patterson v. Colorado, 205 U.S. 454, 462 (1907).
16. Patterson v. Colorado, 205 U.S. 454, 461 (1907).
17. 249 U.S. 47 (1919).
18. *Id.* at pages 51–52.
19. Debs v. United States, 249 U.S. 211 (1919); Abrams v. United States, 250 U.S. 616 (1919); Schaefer v. United States, 251 U.S. 251 (1920); Pierce v. United States, 252 U.S. 239 (1920); United States *ex rel.* Milwaukee Social Democratic Pub. Co. v. Burleson, 255 U.S. 407 (1921); Gilbert v. Minnesota, 254 U.S. 325 (1920).
20. 274 U.S. 380 (1927).
21. 283 U.S. 359 (1931).

22. Near v. Minnesota *ex rel.* Olson, *infra.*; Herndon v. Lowry, 301 U.S. 242 (1937); De Jonge v. Oregon, 299 U.S. (1937); Lovell v. Griffin, 303 U.S. 444 (1938).
23. Bridges v. California, 314 U.S. 251–68 (1941) (overturning contempt convictions of newspaper editor and others for publishing commentary on pending cases).
24. New York Times Co. v. Sullivan, 376 U.S. 254 (1964).
25. Brandenburg v. Ohio, 395 U.S. 444 (1969).
26. Houchins v. KQED, 438 U.S. 1 (1978) (concurring opinion).
27. First National Bank of Boston v. Bellotti, 435 U.S. 765 (1978).
28. Houchins v. KQED, *infra.*; Saxbe v. Washington Post, 417 U.S. 817 (1974).
29. Branzburg v. Hayes, 408 U.S. 665 (1972); Zurcher v. Stanford Daily, 436 U.S. 547 (1978).
30. 448 U.S. 555 (1980).
31. Mills v. Alabama, 453 U.S. 367 (1981).
32. New York Times Co. v. Sullivan, *infra.*
33. Near v. Minnesota *ex rel.* Olson, *infra.* (1931).
34. Bantam Books v. Sullivan, 372 U.S. 58 (1963).
35. Organization for a Better Austin v. Keefe, 402 U.S. 415 (1971); New York Times Co. v. United States, 403 U.S. 713 (1971).
36. See discussion in Near v. Minnesota *ex rel.* Olson, *infra.*, and in Lovell v. Griffin, 303 U.S. 444 (1938).
37. 283 U.S. 697 (1931).
38. *Id.* at 723, 733–36 (Justice Butler dissenting).
39. *Id.* at 712–13.
40. *Id.* at 719–20.
41. *Id.* at 715–16.
42. See Lovell v. Griffin, *infra*; Cantwell v. Connecticut, 310 U.S. 296 (1940); Kunz v. New York, 340 U.S. 290 (1951); Niemotko v. Maryland, 340 U.S. 268 (1951).
43. See Cox v. New Hampshire, 312 U.S. 569 (1941); Poulos v. New Hampshire, 345 U.S. 395 (1953); Organization for a Better Austin v. Keefe, 402 U.S. 415 (1971); and City of Lakewood v. Plain Dealer Publishing Co., 486 U.S. 750 (1988).
44. Nebraska Press Ass'n. v. Stuart, 427 U.S. 539 (1976).
45. See Dennis v. United States, 183 F.2d 201, 212 (2d Cir. 1950), aff'd., 341 U.S. 539 (1951).
46. Nebraska Press Ass'n v. Stuart, 427 U.S. 539 (1976).
47. See, e.g., Chicago Council of Lawyers v. Bauer, 522 F. 2d 242 (7th Cir. 1975), cert. denied, 427 U.S. 912 (1976).
48. 467 U.S. 20 (1984).
49. 467 U.S. 36.
50. Kingsley Books v. Brown, *infra.*
51. 365 U.S. 43 (1961).
52. 427 U.S. 50 (1976).
53. Kingsley Books v. Brown, 354 U.S. 436 (1957).
54. Freedman v. Maryland, 380 U.S. 51 (1965); Teitel Film Corp. v. Cusack, 390 U.S. 139 (1968); Interstate Circuit v. City of Dallas, 390 U.S. 676 (1968).
55. New York Times Co. v. Sullivan, *infra.*
56. *Id.*
57. Whitney v. California, 274 U.S. 357 at 374.
58. Davis v. Beason, 133 U.S. 333 (1890); Fox v. Washington, 236 U.S. 273 (1915).
59. 249 U.S. 47 (1919).

60. *Id.* at 52.
61. Frohwerk v. United States, 249 U.S., 204, 206 (1919) (citations omitted).
62. 250 U.S. 616 (1919).
63. Schaefer v. United States, 251 U.S. 466 (1920).
64. 268 U.S. 652 (1925).
65. *Id.* at 670–71.
66. *Id.* at 673.
67. 274 U.S. 357–72 (1927).
68. *Id.* at 376.
69. 274 U.S. 380 (1927).
70. *Id.*
71. 299 U.S. 353 (1937). See *id.* at 364–65.
72. 301 U.S. 242 (1937). At another point, clear and present danger was alluded to without any definite indication it was the standard. *Id.* at 261.
73. *Id.*
74. 310 U.S. 88, 105 (1940).
75. 337 U.S. 1 (1949).
76. *Id.* at 4–5.
77. 341 U.S. 494 (1951).
78. Dennis v. United States, 341 U.S. 494, 508 (1951).
79. *Id.* at 508, 509.
80. 339 U.S. 382 (1950).
81. American Communications Ass'n v. Douds, 339 U.S. 382, 396 (1950).
82. 366 U.S. 36 (1961).
83. *Id.* at 50–51.
84. See, e.g., Connally v. General Construction Co., 269 U.S. 385 (1926); Lanzetta v. New Jersey, 306 U.S. 451 (1939); Colautti v. Franklin, 439 U.S. 379 (1979); Village of Hoffman Estates v. Flipside, 455 U.S. 489 (1982).
85. Cramp v. Board of Pub. Instruction, 368 U.S. 278 (1961); Baggett v. Bullitt, 377 U.S. 360 (1964); Keyishian v. Board of Regents, 385 U.S. 589 (1967). See also Gentile v. State Bar of Nevada, 501 U.S. 1030 (1991).
86. Winters v. New York, 333 U.S. 507 (1948); Burstyn v. Wilson, 343 U.S. 495 (1952); Interstate Circuit v. City of Dallas, 390 U.S. 676 (1968).
87. Cantwell v. Connecticut, 310 U.S. 296 (1940); Gregory v. City of Chicago, 394 U.S. 111 (1969); Coates v. City of Cincinnati, 402 U.S. 611 (1971).
88. Shelton v. Tucker, 364 U.S. 479 (1960); United States v. Robel, 389 U.S. 258 (1967); Schneider v. Smith, 390 U.S. 17 (1968); Virginia State Bd. of Pharmacy v. Virginia Citizens Consumer Council, 425 U.S. 748 (1976); Central Hudson Gas & Electric Co. v. PSC, 447 U.S. 557, 564, 565, 569–71 (1980).
89. Roth v. United States, 354 U.S. 476 (1957); Paris Adult Theatre v. Slaton, 413 U.S. 49 (1973), as are malicious defamation, New York Times Co. v. Sullivan, 376 U.S. 254 (1964).
90. Chaplinsky v. New Hampshire, 315 U.S. 568 (1942).
91. See, e.g., Jenkins v. Georgia, 418 U.S. 153 (1974); Gooding v. Wilson, 405 U.S. 518 (1972).

8 Rights of Assembly and Petition

I. BACKGROUND AND DEVELOPMENT

The right of petition rises from the modest provision made for it in Chapter 61 of the Magna Carta (1215). Like the provisions for representatives' legislature, an executive branch, and other rights we hold so dear in our own Constitution, the work of the early English noblemen lay the foundation for our own liberty. In this sense, it is the most basic of propositions that make up the right of the people to be heard by their sovereign. A voice in government is exactly what the Magna Carta was all about.

To this meager beginning are traceable, in some measure, Parliament itself and its procedures in the enactment of legislation, the equity jurisdiction of the Lord Chancellor, and proceedings against the Crown by "petition of right." While the King summoned Parliament for the purpose of supply the House of Commons petitioned the King for a redress of grievances as its price for meeting the financial needs of the monarch. By the fifteenth century the right of the people, in this instance the free noblemen, to be heard in their own government had grown so that the Commons declared itself to be "as well assenters as petitioners."

Two hundred and fifty years later, in 1669, the Commons further resolved that every commoner in England possessed "the inherent right to prepare and present petitions" to it "in case of grievance," and of the Commons "to receive the same" and to judge whether they were "fit" to be received. Finally, Chapter 5 of the Bill of Rights of 1689 asserted the right of the subjects to petition the King and "all commitments and prosecutions for such petitioning to be illegal."[1]

Historically the right of petition is the primary right and is at the heart of both the form of government created by the Magna Carta and that of our own Constitution. Today, however, the right of peaceable assembly is, in the language of the Court:

> cognate to those of free speech and free press and is equally fundamental.... [It] is one that cannot be denied without violating those fundamental principles of liberty and justice which lie at the base of all civil and political institutions — principles which the Fourteenth Amendment embodies in the general terms of its due process clause.... The holding of meetings for peaceable political action cannot be proscribed. Those who assist in the conduct of such meetings cannot be branded as criminals on that score. The question...is not as to the auspices under which the meeting is held but as to its purposes; not as to the relation of the speakers, but whether their utterances transcend the bounds of the freedom of speech which the Constitution protects.[2]

While the historical right of petition has expanded, it is no longer confined to demands for "a redress of grievances," in any accurate meaning of these words, but comprehends demands for an exercise by the government of its powers in furtherance of the interest and prosperity of the petitioners and of their views on politically contentious matters. The right extends to the "approach of citizens or groups of them to administrative agencies (which are both creatures of the legislature, and arms of the executive) and to courts, the third branch of government. Certainly the right to petition extends to all departments of the government. The right of access to the courts is indeed but one aspect of the right of petition.[3]

The right of petition recognized by the First Amendment first came into prominence in the early 1830s, when petitions against slavery in the District of Columbia began flowing into Congress in a constantly increasing stream, which reached its climax in the winter of 1835. Finally on January 28, 1840, the House adopted as a standing rule: "That no petition, memorial, resolution, or other paper praying the abolition of slavery in the District of Columbia, or any State or Territories of the United States in which it now exists, shall be received by this House, or entertained in any way whatever."[4]

Because of the efforts of John Quincy Adams, this rule was repealed five years later. For many years now the rules of the House of Representatives have provided that members with petitions to present may deliver them to the Clerk. Those petitions, except such as in the judgment of the Speaker are of an obscene or insulting character, shall be entered on the Journal, and the Clerk shall furnish a transcript of such record to the official reporters of debates for publication in the Record. Even so, petitions for the repeal of the espionage and sedition laws and against military measures for recruiting resulted, during World War I, in imprisonment.

Processions for the presentation of petitions in the U.S. have not been particularly successful. In 1894 General Coxey of Ohio organized armies of unemployed to march on Washington and present petitions, only to see their leaders arrested for unlawfully walking on the grass of the Capitol.

A 1932 march on Washington of the veterans demanding bonus legislation was defended as an exercise of the right of petition. The administration, however, regarded it as a threat against the Constitution and called out the army to expel the marchers and burn their camps. Marches and encampments have become more common since then, but the results have been mixed.

The right of assembly was before the Supreme Court for the first time in 1876 in the now famous case of *United States v. Cruikshank*.[5] In this case, the Supreme Court examined the Enforcement Act of 1870[6] which forbade conspiring or going onto the highways or onto the premises of another to intimidate any other person from freely exercising and enjoying any right or privilege granted or secured by the Constitution of the United States. Defendants had been indicted under this act on charges of having deprived certain citizens of their right to assemble together peaceably with other citizens "for a peaceful and lawful purpose." While the Court held the indictment inadequate because it did not allege that the attempted assembly was for a purpose related to the federal government, its dicta broadly declared the outlines of the right of assembly.

> The right of the people peaceably to assemble for the purpose of petitioning Congress for a redress of grievances, or for anything else connected with the powers or the duties of the National Government, is an attribute of national citizenship, and, as such,

under the protection of, and guaranteed by, the United States. The very idea of a government, republican in form, implies a right on the part of its citizens to meet peaceably for consultation in respect to public affairs and to petition for a redress of grievances. If it had been alleged in these counts that the object of the defendants was to prevent a meeting for such a purpose, the case would have been within the statute, and within the scope of the sovereignty of the United States.[7]

Over time both the assembly and petition clauses have been absorbed into the liberty protected by the due process clause of the Fourteenth Amendment. As such, the *Cruikshank* limitation is no longer applicable, but it does show how the Court has handled such claims in the past.

In later cases, such as *Hague v. CIO*,[8] the Court, although splintered with regard to reasoning and rationale, struck down an ordinance that vested an uncontrolled discretion in a city official to permit or deny any group the opportunity to conduct a public assembly in a public place. Justice Roberts, in an opinion that Justice Black joined and with which Chief Justice Hughes concurred, found protection against state abridgment of the rights of assembly and petition in the privileges and immunities clause of the Fourteenth Amendment.

"The privilege of a citizen of the United States to use the streets and parks for communication of views on national questions may be regulated in the interest of all; it is not absolute, but relative, and must be exercised in subordination to the general comfort and convenience, and in consonance with peace and good order; but it must not, in the guise of regulation, be abridged or denied."[9]

Justices Stone and Reed invoked the due process clause of the Fourteenth Amendment for the result, thereby claiming the rights of assembly and petition for aliens as well as citizens. "I think respondents' right to maintain it does not depend on their citizenship and cannot rightly be made to turn on the existence or non-existence of a purpose to disseminate information about the National Labor Relations Act. It is enough that petitioners have prevented respondents from holding meetings and disseminating information whether for the organization of labor unions or for any other lawful purpose."[10]

This due process view of Justice Stone has carried the day over the privileges and immunities approach. Later cases tend to merge the rights of assembly and petition into the speech and press clauses, and, indeed, all four rights may well be considered as elements of an inclusive right to freedom of expression.

Certain conduct may call forth a denomination of petition[11] or assembly,[12] but there seems little question that no substantive issue turns upon whether one may be said to be engaged in speech or assembly or petition.

ENDNOTES

1. 12 Encyclopedia of the Social Sciences 98 (1934).
2. De Jonge v. Oregon, 299 U.S. 353, 364, 365 (1937).
3. United States v. Cruikshank, 92 U.S. 542 (1876).
4. The account is told in many sources, e.g., S. Bemis, *John Quincy Adams and the Union,* chs. 17, 18 and pp. 446–47 (1956).

5. 92 U.S. 542 (1876).
6. Act of May 31, 1870, ch. 114, 16 Stat. 141 (1870).
7. United States v. Cruikshank, 92 U.S. 542, 552–53 (1876).
8. Hague v. CIO, 397 U.S. 496 (1939).
9. *Id.* at 515.
10. *Id.* at 525.
11. See United States v. Harriss, 342 U.S. 61 (1954), Eastern R.R. Presidents Conf. v. Noerr Motor Freight, 365 U.S. 127 (1961).
12. Coates v. City of Cincinnati, 402 U.S. 611 (1971).

Section Four

Fourth Amendment — Search and Seizure

Amendment Text

The right of the people to be secure in their persons, houses, papers, and effects, against unreasonable searches and seizures, shall not be violated, and no Warrants shall issue, but upon probable cause, supported by Oath or affirmation, and particularly describing the place to be searched, and the persons or things to be seized.

9 The History and Application of the Fourth Amendment

I. HISTORY OF THE AMENDMENT

Like so many of the protections found in the Bill of Rights, the legal protections contained in the Fourth Amendment can be traced to the days of early English common law. Drawing on the rich English maxim that "Every man's house is his castle"[1] the colonial leaders framed an amendment that stands today as one of the strongest in history. One of the most forceful expressions of the maxim was made by William Pitt in Parliament in 1763:

> The poorest man may in his cottage bid defiance to all the force of the crown. It may be frail — its roof may shake — the wind may blow through it — the storm may enter, the rain may enter — but the King of England cannot enter — all his force dares not cross the threshold of the ruined tenement.

The earliest cases that advocated the sanctity of the home did not arise under our modern system of criminal laws and procedures, but instead arose from civil matters where the King, or his designates, sought to enforce some sovereign interest. One such case, decided in 1603, involved the execution of civil process by the King's agents. Commonly known as *Semayne's Case*,[2] the matter focused on the right of a homeowner to defend his house against unlawful entry by the King's agents.

The case is important in establishing an early right to protect one's property and home from illegal actions by the government. The court held that where the agents lacked proper authority to make an entry the homeowner would be justified in taking action to protect his property. However, the court tempered its holding by recognizing that where the King's agents had lawful cause to enter, such as to arrest or exercise the King's authority in other manners, the homeowner would not be protected by the law if the action was improper.

Over a century later the courts revisited these issues in *Entick v. Carrington*.[3] Like *Semayne's Case*, *Entick* arose from a civil action against state officers who, pursuant to general warrants, had raided many homes and other places searching for political materials critical of the King. Other cases attacking similar actions by the Crown also arose,[4] but it is *Entick* that many commentators hold up as the crucial decision in this area.

Factually, *Entick* is an interesting case because it deals with issues that today also would be attacked under First Amendment claims. During this time the King of England was attacked viciously through pamphlets and other written material of the day by those who opposed his policies. One of the leading critics was John Wilkes. Entick was Wilkes' ally.

Agents of the King forcibly broke into Entick's house searching for pamphlets, charts, and other materials used by Wilkes in his polemical attacks on the king. In their efforts to find the material the agents broke into locked desks, boxes, and other places of safekeeping within the home. Few, if any, hiding places were overlooked in the home, and some have argued that the agents were a bit overzealous in their search.

Although the agents had a warrant the court's opinion was sweeping in its statements against their actions. The court declared that the agents' actions were subversive "of all the comforts of society." The court also attacked the nature of the warrant itself by holding that the issuance of a warrant for the seizure of all a person's papers, rather than only those alleged to be criminal in nature, was "contrary to the genius of the law of England."[5] The court also criticized the agents for obtaining the warrant without a showing of probable cause. Likewise, the court was critical of the fact that no record was required to show what had been seized.

The *Entick* case continues to point the way to the protections now part of our Fourth Amendment, and our own Supreme Court has called the Entick case a "great judgment," "one of the landmarks of English liberty," "one of the permanent monuments of the British Constitution." The Court has also called the case a guide to an understanding of what the Framers meant in writing the Fourth Amendment.[6]

In the colonies, smuggling rather than seditious libel afforded the leading examples of the necessity for protection against unreasonable searches and seizures. In order to enforce the revenue laws, English authorities made use of *Writs of Assistance*, which were general warrants authorizing the bearer to enter any house or other place to search for and seize "prohibited and uncustomed" goods. The writs further commanded all persons to assist in these endeavors. Once issued, the writs remained in force throughout the lifetime of the sovereign and for six months thereafter.

When, upon the death of George II in 1760, the authorities were required to obtain the issuance of new writs, opposition was led by James Otis, who attacked the writs on libertarian grounds and asserted the invalidity of the authorizing statutes because they conflicted with English constitutionalism. Although Otis lost his battle to thwart issuance of new writs his arguments were much cited in the colonies and regarded as a leading argument for the abolition of the writs.[7]

Throughout the colonies the Writs of Assistance were attacked by those who opposed their ever-broadening power. As noted in our opening paragraphs, colonial leaders went so far as to take their complaints directly before Parliament, but little relief was granted. By the time of the American Revolution the abuse of the Writs of Assistance by British authority was a strong rallying point for the colonials.

Following the Revolution it was clear that restrictions were needed to curb broad government authority to search one's home or business. The new states included some provisions in both their new constitutions and charters and in their statutory laws. At the Constitutional Convention in Philadelphia in 1787 there was further discussion of the powers of the government in this area.

As the first Congress considered the various amendments to the new Constitution there was clear consensus on the need for some control. However, the language of the provision, which became the Fourth Amendment, underwent modest changes during its passage through the Congress. Historians have long debated that a part of this was due to the relationship of the distinct clauses in the amendment. The phraseology of these clauses merited much discussion in Congress as to the meaning and consequences of the amendment.[8]

Madison's version stated:

> The rights to be secured in their persons, their houses, their papers, and their other property, from all unreasonable searches and seizures, shall not be violated by warrants issued without probable cause, supported by oath or affirmation, or not particularly describing the places to be searched, or the persons or things to be seized.[9]

In committee the proposed amendment underwent only minor changes. The word "secured" was changed to "secure," and the phrase "against unreasonable searches and seizures," which had been taken out before submission to the full House, was reinserted on the floor of the House.[10] Before the full House there was a motion to substitute "and no warrant shall issue" for "by warrants issuing," but this was quickly defeated.

Another noteworthy peculiarity is the fact that the two clauses of the current amendment were originally offered as one single clause. Madison's intent was an amendment that combined the requirement for a warrant with the ban on unreasonable searches. Many have argued that this is the true meaning of the Fourth Amendment, but, as we shall see, this has not been the applied meaning.

II. APPLICATION OF THE AMENDMENT

A. SEARCH WITHOUT A WARRANT

One of the early and lingering problems with the Fourth Amendment was the proper interpretation of the two clauses within the amendment. As set forth above, the two clauses were once combined in the proposed amendment, but an "error" on the floor of the House led to the insertion of specific language that created two distinct clauses. This is where the first issue with the Fourth Amendment arises: Should the two clauses be read together, or should they stand apart?

As one will quickly recognize, the first clause protects citizens from "unreasonable" searches and seizures, and some would argue that this applies to all acts — either with or without a warrant — that are unreasonable. The second clause addresses the more technical aspect of the warrant requirements themselves. By reading the clauses separately one may argue that the Fourth Amendment allows for searches without a warrant as long as the search is reasonable. On the other hand, one may also argue that the two clauses dictate the need for a warrant, and that only those instances of unreasonable warrant — or search pursuant to an unreasonably issued warrant — are to be attacked.

The issue of warrantless searches has been addressed in various fashions by the Court over the years, but there has been little guidance in the area of warrantless searches. In early litigation the Court failed to establish a clear standard for requiring a warrant in all instances of search, and many argue that this oversight has led to the continual dispute we see even today. Not until the last 40 years have we begun to see some clear lines drawn in the debate over reasonable and unreasonable searches with and without warrants.

Part of the convergence came after World War II when the Supreme Court took a clear turn toward the allowance of government intrusion onto what was otherwise considered protected ground. Early on there was consensus that police could search a person contemporaneous with a valid arrest. This right was expanded in *Harris v. United States*,[11] when the Supreme Court approved as "reasonable" the warrantless search of a four-room apartment pursuant to the arrest of the man found inside.

In this case the defendant was arrested by police while still inside the apartment. Concurrent with the arrest the police conducted a search of the apartment, including the room in which the defendant was arrested and the adjoining rooms. Although no warrant was issued, and in fact there was no real "probable cause" to support issuance of a warrant, the Court clearly extended the meaning of "reasonableness" under the Fourth Amendment.

This is a clear expansion of the government's ability to search without a warrant and went well beyond the traditional exception allowing a search of the arrestee only. While this holding expanded the ability of the police to make such a warrantless search, the Court quickly modified the concept the following year.

In *Trupiano v. United States*[12] a reconstituted majority set aside a conviction based on evidence seized by a warrantless search pursuant to an arrest. Where the Court had broadened the police power to conduct a warrantless search of the adjoining four rooms of the apartment in the *Harris* case it now narrowed the ability to search such a wide area in the *Trupiano* case. In doing so, the Court established what some would argue was a new standard when it held the "cardinal rule that, in seizing goods and articles, law enforcement agents must secure and use search warrants wherever reasonably practicable."[13]

This new "cardinal rule," however, was not long-lived. Two years later it was set aside by another reconstituted majority, which adopted the premise that the test "is not whether it is reasonable to procure a search warrant, but whether the search was reasonable." In this sense the Court focused not on the requirement for a warrant but on the probable exceptions to such a requirement. The Court held that the issue of whether a search is reasonable "must find resolution in the facts and circumstances of each case."[14] In this sense the Court now focused on a divided amendment that allowed reasonable searches without a warrant.

In a single three-year period we see the Court extend the ability to search beyond the person of the arrestee, take back such authority, and then extend it again. This psychosis was common among search and seizure cases of the time, and it is not until the 1960s that we see a significant shift in political and social thinking. Where the Court had expanded the ability of the police to search without a warrant in the post-war era we now see it again begin to curtail that power in the "Decade of Peace."

The Court reemphasized the warrant requirement when it held that "[t]he [Fourth] Amendment was in large part a reaction to the general warrants and warrantless searches that had so alienated the colonists and had helped speed the movement for independence. In the scheme of the Amendment, therefore, the requirement that 'no Warrants shall issue, but upon probable cause,' plays a crucial part."[15] The Court further stated that "the police must, whenever practicable, obtain advance judicial approval of searches and seizures through a warrant procedure."[16]

During this same time the Court established many "new" standards for application of the Fourth Amendment. Some have argued that the Court went too far during this era to protect the "rights of the criminals" rather than strengthen the power of the police. By the 1970s the Court was closely divided on which standard to apply, and for a while the balance tipped in favor of the view that warrantless searches are per se unreasonable. There were, however, a few carefully prescribed exceptions to this perception.[17]

Guided by the variable expectation of privacy approach to coverage of the Fourth Amendment, the Court gradually broadened its view of permissible exceptions and of the scope of those exceptions. By 1992, the Court no longer viewed the warrant requirement as superior and the warrantless search as a true exception. The standard moved from a preference for warrants with narrowly tailored exceptions to one of "reasonableness" in allowing warrantless searches.[18]

While the Court appears to follow the standard that a warrant is required, it is also clear that the exceptions to the warrant requirement have multiplied. Today it may easily be said that a warrant is required where practical, but that the issue of practicality will often be measured with a very narrow yardstick.

B. WHO IS PROTECTED UNDER THE AMENDMENT?

When the Fourth Amendment spells out the "right of the people" to be free from unreasonable search and seizure the question arises as to who exactly are "the people." Are only the citizens of the U.S. considered in this elite group, or does the term "the people" have a broader definition? In addressing this issue, the Court determined that the phrase "refers to a class of persons who are part of a national community or who have otherwise developed sufficient connection with [the United States] to be considered part of that community."[19]

In this sense the term "the people" has been interpreted to mean not only all citizens of the U.S. but also anyone within the borders of the U.S. Even a visiting foreign national would protected from an unreasonable search and seizure. The community of protected people includes U.S. citizens, legal visitors to the U.S., and are permanent residents of the U.S. The protection even extends, in most instances, to those within the country illegally. In other words, even an illegal immigrant is protected from unreasonable search and seizure. The amendment does not, however, protect U.S. citizens in foreign countries unless they are within U.S.-held facilities such as military bases, embassies, or similar areas.

C. THE INTEREST PROTECTED

For the Fourth Amendment to be applicable to a particular set of facts, there must be a "search" and a "seizure," occurring typically in a criminal case, with a subsequent attempt to use judicially what was seized. Whether there was a search and seizure within the meaning of the amendment or, whether a complainant's interests were constitutionally infringed, will often turn upon consideration of the complainant's interest and whether it was officially abused.

Under the common law, there was no doubt, said Lord Camden in *Entick v. Carrington*,[20] that: "The great end for which men entered in society was to secure their property. That right is preserved sacred and incommunicable in all instances where it has not been taken away or abridged by some public law for the good of the whole.... By the laws of England, every invasion of private property, be it ever so minute, is a trespass. No man can set foot upon my ground without my license but he is liable to an action though the damage be nothing ...."

This concept has carried forward to the modern protections of the Fourth Amendment. Protection of property interests is at the heart of the Fourth Amendment and has long been recognized by the Supreme Court. In fact, this recognition of a unique property interest has controlled decisions in numerous cases.

For example, in *Olmstead v. United States*[21] one of the two premises underlying the holding that wiretapping was not covered by the Fourth Amendment was that there had been no actual physical invasion of the defendant's premises. The Court has since held that where there had been an invasion there would be a technical trespass and the electronic surveillance would be deemed subject to Fourth Amendment restrictions.[22]

The Court later rejected this approach, however, when it stated: "The premise that property interests control the right of the Government to search and seize has been discredited.... We have recognized that the principal object of the Fourth Amendment is the protection of privacy rather than property, and have increasingly discarded fictional and procedural barriers rested on property concepts."[23] The Court also clarified that the Fourth Amendment "protects people, not places" and, as such, the requirement of actual physical trespass is dispensed with and electronic surveillance was made subject to Fourth Amendment requirements because of the perceived need to protect the individual rather than the property in question.[24]

The test propounded in *Katz v. United States*[25] is whether there is an expectation of privacy upon which one may "justifiably" rely. "What a person knowingly exposes to the public, even in his own home or office, is not a subject of Fourth Amendment protection," the Court wrote. "But what he seeks to preserve as private, even in an area accessible to the public, may be constitutionally protected."

The Court further clarified the protection when it stated that the "capacity to claim the protection of the Amendment depends not upon a property right in the invaded place but upon whether the area was one in which there was reasonable expectation of freedom from governmental intrusion." Thus, in *Mancusi v. DeForte*[26] the Court held that an individual had a reasonable expectation of privacy in an office he shared with others, although he owned neither the premises nor the papers seized. Likewise, in *Minnesota v. Olson*[27] the Court held that even an overnight houseguest has a reasonable expectation of privacy.

While the "expectations of privacy" standards announced in *Katz* appear to draw a bright line for weighing future search and seizure cases it must be pointed out that the Court has not always stayed with these standards. For instance, the first element, the "subjective expectation" of privacy, has largely dwindled as a viable standard, because, as Justice Harlan noted in a subsequent case, "our expectations, and the risks we assume, are in large part reflections of laws that translate into rules the customs and values of the past and present."[28]

As for the second element, whether one has a "legitimate" expectation of privacy that society finds "reasonable" to recognize, the Court has said that "[l]egitimation of expectations of privacy by law must have a source outside of the Fourth Amendment, either by reference to concepts of real or personal property law or to understandings that are recognized and permitted by society."[29] In this sense the protection of the home is at the apex of Fourth Amendment coverage because of the right associated with ownership to exclude others,[30] but ownership of other things, e.g., automobiles, does not carry a similar high degree of protection.[31]

In the modern scheme of search and seizure law it is often sufficient that a person has taken normal precautions to maintain his or her privacy. Fourth Amendment protections are afforded those who use the precautions customarily taken by those seeking to exclude others. Locking doors, securing containers, and concealing items in a manner that requires concerted effort to access the goods may be enough to trigger Fourth Amendment protections.[32]

While customary precautions may trigger those protections, they are not always enough. The Court has indicated that some expectations fall outside those society is willing to accept in activating the protections. Items such as bank records,[33] numbers dialed from one's telephone,[34] materials sent from a prison cell,[35] or garbage left at the curb for collection[36] may not have the privacy protections afforded other matters.

While perhaps not clearly expressed in the opinions, what seems to have emerged is a balancing standard, which requires "an assessing of the nature of a particular practice and the likely extent of its impact on the individual's sense of security balanced against the utility of the conduct as a technique of law enforcement."[37] As the intrusions grow more extensive and significantly jeopardize the sense of security of the individual, greater restraint of police officers through the warrant requirement may be deemed necessary.

Over the years a two-tiered test of privacy interests has been created. Application of this balancing test requires the Court to weigh law enforcement's investigative needs against the subjective expectation of privacy.[38]

The privacy test was originally designed to permit a determination that a Fourth Amendment protected interest had been invaded. If it had been, then ordinarily a warrant was required, subject only to the narrowly defined exceptions, and the scope of the search under those exceptions was "strictly tied to and justified by the circumstances which rendered its initiation permissible."[39]

The Court now uses the test to determine whether the interest invaded is important or persuasive enough so that a warrant is required to justify it. One example of this is seen in the ability of law enforcement to enter into a house for purposes of conducting a search. A tradition has long been held, and remains steadfastly held today, that such entry will not be allowed except with a warrant or some exigent circumstance.[40] The "Fourth Amendment has drawn a firm line at the entrance to the house. Absent exigent circumstances, that threshold may not reasonably be crossed without a warrant."[41]

While some instances clearly demonstrate a preference for a warrant before a search can be had, others seem to require little to allow the exception. If the individual has a lesser expectation of privacy, then the invasion may be justified, absent a warrant, by the reasonableness of the intrusion. Exceptions to the warrant requirement are no longer evaluated solely by the justifications for the exception, e.g., exigent circumstances, and the scope of the search is no longer tied to and limited by the justification for the exception.

We see such exceptions in the more recent cases. For instance, in *Texas v. White*[42] the Court held that if probable cause to search an automobile existed at the scene then the automobile could be removed to the police station and searched without warrant. In *United States v. Robinson*[43] the Court held that once a valid arrest has been made a search pursuant to that arrest is so minimally intrusive that the scope of the search is not limited only to those items that affect the security of the officer. In this sense, the Court extended the right of an officer to search the person arrested for weapons to allow the police to conduct a full search for illegal material of all types.

The Court also held that officers do not need a warrant to search an incarcerated suspect and they may have a right to order the suspect to remove his or her clothes so they may be taken for forensic testing.[44] In this sense the Court held that not only did it not violate the Fifth Amendment to require the suspect to give evidence against himself but it also did not violate the Fourth Amendment unreasonable search or seizure clause. As we enter the twenty-first century it appears that the right of police to search without a warrant has been slightly expanded in comparison to past eras. However, when one considers the restrictions put in place during the 1960s it is easy to see that these rights have not been overly expanded. Some commentators do expect the rights to be curtailed in future decisions, but it is unlikely that we will see the restrictions that we had just 40 years ago. Of course, political and social attitudes will help guide the future decisions of the Court and will certainly affect the trends we see in the future of search and seizure law.

ENDNOTES

1. 5 Coke's Rep. 91a, 77 Eng. Rep. 194 (K.B. 1604).
2. *Id.*
3. 19 Howell's State Trials 1029, 95 Eng. 807 (1705).
4. See also Wilkes v. Wood, 98 Eng. 489 (C.P. 1763); Huckle v. Money, 95 Eng. Rep. 768 (K.B. 1763), aff'd 19 Howell's State Trials 1002, 1028; 97 Eng. Rep. 1075 (K.B. 1765).
5. 5 Eng. Rep. 817, 818.
6. Boyd v. United States, 116 U.S. 616, 626 (1886).
7. Quincy's Massachusetts Reports, 1761–1772, App. I, pp. 395–540, and in 2 Legal Papers of John Adams 106–47 (Wroth and Zobel eds., 1965). See also Dickerson, "Writs of Assistance as a Cause of the American Revolution," in The Era of the American Revolution: Studies Inscribed to Evarts Boutell Greene 40 (R. Morris, ed., 1939).

8. 1 Annals of Congress 434–54 (June 8, 1789).
9. 1 Annals of Congress 434 (June 8, 1789).
10. *Id.* at 754 (August 17, 1789).
11. 331 U.S. 145 (1947).
12. 334 U.S. 699 (1948).
13. *Id.* at 705.
14. United States v. Rabinowitz, 339 U.S. 56, 66 (1950).
15. Chimel v. California, 395 U.S. 752, 761 (1969).
16. Terry v. Ohio, 392 U.S. 1, 20 (1968).
17. See G.M. Leasing Corp. v. United States, 429 U.S. 338, 352–53 (1977) (unanimous); Marshall v. Barlow's, Inc., 436 U.S. 307, 312 (1978); Michigan v. Tyler, 436 U.S. 499, 506 (1978); Mincey v. Arizona, 437 U.S. 385, 390 (1978) (unanimous); Arkansas v. Sanders, 442 U.S. 743, 758 (1979); United States v. Ross, 456 U.S. 798, 824–25 (1982).
18. See Illinois v. Rodriguez, 497 U.S. 177, 189 (Justice Stevens joining Justice Marshall's dissent); New Jersey v. T.L.O., 469 U.S. 325, 370 (1985) (Justice Stevens dissenting); California v. Acevedo, 500 U.S. 565, 585 (1991) (Justice Stevens dissenting).
19. United States v. Verdugo-Urquidez, 494 U.S. 259, 265 (1990).
20. 19 Howell's State Trials 1029, 95 Eng. 807 (1705).
21. 277 U.S. 438 (1928).
22. Silverman v. United States, 365 U.S. 505 (1961).
23. Warden v. Hayden, 387 U.S. 294, 304 (1967).
24. Katz v. United States, 389 U.S. 347, 353 (1967).
25. *Id.*
26. 392 U.S. 364, 368 (1968).
27. 495 U.S. 91 (1990).
28. United States v. White, 401 U.S. 745, 786 (1971).
29. Rakas v. Illinois, 439 U.S. 128, 144 n.12 (1978).
30. Alderman v. United States, 394 U.S. 165 (1969); Mincey v. Arizona, 437 U.S. 385 (1978); Payton v. New York, 445 U.S. 573 (1980).
31. United States v. Ross, 456 U.S. 798 (1982); Donovan v. Dewey, 452 U.S. 594 (1981); and Maryland v. Macon, 472 U.S. 463 (1985).
32. United States v. Chadwick, 433 U.S. 1, 11 (1977); Katz v. United States, 389 U.S. 347, 352 (1967).
33. United States v. Miller, 425 U.S. 435 (1976).
34. Smith v. Maryland, 442 U.S. 735 (1979).
35. Hudson v. Palmer, 468 U.S. 517 (1984).
36. California v. Greenwood, 486 U.S. 35 (1988).
37. United States v. White, 401 U.S. 745, 786–87 (1971) (Justice Harlan dissenting).
38. Robbins v. California, 453 U.S. 420, 429, 433–34 (1981) and United States v. Ross, 456 U.S. 798, 815–16 and n.21 (1982).
39. Terry v. Ohio, 392 U.S. 1, 19 (1968).
40. Payton v. New York, 445 U.S. 573, 590 (1980); Steagald v. United States, 451 U.S. 204, 212 (1981). And see Mincey v. Arizona, 437 U.S. 385 (1978).
41. Payton v. New York, 445 U.S. 573, 590 (1980).
42. 423 U.S. 67 (1975).
43. 414 U.S. 218 (1973).
44. United States v. Edwards, 415 U.S. 800 (1974).

10 Arrests and Other Detentions

I. WHAT IS A SEIZURE?

From the outset it is important to note that the seizure clause of the Fourth Amendment was intended to protect against arbitrary arrests as well as against unreasonable searches. Chief Justice Marshall[1] noted this fact as early as 1806, and the concept is now considered well-established law.[2]

The principle arises from early common law when it was proper to arrest someone who committed a breach of the peace or a felony, and such arrests could be made without a warrant. This same principle is practiced today. It allows the police to arrest for felony crimes and for certain misdemeanors when the arrest is made in a public place on probable cause grounds, regardless of whether a warrant has been obtained.[3]

Until recently, arrests and other detentions were rarely prosecuted to the Supreme Court. Part of the reason is that, when a person is seized by police and released, there is little to litigate that requires review above the intermediate appellate courts. Likewise, when a person was wrongfully held or arrested, the issue tended to be reconciled at the lower levels, most notably at the trial level. Part of the reasoning for this was that the seizure, unlike the improper search, required presentation of the seized party before a judicial officer very early in the case. This opportunity for the seized party to attack the state's actions was a practice not normally allowed when dealing with a search.

It must also be noted that in order to effectuate an arrest in the home, absent consent or exigent circumstances, police officers must have a warrant.[4] There are exceptions to this rule, and as we will see in upcoming sections, these exceptions have been narrowly tailored to address specific needs. For the most part, however, no arrest can be made in the home without a warrant or other exigent circumstances.

It is also important to recognize that the Fourth Amendment applies to "seizures," but this does not necessarily mean the formal detention of arrest. In establishing a standard the Court has indicated that "a person has been 'seized' within the meaning of the Fourth Amendment only if, in view of all the circumstances surrounding the incident, a reasonable person would have believed that he was not free to leave."[5] Thus, it may be held that when the person's freedom of movement is restricted he or she has been seized, and in certain instances the seizure — not just an arrest — will trigger the protections of the Fourth Amendment.

One should also recognize that a seizure need not be for an extended period of time or require the police to remove the person seized from the location of the seizure. A brief detention such as a traffic stop is often enough to create a seizure. When such action is taken, the police must be able to show some objective justification to validate the seizure of the person; however, the nature of the detention will determine whether probable cause or some reasonable and articulable suspicion is necessary.[6]

One area that has impacted the issues of seizure arises from the application of self-incrimination and other exclusionary rules to the states. The heightening of the scope of these protections in state and federal cases alike has brought forth a rule that verbal evidence, confessions, and other admissions, like all derivative evidence obtained as a result of unlawful seizures, could be excluded.[7]

Over the years the issue of detention has slowly been shaped to today's standard. Those instances that create an unlawful detention trigger the protections of the Fourth Amendment — as well as others — and may result in the exclusion of any evidence obtained in conjunction with the illegal detention.

For instance, a confession made by someone illegally in custody must be suppressed, unless the causal connection between the illegal arrest and the confession had become so attenuated that the latter should not be deemed "tainted" by the former.[8] Similarly, fingerprints and other physical evidence obtained as a result of an unlawful arrest must be suppressed.[9]

II. DETENTION SHORT OF ARREST: STOP-AND-FRISK

We have already established that arrests are subject to Fourth Amendment requirements, and in some respects we have also demonstrated that detentions may trigger application of the amendment. The standard for making an arrest, and, in fact, for making a legal detention, is "probable cause." Where an officer has "probable cause" to believe that a crime has been committed and that the accused has committed that crime then the officer may have the right to arrest the person. There are, however, instances when a policeman's suspicions are aroused by someone's conduct or manner, but probable cause for placing such a person under arrest is lacking. In these situations what may a law enforcement officer do to further his or her investigation?

Terry v. Ohio, the most influential case in this area, arose from an incident in Ohio where a Cleveland detective, on a downtown beat he had patrolled for many years, observed two strangers on a street corner.[10] The detective saw the men alternately walk back and forth along an identical route in front of the business. The men paused each time to stare in the same store window. This pattern continued for at least 24 individual trips up and down the sidewalk. With each completion of the route the men stood in "conference" together on a corner where they could watch the store. They were briefly joined by a third man, who left swiftly.

Suspecting the two men of "casing a job" or preparing for "a stick-up" the officer followed them and saw them rejoin the third man a couple of blocks away in front of a different store. The officer approached the three, identified himself as a policeman, and asked their names. The men "mumbled something" and tried to avoid direct contact with the officer. The officer then spun the defendant (Terry) around, patted down his outside clothing, and found a pistol in Terry's overcoat pocket, which the officer was unable to remove.

Watching the three men closely, the officer ordered them into the store. Once inside, the officer removed Terry's overcoat, took out a revolver, and ordered the three to face the wall with their hands raised. The officer then patted down the outer clothing of the other two men, and seized a revolver from an outside overcoat pocket of one of the other men. The officer did not put his hands under the outer garments of the third man (since he discovered nothing in his pat-down which might have been a weapon), or under the outer garments of Terry or the second man until after he felt the guns.

Chief Justice Warren wrote the opinion for the Court and held that the Fourth Amendment was applicable in this situation. The Chief Justice wrote that the amendment is applicable "whenever a police officer accosts an individual and restrains his freedom to walk away."[11]

In analyzing the case and the application of the warrant clause the Court focused on the question of whether the police officer's actions were "reasonable." The test of reasonableness in this sort of situation is whether the police officer can point to "specific and articulable facts which, taken together with rational inferences from those facts," would lead a neutral magistrate on review to conclude that a man of reasonable caution would act in a similar fashion. The issue was whether the officer was justified in believing that possible criminal behavior was at hand and that both an investigative stop and a "frisk" were required.[12]

In addressing the specifics of this case the Court held that a reasonable police officer, with similar training and experience, would likely conclude that an armed robbery or other illegal act was about to take place. As such, the officer had a duty to investigate and, upon confronting the suspected individuals, would have reasonably believed that the men were armed and probably dangerous. Such belief would then justify the "frisk" type search of the individuals for the officer's safety.

Because the object of the "frisk" is the discovery of dangerous weapons, "it must therefore be confined in scope to an intrusion reasonably designed to discover guns, knives, clubs, or other hidden instruments for the assault of the police officer." In this sense, an officer would not be justified in searching for smaller items, such as bindles of drugs or other contraband which would not be considered "threatening," and such a search would violate the protections of the Fourth Amendment.

While *Terry* does provide some guidelines for the search short of an arrest, it did not pass on a host of problems, including the grounds that could permissibly lead an officer to momentarily stop a person on the street or elsewhere. It also left unanswered questions as to the right of the stopped individual to refuse to cooperate, and the permissible response of the police to that refusal.

Following that decision, the standard for stops for investigative purposes evolved into one of "reasonable suspicion of criminal activity." That test permits some stops and questioning without probable cause in order to allow police officers to explore the foundations of their suspicions. Initially the Court was restrictive in allowing permissible intrusions.

The *Terry* Court recognized in dictum that "not all personal intercourse between policemen and citizens involves 'seizures' of persons," and suggested that "[o]nly when the officer, by means of physical force or show of authority, has in some way restrained the liberty of a citizen may we conclude that a 'seizure' has occurred." Years later Justice Stewart proposed a similar standard, that a person has been seized "only if, in view of all of the circumstances surrounding the incident, a reasonable person would have believed that he was not free to leave."[13]

This standard was eventually endorsed by a majority of Justices in later cases. The standard was most notably applied in cases where the admissibility of evidence relied on an analysis of whether the probable cause for the seizure of the person was developed prior to the actual seizure. In cases where the cause was contemporaneous or even subsequent to the stop then the evidence would be excluded.[14]

In one instance where the standard was applied the Court ruled that no seizure had occurred when police in a squad car drove alongside a suspect who had turned and run down the sidewalk when he saw the squad car approach. Under the circumstances (no siren, flashing lights, display of a weapon, or blocking of the suspect's path), the Court concluded, the police conduct "would not have communicated to the reasonable person an attempt to capture or otherwise intrude upon [one's] freedom of movement."[15]

Not long after this case, however, the Court departed from the *Mendenhall* reasonable perception standard and adopted a more formalistic approach. In *California v. Hodari*, the Court held that an actual chase with evident intent to capture did not amount to a "seizure" because the suspect did not comply with the officer's order to halt.[16] A Fourth Amendment "seizure" of the person, the Court determined, is the same as a common law arrest and there must be either application of physical force (or the laying on of hands), or submission to the assertion of authority by the person being detained.[17]

While the *Hodari* standard does appear to alter the "reasonable perception" standard of *Mendenhall* there is reason to believe that it in fact merely carves an exception for those cases involving chases. Part of the reason for this perception arises from cases decided after *Hodari*. For example, in the same term, the Court ruled that the *Mendenhall* "free-to-leave" inquiry was misplaced in the context of a police sweep of a bus, but that a modified reasonable perception approach still governed.[18]

A *Terry* search need not be limited to a stop-and-frisk of the person but may extend as well to a protective search of the passenger compartment of a car if an officer possesses "a reasonable belief, based on specific and articulable facts...that the suspect is dangerous and...may gain immediate control of weapons."[19] In this sense an officer who has "articulable" belief that a detained motorist has access to a weapon, and may be dangerous to the officer or others, may not only order the motorist from the vehicle but may also conduct a cursory search of the vehicle in order to locate the weapon. Such a search would commonly include looking under and around the driver's seat, in the glove compartment or console, and examining all areas immediately accessible to the driver.

One issue that arises in these situations, however, is just how long an officer may make such a search. In answering this, the Court has indicated that the duration may vary, depending on the specific circumstances of the detention. In one case the Court approved a 20-minute detention of a driver necessitated by the driver's own evasion of drug agents and a state police decision to hold the driver until the agents could arrive on the scene. The Court indicated that it is "appropriate to examine whether the police diligently pursued a means of investigation that was likely to confirm or dispel their suspicions quickly, during which time it was necessary to detain the defendant."[20]

A similar standard, although more relaxed, has been applied to detention of travelers at the border. In these cases the Court weighed the reasonableness in terms of "the period of time necessary to either verify or dispel the suspicion" in question. In *United States v. Montoya de Hernandez*[21] the Court approved the warrantless detention of the defendant for more than 24 hours when the traveler was suspected of alimentary canal drug smuggling. In such a case the time was needed to allow the suspected drugs to move from the intestines and be passed with fecal material.

Similar principles govern detention of luggage at airports in order to detect the presence of drugs. The Court has held that *Terry* "limitations applicable to investigative detentions of the person should define the permissible scope of an investigative detention of the person's luggage on less than probable cause."[22] The general rule is that "when an officer's observations lead him reasonably to believe that a traveler is carrying luggage that contains narcotics, the principles of Terry... would permit the officer to detain the luggage briefly to investigate the circumstances that aroused his suspicion, provided that the investigative detention is properly limited in scope."

In recent years the use of canines to detect smuggled narcotics (and other materials) has led to some expansion of the *Terry* standards. Seizure of luggage for an expeditious "canine sniff" by a trained dog can satisfy the test although seizure of luggage is in effect detention of the traveler. Because the procedure results in "limited disclosure," the Court had ruled that it impinges only slightly on a traveler's privacy interest in the contents of personal luggage. Such actions by the police do not constitute a search within the meaning of the Fourth Amendment.

This does not mean the officers using the dogs have unlimited access to the traveler or their luggage. For example, in *United States v. Place*[23] the Court held the actions of the agents in transporting the traveler's luggage to another airport in order to have it "sniffed" by the dog were unreasonable when it took over 90 minutes to accomplish the task. A question remains, however, whether a shorter delay may have been allowable.

The pivotal issue is the degree of intrusion upon the expectation of privacy and freedom to the detained person. An articulable reason may exist and allow a *Terry*-type search where such search can be conducted without undue burden on the individual. It is clear that time, inconvenience, and methods of search all play a vital role in the analysis.

ENDNOTES

1. Ex parte Burford, 7 U.S. (3 Cr.) 448 (1806).
2. Giordenello v. United States, 357 U.S. 480, 485–86 (1958); United States v. Watson, 423 U.S. 411, 416–18 (1976); Payton v. New York, 445 U.S. 573, 583–86 (1980).
3. United States v. Watson, 423 U.S. 411 (1976).
4. Payton v. New York, 445 U.S. 573 (1980).
5. United States v. Mendenhall, 446 U.S. 544, 554 (1980).
6. Adams v. Williams, 407 U.S. 143, 146–49 (1972); Delaware v. Prouse, 440 U.S. 648, 661 (1979); Brown v. Texas, 443 U.S. 47, 51 (1979); Reid v. Georgia, 448 U.S. 438, 440 (1980); Michigan v. Summers, 452 U.S. 692 (1981).
7. Wong Sun v. United States, 371 U.S. 471 (1963).

8. Brown v. Illinois, 422 U.S. 590 (1975).
9. Davis v. Mississippi, 394 U.S. 721 (1969); Taylor v. Alabama, 457 U.S. 687 (1982); and United States v. Crews, 445 U.S. 463 (1980).
10. Terry v. Ohio, 392 U.S. 1 (1968).
11. *Id.* at 16.
12. *Id.* at pp. 20–27.
13. United States v. Mendenhall, 446 U.S. 544, 554 (1980).
14. INS v. Delgado, 466 U.S. 210 (1984).
15. Michigan v. Chesternut, 486 U.S. 567, 575 (1988).
16. California v. Hodari, 499 U.S. 621, 628 (1991).
17. *Id.*
18. Florida v. Bostick (1991).
19. Michigan v. Long, 463 U.S. 1032 (1983).
20. United States v. Sharpe, 470 U.S. 675, 686 (1985).
21. 473 U.S. 531, 544 (1985).
22. United States v. Place, 462 U.S. 696, 709 (1983).
23. 462 U.S. 696, 709 (1983).

11 Searches and Seizures Pursuant to Warrant

I. INTRODUCTION

The second clause of the Fourth Amendment sets forth specific requirements for the issuance and use of a warrant:

> [N]o Warrants shall issue, but upon probable cause, supported by Oath or affirmation, and particularly describing the place to be searched, and the persons or things to be seized.

Although the amendment does not specifically name the judicial officer before whom a warrant shall be sought, the courts have long held that the purpose of the amendment is to place the judgment of an independent magistrate between law enforcement officers and the privacy of citizens. The courts have also held that the Fourth Amendment authorizes invasion of that privacy only upon a showing that constitutes probable cause. It limits that invasion by specifying the person to be seized, the place to be searched, and the evidence to be sought.

While a warrant is issued *ex parte* — that is, in a judicial hearing brought on behalf of one party to the suit alone — its validity may be contested in a subsequent suppression hearing if incriminating evidence is found and a prosecution is brought.[1] For this reason, the warrant requirement of the Fourth Amendment has been strictly applied in cases where the warrant was necessary. For that reason it is important that criminal justice professionals understand not only the requirements for obtaining the warrant but also the traditional methods for seeking the warrant.

II. ISSUANCE BY NEUTRAL MAGISTRATE

It is well established that warrants be issued by a "judicial officer" or a "magistrate."[2] This means that a police officer seeking a warrant must present the evidence to a judicial officer designated by the local court for the purpose of evaluating the need to issue a warrant. This is the first line of protection against an overzealous government agent and the infringement of a right to privacy or protection from unreasonable search.

The purpose of this requirement is to remove from the investigating officer the ability to judge those facts he has gathered and to place those facts before a neutral party for proper evaluation. "Any assumption that evidence sufficient to support a magistrate's disinterested determination to issue a search warrant will justify the officers in making a search without a warrant would reduce the Amendment to a nullity and leave the people's homes secure only in the discretion of police officers."[3]

There are two requirements for the judicial officer in question to fill his role. First, the judicial officer must be "neutral and detached."[4] This means the magistrate or other judicial officer cannot be an employee of, or in any other way linked to, the agency seeking the warrant. It does not mean, however, that the agent seeking the warrant and the magistrate before whom it is sought cannot work for the same governmental body. In other words, a judge working for the state may review an affidavit presented by a police agent working for the state bureau of investigation. The issue of neutrality is one of office, not necessarily of governmental employment.

The judicial officer must also "be capable of determining whether probable cause exists for the requested arrest or search."[5] One must remember, however, that probable cause is not the same as "beyond a reasonable doubt," which is the standard necessary in most jurisdictions for conviction. As such, the courts have been pragmatic in assessing whether the issuing party possesses the capacity to determine probable cause.[6]

III. PROBABLE CAUSE

The concept of "probable cause" is central to the meaning of the warrant clause. Neither the Fourth Amendment nor the federal statutory provisions relevant to the area define "probable cause." The definition is entirely a judicial construct, and an applicant for a warrant must present to the magistrate facts sufficient to enable the officer himself to make a determination of probable cause. The Court has given some guidance for determining this standard:

> In determining what is probable cause... [w]e are concerned only with the question whether the affiant had reasonable grounds at the time of his affidavit... for the belief that the law was being violated on the premises to be searched; and if the apparent facts set out in the affidavit are such that a reasonably discreet and prudent man would be led to believe that there was a commission of the offense charged, there is probable cause justifying the issuance of a warrant.[7]

Probable cause is to be determined according to "the factual and practical considerations of everyday life on which reasonable and prudent men, not legal technicians, act."[8] Warrants are favored in the law and their utilization will not be thwarted by a hypertechnical reading of the supporting affidavit and supporting testimony.[9] For the same reason, reviewing courts will accept evidence of a less "judicially competent or persuasive character than would have justified an officer in acting on his own without a warrant."[10]

From a practical standpoint one may say that probable cause is that evidence, when viewed after the fact, that would allow a reasonable person similarly situated to conclude that it is likely that a fact exists. This is not a bright line standard where the summation of various evidence always leads to a finding of probable cause, but rather a loose method for ensuring that at least minimal standards are applied in order to protect the truly innocent.

Litigation in this area has led to some basic standards for determining probable cause. In one sense we can say that it has been well established that mere conclusory assertions are not enough, but that does not necessarily mean that a "belief" rather than a conclusion will not suffice. For example, in *United States v. Ventresca*,[11] an affidavit by a law enforcement officer asserting his belief that an illegal distillery was being operated in a certain place, explaining that the belief was based upon his own observations and upon those of fellow investigators, and detailing a substantial number of these personal observations clearly supporting the stated belief, was held to be sufficient to constitute probable cause.

In upholding the warrant the Court stated that "[r]ecital of some of the underlying circumstances in the affidavit is essential." The Court also noted that "where these circumstances are detailed, where reason for crediting the source of the information is given, and when a magistrate has found probable cause," the reliance on the warrant process should not be deterred by insistence on too stringent a showing.[12] As such, it can be argued that probable cause is a high enough standard to protect the truly innocent, but low enough to allow the police to pursue reasonable leads in fighting crime.

Requirements for establishing probable cause through reliance on information received from an informant has divided the Court in several cases. In *Draper v. United States*[13] the Court began the analysis when it held that a previously reliable informant could supply sufficient cause belief a criminal act was about to take place. Although this case did not involve a warrant it did involve a basic issue addressed in cases measuring probable cause from informants.

In addressing the issue the Court held that an officer may have probable cause even when such cause comes from a third party such as a reliable informant. In *Draper* the informant reported that narcotics would arrive by courier on a particular train, and described the clothes the courier would be wearing and the bag he would be carrying. FBI agents met the train, observed that the defendant matched the description in all respects, and arrested him. The Court held that the corroboration of part of the informer's tip established probable cause to support the arrest.

A later case involving a search warrant, which helped establish the standard, was *Jones v. United States*.[14] In this case the Court utilized a test of considering the affidavit as a whole to see whether the tip plus the corroborating information provided a substantial basis for finding probable cause. The Court held that probable cause did exist because the affidavit also set forth the reliability of the informer and sufficient detail to indicate that the tip was based on the informant's personal observation, which later proved to be true.

Mere assertion that "reliable information from a credible person" exists may not be enough. In *Aguilar v. Texas*[15] the police made such an assertion where the informant gave information that narcotics were in a certain place. The Court, however, held insufficient the affidavit and stated that when the affiant relies on an informant's tip he must present two types of evidence to the magistrate. The affidavit must first indicate the informant's basis of knowledge, i.e., the circumstances from which the informant concluded that evidence was present or that crimes had been committed. The affiant must also present information that would permit the magistrate to decide whether or not the informant was trustworthy.

The Court later modified this standard when it held in *Spinelli v. United States*[16] that the informant's tip and the corroborating evidence must be considered separately. The Court later returned to the "totality test" in *United States v. Harris*.[17]

In *Illinois v. Gates*[18] the Court abandoned the two-part *Aguilar-Spinelli* test and returned to the "totality of the circumstances" approach to evaluate probable cause based on an informant's tip. The main defect of the two-part test, Justice Rehnquist concluded for the Court, was in treating an informant's reliability and his basis for knowledge as independent requirements. Instead, "a deficiency in one may be compensated for, in determining the overall reliability of a tip, by a strong showing as to the other, or by some other indicia of reliability."

The Court has stated that, when evaluating probable cause, "[t]he task of the issuing magistrate is simply to make a practical, commonsense decision whether, given all the circumstances set forth in the affidavit before him, including the 'veracity' and 'basis of knowledge' of persons supplying hearsay information, there is a fair probability that contraband or evidence of a crime will be found in a particular place."[19] This standard follows more closely the "totality" standard of earlier years and allows the magistrate great latitude in determining when probable cause may exist.

IV. PARTICULARITY

One area of the Fourth Amendment of minimal controversy is the requirement that a warrant describe with particularity the place to be searched and the items to be seized. "The requirement that warrants shall particularly describe the things to be seized makes general searches under them impossible and prevents the seizure of one thing under a warrant describing another. As to what is to be taken, nothing is left to the discretion of the officer executing the warrant."[20]

This requirement thus acts to limit the scope of the search, inasmuch as the executing officers should be limited to looking in places where the described object could be expected to be found. Thus, a warrant authorizing the search of an apartment for a stolen grand piano will limit the officers to searching only those places within the apartment where a grand piano reasonably could be hidden. Desk drawers, kitchen cabinets, and other areas may be fully off limits, and officers violating this provision would be hard put to qualify their intrusion into such locations. The scope of the search must be "strictly tied to and justified by" the circumstances that rendered its initiation permissible.[21]

This does not mean, however, that an officer who is rightfully in a location to see illegal contraband cannot seize such even though the illegal item is not specifically named in the warrant. On the contrary, police who are lawfully on the premises pursuant to a warrant may seize evidence of crime in "plain view" even if that evidence is not described in the warrant.[22]

V. FIRST AMENDMENT BEARING ON PROBABLE CAUSE AND PARTICULARITY

One area where the courts have long held the government to narrow standards has been in cases where the warrant process is used to authorize seizure of books and other items. Such items, often protected by the First Amendment or at least entitled to some First Amendment consideration, demand a more exacting standard. Seizure of materials arguably protected by the First Amendment is a form of prior restraint that requires strict observance of the Fourth Amendment.[23]

The Court has previously held that, at a minimum, a warrant is required and additional safeguards may be required for large-scale seizures. Such a standard was applied in *Marcus v. Search Warrant*,[24] where agents, pursuant to a warrant issued *ex parte* by a magistrate, seized 11,000 copies of some 280 publications alleged to be obscene. Although copies of the seized documents were available through other means, and could have been reviewed by the magistrate before issuing the warrant, the magistrate chose instead to rely on the conclusory statements of the officer in the affidavit.

In setting aside the warrant the Supreme Court stated that the failure to scrutinize the materials and to particularize the items to be seized was inadequate. It was further noted that police "were provided with no guide to the exercise of informed discretion, because there was no step in the procedure before seizure designed to focus searchingly on the question of obscenity."

In *A Quantity of Books v. Kansas*[25] a state procedure designed to comply with *Marcus* was set aside as being inadequate for protecting First Amendment rights. A Kansas procedure required the presentation of copies of books (or other material) to be seized to the magistrate for the magistrate's scrutiny prior to issuance of a warrant. In this case, however, the magistrate examined only 7 of the 59 listed titles to be seized.

The Supreme Court concluded that since the warrant "authorized the sheriff to seize all copies of the specified titles, and since [appellant] was not afforded a hearing on the question of the obscenity even of the seven novels ... before the warrant issued, the procedure was ... constitutionally deficient."[26]

Confusion remains, however, about the necessity for and the character of prior adversary hearings on the issue of obscenity. In a later decision the Court held that, with adequate safeguards, no pre-seizure adversary hearing on the issue of obscenity is required if the film is seized not for the purpose of destruction as contraband (the purpose in *Marcus* and *A Quantity of Books*), but instead to preserve a copy for evidence.[27]

It is constitutionally permissible to seize a copy of a film pursuant to a warrant as long as there is a prompt post-seizure adversary hearing on the obscenity issue. Until there is a judicial determination of obscenity, the Court advised, the film may continue to be exhibited; if no other copy is available either a copy must be made from the seized film or the film itself must be returned.[28]

A warrant seeking the seizure of items that fall within the protections of the First Amendment must be "supported by affidavits setting forth specific facts in order that the issuing magistrate may 'focus searchingly on the question of obscenity.'"[29] This does not mean, however, that a higher standard of probable cause is required in order to obtain a warrant to seize materials protected by the First Amendment.

These standards apply in cases other than obscenity as well. For example, in *Stanford v. Texas*[30] a seizure of more than 2,000 books, pamphlets, and other documents "concerning the Communist Party of Texas" was voided by the Court on particularity grounds. "[T]he constitutional requirement that warrants must particularly describe the 'things to be seized' is to be accorded the most scrupulous exactitude when the 'things' are books, and the basis for their seizure is the ideas which they contain.... No less a standard could be faithful to First Amendment freedoms."[31]

First Amendment protections do not extend to everything that may be published. For instance, the First Amendment does not bar the issuance or execution of a warrant to search a newsroom to obtain photographs of demonstrators who had injured several policemen.[32] In upholding the warrant the Court appeared to suggest that a magistrate asked to issue such a warrant should guard against interference with press freedoms through limits on type, scope, and intrusiveness of the search, but the issuance of such a warrant would not be thwarted simply because the press was involved. It might be noted, however, that Congress later implemented specific protections through statute.[33]

VI. PROPERTY SUBJECT TO SEIZURE

It has long been accepted that search warrants may be issued for the seizure of the "fruits of crimes." Likewise, there has been little debate that a warrant may be issued to seize the "instrumentality" of a criminal act.[34] There has been some limitation, however, on certain classes of property which may be seized when they constitute "mere evidence."[35]

In this sense the use of a warrant is often limited to that evidence to which the government has a superior right. While a particular item may be "evidence" of a crime it may not always fall into the categories of "fruits of the crime" or "instrumentality" of the crime, and as such may not be subject to seizure by warrant.[36]

While there are some restrictions on what may be seized there are also items that may be taken either through the warrant clause or where "special needs" of government are shown. For instance, evidentiary items such as fingerprints,[37] blood,[38] urine samples,[39] fingernail and skin scrapings,[40] voice and handwriting exemplars,[41] conversations,[42] and other demonstrative evidence may be obtained both through the warrant process and without a warrant.

A fine line has appeared in recent years that suggests that some medically assisted bodily intrusions may be impermissible without a warrant. For example, forcible administration of an emetic to induce vomiting[43] and surgery under general anesthetic to remove a bullet lodged in a suspect's chest[44] have been held invalid without a warrant.

Factors to be weighed in determining which medical tests and procedures are reasonable include the extent to which the procedure threatens the individual's safety or health, "the extent of the intrusion upon the individual's dignitary interests in personal privacy and bodily integrity," and the importance of the evidence to the prosecution's case.[45]

ENDNOTES

1. Spinelli v. United States, 393 U.S. 410 (1969); United States v. Harris, 403 U.S. 573 (1971).
2. United States v. Lefkowitz, 285 U.S. 452, 464 (1932); Giordenello v. United States, 357 U.S. 480, 486 (1958); Jones v. United States, 362 U.S. 257, 270 (1960); Katz v. United States, 389 U.S. 347, 356 (1967); United States v. United States District Court, 407 U.S. 297, 321 (1972); United States v. Chadwick, 433 U.S. 1, 9 (1977); Lo-Ji Sales v. New York, 442 U.S. 319, 326 (1979).
3. Johnson v. United States, 333 U.S. 10, 13–14 (1948).
4. Shadwick v. City of Tampa, 407 U.S. 345, 354 (1972).
5. Id.
6. Connally v. Georgia, 429 U.S. 245 (1977).
7. Dumbra v. United States, 268 U.S. 435, 439, 441 (1925).
8. Brinegar v. United States, 338 U.S. 160, 175 (1949).
9. United States v. Ventresca, 380 U.S. 102, 108–09 (1965).
10. Jones v. United States, 362 U.S. 257, 270–71 (1960).
11. 380 U.S. 102 (1965).
12. Id. at 109.
13. 358 U.S. 307 (1959).
14. 362 U.S. 257 (1960).
15. 378 U.S. 108 (1964).
16. 393 U.S. 410 (1969).
17. 403 U.S. 573 (1971).
18. 462 U.S. at 213 (1983).
19. 462 U.S. at 238.
20. Marron v. United States, 275 U.S. 192, 196 (1927).
21. Warden v. Hayden, 387 U.S. 294, 310 (1967).
22. Coolidge v. New Hampshire, 403, U.S. 443, 464–71 (1971).
23. Marcus v. Search Warrant, 367 U.S. 717, 730–31 (1961); Stanford v. Texas, 379 U.S. 476, 485 (1965).
24. 367 U.S. 717 (1961).
25. A Quantity of Books v. Kansas, 378 U.S. 205, 210 (1964).
26. Id.
27. Heller v. New York, 413 U.S. 483 (1973).
28. Id. at 492–93.
29. Roaden v. Kentucky, 413 U.S. 496 (1973). See also Lo-Ji Sales v. New York, 442 U.S. 319 (1979); Walter v. United States, 447 U.S. 649 (1980).
30. 379 U.S. 476 (1965).
31. Id. at 485–86.
32. Zurcher v. Stanford Daily, 436 U.S. 547 (1978).
33. Privacy Protection Act, Pub. L. No. 96–440, 94 Stat. 1879 (1980), 42 U.S.C. §2000aa.
34. United States v. Lefkowitz, 285 U.S. 452, 465–66 (1932).
35. Gouled v. United States, 255 U.S. 298 (1921).
36. Warden v. Hayden, 387 U.S. 294, 303 (1967). See Gouled v. United States, 255 U.S. 298, 309 (1921).
37. Davis v. Mississippi, 394 U.S. 721 (1969).

38. Schmerber v. California, 384 U.S. 757 (1966). Skinner v. Railway Labor Executives' Ass'n, 489 U.S. 602 (1989) (warrantless blood testing for drug use by railroad employee involved in accident).
39. Skinner v. Railway Labor Executives' Ass'n, 489 U.S. 602 (1989).
40. Cupp v. Murphy, 412 U.S. 291 (1973).
41. United States v. Dionisio, 410 U.S. 1 (1973); United States v. Mara, 410 U.S. 19 (1973).
42. Berger v. New York, 388 U.S. 41 (1967).
43. Rochin v. California, 342 U.S. 165 (1952).
44. Winston v. Lee, 470 U.S. 753 (1985).
45. Winston v. Lee, 470 U.S. 753, 761–63 (1985).

12 Execution of Warrants

I. KNOCK AND ANNOUNCE

The Constitution is virtually silent on the issues of execution of the warrant. The methods employed by law enforcement are generally governed by statute and specific rules established through case law.

One of the more common rules in executing the warrant has been the common law requirement that an officer, before being allowed to break and enter when serving a warrant, must first identify his or her office, authority, and purpose. It was commonly held that an officer must have been refused entry before he or she could resort to force to make entry.[1]

Recently these requirements have been relaxed significantly to allow officers to forcibly enter a dwelling or other structure when serving a warrant. In *Ker v. California*[2] the Court considered the rule of announcement as a constitutional requirement. Although a majority of the Court found circumstances justifying entry without announcement, the analysis of the past requirement indicated that the "knock and announce" rule was alive and well when police served warrants.

In *Wilson v. Arkansas*[3] the Supreme Court held that the Fourth Amendment incorporates the common law requirement that police must knock on a dwelling door and announce their identity and purpose before attempting forcible entry. The case also recognized the need for a flexible reasonableness standard allowing magistrates to weigh countervailing law enforcement interests such as safety and protection of potential evidence. The Court left the specifics of such standards to the lower courts and legislative bodies.

Statutory provisions soon evolved at both the state and federal levels providing guidelines for the issuance of what are commonly called "no-knock" warrants. For instance, in narcotics cases, magistrates are authorized to issue "no-knock" warrants if they find probable cause to believe: (1) the property sought may, and if notice is given will, be easily and quickly destroyed or (2) giving notice will endanger the life or safety of the executing officer or another person.[4] Similar provisions were created by state legislative bodies or through court rulings.

By 1997 there were various standards across the country, and the Supreme Court once again addressed the issue in a case from Wisconsin.

In *Richards v. Wisconsin*[5] officers from the Madison, Wisconsin, police department obtained a warrant to search Richards' hotel room for drugs and related paraphernalia. The magistrate refused to give advance authorization for a "no-knock" entry.

When the officers arrived at the hotel they approached the room with one of the officers dressed as a maintenance man, who knocked on Richards' door and identified himself as "maintenance." When Richards opened the door he saw the officer in the maintenance uniform and a uniformed officer. Richards quickly closed the door.

Fearing Richards might try to destroy evidence or escape the officers kicked down the door. Upon entry they caught Richards trying to escape and found cash and cocaine in the bathroom. In denying Richards' motion to suppress the evidence on the ground that the officers did not knock and announce their presence before forcing entry, the trial court found that they could gather from Richards' strange behavior that he might try to destroy evidence or escape and that the disposable nature of the drugs further justified their decision not to knock and announce.

The State Supreme Court affirmed, concluding that *Wilson* did not preclude the state court's pre-*Wilson* rule that police officers are never required to knock and announce when executing a search warrant in a felony drug investigation. The state court had reasoned that because of the special circumstances of today's drug culture the need to serve a warrant without knocking was a basic part of police work.

In its ruling the Supreme Court held that the Fourth Amendment does not permit a blanket exception to the knock and announce requirement for felony drug investigations. The knock and announce requirement may be lifted under circumstances presenting a threat of physical violence or where officers believe that evidence would be destroyed if advance notice were given, but this was not a blanket rule for all drug cases.

The fact that felony drug investigations may frequently present such circumstances cannot remove from the neutral scrutiny of a reviewing court the reasonableness of the police decision not to knock and announce in a particular case. Creating exceptions to the requirement based on the culture surrounding a general category of criminal behavior presents at least two serious concerns. First, the exception contains considerable overgeneralization that would impermissibly insulate from judicial review cases in which a drug investigation does not pose special risks. Second, an exception created in one category can, relatively easily, then be applied to other categories.

The Court also held that if a per se exception were allowed for each criminal activity category that included a considerable risk of danger to officers or destruction of evidence, the knock and announce requirement would be meaningless. The trial court confronting this question has a duty to determine whether the facts and circumstances of the particular entry justified dispensing with the requirement.

A "no-knock" entry is justified when the police have a reasonable suspicion that knocking and announcing their presence, under the particular circumstances, would be dangerous or futile, or would inhibit the effective investigation of the crime. This standard strikes the appropriate balance between the legitimate law enforcement concerns at issue in the execution of search warrants and the individual privacy interests affected by "no-knock" entries.[6]

The Court also held that because the evidence in this case establishes that the decision not to knock and announce was a reasonable one under the circumstances, the officers' entry into the hotel room did not violate the Fourth Amendment. That the magistrate had originally refused to issue a "no-knock" warrant means only that at the time the warrant was requested there was insufficient evidence for a "no-knock" entry. This means that even where the "no-knock" warrant is denied by the issuing magistrate conditions may exists at the time of the execution of the warrant to justify a "no-knock" entry. In this case the fact that Richards had acted in a manner consistent with someone attempting to escape and/or dispose of evidence supported the decision to make a dynamic entry into the room.

One issue must be noted from this portion of the Court's holding. The events that exist at the time of the warrant application do not always control. As in this case, events at the time of execution may lead to certain actions by police, but police officers serving such warrants must be able to reasonably articulate their grounds for taking action to enter without first knocking and announcing.

Another issue worthy of evaluation from this case is the circumstances of the initial contact with Richards. As noted, the initial contact was made by a policeman who identified himself as a maintenance man rather than a police officer. Had the officer identified himself as a police officer first, and Richards then had taken the action he did, then there would have been little if any grounds for seeking to quash the warrant. The action of the police identifying themselves as personnel other than legal authority may have jeopardized the arrests had it not been for Richards' bizarre reaction. From a tactical standpoint the police must recognize that decisions of this nature will ultimately be weighed by courts later, and such actions do not meet the requirements for knock and announce.

II. TIMELINESS

The officers generally should execute a warrant in a timely fashion. In many juris-dictions the time period within which a warrant may be executed is statutorily mandated. While the courts have held that a statute regulating the expiration of a warrant and issuance of another "should be liberally construed in favor of the individual,"[7] there are instances when a delay in serving the warrant has resulted in loss of the evidence obtained.

While the existence of probable cause for issuance of a warrant must be estab-lished by fresh facts it may also be held that the execution of the warrant should be done in timely fashion so as to ensure the continued existence of probable cause.[8]

III. THIRD PARTIES ON THE PREMISES

As a general rule, when executing a warrant for a search of premises and of named persons on the premises, police officers may not automatically search someone else found on the premises.[9] This means that if the warrant names a specific person at the premises the officers conducting the search may not use the warrant for an unrestricted search of everyone found at the scene.

The police may search third parties found on the scene of warrant search when they can articulate some reasonable basis for the search. An example would be the reasonable need to search for safety purposes such as may arise at the home of a known illegal gun dealer. Similarly, police may conduct a "pat-down" type search where other safety issues arise. If facts so warrant, the officers may also conduct a Terry-type search where facts exist to support such action.

The Court addressed similar issues in Michigan v. Summers,[10] when it held that officers arriving to execute a warrant for the search of a house could detain — without being required to articulate any reasonable basis and necessarily therefore without probable cause — the house owner or occupant, whom they encountered on the front porch leaving the premises. Applying what has commonly been called the "intrusiveness test" the Court determined that such a detention was "substantially less intrusive" than an arrest and that such action was justified because of the law enforcement interests in minimizing the risk of harm to officers, facilitating entry and conduct of the search, and preventing flight in the event incriminating evidence is found. Also, under some circumstances, officers may search premises on the mistaken but reasonable belief that the premises are described in an otherwise valid warrant.[11]

While officers are restricted in the extent to which a search may expand during execution of a warrant, one other noteworthy exception may arise. As with the above case, it has been noted that where there is a danger of loss of evidence by third parties the police may not only control third party movement while on the scene but may, where an articulable reason exists, conduct a search of those leaving the premises in order to protect any evidence that may be removed.

As for many other matters, for purposes of execution there is little difference between search warrants and arrest warrants, but one significant difference is that possession of a valid arrest warrant cannot authorize authorities to enter the home of a third party looking for the person named in the warrant. In order to do that, the authorities must obtain a search warrant signifying that a magistrate has determined that there is probable cause to believe the person named is on the premises.[12]

ENDNOTES

1. Semayne's Case, 5 Coke's Rep. 91a, 77 Eng. Rep. 194 (K.B. 1604).
2. 374 U.S. 23 (1963).
3. 514 U.S. 927.
4. 21 U.S.C. §879(b). See also D.C. Code §23–591.
5. 96-5955. Argued March 24, 1997 — Decided April 28, 1997.
6. Maryland v. Buie, 494 U.S. 325, 337, pp. 5–9.
7. Lankford v. Gelston, 364 F.2d 197 (4th Cir. 1966); Wheeler v. Goodman, 298 F. Supp. 935 (preliminary injunction), 306 F. Supp. 58 (permanent injunction) (W.D.N.C. 1969), vacated on jurisdictional grounds, 401 U.S. 987 (1971).
8. 42 U.S.C. §1983 (1964). See Monroe v. Pape, 365 U.S. 167 (1961).
9. Ybarra v. Illinois, 444 U.S. 85 (1979) (patron in a bar), relying on and reaffirming United States v. Di Re, 332 U.S. 581 (1948) (occupant of vehicle may not be searched merely because there are grounds to search the automobile).
10. 452 U.S. 692 (1981).
11. Maryland v. Garrison, 480 U.S. 79 (1987) (officers reasonably believed there was only one "third floor apartment" in city row house when in fact there were two).
12. Steagald v. United States, 451 U.S. 204 (1981).

13 Warrantless Searches and Exceptions to the Warrant Requirements

I. INTRODUCTION

It is clear that the Supreme Court has a preference for searches conducted under color of a valid warrant; however, it is recognized that not all searches fall within this category. The Supreme Court frequently asserts that "the most basic constitutional rule in this area is that 'searches conducted outside the judicial process, without prior approval by judge or magistrate, are per se unreasonable under the Fourth Amendment — subject only to a few specially established and well-delineated exceptions.'"[1]

The exceptions are said to be "jealously and carefully drawn,"[2] and there must be "a showing by those who seek exemption...that the exigencies of the situation made that course [the warrantless search] imperative."[3]

Today there is an effort to categorize the many exceptions allowed to the warrant requirements, but as we will see in upcoming sections there are more now than at any time in our history. Some argue that there is a growing need for such exceptions, and that without them law enforcement would be unable to keep up with the steady growth of crime in our country. Others argue that the exceptions are burdening our society by restricting our glorious personal liberties. Whichever side of the debate you take it is clear that tomorrow's criminal justice professional must be knowledgeable not only in the principle of the exception but also in the application.

II. SEARCH INCIDENT TO ARREST

As discussed in other areas, the common-law rule permitting searches of the person arrested as an incident to the arrest has elicited little controversy in the Court.[4] The general dispute in this area often has centered on the scope of the search rather than the right to search. From a practical standpoint the rule for such warrantless searches has been that any search must be strictly tied to and justified by the circumstances leading to the arrest. In recent years, however, such justification has come under scrutiny and the courts have expanded the police officer's right to search pursuant to an arrest.

In its simplest terms the rule allowing a search at the time of arrest was needed to prevent destruction of evidence and to prevent access to a weapon.[5] This justification has been attacked numerous times, and been questioned, especially in instances such as traffic stops where the alleged threat to the police officer's safety is said to be at its lowest.

As most who study police murders or assaults know, there is no such thing as a safe police contact. Officers have been killed or injured by all age groups and races, both sexes, and by individuals normally not prone to violence. For this reason, many courts recognize that the traffic stop can be just as dangerous to the police officer as the execution of a felony arrest warrant.

Past cases have argued that a search arising from "routine" matters, such as traffic stops, should be impermissible. While it is recognized that most traffic stops do not rise to the level of a full arrest, it is also clear that the traffic stop is a detention and for purposes of the enforcement of the law the officer has taken the driver into custody. In such cases the Court has found that the traffic stop constitutes an arrest for purposes of the Fourth Amendment.

One such case involved the stop of a motorist for a traffic violation, and, upon a pat-down search, the officer retrieved a crumpled cigarette package containing heroin. The defendant argued that such a search was unreasonable since no evidence related to the original offense would be found in the crumpled cigarette package. Likewise, no legitimate weapon could be reasonably concealed in the package, and as such the search was unreasonable. The Court, however, rejected this argument, ruling that "no additional justification" is required for a custodial arrest of a suspect based on probable cause.[6]

Over the years the Court has found itself embroiled in a continuing debate on when a police officer may search motorists stopped for simple traffic violations. Some argue that such actions are often taken as a pretextual means of conducting a search. In other words, it is argued that the traffic violation is not the real reason the officer is stopping the motorist but that the search — and subsequent discovery of illegal items — is the heart of the stop. The traffic stop is used as a means to the end. At this time no clear, bright line has been drawn indicating that police cannot conduct such searches of the person being stopped.

Under certain circumstances, the search may also be extended to the automobile. This is similar to the justifications for allowing the officer to search the immediate area around an arrested individual. The Court has long struggled to establish some clear guidelines in this area. Certain early cases went both ways on the basis of some fine distinctions,[7] and it has only been in the last few decades that we see some clear rules being applied.

In *Harris v. United States*[8] the Court approved a search of a four-room apartment pursuant to an arrest under warrant for one crime and in which the search turned up evidence of another crime. A year later, in *Trupiano v. United States*[9] a raid on a distillery resulted in the arrest of a man found on the premises and a seizure of the equipment. The Court reversed the conviction because the officers had had time to obtain a search warrant and had not done so. In announcing its decision, the Court stated that "A search or seizure without a warrant as an incident to a lawful arrest has always been considered to be a strictly limited right. It grows out of the inherent necessities of the situation at the time of the arrest. But there must be something more in the way of necessity than merely a lawful arrest."[10]

This decision was overruled in *United States v. Rabinowitz*,[11] in which officers arrested the defendant in his one-room office pursuant to an arrest warrant and proceeded to search the room completely. The Court observed that the issue was not whether the officers had the time and opportunity to obtain a search warrant but whether the search incident to arrest was reasonable. Although *Rabinowitz* referred to searches of the area within the arrestee's "immediate control," it provided no standard by which to determine this area, and extensive searches were later permitted under the rule.[12]

By 1969, when *Chimel v. California*[13] was decided, a narrower view was asserted in which the primacy of warrants was again emphasized. For the first time it appeared that a standard by which the scope of searches pursuant to arrest could be ascertained was set out. The Court stated:

> When an arrest is made, it is reasonable for the arresting officer to search the person arrested in order to remove any weapons that the latter might seek to use in order to resist arrest or effect his escape. Otherwise, the officer's safety might well be endangered, and the arrest itself frustrated. In addition, it is entirely reasonable for the arresting officer to search for and seize any evidence on the arrestee's person in order to prevent its concealment or destruction. And the area into which an arrestee might reach in order to grab a weapon or evidentiary items must, of course, be governed by a like rule. A gun on a table or in a drawer in front of one who is arrested can be as dangerous to the arresting officer as one concealed in the clothing of the person arrested. There is ample justification, therefore, for a search of the arrestee's person and the area "within his immediate control."[14]

Since *Chimel* the courts have construed the phrase "within his immediate control" to mean the area from within which an arrested person might gain possession of a weapon or destructible evidence.

Through the years the rationale of *Chimel* has undergone some change, and critics suggest that the case, as applied, does not meet the reasonable and justifiable expectations of privacy.[15] In *Mincey v. Arizona*[16] the Court addressed similar issues arising under a state attempt to create an exception for homicide scenes. Such exceptions would allow police to conduct warrantless searches of an entire home, rather than the restricted area normally prescribed, and the search could spread over several days. In *Mincey* the arrested occupant of an apartment had been removed from the home almost immediately after being arrested. The Court noted that while a person legally taken into custody has a lessened right of privacy in his person he does not necessarily have a lessened right of privacy in his entire house.

The expectation of privacy may also extend the protections of the Fourth Amendment to personal items such as luggage. For example, in *United States v. Chadwick*[17] the defendant, his luggage, and a footlocker were taken by police to the station where a search of the defendant and his property was conducted. In addressing the issues the Court emphasized a person's reasonable expectation of privacy in his luggage or other baggage. The Court held that, once police have arrested and immobilized a suspect, validly seized bags are not subject to search without a warrant.

Police may, however, in the course of jailing an arrested suspect, conduct an inventory search of the individual's personal effects, including the contents of a shoulder bag, since "the scope of a station-house search may in some circumstances be even greater than those supporting a search immediately following arrest."[18]

The Court has also held that an inventory search of an impounded vehicle may include the contents of a closed container.[19] Inventory searches of closed containers must, however, be guided by a police policy containing standardized criteria for exercise of discretion.[20]

Other cases also address the issues of *Chimel*. For example, in *New York v. Belton*[21] the Court held that police officers who had made a valid arrest of the occupant of a vehicle could make a contemporaneous search of the entire passenger compartment of the automobile, including containers found therein. Believing that a fairly simple rule understandable to authorities in the field was desirable, the Court ruled "that articles inside the relatively narrow compass of the passenger compartment of an automobile are in fact generally, if not inevitably, within 'the area into which an arrestee might reach in order to grab a weapon or evidentiary item.'"

The ability to search not only an arrested person but also the surrounding area has been extended in later cases. Not only may officers search areas within the arrestee's immediate control in order to alleviate any threat posed by the arrestee, but they may extend that search if "unseen third parties in the house" may pose a threat. Such searches, commonly known as a "protective sweep," are often undertaken on less than probable cause if officers have a "reasonable belief," based on "articulable facts," that the area to be swept may harbor an individual posing a danger to those on the arrest scene.[22]

It should be noted, however, that such a search cannot be "full blown" in the sense that officers may look in all containers or other areas. The officers are allowed to make a reasonable search for persons and are thereby limited to searching those places where persons might conceal themselves. Items of contraband or other illegal substances found during such searches are commonly admissible so long as the officer was making the search in good faith and the item seized was in "plain view" during the search. An example would be the seizure of an illegal firearm in plain view inside a closet of the home when the officers were, in good faith, sweeping the home for third parties.

III. VEHICULAR SEARCHES

Almost from the beginning of the age of the automobile the car has presented peculiar problems for law enforcement. The more influential cases dealing with searches of an automobile arise during the Prohibition Era of the 1920s. One such case, *Carroll v. United States*,[23] established that a vehicle may be searched without warrant if the officer undertaking the search has probable cause to believe that the vehicle contains contraband. The Court explained that the mobility of vehicles allows them to be quickly moved from the jurisdiction if time were taken to obtain a warrant, and for that reason an exception to the warrant requirement was logical and necessary.

Almost immediately there was controversy over this new standard. In *Coolidge v. New Hampshire*[24] the Court limited *Carroll*'s reach by holding impermissible the warrantless seizure of a parked automobile merely because it is movable. The Court indicated that the exception would apply only when the vehicle in question was originally moving, as in a traffic stop, or when it was likely that the vehicle would be moved.

In later cases the Court clarified the *Carroll* doctrine further when it held that any search of an automobile must be made contemporaneous with the stop or seizure. This meant that the police could not seize the vehicle and then remove it to the station house for a warrantless search at the convenience of the police.[25]

The Court also developed a reduced privacy rationale to supplement the mobility rationale, explaining that "the configuration, use, and regulation of automobiles often may dilute the reasonable expectation of privacy that exists with respect to differently situated property."[26] The Court felt that one had a reduced expectation of privacy in a motor vehicle because its primary function was transportation rather than personal storage or housing unit.[27]

While motor homes do serve as residences and as repositories for personal effects, and while their contents are often shielded from public view, the Court extended the automobile exception to them as well, holding that there is a diminished expectation of privacy in a mobile home parked in a parking lot and licensed for vehicular travel, hence "readily mobile."[28] The Court has yet to decide what level of protection might be afforded a "motor home" parked in a permanent space and thus not as readily mobile.

While this "reduced expectancy of privacy" concept has broadened police powers to conduct automobile searches without warrants it has not lessened the need to have valid probable cause to establish the need for a search.[29] Officers must still have an "articulable suspicion" of criminal activity in order to make random stops of vehicles on the roads.[30]

Once police have validly stopped a vehicle, they may also, based on articulable facts warranting a reasonable belief that weapons may be present, conduct a *Terry*-type protective search of those portions of the passenger compartment in which a weapon could be placed or hidden.[31] Even absent such "reasonable suspicion" police may seize contraband and suspicious items "in plain view" inside the passenger compartment.[32]

Another item that police may use that is commonly in plain view is the Vehicle Identification Number (VIN), which is placed on the dashboard of all automobiles. So long as the officer has the right to be where the automobile is, such as in a public parking lot or during a routine traffic stop, then the officer may obtain the VIN by looking through the window. Police may also reach into the passenger compartment to remove items obscuring the number and may seize items in plain view while doing so.[33]

The vehicle exception also gives police expanded power once they have probable cause to believe contraband is in a vehicle. In *Michigan v. Thomas*[34] the Court held that police may remove a vehicle from the scene to the station house in order to conduct a search where they have probable cause to believe illegal evidence is inside. "[T]he justification to conduct such a warrantless search does not vanish once the car has been immobilized; nor does it depend upon a reviewing court's assessment of the likelihood in each particular case that the car would have been driven away, or that its contents would have been tampered with, during the period required for the police to obtain a warrant."

Vehicles to be impounded may also be searched by way of an inventory of the contents. Such searches are justified on two grounds. First, since the vehicle is being removed from the owner's custody there is an interest in ensuring public safety. A vehicle carrying flammable or caustic material, for instance, must be stored in conditions different from an empty vehicle. Likewise, the search is justified by a need to protect the owner's interest in safeguarding the property inside the vehicle at time of the impound.[35]

While the automobile does extend to the police some exceptions to the warrant requirements these exceptions do not extend beyond the vehicle. For example, the police may not use the automobile exception to justify a search of the persons inside the vehicle.[36] This does not mean, however, that the police cannot search the interior area of the vehicle around which the passenger is seated or has been sitting. In *Rakas v. Illinois*[37] the Court held that passengers in an automobile have no reasonable expectation of privacy in the interior area of the car, and as such a warrantless search of the glove compartment and the spaces under the seats would not violate the Fourth Amendment interest of the passenger.

Luggage and other closed containers found in automobiles also may be subjected to warrantless searches based on probable cause. *California v. Acevedo*[38] overruled an earlier proscription of such searches found in *Arkansas v. Sanders*.[39] This means that police may search the containers contained in the vehicle as well as the vehicle itself.

Likewise, in *United States v. Ross*[40] the Court extended the right to search to include the automobile for something capable of being held in the container. In fact, a *Ross* search of a container found in an automobile need not occur contemporaneous with the stop, and, in at least one case, the search was conducted three days after the vehicle was seized.[41] The Court has also held that a consent to search the automobile for drugs constitutes consent to open containers within the car that might contain drugs.[42]

IV. VESSEL SEARCHES

Vehicles are not the only transportation means in our society that require exceptions to the warrant requirements of the Fourth Amendment. Exceptions include the stop and boarding of a vessel by U.S. Customs agents for purposes of checking documentation[43] and cargo and to conduct searches where probable cause exists. Because there is a "substantial" governmental interest in enforcing documentation laws, "especially in waters where the need to deter or apprehend smugglers is great," the Court found the "limited" but not "minimal" intrusion occasioned by boarding for documentation inspection to be reasonable.[44]

Agents may also have a statutory right to board vessels arriving in U.S. harbors, ports, and other inlets. As we will see in later sections, the Court has also authorized searches at border checkpoints where the intent is to prevent smuggling of goods and persons.

V. CONSENT SEARCHES

One of the most overlooked, and often easiest to apply, of the Fourth Amendment exceptions is the consent search. Like all constitutional rights, the Fourth Amendment requirements for a warrant may be waived, and one may consent to search of his or her person or premises by officers who have not complied with the amendment.

In addressing this type of search the Court has continually held that the burden is on the prosecution to prove the voluntariness of the consent.[45] The government will also be required to prove that the defendant knew of his or her right to refuse the search.[46]

Reviewing courts must determine on the basis of the totality of the circumstances whether consent has been freely given or has been coerced. Actual knowledge of the right to refuse consent is not essential to the issue of voluntariness, and therefore police are not required to acquaint a person with his or her rights, as through a Fourth Amendment version of Miranda warnings.[47] Consent will not, however, be regarded as voluntary when the officer asserts his official status or claims a right to search.[48]

The consent search means that an officer may forego the warrant requirements of the Fourth Amendment as long as the officer has a knowing and voluntary consent to search. Should, however, the consent be contested at trial, or even at later hearings such as appeal, then it is the duty of the government — and, in fact, the officer — to prove that the consent was obtained from a person whom both knew they had a right to refuse and that they voluntarily surrendered such right.

Additional issues arise in determining the validity of a consent to search when consent is given not by the suspect but by a third party. In early cases such consent was considered sufficient if that party "possessed common authority over or other sufficient relationship to the premises or effects sought to be inspected."[49] This meant that the officer must ensure that the person giving consent had actual authority to give such consent.

That requirement changed, however, when the Court ruled that an officer merely need have a good faith belief that the person giving consent has authority to act. In this sense, a third party who portrays itself as having authority over the premises may give consent to search even when they do not have such authority in a legal sense. Even if the officer is mistaken in such belief, so long as the belief is held in good faith, the consent may be valid.[50] An officer thus may be deemed to have made a valid lawful search when a third party gives permission to search, even though it is revealed later than the party did not have the right to give such consent.

Recent decisions have extended the consent search principles allowing officers to seek consent even after the reason for the initial contact has lapsed. In *Ohio v. Robinette* the law enforcement officers stopped the defendant for a speeding violation. The officer did not issue a citation, and the facts indicate he appeared to have released the defendant when he returned the driver's license and indicated the traffic matter was over. Before the defendant could walk away, however, the officer asked if the defendant had anything illegal in the car. When the defendant responded that he did not the officer asked permission to search and consent was given.

In upholding the conviction arising from the defendant's arrest following the officer's discovery of illegal drugs in the car the Court held that the defendant was free to leave and that he could have refused permission for the search. Had he done so, there would have been little the officer could have done since there was no probable cause to believe the defendant was transporting illegal items.

The Court also held that the officer had no obligation to tell the defendant that he was free to go. Upholding earlier rulings the Court also found that the officer had no obligation to inform the defendant of his right to refuse the search. The Court was careful not to establish any bright line rules in matters such as this, and it appears that future cases dealing with consent searches are certain to appear in the coming years.

VI. BORDER SEARCHES

> That searches made at the border, pursuant to the longstanding right of the sovereign to protect itself by stopping and examining persons and property crossing into this country, are reasonable simply by virtue of the fact that they occur at the border, should, by now, require no extended demonstration.[51]

With this statement the Supreme Court affirmed the right of the government to conduct warrantless searches at its borders. This power, authorized by the first Congress,[52] allowed customs searches without a warrant or probable cause. In fact, there is not even a requirement for a scintilla of suspicion to justify the search.[53] This means that customs agents and other law enforcement officials may be justified in making a search at the border even if there is no reason to suspect wrongdoing.

There are a few restrictions on this broad power. For example, a prolonged detention of travelers beyond the routine customs search and inspection must be justified by the *Terry* standard of reasonable suspicion.[54] Once the particularized and objective basis is reached, however, the *Terry* protections do not apply.

Another issue that arises when dealing with "border searches" concerns how far inland (or away from the border) the search may be conducted. It is well documented that smugglers go around fixed checkpoints to gain access to the interior of the country. If the government were limited to only those points fixed at the border itself, little could be done about those who skirt the checkpoint. In addressing this issue, the Supreme Court has upheld various schemes that have been used to thwart smuggling and other illegal activity at the borders.

In the broadest sense the border has been held to extend into the interior of the country, and searches conducted within reasonable distances are often found to be legal. For example, in *Almeida-Sanchez v. United States*[55] the Court upheld the use of a "roving patrol" designed to intercept smugglers when the officers stopped the defendant's car 20 miles from the border. In analyzing such searches the Court often looks at the type of activity associated with the stop and the efforts by law enforcement to use other methods.

While it is clear that certain roving patrols will be allowed as an exception, other tactics may not be allowed away from the border. For example, in *United States v. Ortiz*[56] the Court invalidated an automobile search at a fixed checkpoint well removed from the border. The Court agreed that a fixed checkpoint probably gave motorists less cause for alarm than did roving patrols, but it nonetheless held the act of establishing such a checkpoint as violative of the right of privacy protected under the Fourth Amendment. In similar cases the Court has reasoned that fixed checkpoints can be established at the borders and are no better for preventing illegal activity than those set at the border. This means that fixed checkpoints may be improper but not all points will be struck down.

Officers working a border area may be justified in stopping vehicles for purposes of inquiring into residence status. Temporary checkpoints set up along the traffic ways leading from the border have been allowed in the past.[57] Likewise, officers may have a right to conduct searches where they use approved tactics designed to develop probable cause. The use of drug-sniffing dogs is just one such tactic, and the dog may be used on the exterior of a car without interference in the expectation of privacy by the persons inside the car.

Officers may also stop vehicles for purposes of a brief inquiry, provided the interference with Fourth Amendment rights is "modest" and the law enforcement interests served are significant.[58] For example, momentary stops for the purpose of checking driver's license or insurance verification have been upheld in past cases. Probable cause for a search developed during such a stop does not violate the Fourth Amendment.

VII. OPEN FIELDS

Does a person have an expectation of privacy in an open field? The Court answered this question in *Hester v. United States*,[59] when it held that the Fourth Amendment did not protect "open fields" and that police searches in such areas as pastures, wooded areas, open water, and vacant lots need not comply with the requirements of warrants and probable cause. The concept is simple. That which is open to public view — even when away from public access — will not have an expectation of privacy and will not warrant the imposition of Fourth Amendment protections.

One problem with this early decision arose with the Court's announcement in *Katz v. United States*[60] that the Fourth Amendment protects "people not places." One interpretation of this statement cast some doubt on the vitality of the "open fields" principle.

These doubts were dispelled in *Oliver v. United States*,[61] when the Court approved a warrantless intrusion past "No Trespassing" signs and around a locked gate by police officers so that they could view a field not visible from outside property. In upholding such action the Court established that the "open fields" doctrine is alive and well in modern criminal procedure. "[A]n individual may not legitimately demand privacy for activities conducted out of doors in fields, except in the area immediately surrounding the home."[62]

In *United States v. Dunn*[63] the Court expanded the principle when it held that an individual may not demand privacy for activities conducted within outbuildings and visible by trespassers peering into the buildings from just outside. The *Dunn* case involved space immediately outside a barn situated one half mile from the public road and accessible only after crossing a series of "ranch-style" fences. The Court held that such space constitutes unprotected "open field."

At one point the Court had restricted this doctrine when dealing with land near or connected to the dwelling house. This area, commonly referred to as the curtilage, consists of the land within the enclosed area of the dwelling. For instance, a patio is often considered a part of the curtilage when the patio is next to or a part of the house proper. A fenced-in area adjacent to the home may also be considered part of the curtilage.

This principle was modified in recent years when the Court held that even within the curtilage the owner or possessor may have little or no expectation of privacy. In one case the Court held that an area enclosed by a 10-ft high fence and not easily accessible from ground level would not be protected. The Court held that because there was no reasonable expectation of privacy from naked-eye inspection from fixed-wing aircraft flying in navigable airspace there would be little Fourth Amendment protection.[64]

The Court has described four considerations for determining whether an area falls within the curtilage. First, the courts should look at the proximity of the area to the home. Taking this factor into account, a garden area 50 ft from the home may not be protected while one adjacent to the home might be.

Second, the courts are to determine whether the area is included within an enclosure also surrounding the home. A separate fence away from the house will generally not create curtilage, but a fence that surrounds all or a significant part of the house may also create curtilage for that land enclosed.

Third, a court must examine the nature of the uses to which the area is put. There are no hard and fast rules for which uses will or will not be protected. These cases appear to support protection for those uses that are "normally associated" with closeness to the home but exclude those which are not.

Finally, the courts are to look at the steps taken by the resident to shield the area from view of passersby. As noted above, an area surrounded by a 10-ft high privacy fence may be protected curtilage when dealing with a pedestrian but may not be considered protected space when dealing with low-flying aircraft. As such, the naked-eye inspection of property from helicopters contravenes any reasonable expectation of privacy.

Likewise, in *Florida v. Riley*[65] the Court found that a view from a neighbor's second story through a partially open roof of the defendant's greenhouse would not violate Fourth Amendment principles using a curtilage argument because there was no reasonable expectation of privacy.

The Court appears to have drawn a line with this type of invasion, however, when it concerns photographing the area in question. In a commercial sense the Court has refused to extend the principle of the protected curtilage to a business and has allowed the aerial photography of commercial facilities secured from ground-level public view. The Court reasoned that these spaces were more analogous to open fields than to the curtilage of a dwelling.[66] In the same case, however, the Court suggested that aerial photography of the curtilage would be impermissible.

VIII. PLAIN VIEW

On the surface, the "plain view" doctrine appears to be easy to apply but in practice this is sometimes more difficult than the other exceptions. In its simplest form the "plain view" doctrine means that anything in plain view of an officer, who has a right to be where he or she is, may be seized. In practice, however, questions about trespass and pretense often arise to cloud the issues.

The Court has long held that the officer who has a right to be in the position to see the item in plain view also has a right to seize the item. For instance, in *Washington v. Chrisman*[67] the Court upheld the seizure of marijuana seeds and pipe in open view by an officer lawfully in a dorm room for other purposes. Similarly, an officer who, during the impounding of an automobile, opens a door to find contraband or illegal substances in plain view on the car seat has a right to seize the items in question.[68]

Some of the more controversial cases arise when the officer is exercising other authority such as an arrest without a warrant. In *Ker v. California*[69] officers entered a residence without a warrant to make an arrest but they did have "exigent circumstances" for making the warrantless arrest. As such, the Court held that items seized in plain sight during the arrest could be used against the defendant later in related criminal charges.

As we discussed in other sections, when it comes to an arrest an officer may have a right to make a protective sweep of the premises or surrounding area as a safety precaution. Items in plain view during such sweeps may be lawfully seized.[70]

While the "plain view" doctrine does appear to be very broad in its application, some limitations must be addressed. For instance, the doctrine is limited by the probable cause requirement; i.e., officers must have probable cause to believe that items in plain view are contraband before they may search or seize them.[71]

IX. PUBLIC SCHOOLS

The issues arising from warrantless searches in public schools are relatively recent phenomena. Many have argued that since the public schools are supported by tax dollars there is little or no expectation of privacy, and as such school authorities — including school police — should have a right to search anywhere on school grounds.

Opponents have strongly argued that the expectation of privacy does not stop merely because one chooses to use a public facility. It is also argued that if searches are allowed at public schools then they next will be allowed in public restrooms, public recreation areas, and other public places where one might expect a modicum of privacy.

In *New Jersey v. T.L.O.*[72] the Court set forth the principles governing searches by public school authorities. The Court held that the Fourth Amendment does apply to searches conducted by public school officials because "school officials act as representatives of the State, not merely as surrogates for the parents"; however, "the school setting requires some easing of the restrictions to which searches by public authorities are ordinarily subject."

The Court explained that neither the warrant requirement nor the probable cause standard is appropriate when dealing with the public school setting. Instead, a simple reasonableness standard governs all searches of students' persons and effects by school authorities. The Court explained that this single rule will permit school authorities "to regulate their conduct according to the dictates of reason and common sense."[73]

This case does not give school authorities unlimited power to search. From the outset it is clear that a search must be reasonable before it will be allowed. The Court had held that there must be "reasonable grounds for suspecting that the search will turn up evidence that the student has violated or is violating either the law or the rules of the school."[74]

School searches must also be reasonably related in scope to the circumstances justifying the interference, and "not excessively intrusive in light of the age and sex of the student and the nature of the infraction." In applying these rules, the Court upheld as reasonable the search of a student's purse to determine whether the student, accused of violating a school rule by smoking in the lavatory, possessed cigarettes. The search for cigarettes uncovered evidence of drug activity which was later held admissible in a prosecution under the juvenile laws.[75]

X. GOVERNMENT OFFICES

Not unlike the public school searches there are also specific standards that apply to a public employer's work-related search of its employees' offices, desks, or file cabinets. In *O'Connor v. Ortega*[76] a majority of Justices agreed, albeit with somewhat differing rationales, that neither a warrant nor a probable cause requirement should apply to employer searches "for non-investigatory, work-related purposes, as well as for investigations of work-related misconduct." Four Justices suggested there be a case-by-case inquiry into the reasonableness of such searches while one would hold that such searches flatly "do not violate the Fourth Amendment."[77]

It must be noted that this application affects only government-owned office buildings and work environments. Private offices and environments fall under different standards, and a search by police of such facilities may trigger the protections of the Fourth Amendment, absent exceptions as noted above.

XI. PRISONS AND REGULATION OF PROBATION

The Supreme Court has long held that "the Fourth Amendment proscription against unreasonable searches does not apply within the confines of the prison cell."[78] Thus, prison administrators may conduct random "shakedown" searches of inmates' cells without the need to adopt any established practice or plan. Inmates must then look to the Eighth Amendment or to state tort law for redress against harassment, malicious property destruction, and the like.

Likewise, neither a warrant nor probable cause is needed for an administrative search of a probationer's home. The Court ruled in *Griffin v. Wisconsin* that it is enough that such a search was conducted pursuant to a valid regulation that itself satisfies the Fourth Amendment's reasonableness standard (e.g., by requiring "reasonable grounds" for a search).[79] "A State's operation of a probation system, like its operation of a school, government office or prison, or its supervision of a regulated industry,... presents 'special needs' beyond normal law enforcement that may justify departures from the usual warrant and probable cause requirements."

The Court further noted that "Probation, like incarceration, is a form of criminal sanction." As such, a warrant or probable cause requirement would interfere with the "ongoing [non-adversarial] supervisory relationship" required for proper functioning of the system.[80]

XII. DRUG TESTING

Drug testing may be allowable, without probable cause or even individualized suspicion, for certain categories of public employees. In reaching this decision the Court stated that, in each case, "special needs beyond the normal need for law enforcement" were identified as justifying the drug testing. In *Skinner v. Railway Labor Executives' Ass'n*[81] the Court upheld regulations requiring railroads to administer blood, urine, and breath tests to employees involved in certain train accidents or violating certain safety rules. The justification for such an exception lay in the special needs of the public to be safe when traveling.

The Court also upheld drug tests as a screening program in *National Treasury Employees Union v. Von Raab.*[82] In this case a Customs Service requirement for urinalysis testing of employees seeking transfer or promotion to positions having direct involvement with drug interdiction, or to positions requiring the agent to carry firearms, was upheld due to the unique nature of the jobs at hand.

In both cases the Court looked at "compelling" governmental interest in testing the employees without any showing of individualized suspicion. In *Skinner* the Court held such an interest existed since the operation of trains by anyone impaired by drugs "can cause great human loss before any signs of impairment become noticeable."[83]

The Court also held that the intrusions on privacy were "limited" when compared to the potential costs of harm. Blood and breath tests were considered as routine. The urine test, while more intrusive, was deemed permissible because of the "diminished expectation of privacy" in employees having some responsibility for safety in a pervasively regulated industry.

In *Von Raab* the governmental interests underlying the Customs Service's screening program were also termed "compelling" since they were necessary to ensure that persons entrusted with a firearm and the possible use of deadly force did not suffer from drug-induced impairment of perception and judgment. The Court also held that "front-line [drug] interdiction personnel [be] physically fit, and have unimpeachable integrity and judgment."[84]

Since these two cases the Court has been careful in selecting other drug testing cases. While the cases do present some guidelines for when test can be made they do not go far enough in describing the standards so that they can be easily applied to other positions. Left unanswered are questions about drug testing where safety and security are not such high priorities. It appears that these standards will only be set as cases arise in the courts.

ENDNOTES

1. Coolidge v. New Hampshire, 403 U.S. 443, 454–55 (1971) (quoting Katz v. United States, 389 U.S. 347, 357 (1967)); G.M. Leasing Corp. v. United States, 429 U.S. 338, 352–53, 358 (1977).
2. Jones v. United States, 357 U.S. 493, 499 (1958).
3. McDonald v. United States, 335 U.S. 451, 456 (1948).
4. Weeks v. United States, 232 U.S. 383, 392 (1914); Carroll v. United States, 267 U.S. 132, 158 (1925); Agnello v. United States, 269 U.S. 20, 30 (1925).
5. Terry v. Ohio, 392 U.S. 1, 19 (1968); Chimel v. California, 395 U.S. 752, 762, 763 (1969).
6. United States v. Robinson, 414 U.S. 218, 235 (1973); see also United States v. Edwards, 415 U.S. 800 (1974).
7. Compare Marron v. United States, 275 U.S. 192 (1927), with Go-Bart Importing Co. v. United States, 282 U.S. 344 (1931), and United States v. Lefkowitz, 285 U.S. 452 (1932).
8. 331 U.S. 145 (1947).
9. 334 U.S. 699 (1948).
10. *Id.* at 708.
11. 339 U.S. 56 (1950).
12. Chimel v. California, 395 U.S. 752 (1969); compare Kremen v. United States, 353 U.S. 346 (1957).
13. 395 U.S. 752 (1969).
14. *Id.*
15. See Coolidge v. New Hampshire, 403 U.S. 443 (1971), in which the four dissenters advocated the reasonableness argument rejected in Chimel.
16. 437 U.S. 385 (1978).
17. 433 U.S. 1 (1977).
18. Illinois v. LaFayette, 462 U.S. 640, 645 (1983).
19. Colorado v. Bertine, 479 U.S. 367 (1987).
20. Florida v. Wells, 495 U.S. 1 (1990).
21. 453 U.S. 454 (1981).
22. Maryland v. Buie, 494 U.S. 325, 334 (1990).
23. 267 U.S. 132 (1925).
24. 403 U.S. 443 (1971).
25. Preston v. United States, 376 U.S. 364 (1964); Dyke v. Taylor Implement Mfg. Co., 391 U.S. 216 (1968).
26. Arkansas v. Sanders, 442 U.S. 753, 761 (1979).
27. Cardwell v. Lewis, 417 U.S. 583, 590 (1974) (plurality opinion), quoted in United States v. Chadwick, 433 U.S. 1, 12 (1977).
28. California v. Carney, 471 U.S. 386, 393 (1985).
29. United States v. Ortiz, 422 U.S. 891 (1975).
30. Delaware v. Prouse, 440 U.S. 648 (1979); United States v. Brignoni-Ponce, 422 U.S. 873 (1975).
31. Michigan v. Long, 463 U.S. 1032, 1049 (1983).
32. Texas v. Brown, 460 U.S. 730 (1983).
33. New York v. Class, 475 U.S. 106 (1986).
34. 458 U.S. 259, 261 (1982).
35. Cady v. Dombrowski, 413 U.S. 433 (1973); South Dakota v. Opperman, 428 U.S. 364 (1976).

36. Ybarra v. Illinois, 444 U.S. 85 (1979).
37. 439 U.S. 128 (1978).
38. 500 U.S. 565 (1991).
39. 442 U.S. 753 (1979).
40. 456 U.S. 798 (1982).
41. United States v. Johns, 469 U.S. 478 (1985).
42. Florida v. Jimeno, 500 U.S. 248 (1991).
43. United States v. Villamonte-Marquez, 462 U.S. 579 (1983).
44. 462 U.S. at 593.
45. Bumper v. North Carolina, 391 U.S. 543 (1968).
46. Johnson v. United States, 333 U.S. 10, 13 (1948).
47. Schneckloth v. Bustamonte, 412 U.S. 218, 231–33 (1973).
48. Amos v. United States, 255 U.S. 313 (1921); Johnson v. United States, 333 U.S. 10 (1948); Bumper v. North Carolina, 391 U.S. 543 (1968).
49. United States v. Matlock, 415 U.S. 164, 171 (1974) (valid consent by woman with whom defendant was living and sharing the bedroom searched). See also Chapman v. United States, 365 U.S. 610 (1961) (landlord's consent insufficient); Stoner v. California, 376 U.S. 483 (1964) (hotel desk clerk lacked authority to consent to search of guest's room); Frazier v. Culp, 394 U.S. 731 (1969) (joint user of duffel bag had authority to consent to search).
50. Illinois v. Rodriguez, 497 U.S. 177 (1990). See also Florida v. Jimeno, 500 U.S. 248, 251 (1991) (it was "objectively reasonable" for officer to believe that suspect's consent to search his car for narcotics included consent to search containers found within the car).
51. United States v. Ramsey, 431 U.S. 606, 616 (1977).
52. Act of July 31, 1789, ch.5, §§23–24, 1 Stat. 43. See 19 U.S.C. §§507, 1581, 1582.
53. Carroll v. United States, 267 U.S. 132, 154 (1925); United States v. Thirty-Seven Photographs, 402 U.S. 363, 376 (1971); Almeida-Sanchez v. United States, 413 U.S. 266, 272 (1973).
54. United States v. Montoya de Hernandez, 473 U.S. 531 (1985).
55. Almeida-Sanchez v. United States, 413 U.S. 266 (1973).
56. 422 U.S. 891 (1975).
57. United States v. Brignoni-Ponce, 422 U.S. 873 (1975).
58. United States v. Cortez, 449 U.S. 411 (1981).
59. 265 U.S. 57 (1924).
60. 389 U.S. 347, 353 (1967).
61. 466 U.S. 170 (1984).
62. *Id.* at 178. See also California v. Greenwood, 486 U.S. 35 (1988) (approving warrantless search of garbage left curbside "readily accessible to animals, children, scavengers, snoops, and other members of the public").
63. 480 U.S. 294 (1987).
64. California v. Ciraolo, 476 U.S. 207 (1986).
65. 488 U.S. 445 (1989).
66. Dow Chemical Co. v. United States, 476 U.S. 227 (1986).
67. 455 U.S. 1 (1982).
68. Harris v. United States, 390 U.S. 234 (1968).
69. 374 U.S. 23 (1963).
70. Maryland v. Buie, 494 U.S. 325 (1990).
71. Arizona v. Hicks, 480 U.S. 321 (1987).
72. 469 U.S. 325 (1985).

73. 469 U.S. at 343.
74. *Id.* at 342.
75. *Id.*
76. 480 U.S. 709 (1987).
77. Justice O'Connor's plurality opinion, joined by Chief Justice Rehnquist and by Justices White and Powell with Justice Scalia concurring in judgment.
78. Hudson v. Palmer, 468 U.S. 517, 526 (1984).
79. 483 U.S. 868 (1987).
80. *Id.* at 718, 721.
81. 489 U.S. 602 (1989).
82. 489 U.S. 656 (1989).
83. 489 U.S. at 628.
84. Von Raab, 489 U.S. at 670–71.

14 Electronic Surveillance under the Fourth Amendment

I. DEVELOPMENT OF THE EARLY STANDARD

The art of listening in on another conversation is a long-practiced means of surveillance and intelligence gathering, but the invention of the microphone and related electronic devices has turned the art into a science. Today it is much easier to "eavesdrop" than at any time in our prior history. With this increased ability have come some unique applications of the Fourth Amendment.

Use of electronic means by law enforcement began in the early twentieth century. In 1928 the Supreme Court reviewed several convictions obtained on the basis of evidence gained through taps on telephone wires that had been placed by police in violation of state law. Prominent among these cases was *Olmstead v. United States.*[1]

In a 5–4 vote, the Court held that wiretapping was not within the confines of the Fourth Amendment. Chief Justice Taft, writing the opinion of the Court, relied on two lines of argument for the conclusion. First, inasmuch as the Fourth Amendment was designed to protect one's property interest in one's premises, there was no search as long as there was no physical trespass on the premises owned or controlled by a defendant. Second, all the evidence obtained had been secured by hearing, which does not constitute a trespass, and the interception of a conversation could not qualify as a seizure since a conversation is not a tangible thing and therefore not covered by the Fourth Amendment.

The Court held that the violation of state law did not render the evidence excludable because the exclusionary rule operated to exclude evidence seized in violation of the Constitution. Since the acts of the police officer did not constitute a trespass, as long as they did not enter the dwelling or other place to be bugged, there was no seizure.

The Court's ruling came under fire almost immediately from various entities. Within six years of the decision Congress enacted the Federal Communications Act[2] and included in Section 605 of the act a broadly worded proscription of acts like those in *Olmstead.*

The Court used this new act to place some limitation upon governmental wiretapping. In *Nardone v. United States*[3] the Court held that wiretapping by federal officers may violate Section 605 if the officers both intercepted and then divulged the contents of the conversation they overheard. The Court also held that testimony in court would constitute a form of prohibited divulgence, and where such a violation occurs then the evidence should be excluded.

Under the Court's interpretation of the new statute wiretapping would not be illegal if the information was not used outside the governmental agency. As such, many wiretaps were placed to gain valuable information then used to uncover other evidence. For example, where the government investigated illegal gambling operations the wiretap might reveal information on bets being placed and times. With such information the government agents could plan specific legal raids in order to seize material related to gambling. While the intercepted conversations would not be admissible, the seized evidence, obtained by information gathered through the wiretap, would be admissible.

Since the new statute also applied to both interstate and intrastate communications, there was little debate as to whether the ban applied to state police officers. The Court, however, declined to apply either the statute or the due process clause to require the exclusion of such evidence from state criminal trials.[4]

Other electronic listening devices have had their day in court as well. In *Goldman v. United States*[5] the Court addressed the use of a listening device placed against a party wall in order to overhear conversations from the neighboring room. Like the *Olmstead* case, the Court in *Goldman* focused on the actual intrusion by police in order to hear the conversations. Because the device used remained on the officer's side of the wall, there was no real intrusion, and the Court ruled that no Fourth Amendment violation had occurred.

In a later case, involving the use of a "spike mike" to overhear conversations, the Court focused on the acts of the police in driving the microphone into the wall so that it would contact a heating duct and thereby broadcast the conversation from the neighboring room. The Court determined that the act of placing the microphone in the heating duct constituted a trespass and therefore brought the case within the confines of the Fourth Amendment.[6] In so holding, the Court overruled the second rationale of *Olmstead* when it alluded to the possibility that conversations could in fact be seized.

In a similar case the Court ruled that a physical trespass occurred when police stuck a thumbtack into a partition wall to help amplify the conversation on the other side.[7] This line of cases slowly led the Court to two distinct conclusions. First, the earlier rulings that held conversations could not be seized gradually were being eroded. Second, a physical intrusion, however slight, might be enough to constitute a trespass. These principles were later amplified and the earlier standards all but abraded with changes in technology and police tactics.

One of the primary cases that set the stage for future Fourth Amendment litigation arose in New York and effectively brought an end to the *Olmstead* standard on seized conversations. In *Berger v. New York*[8] the Court held unconstitutional on its face a state eavesdropping statute which authorized judges to issue warrants permitting police officers to trespass on private premises to install listening devices. The warrants were to be issued upon a showing of "reasonable ground to believe that evidence of crime may be thus obtained, and particularly describing the person or persons whose communications, conversations or discussions are to be overheard or recorded."

A five-Justice majority, lead by Justice Clark, discerned several constitutional defects in the law. "First, ... eavesdropping is authorized without requiring belief that any particular offense has been or is being committed; nor that the 'property' sought, the conversations, be particularly described." This Court's ruling verifies that, for purposes of a Fourth Amendment analysis, a conversation would now be considered property.

The Court continued: "The purpose of the probable-cause requirement of the Fourth Amendment to keep the state out of constitutionally protected areas until it has reason to believe that a specific crime has been or is being committed is thereby wholly aborted. Likewise the statute's failure to describe with particularity the conversations sought gives the officer a roving commission to 'seize' any and all conversations." This meant the end of *Olmstead*.

"It is true," continued the Court, "that the statute requires the naming of 'the person or persons whose communications, conversations or discussions are to be overheard or recorded....' But this does no more than identify the person whose constitutionally protected area is to be invaded rather than 'particularly describing' the communications, conversations, or discussions to be seized...."[9]

The majority opinion effectively set a burden on the states to create eavesdropping statutes which would pass a new Fourth Amendment standard. Where *Olmstead* all but rubber-stamped virtually any state scheme as sound, the new holding in *Berger* created a standard that would allow the Court to strike down future statutes almost at will.

In their dissent, both Justices Black and White accused the *Berger* majority of so construing the Fourth Amendment as to effectively preclude future wiretapping-eavesdropping statutes. The dissenting Justices suggested that no reasonable statute would now be able to pass constitutional scrutiny, and that law enforcement would be thwarted beyond repair.[10] In this sense it was clear that the standards had migrated from one extreme to the other, and the dissenting Justices saw further need to modify the standards to more neutral ground.

II. EVOLUTION TO A MODERN STANDARD OF JUDICIAL SCRUTINY

These concerns expressed by the Court were addressed and the limitations of *Berger* modified in *Katz v. United States*.[11] In an opinion by Justice Stewart, one of the *Berger* dissenters, the Court adjusted the strict language of *Berger* and effectively pointed to Court approval of some types of statutorily-authorized electronic surveillance. Just as *Berger* had confirmed that one rationale of the *Olmstead* decision, the inapplicability of "seizure" to conversations, was no longer valid, *Katz* disposed of the other rationale.

In *Katz* officers affixed a listening device to the outside wall of a telephone booth regularly used by Katz and activated it each time he entered. By attaching the bug to the outside of the telephone booth the officers did not make a physical trespass into the booth. Because of this distinction, the lower courts held the Fourth Amendment not relevant. The Supreme Court disagreed, saying that "once it is recognized that the Fourth Amendment protects people — and not simply 'areas' — against unreasonable searches and seizures, it becomes clear that the reach of that Amendment cannot turn upon the presence or absence of a physical intrusion into any given enclosure."[12]

What is also of importance in *Katz* is the language the Court used in describing how easy it might be for an officer to obtain a warrant allowing the same type of intrusion, but under the shielding of the Fourth Amendment. The Court effectively pointed the way when it stated, "it is clear that this surveillance was so narrowly circumscribed that a duly authorized magistrate, properly notified of the need for such investigation, specifically informed of the basis on which it was to proceed, and clearly apprised of the precise intrusion it would entail, could constitutionally have authorized, with appropriate safeguards, the very limited search and seizure that the Government asserts in fact took place."

The *Katz* case clarified that electronic interception of conversations can be constitutional and at the same time gave some guidance on the means of obtaining judicial approval for such actions. In essence, the Court was telling law enforcement personnel that if they want to tap a phone or use other electronic means to "seize" a conversation then they must seek a warrant and narrowly tailor the time, place, and manner of the interception.

Katz summarily disposed of the notice requirement, which had loomed in *Berger* as an obstacle to successful electronic surveillance. Similarly, Justice Stewart also signified that it was unlikely that electronic surveillance would ever come under any of the established exceptions to the Fourth Amendment, and as such it was also unlikely that it could be conducted without prior judicial approval.[13]

The *Katz* decision was not accepted lightly. In 1968 Congress enacted a comprehensive statute authorizing federal officers to seek warrants for electronic surveillance to investigate violations of prescribed classes of criminal legislation.[14] This new statute also allowed states to establish their own versions of such legislation, provided the state scheme follow the federal scheme in scope and application. Congress thus broadened what *Katz* effectively limited.

The Congressional answer to *Berger* and *Katz* has made its way to the Supreme Court as a secondary issue but has yet to face a true constitutional challenge. The Court has interpreted the statute several times without facing the constitutional questions.[15] It also appears unlikely that such a challenge will be mounted under current operations by law enforcement. One may argue that the varied opinions in *Olmstead, Berger, Katz,* and others have explored the issues sufficiently, but that appears unlikely with the ever-changing world of electronic technology.

III. WARRANTLESS "NATIONAL SECURITY" ELECTRONIC SURVEILLANCE

Another significant event in the *Katz* decision was Justice White's attempt to preserve for a future decision the possibility that in "national security cases" electronic surveillance may fall under a different standard. Justice White suggested that upon the authorization of the President or the Attorney General electronic surveillance would be permissible without prior judicial approval.[16]

Following the *Katz* decision and Justice White's statements, the Executive Branch asserted the power to wiretap and to "bug" in two types of national security situations: against domestic subversion and against foreign intelligence operations. The Executive Branch based its authority on a theory of "inherent" presidential power. It also argued that the Supreme Court's holding effectively meant that such surveillance was a "reasonable" search and seizure and therefore valid under the Fourth Amendment.

The Supreme Court addressed this issue in *United States v. United States District Court*,[17] when it held that at least in cases of domestic subversive investigations, compliance with the warrant provisions of the Fourth Amendment was required. Whether or not a search was reasonable, wrote Justice Powell for a unanimous Court, was a question which derived much of its answer from the warrant clause. Except in a few narrowly circumscribed classes of situations, only those searches conducted pursuant to warrants were reasonable.

The government's duty to preserve the national security did not override the guarantee against invasion of privacy by the government. Thus, before the government could use electronic surveillance techniques they must meet the standards of the Fourth Amendment. In other words, the government must present to a neutral magistrate evidence sufficient to support issuance of a warrant authorizing that invasion of privacy.

It should be noted that while this case places on the government the requirement of complying with the Fourth Amendment, it does not preclude Congress from creating a different standard of probable cause in national security cases. In pertinent part the Court stated:

> We recognize that domestic security surveillance may involve different policy and practical considerations from the surveillance of 'ordinary crime.' The gathering of security intelligence is often long range and involves the interrelation of various sources and types of information. The exact targets of such surveillance may be more difficult to identify than in surveillance operations against many types of crimes specified in Title III. Often, too, the emphasis of domestic intelligence gathering is on the prevention of unlawful activity or the enhancement of the Government's preparedness for some future crisis or emergency.... Different standards may be compatible with the Fourth Amendment if they are reasonable both in relation to the legitimate need of Government for intelligence information and the protected rights of our citizens. For the warrant application may vary according to the governmental interest to be enforced and the nature of citizen rights deserving protection.... It may be that Congress, for example, would judge that the application and affidavit showing probable cause need not follow the exact requirements of Sec. 2518 but should allege other circumstances more appropriate to domestic security cases....[18]

Congress has acted by providing for a special court to hear requests for warrants for electronic surveillance in foreign intelligence situations. Congress has also empowered the President to authorize warrantless surveillance to acquire foreign intelligence information provided that the communications to be monitored are exclusively between or among foreign powers and there is no substantial likelihood any "United States person" will be overheard.[19]

ENDNOTES

1. 277 U.S. 438 (1928).
2. The section, which appeared at 47 U.S.C. §605, was rewritten by Title III of the Omnibus Crime Act of 1968, 82 Stat. 22, §803, so that the "regulation of the interception of wire or oral communications in the future is to be governed by" the provisions of Title III. S. Rep. No. 1097, 90th Cong., 2d sess. 107–08 (1968).
3. 302 U.S. 379 (1937).
4. Schwartz v. Texas, 344 U.S. 199 (1952).
5. 316 U.S. 129 (1942).
6. Silverman v. United States, 365 U.S. 505 (1961).
7. Clinton v. Virginia, 377 U.S. 158 (1964).
8. 388 U.S. 41 (1967).
9. *Id.* at 58–60.
10. *Id.* at 71 and 113.
11. 389 U.S. 347 (1967).
12. *Id.* at 353.
13. *Id.* at 357–58.
14. Title III of the Omnibus Crime Control and Safe Streets Act of 1968, 82 Stat. 211, 18 U.S.C. §§2510–20.
15. United States v. Kahn, 415 U.S. 143 (1974); United States v. Giordano, 416 U.S. 505 (1974); United States v. Chavez, 416 U.S. 562 (1974); United States v. Donovan, 429 U.S. 413 (1977); Scott v. United States, 436 U.S. 128 (1978); Dalia v. United States, 441 U.S. 238 (1979); United States v. New York Telephone Co., 434 U.S. 159 (1977); United States v. Caceres, 440 U.S. 741 (1979).
16. 389 U.S. 347, 363–64 (1967) (concurring opinion).
17. 407 U.S. 297 (1972).
18. *Id.* at 322–23.
19. Foreign Intelligence Surveillance Act of 1978, Pub. L. No. 95-511, 92 Stat. 1797, 50 U.S.C. §§1801–11. See United States v. Belfield, 692 F.2d 141 (D.C. Cir. 1982) (upholding constitutionality of disclosure restrictions in Act).

15 Enforcing the Fourth Amendment

I. THE EXCLUSIONARY RULE

While it is clear that the Fourth Amendment provides a right to be free from unreasonable searches and seizures it is also clear that there is no remedy designated in the Constitution. Several possible methods of enforcement have been suggested over time, but none have been as broad of exception as that adopted by the Supreme Court relatively early in constitutional litigation history.

From the outset there has been controversy about what means are necessary to protect the rights of the citizen from an overzealous government. In the area of search and seizure one standard rose above all others. This standard, which has come to be known as the exclusionary rule, began in *Boyd v. United States*.[1]

From a historical standpoint the *Boyd* case is interesting because it was not a true search and seizure case. The case focused on the compulsory production of business papers — recently attacked under the Fifth Amendment — but likened by the Court to a search and seizure.

By analogizing the Fifth Amendment's self-incrimination provisions to the Fourth Amendment's protections the Court developed a rule that required exclusion of compelled evidence based on the fact that the defendant had been compelled to self-incrimination. What is important, at least for Fourth Amendment purposes, is not the analogy to the Fifth Amendment, but the creation of a rule of exclusion in order to remedy a constitutional violation.

While the rule was created in the *Boyd* case, and effectively applied through the analogy method, the exclusionary rule was later rejected by the Court in a pure Fourth Amendment context. Instead, the Justices applied the common law rule that evidence was admissible however acquired.[2] Ten years later the common law view was itself rejected and an exclusionary rule propounded in *Weeks v. United States*.[3]

In *Weeks*, the defendant had been convicted on the basis of evidence seized from his home in the course of two warrantless searches. Among other items, the seized evidence included private papers, like those sought to be compelled in the *Boyd* case. A unanimous Court held that the evidence should have been excluded by the trial court because the Fourth Amendment placed on both the courts and law enforcement officers restraints on the exercise of power compatible with its guarantees.

Writing for the majority, Justice Day said, "The tendency of those who execute the criminal laws of the country to obtain convictions by means of unlawful searches and enforced confessions...should find no sanction in the judgment of the courts which are charged at all times with the support of the Constitution and to which people of all conditions have a right to appeal for the maintenance of such fundamental rights."[4]

In strong language the Court took to task both the lower courts and law enforcement when it wrote: "The efforts of the courts and their officials to bring the guilty to punishment, praiseworthy as they are, are not to be aided by the sacrifice of those great principles established by years of endeavor and suffering which have resulted in their embodiment in the fundamental law of the land."

These early cases helped develop the rule of exclusion for illegally obtained evidence, but did the rule apply to the states as well as to the federal government? In at least one case this issue arose as a mandate of the federal Constitution.[5] The Court clarified this in *Wolf v. Colorado*,[6] when a unanimous Court held that freedom from unreasonable searches and seizures was such a fundamental right as to be protected against state violations by the due process clause of the Fourteenth Amendment.

It should be noted that the Court also held that the right thus guaranteed did not require that the exclusionary rule be applied in the state courts. The court reasoned that the rule could be used, but since there were other means to observe and enforce the right it would not be the only means available for enforcing the Fourth Amendment.

The issues of the exclusionary rule floundered in the Court for some time until a clearer standard was developed in *Mapp v. Ohio*.[7] In this case the Court held that the exclusionary rule should and did apply to the states. It was "logically and constitutionally necessary," wrote Justice Clark for the majority, "that the exclusion doctrine — an essential part of the right to privacy — be also insisted upon as an essential ingredient of the right" to be secure from unreasonable searches and seizures. "To hold otherwise is to grant the right but in reality to withhold its privilege and enjoyment."[8]

In *Ker v. California*[9] the Court extended the application of the rule when it held that since illegally seized evidence was to be excluded from both federal and state courts, the standards by which the question of legality was to be determined should be the same, regardless of whether the court in which the evidence was offered was state or federal. This decision effectively limited the state courts to an application of the exclusionary rule absent other constitutionally approved methods. As we will see in the coming sections, such methods have been employed and a debate on the application of the rule continues today.

II. THE FOUNDATIONS OF THE EXCLUSIONARY RULE

One of the common issues in debates surrounding the exclusionary rule is the foundation for the rule. Where did the rule come from? Is it a creation of constitutional mandate or merely a method of federal supervision over the state courts? Answers to these questions will determine the applicability of the rule to the state courts. If it is determined that the rule is not constitutionally mandated then there are those who would argue that it should not apply to the states.

As was set out in the above section, the rule appears to have first evolved from a blending of Fifth and Fourth Amendment principles. Later, the rule was applied specifically to the Fourth Amendment, but not initially to the states. After passage of the Fourteenth Amendment, which made all the provisions of the Bill of Rights applicable to the states, it appears more likely that the rule will apply to the states.

An example of an exclusionary rule not based on constitutional grounds may be found in *McNabb v. United States*[10] and *Mallory v. United States*.[11] In both cases the Court enforced a requirement that arrestees be promptly presented to a magistrate by holding that incriminating admissions obtained during the period beyond a reasonable time for presentation would be inadmissible. The rule was not immediately extended to the states, but the Court's resort to the self-incrimination clause in reviewing confessions made such application irrelevant, in any event, in most cases. For an example of a transmutation of a supervisory rule into a constitutional rule one may also wish to read *McCarthy v. United States*[12] and *Boykin v. Alabama*.[13]

With the decision in *Mapp* it appears that the question of constitutional origin has been laid to rest. The *Mapp* decision, however, does not necessarily mean that the rule is immune to statutory revision. In this sense, Congress — or conceivably a state legislative body — could modify the rule and its application in state courts.

One means by which the exclusionary rule would always apply, even in state courts, is through a Supreme Court finding that the admission of illegally obtained evidence is itself violative of the Fourth Amendment. Suggestions that admission of illegally seized evidence is itself unconstitutional appear in a number of cases.[14] Such suggestions are often combined with a rationale emphasizing "judicial integrity" as a reason to reject the tender of illegally obtained evidence. No clear standard or scheme has yet developed.

III. NARROWING APPLICATION OF THE EXCLUSIONARY RULE

While the exclusionary rule has not been wholly overturned there have been successful attacks against it and some narrowing of its application. By the early 1980s a majority of Justices had stated a desire either to abolish the rule or to sharply curtail its operation,[15] and numerous opinions had rejected all doctrinal bases save that of deterrence.

For example, in *United States v. Janis*[16] the Court ruled that deterrence is the "prime purpose" of the rule, "if not the sole one." Other cases have held that admission of the fruits of an unlawful search or seizure "work no new Fourth Amendment wrong" and that the wrong is "fully accomplished by the unlawful search or seizure itself."[17]

The Court has also held that the exclusionary rule does not "cure the invasion of the defendant's rights which he has already suffered."[18] Judicial integrity is not infringed by the mere admission of evidence seized wrongfully. "[T]he courts must not commit or encourage violations of the Constitution," and the integrity issue is answered by whether exclusion would deter violations by others.[19]

These opinions also voiced strong doubts about the effectiveness of the rule as a deterrent, and advanced public interest values in effective law enforcement and public safety as reasons to discard the rule altogether or curtail its application. The Court emphasized the high costs of enforcing the rule to exclude reliable and trustworthy evidence, even when violations have been technical or in good faith, and suggested that such use of the rule may well "generat[e] disrespect for the law and administration of justice."[20]

The Court has also noted that zealous application of the rule would effectively set free many defendants who were in fact guilty, and as such the public interest is not best served by a strict application of the rule. In this sense, the strength of the Fourth Amendment has been curtailed and is now more of a potential for deterrence than a means of exclusion. Although the exclusionary rule has not been completely rejected, its application has been extensively reduced.

Several decisions have allowed otherwise excludable evidence under this new application. Defendants may no longer exclude evidence against themselves that was actually obtained through an illegal search and seizure of a co-conspirator or codefendants.[21] Illegally seized evidence may also be admitted when its purpose is to impeach the testimony of the defendant.[22] The Court has also held that where defendants have been convicted after trials in which they were given a full and fair opportunity to raise claims of Fourth Amendment violations they may not subsequently raise those claims on federal habeas corpus actions.[23]

Probably the most effective curtailment of the rule came in 1984 with adoption of a "good faith" exception. In *United States v. Leon*[24] the Court created an exception for evidence obtained as a result of officers' objective, good-faith reliance on a warrant even when the warrant was later found to be defective. The Court noted that the warrant met most of the Fourth Amendment requirements, i.e., signed affidavit, presented to a neutral magistrate, and definite as to time and place of search. In writing for the majority, Justice White said that the "exclusionary rule is designed to deter police misconduct rather than to punish the errors of judges and magistrates."

Justice White also suggested that the rule should not be applied "to deter objectively reasonable law enforcement activity," and that "[p]enalizing the officer for the magistrate's error... cannot logically contribute to the deterrence of Fourth Amendment violations."[25]

The Court applied the *Leon* standard in *Massachusetts v. Sheppard*,[26] where an officer, during the application process, pointed out to the magistrate that he had not used the "standard form." The magistrate indicated that the necessary changes had been incorporated in the issued warrant, and this gave the officer grounds to believe that the warrant was in fact valid. Though it was technically invalid, the actions of the officer and magistrate would leave a reasonable person to believe, especially considering the fact the warrant was issued, that the warrant was in fact valid.

The Court then extended *Leon* to hold that the exclusionary rule is inapplicable to evidence obtained by an officer acting in objectively reasonable reliance on a statute later held violative of the Fourth Amendment.[27] Justice Blackmun's opinion for the Court reasoned that application of the exclusionary rule in such circumstances would have no more deterrent effect on officers than it would when officers reasonably rely on an invalid warrant, and no more deterrent effect on legislators who enact invalid statutes than on magistrates who issue invalid warrants.

IV. ALTERNATIVES TO THE EXCLUSIONARY RULE

Opponents of the exclusionary rule have long pointed to the several alternatives available for violations of the Fourth Amendment. Such alternatives have within them various means of enforcement that can be applied directly to the officer who violates the amendment or to the department who employs such an officer. Few of these alternatives, however, provide as caustic a remedy as does the exclusionary rule.

Many of the alternatives focus on the individual officer. For instance, an illegal search and seizure may be criminally actionable where the officers act with malice or reckless disregard for another's rights. Likewise, civil sanctions under various statutory schemes allow the citizen to seek redress directly from the officer who violates constitutional rights.

Officers may also be subject to internal, department-sanctioned discipline for violations. State law may also provide specific remedies for violations as well as guidelines for proper use of evidence seized illegally. Persons who have been illegally arrested or who have had their privacy invaded will usually have a tort action available under state statutory or common law.

As we consider the various formulas and potential for future alternatives it is imperative that we consider both the method for protecting future citizen rights and the means of safeguarding the individual's rights currently involved. We must also add to that equation the need to protect society from harm due to crime. This balancing act of rights is not easily accomplished, and it appears likely that the issues will not find quick answers. For that reason, both today and tomorrow's criminal justice professional must be cognizant of the past application of the Fourth Amendment as well as the future trend likely to preserve the protections.

ENDNOTES

1. 116 U.S. 616 (1886).
2. Adams v. New York, 192 U.S. 585 (1904).
3. 232 U.S. 383 (1914).
4. *Id.* at 392.
5. Elkins v. United States, 364 U.S. 206, 224–32 (1960).
6. 338 U.S. 25 (1949).
7. 367 U.S. 643 (1961).
8. *Id.* at 655–56.
9. 374 U.S. 23 (1963).
10. 318 U.S. 332 (1943).
11. 354 U.S. 449 (1957).
12. 394 U.S. 459 (1969).
13. 395 U.S. 238 (1969).
14. See Weeks v. United States, 232 U.S. 383, 392 (1914); Mapp v. Ohio, 367 U.S. 643, 655, 657 (1961); and Terry v. Ohio, 392 U.S. 1, 12, 13 (1968).
15. See Stone v. Powell, 428 U.S. 465, 496 (1976); Schneckloth v. Bustamonte, 412 U.S. 218, 261 (1973); Brown v. Illinois, 422 U.S. 590, 609 (1975); Robbins v. California, 453 U.S. 420, 437 (1981); California v. Minjares, 443 U.S. 916 (1979); and Coolidge v. New Hampshire, 403 U.S. 443, 510 (1971).
16. 428 U.S. 433, 446 (1976).
17. United States v. Calandara, 414 U.S. 338, 347–48 (1974).
18. Stone v. Powell, 428 U.S. 465, 486 (1976).

19. See United States v. Peltier, 422 U.S. 531, 536–39 (1975); Rakas v. Illinois, 439 U.S. 128, 134 n.3, 137–38 (1978); Michigan v. DeFillippo, 443 U.S. 31, 38 n.3 (1979).
20. Stone v. Powell, 428 U.S. at 490, 491.
21. Rakas v. Illinois, 439 U.S. 128 (1978); United States v. Salvucci, 448 U.S. 83 (1980); Rawlings v. Kentucky, 448 U.S. 98 (1980); and United States v. Payner, 447 U.S. 727 (1980).
22. United States v. Havens, 446 U.S. 620 (1980).
23. Stone v. Powell, 428 U.S. 465 (1976).
24. 468 U.S. 897 (1984).
25. 468 U.S. at 919, 921.
26. 468 U.S. 981 (1984).
27. Illinois v. Krull, 480 U.S. 340 (1987).

Section Five

Fifth Amendment — Rights of Persons

Amendment Text

No person shall be held to answer for a capital, or otherwise infamous crime, unless on a presentment or indictment of a Grand Jury, except in cases arising in the land or naval forces, or in the Militia, when in actual service in time of War or public danger; nor shall any person be subject for the same offence to be twice put in jeopardy of life or limb; nor shall be compelled in any criminal case to be a witness against himself, nor be deprived of life, liberty, or property, without due process of law; nor shall private property be taken for public use, without just compensation.

16 Indictment by Grand Jury

I. DEVELOPING A RIGHT

The Fifth Amendment to the U.S. Constitution offers criminal defendants protections under five broad clauses. The first clause provides protection from being charged without an indictment or other charging instrument. The second clause deals with an issue known today as "double jeopardy." The third clause deals with self-incrimination. The fourth and fifth protections, contained in the final clause of the amendment, deal with due process and the taking of property by the government.

Like much of constitutional history, the history of the grand jury is rooted in the earliest forms of western civilization. Historians have traced the right back to Athens, pre-Norman England, and the Assize of Clarendon promulgated by Henry II. Within the colonies the right first appears in the Charter of Liberties and Privileges of 1683. This charter, which established a number of rights, was passed by the first assembly permitted to be elected in the colony of New York.[1]

By 1787 the right had made its way into many of the early charters of the colonies. Madison introduced the right as part of the initial Bill of Rights, and there is no record of either debate or opposition to the provision. Part of the reason for its easy acceptance is that the right had a long history within the English common law system. There would have been every reason to believe that our constitutional grand jury was intended to operate substantially like its English progenitor.

The heart of the right has the basic purpose of providing a fair method for instituting criminal proceedings. Grand jurors were selected from the body of the people, and their work was not hampered by rigid procedural or evidentiary rules. In fact, grand jurors could act on their own knowledge and were free to make their presentments or indictments on such information as they deemed satisfactory. The issue was not guilt or innocence but merely whether sufficient evidence existed to believe the person should be charged with a crime.

In England the grand jury acquired an independence free from control by the Crown or judges. This power was maintained by grand juries in the colonies. Despite its broad power to institute criminal proceedings, the grand jury grew in popularity over the years. Its adoption in our Constitution as the sole method for preferring charges in serious criminal cases shows the high place it held as an instrument of justice.[2]

The grand jury is an integral part of our constitutional heritage, which was brought to this country with the common law. The Framers, most of them trained in the English law and traditions, accepted the grand jury as a basic guarantee of individual liberty. Its historic office has been to provide a shield against arbitrary or oppressive action, by ensuring that serious criminal accusations will be brought only upon the considered judgment of a representative body of citizens acting under oath and under judicial instruction and guidance.[3]

The traditional constitutional function of grand juries in federal courts is to return criminal indictments,[4] but the juries serve a considerably broader series of purposes as well. The primary task of the grand jury is an investigative function, which is exercised by the individual juries when they summon witnesses by process and compel testimony. A grand jury may also compel the production of evidence.

Grand juries operate in secrecy, but are generally under the direction — but not control — of a federal prosecutor from the U.S. Attorney's office. The juries are not bound by many evidentiary or constitutional restrictions, and juries may examine witnesses in the absence of their counsel.[5] From a practical standpoint the witnesses, including any who themselves may be under investigation, may have counsel available, but the attorney may not go into the grand jury hearing room.

The Court addressed this issue in *Coleman v. Alabama*,[6] deeming the preliminary hearing a "critical stage of the prosecution," at which counsel must be provided. In this sense the Court recognized that counsel was important and could not be denied altogether. In *United States v. Mandujano*,[7] however, the Court clarified that while legal counsel may be available there was no requirement that counsel be allowed into the room while testimony was being taken. The primary purpose for this was that the grand jury proceedings were investigatory in nature, and since no criminal charges were yet pending then no Sixth Amendment rights to counsel attached.

This decision not only emphasized the point that legal counsel was not allowed in the room during questioning but also cast doubt upon the existence of any constitutional requirement that a grand jury witness be permitted to consult with counsel outside the room. In other words, once the witness has entered the closed-door session of the grand jury inquiry there may be no provision allowing that person to stop the hearing/testimony in order to consult with counsel. This case further raised the implication that a witness or putative defendant unable to afford counsel would have no right to appointed counsel at this stage.

Concurring, Justice Brennan argued that it was essential and constitutionally required for the protection of one's constitutional rights that a witness have access to counsel and suggested that this even extends to the appointment of counsel if the person is indigent or otherwise unable to provide for his or her own. Justice Brennan also addressed, although briefly, the concept that one could consult with counsel and that it may be necessary in some instances in order to preserve a witness' rights.[8] These issues have not been settled fully. In recent years there has been movement that has extended the ability of a witness to testify with counsel present.

In August 1998, President Bill Clinton was under investigation and was called before a Washington grand jury by Special Prosecutor Kenneth Starr. A subpoena had been issued for the president's appearance before the grand jury, but negotiations between the president's counsel and the Office of the Special Prosecutor led to a unique situation in grand jury investigations. The president was allowed to testify, but instead of being in the closed environs of the grand jury room at the court house, the president testified from the comfort of his own office via closed-circuit television.

What also made this grand jury testimony unique was the fact that the president had his legal counsel with him as he testified. Counsel was able to advise the president at the moment the questions of the grand jury were being asked. Unlike any such prior situation, the witness, a sitting president, had — for the first time — the benefit of counsel at his side, unlike any witness who has appeared before a grand jury. This procedure, however, was highly unusual and was agreed to by the Special Prosecutor in order to prevent the protracted legal battle that would have taken place had the president refused to testify. Witnesses of lower social and political position should not expect such special treatment when dealing with a grand jury.

As indicated above, a grand jury may subpoena any witness necessary for its investigation, including the person who may be a putative defendant. Likewise, a grand jury may summon witnesses without informing them of the object of the investigation or the involvement of the witnesses within the investigation. In this sense, the secrecy surrounding the work of a grand jury often takes on ominous tones in that few outside the prosecutor's office or the grand jury itself will know for certain what the grand jury is investigating.

One exception to this rule is noteworthy. Where a grand jury is investigating an individual for specific criminal acts, and where this investigation could result in criminal charges, the grand jury is required to notify the witness of his or her rights against self-incrimination.[9] This does not mean that the grand jury must inform the person that he or she is in fact being investigated or may be indicted as a result of the investigation. In other words, a grand jury may subpoena as witness the person whom it is investigating. The grand jury is required to inform this person, as a witness, that he or she has a right against self-incrimination, but the grand jury does not have to tell the witness that the grand jury will in fact be focusing on him or her specifically for criminal purposes.[10]

In previous sections covering the protections of the Fourth Amendment we explored the use of the exclusionary rule to limit introduction of tainted evidence in a judicial proceeding. This rule is inapplicable in grand jury proceedings, and the result is that a witness called before a grand jury may be questioned on the basis of knowledge obtained through the use of illegally seized evidence.[11]

The power of the grand jury even reaches other constitutional provisions. For example, the Court has held that the Fourth Amendment is inapplicable to grand jury subpoenas requiring named parties to give voice exemplars and handwriting samples to the grand jury for identification purposes.[12] In addressing this issue the Court applied a two-tiered analysis: "whether either the initial compulsion of the person to appear before the grand jury, or the subsequent directive to make a voice recording is an unreasonable 'seizure' within the meaning of the Fourth Amendment."[13]

In addressing the issues the Court first established that a subpoena to appear was not a seizure in the Fourth Amendment context. The Court reasoned that because the subpoena to appear before a grand jury entailed significantly less social and personal affront than did an arrest the Fourth Amendment protections did not apply. The Court also held that every citizen has an obligation, which may be onerous at times, to appear and give whatever aid he or she may to a grand jury.[14] The Court next established that the directive to make a voice recording or to produce handwriting samples did not bring the Fourth Amendment into play because the defendant would have no expectation of privacy in the characteristics of either his or her voice or handwriting.[15]

Besides indictments, grand juries may also take other actions such as the issuance of reports that indicate non-indictable misbehavior. For example, the inability of a public officer to perform his or her job is not usually a criminal act, but it may be investigated by a grand jury and a civil indictment issued. Misfeasance and malfeasance of public officers are both considered fair game for the jury. Likewise, objectionable conduct may also be subject to grand jury report. Congress has now specifically authorized issuance of reports in cases concerning public officers and organized crime.[16]

Despite the vast power of grand juries, there is little in the way of judicial or legislative response designed to impose some supervisory restrictions on them. Congress has required that, in the selection of federal grand juries as well as petit juries, random selection of a fair cross section of the community is to take place, and has provided a procedure for challenging discriminatory selection by moving to dismiss the indictment.[17] In this sense, it is not the grand jury itself that may be challenged but the ultimate product of the grand jury.

These expanded powers have been supported in a number of cases. In one such case, the Supreme Court held the grand jury "is a grand inquest, a body with powers of investigation and inquisition, the scope of whose inquiries is not to be limited narrowly by questions of propriety or forecasts of whether any particular individual will be found properly subject to an accusation of crime."[18]

II. INDICTMENT AND INFAMOUS CRIMES

The ultimate authority of a grand jury is most evident with the issuance of an indictment. The indictment is the means by which the grand jury formally accuses a person of criminal wrongdoing. It is the means by which a person may be charged with a crime and to which a defendant must answer. Under the Fifth Amendment no "infamous" crime may be charged without first being subject to the grand jury.

Within the meaning of the amendment, a crime is made "infamous" by the type punishment that may be imposed.[19] The Supreme Court has indicated that "What punishments shall be considered as infamous may be affected by the changes of public opinion from one age to another."[20] In this sense, what may be considered an "infamous" crime in the nineteenth century may not be so infamous in the late twentieth century.

Within the federal system and those states following that system, an accused in danger of being subjected to an infamous punishment if convicted has the right to insist that he or she shall not be put on trial except on the accusation of a grand jury.[21] Thus, the issue is not merely the severity of the crime, but the severity of the punishment. One such example arises where the accused, if convicted, could be imprisoned at hard labor for one year as well as deported merely for being an illegal alien. While the crime of being an "illegal alien" may not be an "infamous" crime in the grandest sense of the word, it may be considered an infamous crime because of the nature of punishment.[22]

Other crimes, which on their face appear to be anything but infamous, also fit within this category. These include counterfeiting,[23] fraudulent alteration of poll books,[24] fraudulent voting,[25] and embezzlement.[26] The Court has held that it is also immaterial how Congress has classified the offense, i.e., felony, misdemeanor, etc.[27]

The protection of indictment by grand jury extends to all persons except those serving in the armed forces. All persons in the regular armed forces are subject to court martial rather than grand jury indictment or trial by jury.[28] The Court has held that the limiting words "when in actual service in time of war or public danger" apply only to members of the militia and not to members of the regular armed forces.

In 1969 the Court held in *O'Callahan v. Parker*[29] that offenses that are not "service connected" may not be punished under military law but instead must be tried in the civil courts in the jurisdiction where the acts took place. This decision was overruled, however, in 1987, with the Court emphasizing the "plain language" of Art. I, Sec. 8, Cl. 14, which confers power on Congress to "make rules for the government and regulation of the land and naval forces."

ENDNOTES

1. The provision read: "That in all Cases Capitall or Criminall there shall be a grand Inquest who shall first present the offence...."
2. Costello v. United States, 350 U.S. 359, 362 (1956).
3. United States v. Mandujano, 425 U.S. 564, 571 (1976).
4. Hurtado v. California, 110 U.S. 516 (1884); Palko v. Connecticut, 302 U.S. 319, 323 (1937); Alexander v. Louisiana, 405 U.S. 625, 633 (1972).
5. Fed. R. Civ. P. 6(d). The validity of this restriction was asserted in dictum in *In re Groban*, 352 U.S. 330, 333 (1957).
6. 399 U.S. 1 (1970).
7. 425 U.S. 564 (1976) (plurality opinion).
8. *Id.* at 602–09 (with Justice Marshall).
9. United States v. Washington, 431 U.S. 181 (1977).
10. *Id.*
11. United States v. Calandra, 414 U.S. 338 (1974).
12. United States v. Dionisio, 410 U.S. 1 (1973); United States v. Mara, 410 U.S. 19 (1973).
13. United States v. Dionisio, 410 U.S. 1 (1973).
14. *Id.* at 9–13.
15. *Id.* at 13–15. For further discussion of this rationale, see the Chapter 14 discussion of the Fourth Amendment and Katz v. United States, 389 U.S. 347 (1967).
16. 18 U.S.C. §333.
17. 28 U.S.C. §§1861–68.
18. Blair v. United States, 250 U.S. 273, 281 (1919).
19. Ex parte Wilson, 114 U.S. 417 (1885).
20. *Id.* at 427.
21. Ex parte Wilson, 114 U.S. 417, 426 (1885).
22. Wong Wing v. United States, 163 U.S. 228, 237 (1896).
23. Ex parte Wilson, 114 U.S. 417 (1885).
24. Mackin v. United States, 117 U.S. 348 (1886).
25. Parkinson v. United States, 121 U.S. 281 (1887).
26. United States v. DeWalt, 128 U.S. 393 (1888).
27. Ex parte Wilson, 114 U.S. 417, 426 (1885).
28. Johnson v. Sayre, 158 U.S. 109, 114 (1895).
29. 395 U.S. 258 (1969).

17 Double Jeopardy

I. DEVELOPMENT AND SCOPE

The Fifth Amendment also provides protections from facing the same charge more than once. This principle is known as "double jeopardy." The underlying idea, one deeply ingrained in at least the Anglo-American system of jurisprudence, is that the state with all its resources and power should not be allowed to make repeated attempts to convict an individual for an alleged offense. Without such limitation, the Court has held, an accused would be forced "to live in a continuing state of anxiety and insecurity, as well as enhancing the possibility that even though innocent he may be found guilty."[1]

While the concept of double jeopardy goes far back in our legal history it is clear that the development of the right was bumpy and establishing a clear meaning was difficult. Early development of the concept in England came under the influence of Coke and Blackstone. Over time the right gradually came to mean that a defendant at trial could plead former conviction or former acquittal as a special plea to defeat the prosecution.[2]

Development of the right followed similar lines in this country. The basic rule extended to bar a new trial although the former trial had not concluded in either an acquittal or a conviction. Inclusion of the rule in several state bills of rights following the American Revolution elevated its fundamental status, and the differing approaches continued.

The first bill of rights that expressly adopted a double jeopardy clause was the New Hampshire constitution of 1784. This state constitution held that "No subject shall be liable to be tried, after an acquittal, for the same crime or offence."[3] A more comprehensive protection was included in the Pennsylvania Declaration of Rights of 1790, which had language almost identical to the present Fifth Amendment provision.[4]

Madison's version of the guarantee as introduced in the House of Representatives read: "No person shall be subject, except in cases of impeachment, to more than one punishment or trial for the same offense."[5] Opposition focused on the language of the amendment rather than its intent. The proposed amendment allowed the defendant to escape a second trial where an appeal, following an initial conviction, was successful. Many argued that such protection would either constitute a hazard to the public by freeing the guilty or, more likely, result in a detriment to defendants because appellate courts would be loath to reverse convictions if no new trial could follow. A motion to strike the phrase "or trial" from the clause failed.[6] The language was modified, however, by the Senate and accepted by the House for referral to the states.

Throughout most of its history, this clause was binding only against the federal government. After ratification of the Fourteenth Amendment the double jeopardy clause remained purely a federal issue, but by 1937 there was a steady effort to apply the provisions in both the federal and state courts.

One of the more meaningful attempts came in *Palko v. Connecticut*.[7] The Court rejected an argument that the Fourteenth Amendment incorporated all the provisions of the first eight amendments as limitations on the states and enunciated the due process theory under which most of those amendments do now apply to the states. Some guarantees in the Bill of Rights, Justice Cardozo wrote, were so fundamental that they are "of the very essence of the scheme of ordered liberty" and "neither liberty nor justice would exist if they were sacrificed."[8] For the Justices, there were certain rights so fundamental that they did not need the Fourteenth Amendment to be applied; however, the double jeopardy clause, like many other procedural rights of defendants, was not one of them.

The Court did offer a tidbit, however, when it held that a defendant's due process rights, absent double jeopardy consideration per se, might be violated if the State "creat[ed] a hardship so acute and shocking as to be unendurable."[9] While *Palko* was not the case for such application it was important in laying the foundation for later application of the principle.

It would be more than 30 years later before a clear standard was created. In *Benton v. Maryland*[10] the Court concluded "that the double jeopardy prohibition... represents a fundamental ideal in our constitutional heritage.... Once it is decided that a particular Bill of Rights guarantee is 'fundamental to the American scheme of justice,'... the same constitutional standards apply against both the State and Federal Governments."[11] As such, the double jeopardy limitation now applies to both federal and state governments. State rules on double jeopardy, with regard to such matters as when jeopardy attaches, must be considered in the light of federal standards.[12]

II. JEOPARDY AT PRETRIAL PROCEEDINGS

It is well established that jeopardy does not attach at proceedings held before a trial; however, a few of these proceedings do merit a brief glance. Jeopardy will not attach where an accused has been before a court on a preliminary examination and subsequently discharged by the examining magistrate.[13] Likewise, where an indictment has been quashed by defense action no jeopardy shall attach.[14] Jeopardy will also not attach by arraignment and pleading to the indictment.[15]

III. CONCURRENT AND OVERLAPPING JURISDICTIONS

When dealing with double jeopardy one issue that arises often is whether both federal and state governments can charge a person with the same crime. Because both federal and state governments may have differing definitions of crimes, and because they may have differing perceptions on the enforcement of their laws, there are instances when one act may subject the criminal defendant to liability based on overlapping jurisdiction.

The problem of competing prosecutions was recognized as early as 1820,[16] and relatively soon thereafter the Court established the standard that prosecution by two governments of the same defendant for the same conduct would not constitute double jeopardy.[17] For the next century the Court would only address the issue in dicta, but by 1922 the time had come to establish the principle more clearly.

The Supreme Court created what is known as the "dual sovereignty" doctrine when it held that a defendant convicted in a state court may be later charged and convicted in federal court for performing the same acts.[18] "We have here two sovereignties, deriving power from different sources, capable of dealing with the same subject-matter within the same territory... Each government in determining what shall be an offense against its peace and dignity is exercising its own sovereignty, not that of the other."[19]

The foundation of the "dual sovereignty" doctrine lies in the recognition of the existence of two sets of laws often serving different federal-state purposes. In essence, the doctrine reflects practical considerations that undesirable consequences could follow, were the double jeopardy clause applied in such circumstances. Thus, a state might preempt federal authority by first prosecuting and providing for a lenient sentence (as compared to the possible federal sentence) or acquitting defendants who had the sympathy of state authorities as against federal law enforcement.[20]

The dual sovereignty doctrine has also been applied to permit successive prosecutions by two states for the same conduct.[21] For example, a defendant who kidnaps someone in State "A" and crosses into State "B" may be tried for the crime in both states, provided elements of the crime are present. Such a case would require each state to establish, beyond a reasonable doubt, that the particular elements of the crime occurred within its jurisdiction, even when the elements for kidnapping may differ slightly from one state to another.

Because one prime purpose of the clause is the protection against the burden of multiple trials, a defendant who raises and loses a double jeopardy claim during pretrial or trial may immediately appeal the ruling, a rare exception to the general rule prohibiting appeals from non-final orders.[22] During the 1970s especially, the Court decided an uncommonly large number of cases raising double jeopardy claims.[23] Instead of the clarity that often emerges from intense consideration of a particular issue, however, double jeopardy doctrine has descended into a state of "confusion," with the Court acknowledging that its decisions "can hardly be characterized as models of consistency and clarity."[24] This means that while the concept of double jeopardy has been well litigated, the actual principles have not been fully established to allow one an instant and clear definition. Some rules were clarified, and it is to these that we now turn.

IV. SUBSEQUENT PROSECUTION
FOLLOWING MISTRIAL

The original concept of double jeopardy, under the common law, generally held that no jeopardy attached until the trial had ended. In this circumstance, a defendant could be charged with a crime, taken before a jury, presented for trial up to the time of judgment, and, as long as no final judgment was entered, no jeopardy had attached. A prosecutor was presented with a unique advantage in having the ability to present a case before a jury, gauge jury members' reactions, and then, if the prosecutor was not satisfied that a conviction would be forthcoming, dismiss the case and refile a new charge.

The modern, constitutional scheme of double jeopardy does not go as far before recognizing that jeopardy has attached. In fact, where the defendant is to be tried by jury, jeopardy attaches at the time the jury is sworn. For trials before a judge alone (commonly known as a bench trial), jeopardy attaches when the first evidence is presented.[25] While this standard has certainly protected defendants from facing multiple trials without judgment, it has also created some interesting problems for the courts.

In some instances, if, after jeopardy attaches, the trial is terminated for some reason, a second trial may be barred even if the termination was erroneous.[26] The Court has reasoned that even

> if the first trial is not completed, a second prosecution may be grossly unfair. It increases the financial and emotional burden on the accused, prolongs the period in which he is stigmatized by an unresolved accusation of wrongdoing, and may even enhance the risk that an innocent defendant may be convicted. The danger of such unfairness to the defendant exists whenever a trial is aborted before it is completed. Consequently, as a general rule, the prosecutor is entitled to one, and only one, opportunity to require an accused to stand trial.[27]

The reasons the Court has given for fixing the attachment of jeopardy at a point prior to judgment and thus making some terminations of trials before judgment final insofar as the defendant is concerned is that a defendant has a "valued right to have his trial completed by a particular tribunal."[28] Problems with such a standard arise where the mistrial may be the result of "manifest necessity."[29] Examples include cases where the jury cannot reach a verdict[30] or external circumstances prevent the continuation of the trial. For example, a juror's impartiality becomes questionable during the trial[31] or there is a discovery during trial that one of the jurors had served on the grand jury that indicted the defendant and that juror was therefore disqualified.[32] One of the more interesting cases came during World War II when a mistrial was declared due to the advances of the enemy on the site of the trial.[33]

Not all matters that lead to a mistrial, however, will result in the attachment of jeopardy and subsequent barring of a second trial. There must ordinarily be a balancing of the defendant's right in having the trial completed against the public's interest in fair trials designed to end in just judgments. Thus, when a mistrial is granted because of a defective indictment (or similar charging instrument) retrial will not be barred.[34]

In such instances the Supreme Court has held that where a trial judge "properly exercises his discretion" in cases in which an impartial verdict cannot be reached or in which a verdict on conviction would have to be reversed on appeal because of an obvious error, then a mistrial would be proper and the defendant may be charged a second time. "If an error could make reversal on appeal a certainty, it would not serve 'the ends of public justice' to require that the Government proceed with its proof when, if it succeeded before the jury, it would automatically be stripped of that success by an appellate court."[35]

On the other hand, when, after jeopardy attached, a prosecutor successfully moved for a mistrial because a key witness had inadvertently not been served with subpoena, and could not be found, the Court barred a retrial. The Court held that because the prosecutor knew prior to the selection and swearing of the jury that the witness was unavailable the state would not get a second shot.[36]

A different issue arises when the prosecutor moves for mistrial because of prejudicial misconduct by the defense. In *Arizona v. Washington*[37] defense counsel in his opening statement made prejudicial comments about the prosecutor's past conduct, and the prosecutor's motion for a mistrial was granted over defendant's objections. The Court ruled that retrial was not barred by double jeopardy, holding that, in a strict, literal sense, mistrial was not necessary because the trial judge could have given limiting instructions to the jury. The Court also held that the highest degree of respect should be given to the trial judge's evaluation of the likelihood of the impairment of the impartiality of one or more jurors, and that as long as support for a mistrial order can be found in the trial record, no specific statement of "manifest necessity" need be made by the trial judge.[38]

The effect of a mistrial shifts when it is the judge who takes the action *sua sponte*. In *Gori v. United States*[39] the trial judge, on his own motion and with no indication of the wishes of defense counsel, declared a mistrial because he thought the prosecutor's line of questioning improper and prejudicial. The questioning was intended to expose the defendant's criminal record, which would have constituted prejudicial error, and the judge interceded without request from the defense.

The Supreme Court thought the judge's action was an abuse of discretion and approved retrial on the conclusion that the judge's decision had been made for the defendant's benefit. The rationale was that because the defendant had not sought corrective action, either by instruction to the prosecutor, the jury, or mistrial, the actions of the judge were excessive.

A different approach was used in the next case. In *United States v. Jorn*[40] the trial judge discharged the jury when he discovered that certain witnesses for the prosecution had not been properly apprised of their constitutional rights.[41] Like the above case, the court acted on its own motion. But unlike the above case, the Supreme Court found that the judge's action was not an abuse of his discretion and refused to permit retrial. The Court observed that the "doctrine of manifest necessity stands as a command to trial judges not to foreclose the defendant's option [to go to the first jury and perhaps obtain an acquittal] until a scrupulous exercise of judicial discretion leads to the conclusion that the ends of public justice would not be served by a continuation of the proceedings."[42]

For our purposes we see that reprosecution is not foreclosed even when a jury has been sworn and testimony begun. In essence, "a motion by the defendant for mistrial is ordinarily assumed to remove any barrier to reprosecution, even if the defendant's motion is necessitated by a prosecutorial or judicial error."[43] "Such a motion by the defendant is deemed to be a deliberate election on his part to forgo his valued right to have his guilt or innocence determined before the first trier of fact."[44] In this sense the Court has put upon the defendant the burden of deciding to proceed with the trial, although possibly tainted by misconduct, in hopes of an acquittal or the sure reprosecution after the granting of a mistrial when sought by the defendant.

Recognizing that the above standard may create an undue risk of facing multiple trials when a defendant elects to seek a mistrial, the Court has set some limitations on when reprosecution in available. For instance, where a prosecutor's intentional misconduct is such that it is seen as an attempt to "goad the defendant into moving for a mistrial" then the defendant's act in seeking a mistrial may not be enough to allow reprosecution.[45] Other extrinsic factors may also weigh in this decision. The bottom line, however, is that when the defendant has caused the mistrial, there may be opportunity for reprosecution.

V. SUBSEQUENT PROSECUTION FOLLOWING ACQUITTAL

The concept that a defendant may not be retried following an acquittal is "the most fundamental rule in the history of double jeopardy jurisprudence."[46] "[T]he law attaches particular significance to an acquittal. To permit a second trial after an acquittal, however mistaken the acquittal may have been, would present an unacceptably high risk that the Government, with its vastly superior resources, might wear down the defendant so that even though innocent he may be found guilty."[47]

While in other areas of double jeopardy doctrine consideration is given to the public safety interest in having a criminal trial proceed to an error-free conclusion, no such balancing of interests is permitted with respect to acquittals. The rule bars retrial even where the acquittal was "egregiously erroneous."[48]

This rule extends even to cases of improper acquittal. Once a jury has acquitted a defendant the government may not, through appeal of the verdict or institution of a new prosecution, place the defendant on trial again. The Supreme Court relatively early on held that, when the results of a trial are set aside because the first indictment was invalid or the trial's results were voidable for some reason, a judgment of acquittal must nevertheless remain undisturbed.[49]

Similarly, when a trial judge acquits a defendant, that action concludes the matter.[50] Problems arise, however, when the trial judge's actions make it difficult to determine whether the action was in fact an acquittal or a dismissal. For example, in a case in which the deadlocked jury had been discharged, and the trial judge had granted the defendant's motion for a judgment of acquittal under the appropriate federal rule, an appeal by the government may be barred where the actions of the judge terminate the case on a finding the government had not proved facts constituting the offense.[51]

In these instances the question is "whether the ruling of the judge, whatever its label, actually represents a resolution, correct or not, of some or all of the factual elements of the offense charged."[52] In the above case the actions of the judge were to rule on the material presented during the trial. Where the jury was deadlocked and unable to reach a verdict within a reasonable time, the judge is granted discretion to enter an appropriate ruling, and that ruling may be either the entry of judgment or the dismissal of the case on technical grounds, which would allow a retrial. Such authority may be limited within different jurisdictions.

In addressing this issue we must recognize that there are some limited exceptions with respect to the finality of trial judge acquittal. The first of these arises where a trial judge receives a verdict of guilty from the jury but instead enters a verdict of not guilty. Under such circumstances the subsequent appeal is not based on a reversal of the jury verdict, but instead is premised upon reinstatement of the jury's verdict and judgment thereon.[53]

Similarly, where a trial judge grants a motion of acquittal, even one based on the conclusion that the evidence is insufficient to convict, the prosecution may appeal if jeopardy had not yet attached in accordance with the federal standard.[54] State standards, however, may vary.

VI. REPROSECUTION FOLLOWING CONVICTION

We have already established that a basic purpose of the double jeopardy clause is to protect a defendant against a second prosecution for the same offense after acquittal. In this section we shall examine the possibility for subsequent prosecution following a conviction. In addressing this issue one must first recognize that a defendant, following conviction, faces a dilemma in interest.

On the one hand, the defendant has an interest in finality; yet, upon conviction, a defendant is likely to appeal, whereas the prosecution will ordinarily be content with its judgment. In this context, issues of double jeopardy arise, most likely when a defendant has been successful on appeal. Should the defendant lose the appeal then the judgment becomes final and there is no risk of second prosecution. For that reason, we will focus only on the issue of double jeopardy as it relates to subsequent prosecution following reversal on appeal.

Generally, a defendant who is successful in having his or her conviction set aside on appeal may be tried again for the same offense. The assumption is made that by appealing a defendant has "waived" his or her objection to further prosecution by challenging the original conviction.[55] While the Supreme Court has characterized the "waiver" theory as "totally unsound and indefensible,"[56] the Court has been hesitant in formulating a new theory in maintaining the practice. Justice Holmes in dissent in *Kepner v. United States*[57] rejected the "waiver" theory and propounded a theory of "continuing jeopardy," but even this theory continues to be rejected on the whole.

An exception to full application of the retrial rule exists, however, when a defendant on trial for an offense is convicted of a lesser offense and succeeds in having that conviction set aside. One such example is seen in *Green v. United States*,[58] where the defendant had been tried for first-degree murder but was convicted of second-degree murder. The Court held that, following reversal of that conviction, he could not be tried again for first-degree murder, but that he could be tried for second-degree murder on the theory that the first verdict was an implicit acquittal of the first-degree murder charge.[59]

Still another exception arises out of appellate reversals grounded on evidentiary insufficiency. Such a situation arose in *Burks v. United States*,[60] when the appellate court set aside the defendant's conviction on the basis that the prosecution had failed to rebut the defendant's proof of insanity. In finding that the defendant could not be retried the Court observed that if the trial court had so held in the first instance — as the reviewing court said it should have done — a judgment of acquittal would have been entered and, of course, petitioner could not be retried for the same offense. "[I]t should make no difference that the reviewing court, rather than the trial court, determined the evidence to be insufficient."[61]

One of the reasons for denying the prosecution a second chance at trial is to foreclose the opportunity to supply evidence it failed to muster in the first proceeding. A problem arises, however, when a reviewing court reverses a jury conviction because of its disagreement on the weight rather than the sufficiency of the evidence. In such instances retrial is permitted.[62]

Also, the *Burks* rule does not bar reprosecution following a reversal based on erroneous admission of evidence. This rule applies even if the remaining properly admitted evidence would be insufficient to convict.[63]

VII. SENTENCE INCREASES

The double jeopardy clause also protects against imposition of multiple punishments for the same offense.[64] Such cases arise under varied circumstances, and the application of the principle leads to a number of complexities.

The more common example includes cases where a court inadvertently imposed both a fine and imprisonment for a crime for which the law authorized one or the other but not both. In such instances a defendant may have completed one of the two punishments, such as having paid the fine, but not the other. A court could not then recall the defendant to set aside its judgment and then resentence to a stiffer or different punishment.[65]

This concept is altered a bit when the execution of judgment has not been completed. The Court has held that the imposition of a sentence does not, from the moment of imposition, have the finality that a judgment of acquittal has. Thus, it has long been recognized that in the same term of court and before the defendant has begun serving the sentence the court may recall the defendant and increase the defendant's sentence.[66]

Moreover, a defendant who is retried after having successfully overturned his or her first conviction is not protected by the double jeopardy clause against receiving a greater sentence upon the second conviction.[67] An exception exists with respect to capital punishment, the Court having held that government may not again seek the death penalty on retrial when on the first trial the jury had declined to impose a death sentence.[68]

VIII. DOUBLE JEOPARDY AND
"THE SAME OFFENSE"

Determining whether a defendant was placed in jeopardy for the same offense is sometimes as difficult as determining when a defendant has been placed in jeopardy.

As noted in our introductory comments, the same conduct may violate the laws of two different sovereigns, and a defendant may be prosecuted by both. The same conduct may transgress two or more different statutes, because laws reach lesser and greater parts of one item of conduct, or conduct may violate the same statute more than once, as when one robs several people in a group at the same time. As such, the Court has fashioned many principles upon which we may measure when jeopardy has attached.

One of the more interesting areas where we confront the double jeopardy issue is when does one act constitute multiple crimes? In other words, can one activity of a criminal nature violate more than one law?

There are essentially two types of situations that fall within this area. The first is commonly known as a "double-description" case. In such instances the criminal law contains more than one prohibition for conduct arising out of a single transaction. For example, prescription drugs are often highly regulated. Where a defendant knowingly sells a controlled product without a prescription there is a violation. Simultaneously, the drug may be sold without the original packaging, which constitutes a separate offense. In such cases a single act is now chargeable as two separate crimes.[69]

The other common situation is known as the "unit-of-prosecution" case. In these matters the same conduct may violate the same statutory prohibition more than once. An example of this is when a defendant transports two women across state lines for an immoral purpose in one trip in the same car. This violation of the Mann Act would subject the defendant to two separate charges for essentially the same conduct.[70]

In both instances it is well established that the double jeopardy clause does not limit the legislative power to split a single transaction into separate crimes. One of the reasons for this exception is to give the prosecution a choice of charges that may be tried in one proceeding, thereby making multiple punishments possible for essentially one transaction.[71]

The commonly used test for determining whether the legislature intended the law to punish for separate offenses occurring in the same transaction, absent otherwise clearly expressed intent, is the "same evidence" rule. The rule, announced in *Blockburger v. United States*,[72] "is that where the same act or transaction constitutes a violation of two distinct statutory provisions, the test to be applied to determine whether there are two offenses or only one, is whether each provision requires proof of a fact which the other does not."

In *Brown v. Ohio*[73] the Supreme Court applied the same evidence test to bar successive prosecutions in state court for different statutory offenses involving the same conduct. The defendant had been convicted of "joyriding," which amounted to the operation of a motor vehicle without the owner's consent. In a successive trial the defendant was then prosecuted and convicted of stealing the same automobile. In reaching a decision the Court observed that each offense required the same proof and for double jeopardy purposes met the *Blockburger* test. The second conviction was subsequently overturned.

In a separate case the defendant was convicted of a charge of felony murder following the robbery and shooting in an Oklahoma convenience store. He was then charged with a separate charge of robbery. Because the lesser crime of robbery, although a felony, was necessary to convict the defendant on the murder charge, the Court reasoned that there could not be a separate prosecution for the robbery.[74] In this sense the robbery was a necessary element of proof for the felony murder rule, and because it relied on the same evidence for proof it would not allow the separate prosecution.

The rule has been modified over the years by both legislative action and the courts. In *Grady v. Corbin*[75] the Supreme Court modified its approach by stating that the appropriate focus is on same conduct rather than same evidence. A subsequent prosecution is barred, the Court explained, if the government, to establish an essential element of an offense, will prove conduct that constitutes an offense for which the defendant has already been prosecuted.

IX. TWO OR MORE VICTIMS

The same conduct may also give rise to multiple offenses in a way that would satisfy the *Blockburger* test if that conduct victimizes two or more individuals. In such a situation the focus is not on the single act of the defendant but the separate action against two or more individuals. Thus, a defendant who commits a robbery involving two or more persons may be charged with separate counts of robbery for each individual robbed.[76]

An interesting twist to this principle occurred in *Ashe v. Swenson*,[77] where seven poker players at the same table were robbed by a single perpetrator. At the first trial the defendant was acquitted of robbing one player. The defense offered no testimony and did not contest evidence that a robbery had taken place and that each of the players had lost money, but the identification of the assailant was shaky. A second trial was held on a charge that the defendant had robbed a second of the seven poker players, and on the basis of stronger identification testimony the defendant was convicted.

Reversing the conviction, the Court held that the doctrine of collateral estoppel[78] was a constitutional rule made applicable to the states through the double jeopardy clause. Because the only basis upon which the jury could have acquitted the defendant at his first trial was a finding that he was not present at the robbery, hence was not one of the robbers, the state could not relitigate that issue. Such a ruling raises several critical questions for prosecutors. One of the more important questions focuses on the issue of joinder.

In exploring this issue we must establish that in a legal context it is preferred practice that all claims against an individual be joined together in the same action. Thus, where a defendant is claimed to have committed a criminal act against several victims the preference is for a single trial wherein all claims are litigated at once. This practice has been modified in some jurisdictions for criminal cases, but remains a viable issue in most.

Several Justices appear to support compulsory joinder (the requirement that all claims be joined whether the state desires such joinder or not) of all charges against a defendant growing out of a single criminal act, occurrence, episode, or transaction. The exception would be those acts not discovered until after prosecution from the same transaction has begun or where the same jurisdiction does not have cognizance of all the crimes.[79] In jurisdictions that require compulsory joinder the question of double jeopardy is thus often moot since all claims would be tried together. In those jurisdictions that allow multiple claims to be tried in multiple suits, double jeopardy remains an issue.

ENDNOTES

1. Green v. United States, 355 U.S. 184, 187–88 (1957).
2. Crist v. Bretz, 437 U.S. 28, 32–36 (1978); see also United States v. Wilson, 420 U.S. 332, 340 (1975).
3. Art. I, Sec. XCI, 4 F. Thorpe, The Federal and State Constitution, reprinted in H.R. Doc. No. 357, 59th Congress, 2d sess. 2455 (1909).
4. *Id.* at 3100.
5. 1 Annals of Congress 434 (June 8, 1789).
6. *Id.* at 753.
7. 302 U.S. 319 (1937).
8. *Id.* at 325, 326.
9. *Id.* at 328.
10. 395 U.S. 784 (1969).
11. *Id.* at 794–95.
12. Crist v. Bretz, 437 U.S. 28, 37–38 (1978).
13. Collins v. Loisel, 262 U.S. 426 (1923).
14. Taylor v. United States, 207 U.S. 120, 127 (1907).
15. Bassing v. Cady, 208 U.S. 386, 391–92 (1908).
16. Houston v. Moore, 18 U.S. (5 Wheat.) 1 (1820).
17. Fox v. Ohio, 46 U.S. (5 How.) 410 (1847); United States v. Marigold, 50 U.S. (9 How.) 560 (1850); Moore v. Illinois, 55 U.S. (14 How.) 13 (1852).
18. United States v. Lanza, 260 U.S. 377 (1922).
19. *Id.* at 382. See also Hebert v. Louisiana, 272 U.S. 312 (1924); Screws v. United States, 325 U.S. 91, 108 (1945); Jerome v. United States, 318 U.S. 101 (1943).
20. See Abbate v. United States, 359 U.S. 187 (1959), and Bartkus v. Illinois, 359 U.S. 121 (1959).
21. Heath v. Alabama, 474 U.S. 82 (1985).
22. Abney v. United States, 431 U.S. 651 (1977).
23. See United States v. DiFrancesco, 449 U.S. 117, 126–27 (1980) (citing cases).
24. Burks v. United States, 437 U.S. 1, 9, 15 (1978).
25. United States v. Perez, 22 U.S. (9 Wheat.) 579 (1824). See also Kepner v. United States, 195 U.S. 100 (1904); Downum v. United States, 372 U.S. 734 (1963) (trial terminated just after jury sworn but before any testimony taken).
26. Downum v. United States, 372 U.S. 734 (1963).
27. Arizona v. Washington, 434 U.S. 497, 503–05 (1978).
28. Wade v. Hunter, 336 U.S. 684, 689 (1949).
29. United States v. Perez, 22 U.S. (9 Wheat.) 579, 580 (1824).
30. Logan v. United States, 144 U.S. 263 (1892).
31. Simmons v. United States, 142 U.S. 148 (1891).
32. Thompson v. United States, 155 U.S. 271 (1884).
33. Wade v. Hunter, 336 U.S. 684 (1949).
34. Illinois v. Somerville, 410 U.S. 458, 463 (1973).
35. *Id.* at 464.

36. Downum v. United States, 372 U.S. 734 (1963).
37. 434 U.S. 497 (1978).
38. *Id.* at 505–06.
39. 367 U.S. 364 (1961).
40. 400 U.S. 470, 483 (1971).
41. *Id.* at 485.
42. *Id.* at 485.
43. United States v. Jorn, 400 U.S. 470, 485 (1971).
44. United States v. Scott, 437 U.S. 82, 93 (1978).
45. Oregon v. Kennedy, 456 U.S. 667, 676 (1982).
46. United States v. Martin Linen Supply Co., 430 U.S. 564, 571 (1977).
47. United States v. Scott, 437 U.S. 82, 91 (1978).
48. Burks v. United States, 437 U.S. 1, 16 (1978); Fong Foo v. United States, 369 U.S. 141, 143 (1962).
49. United States v. Ball, 163 U.S. 662 (1896).
50. United States v. Martin Linen Supply Co., 430 U.S. 564, 570–72 (1977); Sanabria v. United States 437 U.S. 54, 63–65 (1978); Finch v. United States, 433 U.S. 676 (1977).
51. United States v. Scott, 437 U.S. 82, 87–92 (1978); Smalis v. Pennsylvania, 476 U.S. 140 (1986) (demurrer sustained on basis of insufficiency of evidence is acquittal).
52. United States v. Martin Linen Supply Co., 430 U.S. 564, 571 (1977).
53. United States v. Wilson, 420 U.S. 332 (1975).
54. Serfass v. United States, 420 U.S. 377 (1975); United States v. Sanford, 429 U.S. 14 (1976).
55. United States v. Ball, 163 U.S. 662 (1896).
56. Green v. United States, 355 U.S. 184, 197 (1957).
57. 195 U.S. 100, 134 (1904).
58. 355 U.S. 184 (1957).
59. The decision necessarily overruled Trono v. United States, 199 U.S. 521 (1905), although the Court purported to distinguish the decision. Green v. United States, 355 U.S. 184, 194–97 (1957). See also Brantley v. Georgia, 217 U.S. 284 (1910) (no due process violation where defendant is convicted of higher offense on second trial).
60. 437 U.S. 1 (1978).
61. *Id.* at 10–11.
62. Tibbs v. Florida, 457 U.S. 31 (1982).
63. Lockhart v. Nelson, 488 U.S. 33 (1988).
64. Ex parte Lange, 85 U.S. (18 Wall.) 163, 173 (1874); North Carolina v. Pearce, 395 U.S. 711, 717 (1969).
65. Ex parte Lange, 85 U.S. (18 Wall.) 163 (1874).
66. Bozza v. United States, 330 U.S. 160 (1947). See also Pollard v. United States, 352 U.S. 354, 359–60 (1957) (imposition of prison sentence two years after court imposed an invalid sentence of probation approved). Dicta in some cases had cast doubt on the constitutionality of the practice. United States v. Benz, 282 U.S. 304, 307 (1931). However, United States v. DiFrancesco, 449 U.S. 117, 133–36, 138–39 (1980).
67. North Carolina v. Pearce, 395 U.S. 711, 719–21 (1969). See also Chaffin v. Stynchcombe, 412 U.S. 17, 23–24 (1973).
68. Bullington v. Missouri, 451 U.S. 430 (1981).
69. For another example, see Gore v. United States, 357 U.S. 386, 392–93 (1958).
70. Bell v. United States, 349 U.S. 81 (1955).
71. Albernaz v. United States, 450 U.S. 333, 343–44 (1981).
72. 284 U.S. 299, 304 (1932).

73. 432 U.S. 161 (1977).
74. Harris v. Oklahoma, 433 U.S. 682 (1977).
75. 495 U.S. 508 (1990).
76. Hoag v. New Jersey, 356 U.S. 464 (1958). See also Ciucci v. Illinois, 356 U.S. 571 (1958).
77. 397 U.S. 436 (1970).
78. "'Collateral estoppel' is an awkward phrase…[which] means simply that when an issue of ultimate fact has once been determined by a final judgment, that issue cannot again be litigated between the same parties in any future lawsuit." *Id.* at 443. First developed in civil litigation, the doctrine was applied in a criminal case in United States v. Oppenheimer, 242 U.S. 85 (1916). See also Sealfon v. United States, 332 U.S. 575 (1948).
79. Ashe v. Swenson, 397 U.S. 436, 466 (1970).

18 Self-Incrimination

I. DEVELOPMENT AND SCOPE

The early legal maxim "nemo tenetur seipsum accusare" (no man is bound to accuse himself) is often credited as the founding principle of our current right against self-incrimination. From a historical standpoint the maxim represents one aspect of the often competing systems of law enforcement: the accusatorial and the inquisitorial.

In the accusatorial system, which predates the reign of Henry II, first the community and then the state by grand and petit juries proceeded against alleged wrongdoers through the examination of others. Witnesses were called to testify about personal, and sometimes hearsay, knowledge concerning the alleged criminal act.

The inquisitorial system, which developed in the ecclesiastical courts, compelled the alleged wrongdoer to affirm his culpability through the use of the *oath ex officio*. Through the oath a government official had the power to compel testimony by an accused as to all matters about which he would be questioned. There was no obligation for the official to inform the accused of the charges against him, nor was the accused informed of the nature of the questions to be asked.

The use of this oath in Star Chamber proceedings, especially to root out political heresies, combined with opposition to the ecclesiastical oath ex officio, led over a long period of time to general mistrust of the system. By the time the colonies in America were establishing their first governments the maxim against self-incrimination was well implanted in the thinking of the founders.

Following the Revolution six states incorporated the privilege against self-incrimination into their constitutions. The privilege was also recommended by several state ratifying conventions for inclusion in a federal bill of rights.

Madison's version of the clause read "nor shall be compelled to be a witness against himself."[1] The amendment was changed in the House to insert "in any criminal case" in the provision.[2]

Over the years interpretation of the clause has led to subtle expansion and contraction of the protected rights. Many of these changes derive from the judicial application of the policies underlying the guarantees in the context of new factual patterns and practices. The difficulty is that the Court has generally failed to articulate the policy objectives underlying the privilege, and has routinely held that the complexity itself makes bright line rules virtually impossible.

From the earliest days of the rule certain objectives have been clear, among them the assertion that the amendment is intended to protect the innocent and to further the search for truth.[3] Over the years these principles have declined in importance. The Court has settled upon the principle that the clause serves two interrelated interests: the preservation of an accusatorial system of criminal justice, which goes to the integrity of the judicial system, and the preservation of personal privacy from unwarranted governmental intrusion.

The extent of the privilege is often very broad. The Supreme Court has stated that "The privilege afforded not only extends to answers that would in themselves support a conviction...but likewise embraces those which would furnish a link in the chain of evidence needed to prosecute ...."[4] To sustain the privilege, "it need only be evident from the implications of the question, in the setting in which it is asked, that a responsive answer to the question or an explanation of why it cannot be answered might be dangerous because injurious disclosure could result."[5]

II. APPLICATION OF THE PRIVILEGE: CORPORATIONS AND NON-HUMAN LEGAL ENTITIES

The privilege against self-incrimination is a personal one and cannot be utilized by or on behalf of any organization such as a corporation. A corporation, therefore, cannot object on self-incrimination grounds to a subpoena of its records and books or to the compelled testimony of those corporate agents who have been given personal immunity from criminal prosecution.[6]

A corporate official with custody of corporate documents also may not claim the privilege. This may also extend to circumstances where the corporate documents also incriminate the corporate officer personally.[7] From this standpoint, the privilege is said to apply to persons in the sense of humans alone rather than persons in the broader legal sense.

III. APPLICATION OF THE PRIVILEGE: PERSONS

While many associate the privilege against self-incrimination with a criminal defendant, it may reach farther. For instance, a witness traditionally has been able to claim the privilege in any proceeding in which testimony is legally required and where his or her answer might be used against him or her in a future criminal proceeding. A witness may also claim the protection if his or her answer might be exploited to uncover other evidence against him or her.[8]

This does not mean, however, that the witness may refuse to testify or give information where the information sought can be used in proceedings that are not criminal in nature.[9] For example, where the information may be used to establish civil but not criminal liability against a particular witness then that person may not claim the privilege under the Fifth Amendment.

The Court in recent years has also applied the privilege to situations, such as police interrogation of suspects, in which there is no legal compulsion to speak.[10] What the privilege protects against is compulsion of "testimonial" disclosures. Requiring a person in custody to stand or walk in a police lineup, to speak prescribed words, to model particular clothing, or to give samples of handwriting, fingerprints, or blood does not compel the person to incriminate himself or herself within the meaning of the clause.[11] On the other hand, it does appear that compelling a suspect to produce private papers may violate the clause.[12]

The protection is against "compulsory" incrimination, and traditionally the Court has treated within the clause only those compulsions that arise from legally enforceable obligations, culminating in imprisonment for refusal to testify or produce documents.[13]

It has long been the rule that a defendant who takes the stand on his or her own behalf cannot claim the privilege to defeat cross-examination on matters reasonably related to the subject matter of his direct examination.[14] In this sense, once the defendant elects to testify, either under his or her own direction or that of his or her legal counsel, the defendant has effectively waived his or her rights under the amendment. From a practical standpoint this means that a defendant, once he or she has taken the stand on his or her own behalf, may even be impeached by proof of prior convictions where such evidence would otherwise be limited or excluded altogether.[15]

Where a defendant refuses to take the stand the Court has also limited the prosecution and court from commenting.[16] The Court held that such comment was a "penalty imposed by courts for exercising a constitutional privilege" and "[i]t cuts down on the privilege by making its assertion costly."[17] This means that when a defendant exercises the right not to testify he may not be subjected to ridicule or comment by either the prosecutor or judge.

There has, however, been some limitation to this practice. For example, where a defendant refuses to testify on his or her own behalf the courts have limited the defendant's ability to make comments regarding his or her own version of the facts in a closing argument. Likewise, where the defendant or the defendant's attorney comments — usually during closing arguments — on the defendant's failure to testify, then they may effectively have opened the door for the prosecution to comment as well.[18]

The federal courts have long held to such a standard in following the federal statutory scheme.[19] Likewise, a federal standard requiring the judge to give a cautionary instruction to jurors that they must disregard defendant's failure to testify and draw no adverse inferences therefrom parallels the decision by the Court to require states to do the same thing.[20] This result had also been accomplished in the federal courts through statutory construction. This scheme was extended when the Court held in *Lakeside v. Oregon*[21] that a trial court may give such an instruction, even over the defendant's objection.

Matters grow more complicated when it comes to issues of exercising the right prior to trial. For instance, where a defendant remains silent upon an arrest, and after being advised of the right to remain silent, a prosecutor may not comment on the defendant's exercise of the right. Should the defendant, however, then take the stand voluntarily and testify, a prosecutor may have a right to comment on the defendant's pretrial silence, but only when such silence had in no way been officially encouraged, through a Miranda warning or otherwise.[22]

IV. THE POWER TO COMPEL TESTIMONY AND DISCLOSURE: IMMUNITY

One of the powers the government has is the ability to select who will and who will not be prosecuted. The power of the government to grant to a person an immunity from prosecution in exchange for that person's testimony has long been held to be a valid tactic. Such acts have deep historical roots in Anglo-American jurisprudence and are not incompatible with the values of the self-incrimination clause.

Immunity statutes seek a rational accommodation between the imperatives of the privilege against self-incrimination and the legitimate demands of government to compel citizens to testify. They are based, in part, on a realization that in many cases "the only persons capable of giving useful testimony are those implicated in the crime."[23]

There are in effect two types of immunity in use today. The first of these is known as "transactional immunity." Congress enacted the statute that conferred transactional immunity as the price for being able to compel testimony.[24] Transactional immunity means that once a witness has been compelled to testify about an offense, that witness may never be prosecuted for that offense, regardless of how much independent evidence might come to light. Similar grants of immunity have evolved within the states as well.

The second type of grant of immunity is commonly referred to as "use immunity." The application of use immunity means that none of the testimony — or evidence derived therefrom — may be used in a later prosecution against the defendant. It does not, however, restrict the prosecution based on independent evidence. In this sense a witness may be compelled to testify knowing that the statements made by the witness will not be used against the witness in later prosecution; however, where the prosecutors have obtained other evidence linking the witness to the crime — separate from the testimonial evidence — such evidence may be used against the witness.

Beginning in 1964 the questions of immunity types and application moved to the forefront of criminal litigation. An early issue faced by the Supreme Court dealt with the problem of granting immunity by a state in its courts but that immunity was ineffective in other states or in the federal courts. The Supreme Court extended immunity protection in *Malloy v. Hogan*[25] when it extended the constitutional clause to the states. The Court addressed a similar issue when it held that Congress could immunize a federal witness from state prosecution and, of course, extend use immunity to state courts.[26]

The argument quickly arose that the concept of foreclosing a state from compelling testimony because it could not immunize a witness in a subsequent "foreign" prosecution would severely limit state law enforcement efforts. Based on this problem the Court emphasized the "use" restriction rationale and announced that as a "constitutional rule, a state witness could not be compelled to incriminate himself under federal law unless federal authorities were precluded from using either his testimony or evidence derived from it," and thus formulated a use restriction to that effect.[27]

Congress eventually enacted a statute replacing all prior immunity statutes and adopting a use-immunity restriction only.[28] This statute, soon tested, was sustained in *Kastigar v. United States*.[29] A similar state statute was sustained in *Zicarelli v. New Jersey State Comm'n of Investigation*.[30]

The privilege has never been construed to mean that one who invokes it cannot subsequently be prosecuted. Its sole concern is to afford protection against an individual being forced to give testimony leading to the infliction of "penalties affixed to…criminal acts."[31] Immunity from the use of compelled testimony and evidence derived directly and indirectly therefrom affords this protection. It prohibits the prosecutorial authorities from using the compelled testimony in any respect and therefore ensures that the testimony cannot lead to the infliction of criminal penalties on the witness.

V. REQUIRED RECORDS DOCTRINE

As stated earlier, the privilege against self-incrimination is applicable to one's papers and effects,[32] but it does not extend to corporate persons. As such, corporate records are subject to compelled production. In fact, the Court has greatly narrowed the protection afforded in this area to natural persons by developing the "required records" doctrine.

The required records doctrine in effect establishes a requirement on a given business to maintain certain records used to prove particular business practices. In establishing this doctrine the Court stated "that the privilege which exists as to private papers cannot be maintained in relation to 'records required by law to be kept in order that there may be suitable information of transactions which are the appropriate subjects of governmental regulation and the enforcement of restrictions validly established.'"[33]

This exception developed out of the rule that documents that are part of the official records of government are wholly outside the scope of the privilege. The theory was that public records are the property of government and always accessible to inspection. Because government requires certain records to be kept to facilitate the regulation of the business being conducted, so the reasoning goes, the records become public in the sense that the government always has a right to them without hindrance from the recordkeeper. As such, no protection from self-incrimination is created, and those records that are required by government mandate may be accessible upon simple subpoena. To better understand this principle, we will examine several cases within which the concept has been established.

The line of cases begins with *United States v. Sullivan*,[34] in which a bootlegger refused to file an income tax return. It was argued, unsuccessfully, that had the illegal whiskey runner filed tax returns he, in effect, would have been forced to give evidence of his illegal acts in violation of his Fifth Amendment rights. In addressing this issue a unanimous Court held that the Fifth Amendment did not protect the bootlegger. "It would be an extreme if not an extravagant application of the Fifth Amendment to say that it authorized a man to refuse to state the amount of his income because it had been made in crime."[35]

Recognizing the power of such requirements the government utilized its taxing power to reach other illegal activities in the 1930s and 1940s. For example, Congress enacted a complicated statute imposing an annual occupational tax on gamblers and an excise tax on all their wages. Congress then coupled the tax with an annual registration requirement under which each gambler must file with the IRS a declaration of business with identification of place of business, employees, and agents. These filings were then made available to state and local law enforcement agencies.

These requirements were upheld by the Court against self-incrimination challenges on three grounds: (1) the privilege did not excuse a complete failure to file; (2) since the threshold decision to gamble was voluntary, the required disclosures were not compulsory; and (3) since registration required disclosure only of prospective conduct, the privilege, limited to past or present acts, did not apply.[36]

Constitutional limitations began to appear as the government's newfound power expanded. In *Albertson v. SACB*[37] the self-incrimination clause was used to strike down a statute requiring registration by individual members of the Communist Party or associated organizations.

> In *Sullivan* the questions in the income tax return were neutral on their face and directed at the public at large, but here they are directed at a highly selective group inherently suspect of criminal activities. Petitioners' claims are not asserted in an essentially non-criminal and regulatory area of inquiry, but against an inquiry in an area permeated with criminal statutes, where response to any of the form's questions in context might involve the petitioners in the admission of a crucial element of a crime.[38]

The gambling tax reporting scheme was next struck down by the Court.[39] Because of the pervasiveness of state laws prohibiting gambling, said Justice Harlan for the Court, "the obligations to register and to pay the occupational tax created for petitioner 'real and appreciable,' and not merely 'imaginary and unsubstantial,' hazards of self-incrimination."[40]

Overruling earlier decisions, the Court rejected its original rationales that supported registration schemes. The Court found that registering per se would have exposed a gambler to dangers of state prosecution and so the statutes did not apply. The contentions that the voluntary engagement in gambling "waived" the self-incrimination claim, because there is "no constitutional right to gamble," were held to nullify the privilege.

> The question is not whether petitioner holds a "right" to violate state law, but whether, having done so, he may be compelled to give evidence against himself. The constitutional privilege was intended to shield the guilty and imprudent as well as the innocent and foresighted; if such an inference of antecedent choice were alone enough to abrogate the privilege's protection, it would be excluded from the situations in which it has historically been guaranteed, and withheld from those who most require it.[41]

The more recent of this line of cases is *California v. Byers*,[42] which indicates that the Court has yet to settle on an ascertainable standard for judging self-incrimination claims in cases where government is asserting an interest other than criminal law enforcement. *Byers* sustained the constitutionality of a statute that required the driver of any automobile involved in an accident to stop and give his or her name and address. The state court had held that a driver who reasonably believed that compliance with the statute would result in self-incrimination could refuse to comply, and the matter went to the Supreme Court for further review.

A plurality of the Court determined that *Sullivan* and *Shapiro* applied and not the *Albertson-Marchetti* line of cases, because the purpose of the statute was to promote the satisfaction of civil liabilities resulting from automobile accidents and not criminal prosecutions. In this sense, the Court appears to indicate that statutes that have a motive other than the gathering of criminal information may be upheld. The Court also held that the statute may be applied because it was directed to all drivers and not to a group that was either "highly selective" or "inherently suspect of criminal activities." One may thus interpret that statutes that reach a large portion of the population, if not all of the population, may be constitutional.

Other justices argued that the combination of a non-criminal motive with the general character of the requirement made too slight for reliance the possibility of incrimination.

Justice Harlan concurred to make up the majority on the disposition of the case, but disagreed with the plurality's conclusion that the stop and identification requirement did not compel incrimination. Justice Harlan thought that where there is no governmental purpose to enforce a criminal law and government instead is pursuing other legitimate regulatory interests, it is permissible to apply a balancing test between the government's interest and the individual's interest. When he balanced the interests protected by the amendment — protection of privacy and maintenance of an accusatorial system — with the non-criminal purpose, the necessity for self-reporting as a means of securing information, and the nature of the disclosures required, Justice Harlan voted to sustain the statute. One might speculate, however, that had the statute been somewhat different in the material it sought then the decision from the Court may also have been much different, since Justice Harlan would likely have gone against it.

Byers was later applied in *Baltimore Dep't of Social Services v. Bouknight*[43] to uphold a juvenile court's order that the mother of a child under the court's supervision produce the child. Although in this case the mother was suspected of having abused or murdered her child, the order was justified for "compelling reasons unrelated to criminal law enforcement." In this case the concern for the child's safety was the controlling factor.

Moreover, because the mother had custody of her previously abused child as a result of the juvenile court's order, the Court analogized to the required records cases to conclude that the mother had submitted to the requirements of the civil regulatory regime as the child's "custodian." In such an instance, the Court obviously weighed factors other than criminal prosecution in arriving at its ruling.

VI. CONFESSIONS AND POLICE INTERROGATION: INITIAL APPLICATION OF DUE PROCESS

Up to this point, we have focused on very specialized areas of self-incrimination. One of the more common areas in application of the self-incrimination standards arises from police interrogation. In this section we will focus on that issue.

Early cases examining these issues focused on the question of voluntariness. By 1897, however, we begin to see a change in the Court's focus, with more emphasis on issues related to due process rather than a simple voluntariness standard. This is in part due to the fact that the self-incrimination clause for most of the early years of application was not applicable to the states. Originally, the admissibility of confessions in state courts was determined under due process standards developed from common-law voluntariness principles. It was only after the Court extended the self-incrimination clause to the states that a divided Court extended rulings concerning federal interrogations to the states. These cases now imposed on both federal and state trial courts new rules for admitting or excluding confessions and other admissions made to police during custodial interrogation.[44]

VII. THE COMMON-LAW RULE

Not until the latter part of the eighteenth century did a rule develop excluding coerced confessions from admission at trial. Prior to that time even confessions obtained by torture were admissible. As the rule developed in England and in early United States jurisprudence, the rationale was the unreliability of the contents of the confession when induced by a promise of benefit or a threat of harm.

In its first decision on the admissibility of confessions, the Court adopted the common-law rule, stressing that while a "voluntary confession of guilt is among the most effectual proofs in the law, from the very nature of such evidence it must be subjected to careful scrutiny and received with great caution."[45] The Court further stated, "the presumption upon which weight is given to such evidence, namely, that one who is innocent will not imperil his safety or prejudice his interests by an untrue statement, ceases when the confession appears to have been made either in consequence of inducements of a temporal nature, held out by one in authority, touching the charge preferred, or because of a threat or promise by or in the presence of such person, which, operating upon the fears or hopes of the accused, in reference to the charge, deprives him of that freedom of will or self-control essential to make his confession voluntary within the meaning of the law."[46]

Later, the Court assimilated the common-law rule as a command of the Fifth Amendment and indicated that a broader standard for judging admissibility was to be applied.[47] Although this rule was subsequently approved in several cases, the Court would ultimately hold that a confession should not be excluded merely because the authorities had not warned a suspect of the right to remain silent.[48]

VIII. STATE CONFESSION CASES

The first case dealing with a confession by state authority while under torture or threat of torture was *Brown v. Mississippi.*[49] In this case the confessions of the defendants had been extorted from them through repeated whippings with ropes and studded belts. This was enough, the Court held, to taint the confession and establish grounds upon which the case could be overturned. In so ruling, the Court applied a standard that would later be dubbed the "totality of the circumstances." For some 30 years thereafter the Court attempted through a consideration of the "totality of the circumstances" surrounding interrogation to determine whether a confession was "voluntary" and admissible or "coerced" and inadmissible.

In assessing these early cases Justice Frankfurter explains: "The ultimate test remains that which has been the only clearly established test in Anglo-American courts for two hundred years: the test of voluntariness. Is the confession the product of an essentially free and unconstrained choice by its maker? If it is, if he has willed to confess, it may be used against him. If it is not, if his will has been overborne and his capacity for self-determination critically impaired, the use of his confession offends due process."[50]

Such an analysis was often hampered by the methods employed in seeking confessions. On the one hand the police needed an ability to seek confessions as a means of providing effective law enforcement. On the other hand there was a need to protect the truly innocent from improperly coerced confessions. Another consideration was the fact that most police interrogations (and subsequent confessions) were done in the secured back rooms of police stations. Conditions, often set by the police, were designed from the outset to encourage the confession rather than stifle it. This made the issue of voluntariness all the more difficult. This was especially true when one also considers that, typically, the only persons who witness these confessions are the police officers and the defendant.

The portrayal of police interrogation methods by the film and television industry was not altogether inaccurate. Even through the post-World War II period in America we see methods employed by police that border on coercion. Despite a large number of cases attacking these methods there were few binding precedents from the courts.

Many of the early cases disclosed rather clear instances of coercion of a nature that the Court could little doubt produced involuntary confessions. Not only physical torture, but also other overtly coercive tactics have been condemned, and the Court often fell short of establishing a clear measurement. To make matters worse the Court struggled with the proper standards for measuring such issues.

As stated, "The inquiry whether, in a particular case, a confession was voluntarily or involuntarily made involves, at the least, a three-phased process. First, there is the business of finding the crude historical facts, the external 'phenomenological' occurrences and events surrounding the confession. Second, because the concept of 'voluntariness' is one which concerns a mental state, there is the imaginative recreation, largely inferential, of internal, 'psychological' fact. Third, there is the application to this psychological fact of standards for judgment informed by the larger legal conceptions ordinarily characterized as rules of law but which, also, comprehend both induction from, and anticipation of, factual circumstances."[51]

In fully understanding the state of police interrogations one need look no further than the cases upon which the Court did act. In one instance the defendant was held by the police for a five-day period. Those who inquired were told the defendant was not in police custody. The defendant was also arrested without a warrant so there was no court record to help explain his disappearance. Over that five-day period the defendant was questioned nonstop for up to 16 hours at a time, and, on at least one occasion, for more than 24 hours straight. At no given time did the defendant have more than a few hours of sleep.[52]

In another case the police questioned the defendant for 36 hours straight. The defendant was denied sleep and was constantly exposed to powerful electric lights.

Relays of officers — all of whom were experienced investigators — questioned the defendant continuously during this time. In fact, the defendant was also questioned by trained lawyers brought in by the police to assist with interrogation.[53]

Similarly, the Court voided a conviction based on a confession obtained from a suspect who had been arrested illegally in one county and brought some 100 miles away to a different county where he was subsequently questioned repeatedly over a period of several hours. The defendant was then told that there was a chance of "lynching" and that he would be transported to another county. He was questioned during the entire transfer process, and reminded of the threat of hanging by an angry mob. Over the course of three days the defendant was taken from county to county where he was questioned continuously.[54]

In reaching its conclusion in one case the Court stated it "recognized that coercion can be mental as well as physical and that the blood of the accused is not the only hallmark of an unconstitutional inquisition. A number of cases have demonstrated, if demonstrations were needed, that the efficiency of the rack and thumbscrew can be matched, given the proper subject, by more sophisticated modes of 'persuasion.' A prolonged interrogation of the accused who is ignorant of his rights and who has been cut off from the moral support of friends and relatives is not infrequently an effective technique of terror."[55]

One point, however, stood out among these cases. It was not the prolonged questioning that was most offensive to the Court. Prolonged questioning alone was not enough. In some instances the Court held that intermittent questioning over a period of days may be enough to trigger the protections of the amendment.[56]

Even this standard had some exceptions. In *Stein v. New York*[57] the Court affirmed convictions of experienced criminals who had confessed after 12 hours of intermittent questioning over a period of 32 hours of incommunicado detention. While the questioning was less intensive than in the prior cases, Justice Jackson for the majority stressed that the correct approach was to balance "the circumstances of pressure against the power of resistance of the person confessing. What would be overpowering to the weak of will or mind might be utterly ineffective against an experienced criminal."[58]

In this sense the Court effectively said that one who was able to hold out from such interrogation may very well require the showing of a higher level of coercion than one who was less experienced or had a weak will. The "experienced criminal" principle was quickly applied in many state court cases where interrogations were intensified by police when the suspect had a past criminal record.

Other factors have developed over the years. For instance, the age of a defendant may weigh in the analysis of the voluntary nature of the confession. Much like the "experienced criminal" standard the overall experience of an older person may be used in measuring a person's ability to endure continued interrogation. To this end the older a defendant is the more likely the court will find the confession to be voluntary and not coerced. In appropriate cases this factor has been used to demonstrate the particular susceptibility of the suspects to even mild coercion.[59]

Likewise, the defendant's intelligence may be taken into consideration when weighing the issue of susceptibility to coercion. This factor is not as easy to measure as the age factor. Relative intelligence may vary greatly according to conditions and maturity. Likewise, someone with a relatively low IQ score may not always be an easy target for coercion. The courts recognized early that a criminal with a low IQ but extensive experience could be just as strong as a person with higher intelligence. To this end it must be pointed out that a suspect's mental state alone — even insanity — is insufficient to establish involuntariness absent some coercive police activity.[60]

While it is clear that certain acts by police may be enough to deem the interrogation "inherently coercive," the "totality of the circumstances" is the true measure to apply when looking to determine admissibility. Prolonged interrogation alone is not always enough. Likewise, tender age or low intelligence may also — by themselves — not be enough to show a confession was not voluntary. The courts have traditionally looked at all the factors together, including not only the age and intelligence of the suspect but also the illegality of the arrest, the incommunicado detention, the denial of requested counsel, the denial of access to friends, the employment of trickery, and other factors.[61]

Of course, confessions may be induced through the exploitation of some illegal action, such as an illegal arrest or an unlawful search and seizure, and when that occurs the confession is inadmissible.[62] In this sense the courts may consider such factors as the nature of the crime, the methods of arrests, the methods of incarceration or detention, and the availability of basic services such as bathrooms, food, water, and proper facilities.

As we move toward conclusion of this section it is important to note that having one illegal confession does not necessarily make all later confessions illegal. In other words, where the police use improper coercion to obtain one confession and then obtain a second confession — without coercion — then the subsequent confession will not always be presumed to be tainted or improperly obtained. Each confession is subject to independent analysis, and a defendant claiming an illegally obtained confession carries the burden of showing why it is improper for each confession. The Court will not assume that the subsequent confession was similarly involuntary but will independently evaluate whether the coercive actions which produced the first confession continued to produce the later confession.[63]

ENDNOTES

1. 1 Annals of Congress 434 (June 8, 1789).
2. *Id.* at 753.
3. Twining v. New Jersey, 211 U.S. 78, 91 (1908).
4. Hoffman v. United States, 341 U.S. 479, 486–87 (1951). See also Emspak v. United States, 349 U.S. 190 (1955); Blau v. United States, 340 U.S. 159 (1950).
5. Blau v. United States, 340 U.S. 332 (1951).
6. United States v. White, 322 U.S. 694, 701 (1944); Baltimore & O.R.R. v. ICC, 221 U.S. 612, 622 (1911); Hale v. Henkel, 201 U.S. 43, 69–70, 74–75 (1906).
7. United States v. White, *supra,* 699–700; Wilson v. United States, 221 U.S. 361, 384–385 (1911).

8. In re Gault, 387 U.S. 1, 42–57 (1967), claim the privilege but so may a party or a witness in a civil court proceeding; McCarthy v. Arndstein, 266 U.S. 34 (1924), a potential defendant or any other witness before a grand jury; Reina v. United States, 364 U.S. 507 (1960); Counselman v. Hitchcock, 142 U.S. 547, 563 (1892), or a witness before a legislative inquiry, Watkins v. United States, 354 U.S. 178, 195–96 (1957); Quinn v. United States, 349 U.S. 155 (1955); Emspak v. United States, 349 U.S. 190 (1955), or before an administrative body. In re Groban, 352 U.S. 330, 333, 336–37, 345–46 (1957); ICC v. Brimson, 154 U.S. 447, 478–80 (1894).
9. Minnesota v. Murphy, 465 U.S. 420, 435 n.7 (1984).
10. Miranda v. Arizona, 384 U.S. 436 (1966).
11. Schmerber v. California, 384 U.S. 757, 764 (1966); United States v. Wade, 388 U.S. 218, 221–23 (1967); Holt v. United States, 218 U.S. 245, 252 (1910). In California v. Byers, 402 U.S. 424 (1971).
12. Fisher v. United States, 425 U.S. 391 (1976).
13. Marchetti v. United States, 390 U.S. 39 (1968); Malloy v. Hogan, 378 U.S. 1 (1964); South Dakota v. Neville, 459 U.S. 553 (1983).
14. Brown v. Walker, 161 U.S. 591, 597–98 (1896); Fitzpatrick v. United States, 178 U.S. 304, 314–16 (1900); Brown v. United States, 356 U.S. 148 (1958).
15. Spencer v. Texas, 385 U.S. 554, 561 (1967).
16. Griffin v. California, 380 U.S. 609, 614 (1965).
17. Id.
18. United States v. Robinson, 485 U.S. 25, 32 (1988).
19. 18 U.S.C. §3481.
20. Carter v. Kentucky, 450 U.S. 288 (1981).
21. 435 U.S. 333 (1978).
22. Jenkins v. Anderson, 447 U.S. 231 (1980).
23. Kastigar v. United States, 406 U.S. 441, 445–46 (1972).
24. Ch. 83, 27 Stat. 443 (1893).
25. 378 U.S. 1 (1964).
26. Adams v. Maryland, 347 U.S. 179 (1954).
27. Murphy v. Waterfront Comm'n, 378 U.S. 52, 77–99 (1964).
28. Organized Crime Control Act of 1970, Pub. L. No. 91-452, §201(a), 84 Stat. 922, 18 U.S.C. §§6002–03.
29. 406 U.S. 441 (1972).
30. 406 U.S. 472 (1972).
31. Id.
32. Boyd v. United States, 116 U.S. 616 (1886).
33. Shapiro v. United States, 335 U.S. 1, 33 (1948).
34. 274 U.S. 259, 263, 264 (1927).
35. Id.
36. United States v. Kahriger, 345 U.S. 22 (1953); Lewis v. United States, 348 U.S. 419 (1955).
37. 382 U.S. 70 (1965).
38. Id. at 79. The decision was unanimous, Justice White not participating. The same issue had been held not ripe for adjudication in Communist Party v. SACB, 367 U.S. 1, 105–10 (1961).
39. Marchetti v. United States, 390 U.S. 39 (1968) (occupational tax); Grosso v. United States, 390 U.S. 62 (1968) (wagering excise tax).
40. Marchetti v. United States, 390 U.S. 39, 48 (1968).

41. *Id.* at 51. See also California v. Byers, 402 U.S. 424, 434 (1971) (plurality opinion), in which it is suggested that because there is no "right" to leave the scene of an accident a requirement that a person involved in an accident stop and identify himself does not violate the self-incrimination clause.

42. 402 U.S. 424 (1971).

43. 493 U.S. 549 (1990).

44. Miranda v. Arizona, 384 U.S. 436 (1966).

45. Hopt v. Utah, 110 U.S. 574, 584–85 (1884).

46. *Id.*

47. Bram v. United States, 168 U.S. 532 (1897).

48. Powers v. United States, 223 U.S. 303 (1912).

49. 297 U.S. 278 (1936).

50. *Id.* at 602.

51. *Id.* at 603.

52. Chambers v. Florida, 309 U.S. 227 (1940).

53. Ashcraft v. Tennessee, 322 U.S. 143 (1944).

54. Ward v. Texas, 316 U.S. 547 (1942).

55. Blackburn v. Alabama, 361 U.S. 199, 206 (1960).

56. Lisenba v. California, 314 U.S. 219 (1941).

57. 346 U.S. 156 (1953).

58. *Id.* at 185.

59. Gallegos v. Colorado, 370 U.S. 49 (1962); Blackburn v. Alabama, 361 U.S. 199 (1960); Fikes v. Alabama, 352 U.S. 191 (1957); Payne v. Arkansas, 356 U.S. 560 (1958); Reck v. Pate, 367 U.S. 433 (1961); Culombe v. Connecticut, 367 U.S. 568 (1961).

60. Colorado v. Connelly, 479 U.S. 157 (1986).

61. Johnson v. New Jersey, 384 U.S. 719 (1966); Davis v. North Carolina, 384 U.S. 737 (1966); Ashdown v. Utah, 357 U.S. 426 (1958); Thomas v. Arizona, 356 U.S. 390 (1958).

62. Wong Sun v. United States, 371 U.S. 471 (1963); Fahy v. Connecticut, 375 U.S. 85 (1963).

63. United States v. Bayer, 331 U.S. 532 (1947); Lyons v. Oklahoma, 322 U.S. 596 (1944); Leyra v. Denno, 347 U.S. 556 (1954); Darwin v. Connecticut, 391 U.S. 346 (1968).

19 Self-Incrimination: From Voluntariness Standard to *Miranda*

I. INTRODUCTION

The issues of voluntariness and application of the self-incrimination clause have swayed back and forth for years between a strict standard and one that freed the hands of the police. Standards were established, modified, and later reestablished in more than 150 years of litigation. By the mid-1960s the application of the Fifth Amendment in confession cases was chaotic. Invocation by the Court of a self-incrimination standard for judging the fruits of police interrogation was no unheralded novelty by the time of *Miranda v. Arizona.*[1]

The rationale of the confession cases changed over time to one closely approximating the foundation purposes the Court has attributed to the self-incrimination clause. Historically, the basis of the rule excluding coerced and involuntary confessions was their untrustworthiness and their unreliability. It also appears that this basis formed the Court's judgment in the early state confession cases and the earlier cases from the lower federal courts. This all began to change, however, when the Court drew a distinction between the confession rule and the standard of due process.

In *Lisenba v. California*[2] Justice Roberts, writing for the Court, stated: "[T]he fact that the confessions have been conclusively adjudged by the decision below to be admissible under State law, notwithstanding the circumstances under which they were made, does not answer the question whether due process was lacking. The aim of the rule that a confession is inadmissible unless it was voluntarily made is to exclude false evidence. Tests are invoked to determine whether the inducement to speak was such that there is a fair risk the confession is false.... The aim of the requirement of due process is not to exclude presumptively false evidence, but to prevent fundamental unfairness in the use of evidence, whether true or false."

Over the next several years, while the Justices continued to use the terminology of voluntariness, the Court accepted at different times the different rationales of trustworthiness and constitutional fairness. Ultimately, those Justices who chose to ground the exclusionary rule on the latter consideration prevailed. Justice Frankfurter spoke for six other Justices in writing:

> Our decisions under that [Fourteenth] Amendment have made clear that convictions following the admission into evidence of confessions which are involuntary, i.e., the product of coercion, either physical or psychological, cannot stand. This is so not because such confessions are unlikely to be true but because the methods used to extract them offend an underlying principle in the enforcement of our criminal law:

that ours is an accusatorial and not an inquisitorial system — a system in which the State must establish guilt by evidence independently and freely secured and may not by coercion prove its charges against an accused out of his own mouth.[3]

Nevertheless, the Justice said in another case, "[n]o single litmus-paper test for constitutionally impermissible interrogation has been evolved."[4] Three years later, in *Malloy v. Hogan*[5] Justice Brennan for the Court reinterpreted the line of cases to conclude that the Court had initially based its rulings on the common-law confession rationale, but that beginning with *Lisenba v. California*, a "federal standard" had been developed.

The Court engaged in a "shift [which] reflects recognition that the American system of criminal prosecution is accusatorial, not inquisitorial, and that the Fifth Amendment privilege is its essential mainstay." Today, continued Justice Brennan, "the admissibility of a confession in a state criminal prosecution is tested by the same standard applied in federal prosecutions since 1897," when *Bram v. United States* had announced that the self-incrimination clause furnished the basis for admitting or excluding evidence in federal courts.[6]

One week after the decision in *Malloy v. Hogan*, the Court attempted to define the rules of admissibility of confessions in different terms than its prior decisions; while it continued to emphasize voluntariness, it did so in self-incrimination terms rather than in due process terms. In *Escobedo v. Illinois*[7] the Court held inadmissible the confession obtained from a suspect in custody who repeatedly had requested and repeatedly had been refused an opportunity to consult with his retained counsel, who was present at the police station seeking to gain access to Escobedo. While *Escobedo* appeared to be a primarily Sixth Amendment right-to-counsel case, the Court at several points emphasized, in terms that clearly implicated self-incrimination considerations, that the suspect had not been warned of his constitutional rights.[8] It was clear that the Court was moving again toward the establishment of broader standards, and by the time of *Miranda v. Arizona* it was time to establish those standards.

II. *MIRANDA v. ARIZONA*: THE CASE

The decision in *Miranda* was not a new revelation, or so the Court contended, but instead a restatement of the law as it always had been. For many, however, the specific language of *Miranda* meant that practice and procedure would change for law enforcement. Following the Sixth Amendment holding of *Escobedo* the Court moved to expand the rights of those accused of crimes by shoring up the protections of the Fifth Amendment. In so doing, the Court summarized its holding as follows:

[T]he prosecution may not use statements, whether exculpatory or inculpatory, stemming from custodial interrogation of the defendant unless it demonstrates the use of procedural safeguards effective to secure the privilege against self-incrimination. By custodial interrogation, we mean questioning initiated by law enforcement officers after a person has been taken into custody or otherwise deprived of his freedom of action in any significant way. As for the procedural safeguards to be employed, unless other fully effective means are devised to inform accused persons of their right of silence and to assure a continuous opportunity to exercise it, the following measures are required. Prior to any questioning, the person must be warned that he has a right to remain silent, that any statement he does make may be used as evidence against him, and that he has a right to the presence of an attorney, either retained or appointed. The defendant may waive effectuation of these rights, provided the waiver is made voluntarily, knowingly and intelligently. If, however, he indicates in any manner and at any stage of the process that he wishes to consult with an attorney before speaking there can be no questioning. Likewise, if the individual is alone and indicates in any manner that he does not wish to be interrogated, the police may not question him. The mere fact that he may have answered some questions or volunteered some statements on his own does not deprive him of the right of refrain from answering any further inquiries until he has consulted with an attorney and thereafter consents to be questioned.

Not for the first time, the Court examined the practice of police interrogation and the methods employed by law enforcement in obtaining a confession. Where in the past the Court had steered away from declaring clear standards on what would and would not be considered coercive it now seemed to focus on establishing — at least in some small part — a clear standard for police to follow.

In addressing the issue of police interrogation the Court first found virtually all police interrogation to be inherently coercive. The mere fact that a police officer was asking questions would be considered coercive in nature, but that did not mean that all interrogations rose to the level of being improper. The question, however, was just how to ensure that the statement or confession was in fact being made voluntarily and not because of the coercive nature of the police interrogation.

One method was to construct a practice that guaranteed the voluntariness of the confession. The Court found that the very nature of police interrogations would provoke a confession. The amendment, however, requires that police interrogation practices be so structured as to secure the knowledge that a defendant has not been stripped of the ability to make a free and rational choice between speaking and not speaking.

From the Court's perspective, the practices set forth in the *Miranda* decision had been the law in the federal courts since 1897. The *Miranda* case now allowed the courts to apply the clause to the states through the Fourteenth Amendment and set forth the standards upon which future conduct would be measured.

In addressing the issues presented in *Miranda* the Court established that certain "rights" must be guaranteed to all defendants. These rights included those found in the Fifth and Sixth Amendments. Here the earlier *Escobedo* case merges in forming the rights we know today as the "Miranda warning." The rights include: (1) the right to an attorney; (2) the right to have an attorney present during questioning; (3) the right to remain silent; (4) the right to make a statement, but stop at any point; and (5) the right to have counsel appointed if one cannot afford an attorney.

In 1968, Congress enacted a statute designed to set aside *Miranda* in the federal courts and to reinstate the traditional voluntariness test. An effort to enact a companion provision applicable to the state courts was defeated.[9] The statute applying to the federal courts, however, appears to remain unimplemented because of constitutional doubts about its enforceability.[10]

The application of the *Miranda* provisions may be seen in cases such as *Michigan v. Tucker.*[11] In this case the defendant was improperly advised of his rights through the Miranda warning, and statements by the defendant led to the discovery of witnesses who would help secure a conviction. The issue addressed by the Court was whether the improperly applied warnings would require the exclusion of the witness testimony.[12]

The actual holding of the Court and the concurrence of two Justices turned on the fact that the interrogation preceded *Miranda* and that warnings had been given, although not the full Miranda warnings; thus, in some respects, the decision is in the line of retroactivity cases. But of great possible significance was the language of the Court in considering "whether the police conduct complained of directly infringed upon respondent's rights against compulsory self-incrimination or whether it instead violated only the prophylactic rules developed to protect that right."[13]

In assessing the circumstances the Court found that the defendant's statement had not been coerced or otherwise procured in violation of his privilege. The Court also found that the officer's actions had been in good faith and were an inadvertent error in not fully complying with the "prophylactic" Miranda rules. As such, the provisions of *Miranda* as well as the Fifth Amendment did not require exclusion of the testimony.

In supporting its decision the Court noted that the error preceded *Miranda* and exclusion of the testimony would not deter wrongful conduct by police officers later. Likewise, the Court noted that admission would not implicate the trial court in the use of possibly untrustworthy evidence.[14]

Obviously, dividing the question in this way between a constitutional right and a judicially-created enforcement mechanism permits courts a considerable degree of flexibility to apply or not apply the exclusionary rule previously thought to be fairly rigid under *Miranda*. Those who object to the loosening of earlier *Miranda* standards argue that while the exclusionary rule may not be directly mandated by the constitutional provision in issue, it must be a constitutional standard and must be applied rigidly in cases such as this.[15]

III. OTHER INTERPRETATIONS OF *MIRANDA*

Since its adoption, the holdings in *Miranda* have been under continual scrutiny and interpretation. Over the years the Court has established several lines of decisions interpreting *Miranda*. We begin our analysis with one of the foundational principles of the ruling, i.e., must persons who are questioned while they are in custody be given the Miranda warnings?

Miranda applies to "questioning initiated by law enforcement officers after a person has been taken into custody or otherwise deprived of his freedom of action in any significant way."[16] In applying this language we can clearly see that a person detained in jail is in custody, even if the detention is for some offense other than the one about which he is questioned.[17] Likewise, the language applies to anyone placed "under arrest" or in some other way "deprived of his freedom of action in any significant way." Thus, even if the person is in his own home, the questioning is custodial.[18]

While the above scenarios appear clear on their faces, in some instances it is often unclear whether *Miranda* applies. For instance, a suspect may be present in a police station but not necessarily subject to the warnings. As the Court has held, in the absence of indicia that the suspect was in custody there is no requirement for providing the warnings. The primary issue in such instances is the custody.

This principle is applied firmly in the case of *Oregon v. Mathiason*,[19] in which the defendant voluntarily went to the police station to be questioned. While there, Mathiason was not placed under arrest and was free to leave at any moment. Although he was named by a victim as the culprit, and he was falsely informed his fingerprints had been found at the scene of the crime, he was allowed to leave at the end of interview. Questioning of Mathiason also took place behind closed doors, with only the interrogators and Mathiason present.

In evaluating this case the Court focused on the issues together and separately. The freedom of movement allowed Mathiason appears to have been an important factor. The fact that Mathiason was allowed to leave following the questioning also seems to be important to the Court in determining whether *Miranda* must be applied or not. The Court held that in this case *Miranda* did not apply and the ultimate statements by Mathiason would not be excluded based on a failure to provide the warnings.

The Court has also held that the warnings are not required where the surroundings or circumstances of the interrogation would lead a reasonable person to the belief that they are not in custody. Such circumstances include cases where the suspect was questioned in his or her own home or other familiar surroundings.[20] Again, the focus appears to be on the restriction of freedom of movement and on the ultimate liberty denied or interfered with. If liberty has not been denied, or at least is not reasonably perceived as being denied, then the warnings may not be necessary.

Another situation in which the warnings may not apply, but which the Court has not fully explored, is the street-level interrogation. While most police officers have developed the practice of advising a person of his or her rights regardless of where the interrogation takes place there is some question as to whether Miranda warnings are necessary for questioning on the street and elsewhere in situations in which the police have not asserted authority sufficient to place the citizen in custody.[21]

One such circumstance that has been clarified is the roadside questioning of a motorist in conjunction with a traffic citation. In *Berkemer v. McCarty*[22] the Court held that such questioning of a motorist stopped for a traffic violation is not custodial and thus the interrogation is not subject to the *Miranda* decision. The Court held that until the motorist's "freedom of action is curtailed to a 'degree associated with formal arrest'" there is no reason to require *Miranda*.

Another focal point when applying the warnings is the issue of what constitutes a police custodial interrogation. For many the term "custodial interrogation" brings to mind visions of closed rooms with small tables and a hanging light bulb swinging above the defendant's head. The reality, however, is that the interrogation may take place under a wide variety of circumstances. The issue, breadth of interrogation, has been addressed in *Rhode Island v. Innis*.[23]

In *Innis* the defendant was arrested as a murder suspect. The investigators had been unable to find the weapon used, and while Innis was being transported to police headquarters in a squad car he was advised of the Miranda warnings. The defendant asserted his right to consult a lawyer before submitting to questioning, and he was not asked questions by the officers.

During the ride to the police station the individual police officers engaged in conversation among themselves. In the conversation they indicated that a school for handicapped children was near the crime scene and that they hoped the weapon was found before a child discovered it and was injured. The officers did not directly speak with the defendant, nor did they attempt to question him as to the location of the weapon. The defendant was in a position to clearly hear the conversation, and there is little dispute that he, in fact, did overhear the officers talk. The defendant then "volunteered" to take the officers to the hiding place of the weapon.

Unanimously rejecting a contention that *Miranda* would have been violated only by express questioning, the Court said: "We conclude that the Miranda safeguards come into play whenever a person in custody is subjected to either express questioning or its functional equivalent."[24] The Court held that the term "interrogation" under *Miranda* refers not only to express questioning, but also to any words or actions on the part of the police (other than those normally attendant to arrest and custody) that the police should know are reasonably likely to elicit an incriminating response from the suspect.

In applying this standard one must note that the latter portion of this definition focuses primarily upon the perceptions of the suspect, rather than the intent of the police. This focus reflects the fact that the Miranda safeguards were designed to vest a suspect in custody with an added measure of protection against coercive police practices, without regard to objective proof of the underlying intent of the police.[25] In this case it may be argued that the police were not engaging merely in idle talk while driving to the police station, but were instead using the moment (and Innis' position as a captive audience) to lay a foundation for "coercing" a statement from the suspect.

The Court has also extended the protections to cases where the police did not directly interrogate the defendant. In *Estelle v. Smith*[26] a psychiatrist's conclusions about the defendant's dangerousness were inadmissible at the capital sentencing phase of the trial because the defendant had not been given his Miranda warnings prior to the interview. Part of the reason for this exclusion was based on the fact that the defendant had not raised the issue of insanity or incompetency, and it was the prosecution that ordered the interview. That the defendant had been questioned by a psychiatrist designated to conduct a neutral competency examination, rather than by a police officer, was "immaterial," the Court concluded, since the psychiatrist's testimony at the penalty phase changed his role from one of neutrality to that of an agent of the prosecution.[27]

Another issue that commonly arises when dealing with the warnings under *Miranda* is the question of specificity as to the warnings themselves. Those familiar with the case know that the Court did not require the police to use specific words in providing the warning. While it is clear that a suspect in custody must be given warnings before questioning it is not as clear just what language is required or how detailed the warnings must be. Over time the law enforcement profession has developed an accepted method for providing these warnings, but no one method is preferred by the courts over others.

From a practical standpoint the police now use printed forms or read warnings from a prepared source. Most police officers carry a pocket-size card with the express warnings printed on them. In most instances these warnings appear similar to the following:

1. You have a right to remain silent.
2. Anything you say can and will be used against you in a court of law.
3. You have a right to an attorney and to have an attorney present during any questioning.
4. If you cannot afford an attorney then one may be appointed for you by the courts.
5. You have a right to stop your statement at any time.
6. Do you understand each of these rights?
7. Having these rights in mind do you wish to speak with us now?

While the above statements are similar to those used across the country it is also clear that the Court recognized that "other fully effective means" could be devised to convey the rights. An officer is not required to read the rights from a printed card, but the officer is required to adequately advise the person of those rights. Thus, it is possible for an officer to advise a suspect of his or her rights without resorting to the printed form or card. The burden, however, for showing that the person was adequately advised rests firmly with the officer.[28]

IV. ASSERTION OF THE RIGHTS AND APPLICATION OF THE WARNINGS

Once a warned suspect asserts his or her right to silence and requests counsel, the police must scrupulously respect that assertion of right. The *Miranda* court strongly stated that once a warned suspect "indicates in any manner, at any time prior to or during questioning, that he wishes to remain silent, the interrogation must cease."[29]

Likewise, if the suspect indicates he or she wishes the assistance of counsel before interrogation, the questioning must cease until the suspect has counsel.[30] One area where this right is different from the right to silence is on the issue of reinitiating the interrogation. Where a suspect has indicated the desire to remain silent there has been no hard rule barring the police from later attempting an interrogation. With respect to counsel, however, the Court has created practically a per se rule barring the police from continuing or from reinitiating interrogation with a suspect who has requested counsel. Once counsel is present the police may, through counsel, attempt an interrogation, but they may not directly reinitiate the questioning. Of course, the suspect may initiate further proceedings, but officers should fully document that it was the suspect — and not the officers — who initiated the interrogation.

An example of this type of situation arose in *Edwards v. Arizona*,[31] where the Court ruled that *Miranda* had been violated when police reinitiated questioning after the suspect had requested counsel. Questioning had ceased as soon as the suspect had requested counsel, and the suspect had been returned to his cell. Questioning had resumed the following day only after different police officers had confronted the suspect and again warned him of his rights. During this second attempt the suspect agreed to talk and thereafter incriminated himself.

Although the second questioning was instigated by a second set of officers the Court held "when an accused has invoked his right to have counsel present during custodial interrogation, a valid waiver of that right cannot be established by showing only that he responded to further police-initiated custodial interrogation even if he has been advised of this rights. We further hold that an accused..., having expressed his desire to deal with the police only through counsel, is not subject to further interrogation by the authorities until counsel has been made available to him, unless the accused himself initiates further communication, exchanges, or conversations with the police."[32]

The *Edwards* rule bars police-initiated questioning stemming from a separate investigation as well as questioning relating to the crime for which the suspect was arrested. The suspect, however, must specifically ask for counsel and, if the suspect requests the assistance of someone else he or she thinks may be helpful, that is not a valid assertion of Miranda rights.[33] Moreover, the rigid *Edwards* rule is not applicable to other aspects of the warnings. That is, if the suspect asserts his or her right to remain silent, the questioning must cease, but officers are not precluded from subsequently initiating a new round of interrogation, provided only that they again give the Miranda warnings.[34]

Just as it is clear that a warned suspect may assert his or her rights it is equally clear that a properly warned suspect may waive his or her Miranda rights and submit to custodial interrogation. *Miranda* recognized that a suspect may voluntarily and knowingly give up his or her rights and respond to questioning, but the Court cautioned that the prosecution bore a "heavy burden" to establish that a valid waiver had occurred.[35]

While the waiver need not be express for it to be valid, neither may a suspect's silence or similar conduct constitute a waiver.[36] Silence, "coupled with an understanding of his rights and a course of conduct indicating waiver," may support a conclusion of waiver. The prosecution must show that the suspect was competent to understand and appreciate the warning and to be able to waive his or her rights.[37]

A knowing and intelligent waiver need not be predicated on complete disclosure by police of the intended line of questioning. In other words, the police need merely give adequate warning of the rights and need not inform the suspect of everything that may be covered during the interrogation. As such, the police may inform a subject that they intend to question him or her regarding one crime but they are not precluded from questioning him or her on other crimes as well. The warnings are not intended to thwart the investigation but merely to ensure that a defendant understands his or her rights.[38]

Essentially, resolution of the issue of waiver "must be determined on 'the particular facts and circumstances surrounding that case, including the background, experience, and conduct of the accused.'"[39] In this sense, the earlier standards discussed concerning voluntariness apply equally when examining a *Miranda* issue. The suspect's age, experience, education, and ability to understand others all play a role in determining whether a waiver was sufficient.

Another area where problems often arise is when the warnings are improperly given. May an admission to an unwarned or poorly warned suspect be admitted?

The general rule is that the admissions of an unwarned or improperly warned suspect may not be used directly against the suspect at trial. Similarly, a confession or other incriminating admission obtained in violation of *Miranda* may not be introduced for determining the sentence, at least in bifurcated trials in capital cases. Neither may the "fruits" of such a confession or admission be used.[40] On the other hand, the Court has permitted some use of confessions obtained in this fashion for other purposes such as impeachment.

Where a defendant makes a statement that affects his or her credibility the Court has reasoned that such a statement, although illegally obtained, may be worthy of consideration. In one such case the defendant not only denied the offense of which he was accused (sale of drugs) but also asserted he had never dealt in drugs. The broad statement opened the defendant to questions on credibility since he had in fact been previously convicted of such acts. For that reason, the prosecution was permitted to impeach the suspect concerning heroin seized illegally from his home two years before.

In reaching its decision, the Court observed that the defendant could have denied the offense without making such "sweeping" assertions. Although a denial of the allegations would not have been useful to the prosecution at trial, the broader issue is that the statements made simultaneously were improperly obtained. Had the defendant not opened his credibility up to impeachment the improper statements would not be fodder for the prosecution's cannon.[41]

In *Harris v. New York*[42] the Court held that the prosecution could use statements, obtained in violation of *Miranda*, to impeach the defendant's testimony if he voluntarily took the stand and denied commission of the offense. In this case the defendant had denied only the commission of the offense. The Court observed that it was only "speculative" to think that impermissible police conduct would be encouraged by permitting such impeachment, a resort to deterrence analysis being contemporaneously used to ground the Fourth Amendment exclusionary rule, whereas the defendant's right to testify was the obligation to testify truthfully and the prosecution could impeach him for committing perjury.

Subsequently, in *Oregon v. Hass*[43] the Court permitted impeachment use of a statement made by the defendant after police ignored his request for counsel following his Miranda warning. In ruling on this case the Court held that such impeachment material still must meet the standard of voluntariness associated with the pre-*Miranda* tests for the admission of confessions and statements. The trial courts will thus weigh the issue of voluntariness as it relates to the statements made. Where the court can determine that the statements were made following faulty warnings then they may only be admitted if evidence shows that they were voluntarily made.

The Court has also created a "public safety" exception to the Miranda warning requirement, but this exception generally only applies for high level felony offenses.

In *New York v. Quarles*[44] the defendant was arrested in a public supermarket. The gun used by the suspect during the crimes was hidden or discarded by the suspect, and officers had reason to believe it remained in the supermarket. Believing that public safety was jeopardized, the officers demanded to know where the gun had been placed, and the Court held admissible the suspect's response although the statement fell outside the traditional warnings under *Miranda*.

The Court, in an opinion by Justice Rehnquist, held that a strict application of the *Miranda* principles would place police officers in the "untenable position" of having to choose between public safety or adherence to strict evidentiary standards. While acknowledging that the exception itself will "lessen the desirable clarity of the rule," the Court predicted that confusion would be slight: "[w]e think that police officers can and will distinguish almost instinctively between questions necessary to secure their own safety or the safety of the public and questions designed solely to elicit testimonial evidence from a suspect."[45]

No such compelling justification was offered for a *Miranda* exception for lesser offenses, however, and protecting the "simplicity and clarity" of the rule counseled against creating one. As the Court noted, "[A] person subjected to custodial interrogation is entitled to the benefit of the procedural safeguards enunciated in Miranda, regardless of the nature or severity of the offense of which he is suspected or for which he was arrested."[46]

V. PROCEDURE IN THE TRIAL COURTS

The Court has placed constitutional limitations upon the procedures followed by trial courts for determining the admissibility of confessions and other incriminating admissions. It is at the trial court level that most issues of confession and incriminating admissions arise, and it is at the trial court that decisions affecting these issues are most appropriately applied. With this in mind we now examine the three basic procedures that have developed over time to deal with the question of admissibility when voluntariness was at issue.

The first, and traditional, method applied was rather simple. The trial judge heard all the evidence on voluntariness in a separate or preliminary hearing, and if the judge found the confession involuntary, an order restricting its admission was entered. In this sense, the jury never received the material and there were few issues with which an appellate court had to contend. If the trial judge found the material voluntary, then the jury received the material with the right to consider its weight and credibility. The defendant also was provided opportunity to present, for the jury's consideration, the circumstances of the making of the statement or confession.

This method in effect allowed the defendant an opportunity to explain why the confession was not credible or why it should not be considered in the question of guilt. If a defendant is found not guilty then the issue becomes moot. On the other hand, if the defendant is convicted then the issue of voluntariness is reserved for the appellate court.

A second method, often called the New York method, is similar in that the trial judge hears the evidence related to the confession in a separate hearing. The confession is first weighed as to whether "reasonable men could differ over the [factual] inferences to be drawn" from it. If the confession passes this test, it is submitted to the jury; otherwise, it is excluded.

The jury receives the confession with instructions first to determine its voluntariness. If the jury determines that the confession or statement was made voluntarily then the jury may consider it for purposes of determining guilt. If, on the other hand, the jurors determine that it was not obtained voluntarily then they are instructed to disregard the statement or confession.

A third method, known as the Massachusetts method, also requires the trial judge to determine the voluntariness question. If the judge finds the confession involuntary the jury never receives it. If the judge finds the confession to have been voluntarily made then it is submitted to the jury with instructions that the jurors should make their own independent determination of voluntariness.

Initially, the New York method was upheld against constitutional attack in *Stein v. New York*.[47] Eleven years later a five-to-four decision in *Jackson v. Denno*[48] found it inadequate to protect the due process rights of defendants. The Court held that the procedure did not ensure a "reliable determination on the issue of voluntariness" and did not sufficiently guarantee that convictions would not be grounded on involuntary confessions.

One of the problems with the method was that there was only a general jury verdict of guilty, and it was impossible to determine whether the jury had focused first on the issue of voluntariness. If the jury had properly done its job and weighed the issue of voluntariness then there was no method for determining its decision on that issue. Opponents argued that it was doubtful that a jury could appreciate the values served by the exclusion of involuntary confessions and put out of its collective mind the content of the confession no matter what was determined with regard to its voluntariness.

The rule was reiterated in *Sims v. Georgia*,[49] when the Court voided a state practice permitting the judge to let the confession go to the jury for the ultimate decision on voluntariness. In Georgia the prosecution need merely show grounds upon which to believe the confession was made voluntarily, and the standards for such proof were extremely low. Opponents of the Georgia scheme contended that there was no means for truly protecting the innocent even if the police used overly coercive methods.

While the New York method has been limited, and in some sense was struck down under its traditional application, the Court has not interposed constitutional restrictions on the utilization of either the traditional or the Massachusetts method for determining admissibility. The Court has held that the prosecution bears the burden of establishing voluntariness by a preponderance of the evidence, which rejects earlier contentions that the proof must be "beyond a reasonable doubt,"[50] or by "clear and convincing evidence."[51]

ENDNOTES

1. 384 U.S. 436 (1966).
2. 314 U.S. 219, 236 (1941).
3. Rogers v. Richmond, 365 U.S. 534, 540–41 (1961).

4. Culombe v. Connecticut, 367 U.S. 568, 601 (1961).
5. 378 U.S. 1 (1964).
6. Malloy v. Hogan, 378 U.S. 1, 6–7 (1964).
7. 378 U.S. 478 (1964).
8. Escobedo v. Illinois, 378 U.S. 478, 485, 491 (1964) (both pages containing assertions of the suspect's "absolute right to remain silent" in the context of police warnings prior to interrogation).
9. Pub. L. No. 90-351, Sec. 701(a), 82 Stat. 210, 18 U.S.C. §3501. See S. Rept. No. 1097, 90th Congress, 2d sess. 37–53 (1968).
10. United States v. Crocker, 510 F.2d 1129 (10th Cir. 1975).
11. 417 U.S. 433 (1974).
12. An unresolved issue was whether the witness testimony was suppresible on other grounds such as fourth at is not clear that the witness' testimony was suppressible in any event. Cf. United States v. Ceccolini, 435 U.S. 268 (1978) (a Fourth Amendment case).
13. Michigan v. Tucker, 417 U.S. 433, 439 (1974). Justices Rehnquist, Stewart, Blackmun, Powell, and Chief Justice Burger joined the opinion of the Court. Justices Brennan and Marshall concurred on retroactivity grounds, id. at 453, and Justice Stewart noted he could have joined this opinion as well. Id. Justice White, continuing to think Miranda was wrongly decided, concurred because he did not think the "fruits" of a Miranda violation should be excluded. Id. at 460.
14. Id. at 446–52.
15. See Monaghan, Foreword: Constitutional Common Law, 89 Harv. L. Rev. 1 (1975); Schrock, Welsh & Collins, Interrogational Rights: Reflections on Miranda v. Arizona, 52 So. Cal. L. Rev. 1 (1978).
16. Miranda v. Arizona, 384 U.S. 436, 444 (1966).
17. Mathis v. United States, 391 U.S. 1 (1968) (suspect in state jail questioned by federal officer about a federal crime). Although a suspect is in jail, hence in custody "in a technical sense," a conversation with an undercover agent does not create a coercive, police-dominated environment and does not implicate Miranda if the suspect does not know that he is conversing with a government agent. Illinois v. Perkins, 110 S. Ct. 2394 (1990).
18. Orozco v. Texas, 394 U.S. 324 (1969) (four policemen entered suspect's bedroom at 4 a.m. and questioned him; although not formally arrested, he was in custody).
19. 429 U.S. 492 (1977).
20. Beckwith v. United States, 425 U.S. 341 (1976).
21. See United States v. Mendenhall, 446 U.S. 544 (1980); Reid v. Georgia, 448 U.S. 438 (1980); Brown v. Texas, 443 U.S. 47 (1979); Berkemer v. McCarty, 468 U.S. 420, 440 (1984) (roadside questioning of motorist stopped for traffic violation is not custodial interrogation until his "freedom of action is curtailed to a 'degree associated with formal arrest'").
22. 468 U.S. 420, 440 (1984).
23. 446 U.S. 291 (1980).
24. Rhode Island v. Innis, 446 U.S. 291, 300–01 (1980).
25. Id. at 302–04.
26. 451 U.S. 454 (1981).
27. Id. at 467.

28. California v. Prysock, 453 U.S. 355 (1981). Rephrased, the test is whether the warnings "reasonably conveyed" a suspect's rights, the Court adding that reviewing courts "need not examine Miranda warnings as if construing a will or defining the terms of an easement." Duckworth v. Egan, 492 U.S. 195, 203 (1989) (upholding warning that included possibly misleading statement that a lawyer would be appointed "if and when you go to court").

29. Miranda v. Arizona, 384 U.S. 436, 444 (1966).

30. Miranda v. Arizona, 384 U.S. 436, 472, 473–74 (1966).

31. 451 U.S. 477 (1981).

32. *Id.* at 484–85.

33. Fare v. Michael C., 442 U.S. 707 (1979) (juvenile requested to see his parole officer, rather than counsel). Also, waivers signed by the accused following Miranda warnings are not vitiated by police having kept from the accused information that an attorney had been retained for him by a relative. Moran v. Burbine, 475 U.S. 412 (1986).

34. Michigan v. Mosley, 423 U.S. 96 (1975) (suspect given Miranda warnings at questioning for robbery, requested cessation of interrogation, and police complied; some two hours later, a different policeman interrogated suspect about a murder, gave him a new Miranda warning, and suspect made incriminating admission; since police "scrupulously honored" suspect's request, admission valid).

35. Miranda v. Arizona, 384 U.S. 436, 475 (1966).

36. North Carolina v. Butler, 441 U.S. 369 (1979).

37. Tague v. Louisiana, 444 U.S. 469 (1980).

38. Colorado v. Spring, 479 U.S. 564 (1987).

39. North Carolina v. Butler, 441 U.S. 369, 374–75 (1979) (quoting Johnson v. Zerbst, 304 U.S. 458, 464 [1938]).

40. Harrison v. United States, 392 U.S. 219 (1968).

41. Walter v. United States, 347 U.S. 62 (1954).

42. 401 U.S. 222 (1971).

43. 420 U.S. 714 (1975).

44. 467 U.S. 649 (1984).

45. *Id.* at 658–59.

46. Berkemer v. McCarty, 468 U.S. 420, 432 (1984).

47. 346 U.S. 156, 170–79 (1953).

48. 378 U.S. 368 (1964).

49. 385 U.S. 538 (1967).

50. Lego v. Twomey, 404 U.S. 477 (1972).

51. Colorado v. Connelly, 479 U.S. 157 (1986).

20 Due Process under the Fifth Amendment

I. HISTORY OF THE PROTECTION

It is now the settled doctrine of this Court that the Due Process Clause embodies a system of rights based on moral principles so deeply imbedded in the traditions and feelings of our people as to be deemed fundamental to a civilized society as conceived by our whole history. Due Process is that which comports with the deepest notions of what is fair and right and just.[1]

With these words, Justice Frankfurter has given us a clear understanding of due process from a historical perspective. It is one of our deepest and most sacred traditions within the law.

Like so many principles of our legal system, the content of due process is a historical product that traces its roots all the way back to the Magna Carta. In Chapter 39 of this historic document King John promised that "[n]o free man shall be taken or imprisoned or disseized or exiled or in any way destroyed, nor will we go upon him nor send upon him, except by the lawful judgment of his peers or by the law of the land."[2]

The phrase "due process of law" first appeared in a statutory rendition of this chapter in 1354. "No man of what state or condition he be, shall be put out of his lands or tenements nor taken, nor disinherited, nor put to death, without he be brought to answer by due process of law."[3]

The understanding the founders of the American constitutional system and those who wrote the due process clauses brought to the subject derives in great part from Coke who, in his *Second Institutes*, expounded the proposition that the term "by law of the land" was equivalent to "due process of law." Coke then defined "due process of law" to mean "by due process of the common law," that is, "by the indictment or presentment of good and lawful men ... or by writ original of the Common Law."[4]

In many of the early colonial charters we see the term "law of the land" used in place of the now common "due process of law." In searching these charters one may also find that many charters used both terms, and at times both were used interchangeably. Regardless of which term was favored in the original documents, it is clear that the general intent was to ensure certain precise safeguards to the accused person. We shall also see that, as with the Fifth Amendment, these provisions also suggest some limitations or guarantee of just compensation upon the taking of private property for public use.

For our purposes we may simply say that the safeguards we take from the Fifth Amendment today have had a long history in both development and application.

Protections to the accused are chief among these concerns for the criminal justice professional, but the clause also offers some protection to private property against an overzealous government.

II. SCOPE OF THE GUARANTY

When one examines the term by itself it would seem that "due process" refers solely and exclusively to procedure and the process in court. If so, then process would be nothing more than what the legislature has enacted, but that is not the interpretation the courts have placed on the term. "It is manifest that it was not left to the legislative power to enact any process which might be devised. The article is a restraint on the legislative as well as on the executive and judicial powers of the government, and cannot be so construed as to leave congress free to make any process 'due process of law' by its mere will."[5]

By this statement we see that the Supreme Court views the phrase to encompass more than just what Congress or the individual state legislature has written. For the courts the phrase means that all persons within U.S. territory are entitled to much more than just a literal application of a particular legislative scheme. They are entitled to "the deepest notions of what is fair and right and just."[6]

Early in our judicial history, a number of jurists attempted to formulate a theory of natural rights and natural justice. State courts were the arenas in which this struggle was carried out prior to the Civil War. Opposing the "vested rights" theory of protection of property were jurists who argued first, that the traditionally written constitution was the supreme law of the state and that judicial review could look only to that document in scrutinizing legislation and not to the "unwritten law" of "natural rights"; and second, that the "police power" of government enabled legislatures to regulate the use and holding of property in the public interest, subject only to the specific prohibitions of the state's written constitution.

The "vested rights" jurists thus found in the "law of the land" and the "due process" clauses of the state constitutions a restriction upon the substantive content of legislation, which prohibited, regardless of the matter of procedure, a certain kind or degree of exertion of legislative power altogether.[7] Thus, Chief Justice Taney's opinion in the *Dred Scott* case was not innovative when he pronounced, without elaboration, that one reason the Missouri Compromise was unconstitutional was that an act of Congress that deprived "a citizen of his liberty or property merely because he came himself or brought his property into a particular territory of the United States, and who had committed no offence against the laws, could hardly be dignified with the name of due process of law."[8]

Following the War, with the ratification of the Fourteenth Amendment due process clause, substantive due process interpretations with regard to state legislation were urged on the Supreme Court. The arguments came in time to be accepted, and they imposed upon both federal and state legislation a firm judicial hand that was not to be removed until the 1930s.

One point that must be made in this early portion of the topic is that the protections of due process were not unique by the time of the Constitutional Convention. As we will see in future chapters the application of these standards has long been a process of the courts. By the end of the Civil War, however, we see a marked change in both attitude toward the Constitution and needs of the courts in addressing due process issues. A new amendment was created under which the courts could apply the principles of the Bill of Rights to the states. This amendment, the Fourteenth Amendment, also contains due process requirements, and as we will discover they often go hand in hand with those contained in the Fifth Amendment; however, there are some differences.

The most obvious difference between the two due process clauses is that the Fifth Amendment clause as it binds the Federal Government coexists with a number of other express provisions in the Bill of Rights guaranteeing fair procedure and non-arbitrary action. This is seen in such issues as jury trials, grand jury indictments, non-excessive bail and fines, and in the clauses dealing with just compensation.

The Fourteenth Amendment is a bit different in that it binds the states and is used in many instances to apply the standards of the Bill of Rights to the states. The amendment has been held to contain implicitly not only the standards of fairness and justness found within the Fifth Amendment's clause but also many guarantees that are expressly set out in the Bill of Rights. In that sense, the two clauses are not the same thing, but insofar as they do impose such implicit requirements of fair trials, fair hearings, and the like, the interpretation of the two clauses is substantially if not wholly the same. Save for areas in which the particularly national character of the federal government requires separate treatment, discussion of the meaning of due process is largely reserved for the section on the Fourteenth Amendment. There are, however, some areas of due process that are appropriately discussed as they relate to the Fifth Amendment.

III. PROCEDURAL DUE PROCESS

The simplest definition of the phrase "procedural due process" means that both the letter of the procedural law and its intent will be followed. In 1855, the Supreme Court first attempted to assess its standards for judging this topic. As we have seen in the prior section, the Court first ascertained that Congress was not free to make any process "due process." The Court stated:

> To what principles, then are we to resort to ascertain whether this process, enacted by congress, is due process? To this the answer must be twofold. We must examine the constitution itself, to see whether this process be in conflict with any of its provisions. If not found to be so, we must look to those settled usages and modes of proceedings existing in the common and statute law of England, before the emigration of our ancestors and which are shown not to have been unsuited to their civil and political condition by having been acted on by them after the settlement of this country.[9]

Initially this formal approach to the meaning of due process was seen as limiting both Congress and the state legislatures in the development of procedures unknown to English law. This was clarified, to some extent, by an issue which also arose under the Fifth Amendment: use of the grand jury for indictment. This action was challenged when California abandoned the use of indictment by grand jury as the primary means of indicting. In assessing the change the Court refused to be limited by the fact that such a proceeding was the English practice and that Coke had indicated that it was a proceeding required as "the law of the land."[10]

The Court stated "that a process of law, which is not otherwise forbidden, must be taken to be due process of law, if it can show the sanction of settled usage both in England and in this country; but it by no means follows that nothing else can be due process of law." To hold that only historical, traditional procedures can constitute due process, the Court said, "would be to deny every quality of the law but its age, and to render it incapable of progress or improvement."

In observing the due process guarantee, it was concluded the Court must look "not [to] particular forms of procedures, but [to] the very substance of individual rights to life, liberty, and property."[11] In this sense it follows that any legal proceeding enforced by public authority, whether sanctioned by age and custom, or newly devised by the discretion of the legislative power, in furtherance of the general public good and which regards and preserves the principles of liberty and justice, must be held to be due process of law.[12]

The phrase "due process of law" does not necessarily imply a proceeding in a court or a plenary suit and trial by jury in every case involving personal or property rights. "In all cases, that kind of procedure is due process of law which is suitable and proper to the nature of the case, and sanctioned by the established customs and usages of the courts."[13] To this end, what is unfair in one situation may be fair in another. "The precise nature of the interest that has been adversely affected, the manner in which this was done, the reasons for doing it, the available alternatives to the procedure that was followed, the protection implicit in the office of the functionary whose conduct is challenged, the balance of hurt complained of and good accomplished — these are some of the considerations that must enter into the judicial judgment."[14]

IV. SUBSTANTIVE DUE PROCESS

The constitutional safeguard of substantive due process requires that all legislation be in furtherance of a legitimate governmental objective. To this end, one may say that substantive due process is the means by which we weigh the legitimate acts of our legislative bodies. In areas such as discrimination and police action, due process allows us to measure the intent and breadth of the legislative act. "[Due process] tends to secure equality of law in the sense that it makes a required minimum of protection for every one's right of life, liberty and property, which the Congress or the legislature may not withhold."[15]

Our whole system of law is predicated on the general, fundamental principle of equality of application of the law. The concepts of equal protection and due process, both stemming from our American ideal of fairness, are not mutually exclusive. "Equal protection analysis in the Fifth Amendment area," the Court has said, "is the same as that under the Fourteenth Amendment."[16]

ENDNOTES

1. Solesbee v. Balkcom, 339 U.S. 9, 16 (1950).
2. The chapter became Chapter 29 in the Third Reissue of Henry III in 1225.
3. 28 Edw. III, c. 3.
4. Sir Edward Coke, Institutes of the Laws of England, Part II, 50–51 (London: 1641).
5. Murray's Lessee v. Hoboken Land and Improvement Co. 59 U.S. (18 How.) 272, 276 (1856).
6. Solesbee v. Balkcom, 339 U.S. 9, 16 (1950).
7. Wynhamer v. The People, 13 N.Y. 378 (1856).
8. Scott v. Sandford, 60 U.S. (19 How.) 393, 450 (1857).
9. Murray's Lessee v. Hoboken Land and Improvement Co., 59 U.S. (18 How.) 272, 276–77, 280 (1856). A similar approach was followed in Fourteenth Amendment due process interpretation in Davidson v. City of New Orleans, 96 U.S. 97 (1878), and Munn v. Illinois, 94 U.S. 113 (1877).
10. Hurtado v. California, 110 U.S. 516, 528–29 (1884).
11. *Id.* at 531–32, 535, 537.
12. Twining v. New Jersey, 211 U.S. 78 (1908); Powell v. Alabama, 287 U.S. 45 (1932); Palko v. Connecticut, 302 U.S. 319 (1937).
13. Ex parte Wall, 107 U.S. 265, 289 (1883).
14. Joint Anti-Fascist Refugee Comm. v. McGrath, 341 U.S. 123, 163 (1951).
15. Truax v. Corrigan, 257 U.S. 312, 331 (1921).
16. Buckley v. Valeo, 424 U.S. 1, 93 (1976).

Section Six

Sixth Amendment — Rights of Accused in Criminal Prosecutions

Amendment Text

In all criminal prosecutions, the accused shall enjoy the right to a speedy and public trial, by an impartial jury of the State and district wherein the crime shall have been committed, which district shall have been previously ascertained by law, and to be informed of the nature and cause of the accusation; to be confronted with the witnesses against him; to have compulsory process for obtaining witnesses in his favor, and to have the Assistance of Counsel for his defence.

21 Speedy Public Trial

I. COVERAGE

The Sixth Amendment is one of the few amendments to the Constitution that addresses exclusively criminal matters. From the opening clause, "In all criminal prosecutions," it is clear that the amendment was created to provide minimal protections to those accused of criminal acts. From the outset it was established that the amendment protected those accused of crimes in federal courts. There were questions, however, as to whether the protections extended to the incorporated or unincorporated territories. There was also a question as to any application in the state courts.

By the end of the nineteenth century the Supreme Court had clearly established that the Sixth Amendment did in fact apply to those charged in a federal court of an incorporated territory.[1] Likewise, it was held that the amendment applied to those charged before a court of the District of Columbia.[2] Those charged in the unincorporated territories, however, were left without the protections of the amendment.[3]

The application of the Sixth Amendment within the state courts came some time later. As we discussed in earlier chapters, it was the ratification of the Fourteenth Amendment following the Civil War that led to the application of the Bill of Rights in the state courts. This is true of the Sixth Amendment as well, but it was only to come through individual cases dealing with each of the individual protections found in the amendment's clauses. Today, all of the protections have been firmly established for both federal and state courts.

As for the application of the amendment within the federal courts it is important to remember that there are no "common-law" offenses in federal courts today. All acts against the U.S. are created by legislative act through Congress.[4] Likewise, most, if not all, of the individual states have also done away with common-law criminal acts. One reason for this is a need for uniformity of law, that is, the application of laws that are the same or similar from jurisdiction to jurisdiction.

Another reason for codifying the criminal law is the need for clear and concise standards that will withstand rigorous appellate review upon conviction. At this point, this fact is important more from a historical perspective than from a real legal one but this fact bears mentioning as we begin to explore the protections of the amendment and the cases which have interpreted them.

II. RIGHT TO A SPEEDY AND PUBLIC TRIAL

A. SOURCE AND RATIONALE

Lord Coke once again plays a major role in the development of the early law dealing with the right of trial. Historians believe that a part of this right developed from clauses contained in the Magna Carta,[5] and it was Coke's interpretations of these clauses that set the foundation for later development of the right.[6] In fact, Coke has been credited with much of the early work in developing the right. His writings greatly influenced Madison and others when they began work on the amendment.

There are many reasons for a provision calling for a speedy trial. Chief among these is the need to protect both the defendant and society from the harm that may arise when a trial is unduly delayed. This makes the Sixth Amendment unique in the sense that at least one of its provisions is designed to protect not only the criminally accused but also the society as a whole. For instance, a speedy trial will guarantee that witnesses will be more likely to remember events in question than they might if the trial were delayed. Likewise, the passage of time may lead to the loss of witnesses through death or merely moving geographically away. This is especially important when one considers that today's modern family may simply rent a truck and move thousands of miles away.

The Sixth Amendment is "an important safeguard to prevent undue and oppressive incarceration prior to trial."[7] In other words, a speedy trial lessens the stress on the accused who is without means to make bail or who is denied bail. Being incarcerated while waiting on trial can be burdensome to both accused and his or her family. The Court has also held the amendment is necessary "to minimize anxiety and concern accompanying public accusation and to limit the possibility that long delay will impair the ability of an accused to defend himself."[8]

There is additional societal interest in a speedy trial. Persons in jail must be supported at considerable public expense and their families often must be assisted as well. Even if the person is released from jail while waiting trial there is the risk that a guilty person is avoiding punishment. A speedy trial puts the issues of guilt before a judge or jury in a timely fashion and lessens the likelihood the person may commit additional crimes. Others suggest that a speedy trial also lessens the likelihood that a criminal defendant will "jump" bail. Criminologists point out that a delay often retards the deterrent and rehabilitative effects of the criminal law.[9]

B. APPLICATION AND SCOPE

As set out in the introductory section, the rights of the Sixth Amendment have been applied to all federal and state courts directly or through the provisions of the Fourteenth Amendment.[10] The protection afforded by this guarantee "is activated only when a criminal prosecution has begun and extends only to those persons who have been 'accused' in the course of that prosecution." Invocation of the right need not await indictment, information, or other formal charge but begins with the actual restraints imposed by arrest if those restraints precede the formal preferring of charges.[11]

There are possibilities for delay in presenting formal charges against an individual suspected of a crime. Such delays do not necessarily trigger the protections of the Sixth Amendment. For instance, many crimes carry a statutory scheme known as a "statute of limitations" which places a time frame within which formal charges may be brought. Crimes such as larceny, burglary, and robbery — among others — typically have a limitation of seven years within which charges may be brought. One suspected of a crime may be investigated and charges brought any time within that time frame, but the provisions of the Sixth Amendment will only adhere when the person is arrested or formally charged with the crime.[12] There are, however, some exceptions.

In at least two cases, the Court held that the speedy trial guarantee had been violated by states that preferred criminal charges against persons who were already incarcerated in prisons of other jurisdictions following convictions on other charges when those states ignored the defendants' requests for prompt trials and made no effort through requests to prison authorities to obtain custody of the prisoners for purposes of trial.[13] Many states have implemented statutory schemes that address such issues. Where the person suspected of a crime is in custody of a state facility, and in some instances even in the custody of another state, then the statutory provisions disallow delays in prosecution. This has been brought about in part by the protections of the Sixth Amendment.

Another practice in delaying the charging of a person involves the practice of permitting the prosecutor to take *nolle prosequi* with leave. *Nolle prosequi* typically means that the prosecutor refuses to or is unable to prosecute a given case, and thus in the traditional sense no action to prosecute will be taken. By taking *nolle prosequi* with leave, however, a prosecutor leaves open the opportunity to later file charges against the accused. This is commonly used when the accused is discharged from custody with instructions to act in a particular manner and with the opportunity for prosecution should the accused not comply. For instance, a prosecutor might enter such an agreement based on a promise by the accused to "leave town." The practice itself has not been struck down, but where such agreements or actions in effect toll or stop a statute of limitations from running, the Supreme Court condemned the practice as violative of the Sixth Amendment guarantee.[14]

C. WHEN THE RIGHT IS DENIED

The right of a speedy trial is always relative to other factors concerning the court and the circumstances of a delay. In other words, there has never been a strict interpretation leading to a holding that a trial must be held within a given time frame. The right will be measured against the individual delays and circumstances surrounding the case itself. This means that a delay of 90 days in one jurisdiction might infringe the right, but the same temporal delay in another jurisdiction will not.[15]

In addressing the issues of speedy trial the Supreme Court has adopted an ad hoc balancing approach. In establishing this approach the Court stated: "We can do little more than identify some of the factors which courts should assess in determining whether a particular defendant has been deprived of his right. Though some might express them in different ways, we identify four such factors: Length of delay, the reason for the delay, the defendant's assertion of his right, and prejudice to the defendant."[16]

In assessing these factors the courts will look at the reasons for the delay as well as the circumstances surrounding the case. A deliberate delay by a prosecutor in order to gain tactical advantage will most likely be viewed with a jaundiced eye while a delay due to the legitimate absence of a witness would justify little scrutiny. Factors such as crowded dockets may also weigh into issues of trial delay. Where such delay is caused by an overly busy court the delay often will be overlooked as unavoidable, but where the docket is crowded because of negligence or laziness on the part of court personnel then the delay may trigger the protections of the amendment.[17]

It has long been held that it is the duty of the prosecution to bring a defendant to trial, and the failure of the defendant to demand the right is not to be construed as a waiver of the right to a speedy trial.[18] In this sense, the Court has established that a defendant has no obligation to push a matter to trial, but that does not mean the defendant may use the tactic of acquiescence in delay in order to trigger the amendment protections. A defendant who agrees to continual delays may very well lose the right to raise the speedy trial issue later.

Finally, a court should look to the possible prejudices and disadvantages suffered by a defendant during a delay.[19] If the delay has caused little or no harm to the defendant then the amendment may not be triggered. Delay alone may not be enough to warrant the protections of the amendment. Because a determination that a defendant has been denied his or her right to a speedy trial results in a decision to dismiss the indictment or to reverse a conviction in order that the indictment be dismissed[20] the courts are encouraged to carefully weigh both the need for delay and the results that such delay might cause.

III. PUBLIC TRIAL

The right to a public trial has been a long tradition in the court systems, but it is unclear where such a practice began. It may be assumed that the practice developed as early as the earliest laws, and we know that it was in use 2000 years ago since it is mentioned prominently in the Bible and other religious texts of the time. Likewise, public trials appear in the records of ancient civilizations that date back to the earliest forms of writing.

In this country the guarantee to an accused of the right to a public trial first appeared in various state constitutions during the latter part of the eighteenth century. By 1776 we know that the custom was available in at least three of the original thirteen colonies, and it became a mainstay of the new American system with the 1791 ratification of the Sixth Amendment to the federal Constitution. Most of the original states and those subsequently admitted to the Union adopted similar constitutional provisions. Today almost without exception every state by constitution, statute, or judicial decision requires that all criminal trials be open to the public.

An open trial has many benefits to a society such as ours. Public trial helps to assure the criminal defendant a fair and accurate adjudication of guilt or innocence. It also provides a public demonstration of fairness while discouraging perjury or the misconduct of participants. A public trial also addresses a more psychological issue since society tends to abhor decisions based on secret, bias, or partiality.

Others have suggested that a public trial also serves a societal need to see "justice done." Some argue that there is a therapeutic value to the community since open trials enable the public to see justice and the fulfillment of the urge for retribution that people feel upon the commission of some kinds of crimes. This sociological need has even been addressed by the courts.[21]

Because of the near universality of the guarantee in this country, the Supreme Court has had little occasion to deal with the right. It is a right so fundamental that it is protected against state deprivation by the due process clause,[22] but it is not so absolute that reasonable regulation designed to forestall prejudice from publicity and disorderly trials is foreclosed. In this sense we see that the courts do have some control over the very nature of the publicity or public exposure itself. For example, the banning of television cameras from the courtroom and the precluding of live telecasting of a trial are not denials of the right,[23] although the Court does not inhibit televised trials under the proper circumstances.[24]

The Court has borrowed from First Amendment cases in protecting the right to a public trial. Closure of trials or pretrial proceedings over the objection of the accused may be justified only if the state can show "an overriding interest based on findings that closure is essential to preserve higher values and is narrowly tailored to serve that interest."[25]

The Sixth Amendment guarantee is apparently a personal right of the defendant, which the defendant may in some circumstances waive in conjunction with the prosecution and the court.[26] The First Amendment, however, has been held to protect public and press access to trials in all but the most extraordinary circumstances.[27] As such, a defendant's request for closure of his or her trial must be balanced against the public and press right of access. Before such a request for closure will be honored, there must be "specific findings...demonstrating that first, there is a substantial probability that the defendant's right to a fair trial will be prejudiced by publicity that closure would prevent, and second, reasonable alternatives to closure cannot adequately protect the defendant's fair trial rights."[28]

ENDNOTES

1. Reynolds v. United States, 98 U.S. 145 (1879), and Lovato v. New Mexico, 242 U.S. 199 (1916).
2. Callan v. Wilson, 127 U.S. 540 (1888).
3. Balzac v. Puerto Rico, 258 U.S. 298, 304–05 (1922); Dorr v. United States, 195 U.S. 138 (1904). These holdings are, of course, merely one element of the doctrine of the Insular Cases, De Lima v. Bidwell, 182 U.S. 1 (1901); and Downes v. Bidwell, 182 U.S. 244 (1901), concerned with the "Constitution following the flag." *Supra,* pp. 324–25. Cf. Rassmussen v. United States, 197 U.S. 516 (1905).
4. United States v. Hudson & Goodwin, 11 U.S. (7 Cr.) 32 (1812); United States v. Coolidge, 14 U.S. (1 Wheat.) 415 (1816); United States v. Britton, 108 U.S. 199, 206 (1883); United States v. Eaton, 144 U.S. 677, 687 (1892).
5. Ch. 40 of the 1215 Magna Carta, and a portion of Ch. 29 of the 1225 reissue.
6. For a more detailed discussion of this right and its impact on the Sixth Amendment, see Klopfer v. North Carolina, 386 U.S. 213, 223–24 (1967).
7. *Id.*
8. United States v. Ewell, 383 U.S. 116, 120 (1966). See also Klopfer v. North Carolina, 386 U.S. 213, 221–22 (1967); Smith v. Hooey, 393 U.S. 374, 377–379 (1969); Dickey v. Florida, 389 U.S. 30, 37–38 (1970).

9. Barker v. Wingo, 407 U.S. 514, 519 (1972); Dickey v. Florida, 398 U.S. 30, 42 (1970) (Justice Brennan concurring). Congress by the Speedy Trial Act of 1974, Pub. L. No. 93-619, 88 Stat. 2076, 18 U.S.C. §§3161–74, has codified the law with respect to the right, intending "to give effect to the Sixth Amendment right to a speedy trial." S. Rep. No. 1021, 93d Congress, 2d sess. 1 (1974).
10. Klopfer v. North Carolina, 386 U.S. 213, 226 (1967).
11. United States v. Marion, 404 U.S. 307, 313, 320, 322 (1971).
12. United States v. Marion, 404 U.S. 307, 322–23 (1971).
13. Smith v. Hooey, 393 U.S. 374 (1969); Dickey v. Florida, 398 U.S. 30 (1970).
14. In Pollard v. United States, 352 U.S. 354 (1957).
15. Pollard v. United States, 352 U.S. 354 (1957); United States v. Ewell, 383 U.S. 116 (1966). See also United States v. Provoo, 350 U.S. 857 (1955), aff'g 17 F.R.D. 183 (D. Md. 1955).
16. Barker v. Wingo, 407 U.S. 514, 530 (1972).
17. Barker v. Wingo, 407 U.S. 514, 531 (1972); see also United States v. Loud Hawk, 474 U.S. 302 (1986).
18. Barker v. Wingo, 407 U.S. 514, 528 (1972).
19. Barker v. Wingo, 407 U.S. 514, 532 (1972).
20. Strunk v. United States, 412 U.S. 434 (1973).
21. Estes v. Texas, 381 U.S. 532, 538–39 (1965); Richmond Newspapers v. Virginia, 448 U.S. 555, 569–73 (1980) (plurality opinion of Chief Justice Burger); id. at 593–97 (Justice Brennan concurring).
22. In re Oliver, 333 U.S. 257 (1948); Levine v. United States, 362 U.S. 610 (1960).
23. Estes v. Texas, 381 U.S. 532 (1965). Cf. Nixon v. Warner Communications, 435 U.S. 589, 610 (1978).
24. Chandler v. Florida, 449 U.S. 560 (1981).
25. Press-Enterprise Co. v. Superior Court, 464 U.S. 501, 510 (1984).
26. Gannett Co. v. DePasquale, 443 U.S. 368 (1979).
27. Richmond Newspapers v. Virginia, 448 U.S. 555 (1980); Globe Newspaper Co. v. Superior Court, 457 U.S. 596 (1982). See also Gannett Co. v. DePasquale, 443 U.S. 368, 397 (1979) (Justice Powell concurring).
28. Press-Enterprise Co. v. Superior Court, 478 U.S. 1 (1986).

22 Right to Trial by Impartial Jury

I. DEVELOPMENT OF THE RIGHT

The concept of the jury was started by Frankish conquerors and used initially to discover the King's rights. The jury began in the form of a grand or presentment jury with the role of inquest. Later, Henry II adopted the proceeding to establish royal control over the machinery of justice. The right was first applied in civil trials and later extended to those accused of crimes.

Trial by petit jury was not employed until at least the reign of Henry III. At this time the jury was essentially a body of witnesses. The jurors, called for their knowledge of the case, most often personally knew one or both of the parties to any dispute. The concept was that the jurors, having knowledge of the parties, the dispute, or both would be in a better position than a judge ignorant of the intricacies of the case to determine what was just.

During the reign of Henry VI the jury took on the more traditional role of trier of evidence. It was during the seventeenth century that the jury emerged as a safeguard for the criminally accused. By the eighteenth century the practice was so ingrained that leading commentators such as Blackstone could commemorate the institution as part of a "strong and two-fold barrier...between the liberties of the people and the prerogative of the crown."[1] The other barrier was the presentment of indictment through the grand jury.

In early America the right was guaranteed in the constitutions of the original 13 states, in the body of the Constitution,[2] and in the Sixth Amendment. The right was also guaranteed, in one form or another, by the constitution of every state entering the Union.[3]

Because "a general grant of jury trial for serious offenses is a fundamental right, essential for preventing miscarriages of justice and for assuring that fair trials are provided for all defendants," the Sixth Amendment provision is binding on the States through the due process clause of the Fourteenth Amendment.[4] But inasmuch as it cannot be said that every criminal trial or any particular trial held without a jury is unfair, it is possible for a defendant to waive the right and go to trial before a judge alone. A defendant who waives this important right, however, must appear before a judge and give "express and intelligent consent." The prosecution and judge must also agree that waiver is in the best interest of justice.[5]

II. THE ATTRIBUTES OF THE JURY

It was previously the position of the Court that the right to a jury trial meant "a trial by jury as understood and applied at common law, and includes all the essential elements as they were recognized in this country and England when the Constitution was adopted."[6] This meant that a trial by a jury was held before 12 persons who must reach a unanimous verdict.[7] However, as it extended the guarantee to the states, the Court indicated that at least some of these standards were open to re-examination.[8]

In *Williams v. Florida*[9] the Court held that the fixing of jury size at 12 was "a historical accident" which, while firmly established when the Sixth Amendment was proposed and ratified, was not required as an attribute of the jury system, either as a matter of common-law background or by any ascertainment of the intent of the Framers. The Court added that the size of the jury bore no discernible relationship to the purposes of jury trial, which was the prevention of oppression and the reliability of fact-finding. There was also little reason to believe that any great advantage accrued to the defendant by having a jury composed of 12 rather than 6.

Modern standards dictate that a jury should be large enough to promote group deliberation, free from outside attempts at intimidation, and provide a fair possibility that a cross section of the community will be represented. While the Court did not speculate whether there was a minimum permissible size it did recognize the propriety of conditioning jury size on the seriousness of the offense.[10] In many jurisdictions felony trials often use the traditional 12-person jury while lesser crimes such as misdemeanors operate with as few as 4 jurors. For lesser crimes the more common number of jurors is six.

Another area where tradition has played a strong role in shaping the American jury system is the "unanimity rule." The rule that a jury in a criminal case must reach a unanimous verdict is a holdover from the common-law juries of centuries past. Some have argued that it is unlikely that the Framers of the Sixth Amendment intended to preserve the requirement within the term "jury." For that reason the Supreme Court undertook a functional analysis of the jury and determined that the requirement of unanimity did not materially affect the role of the jury as a barrier against oppression and as a guarantee of a common sense judgment of laymen.[11]

The Justices also determined that the unanimity requirement is not implicated in the constitutional requirement of proof beyond a reasonable doubt and is not necessary to preserve the feature of the requisite cross section representation on the jury. Four dissenting Justices thought that omitting the unanimity requirement would undermine the reasonable doubt standard, would permit a majority of jurors simply to ignore those interpreting the facts differently, and would permit oppression of dissenting minorities.[12]

Absent a specific statutory scheme within the individual states we find that many state courts still follow the traditions of early English common law when it comes to juries. Although the Supreme Court has suggested that jury size and unanimity are not pivotal issues to the effective functioning of a jury, many criminal trials are still held before a jury of 12 members who must agree unanimously. The federal courts, however, have adopted the standards established by the Supreme Court, and one will find federal juries are often a bit different from their state counterparts.

III. CRIMINAL PROCEEDINGS TO WHICH THE GUARANTEE APPLIES

Although the Sixth Amendment provision does not differentiate types of criminal proceedings in which the right to a jury trial is or is not present, the Court has always excluded petty offenses from the guarantee in federal courts. The issue is often defined by the punishment available[13] or by the nature of the offense.[14] This line has been adhered to in the application of the Sixth Amendment to the states,[15] and the Court has held "that no offense can be deemed 'petty' for purposes of the right to trial by jury where imprisonment for more than six months is authorized."[16]

Traditionally, the right to a jury trial also has been held to mean those actions associated with "criminal proceeding." This meant that only those cases in which a defendant was charged by indictment or information carried the right to a jury trial.[17] Thus, a civil action to collect statutory penalties and punitive damages, because it is not technically criminal, has been held to not have a right to jury trial.

More recently the Court has held that certain classes of cases, although not technically criminal in nature, do carry a promise of jury trial. For instance, denationalization carries with it a punishment that reaches the highest level of personal freedom and property rights. Because of this the Court has held that Congress may not impose such punishment without adhering to the guarantees of the Fifth and Sixth Amendments.[18]

Contempt of court proceedings was another area that traditionally held no guaranteed right to jury trial. This was changed when the Court held in *Bloom v. Illinois*[19] that "[o]ur deliberations have convinced us…that serious contempts are so nearly like other serious crimes that they are subject to the jury trial provisions of the Constitution…and that the traditional rule is constitutionally infirm insofar as it permits other than petty contempt to be tried without honoring a demand for a jury trial." Today, contempts that carry the possibility of incarceration for six months or more are typically held to fall within the protections of the Sixth Amendment.

In the area of juvenile law it has long been held that no constitutional right to a jury trial exists.[20] In recent years, however, with the changes in the juvenile systems across the country, that right has been established or is being challenged. In cases involving high felonies and "infamous crimes" there is a movement to provide the protections of the Sixth Amendment to juveniles. We certainly see such protections when the minor is judicially certified as an adult in order to stand trial as an adult for adult crimes. Likewise, in capital cases there appears to be a protected right to jury trial even for juveniles.[21]

IV. IMPARTIAL JURY

One must remember that in the earliest days of the jury system it was often required that the potential juror be knowledgeable of both the circumstances at issue and the parties to the lawsuit. This has slowly changed and today we seek jurors who typically have no knowledge of the case (or who are only minimally knowledgeable) and have little or no familiarity with the parties. The purpose for this is the desire to seat an impartial jury, one that will show no favoritism or prejudice for or against any party to the suit.

From a legal standpoint, impartiality as a principle is served not only by the Sixth Amendment, which is applicable to federal government and to the states through the Fourteenth Amendment,[22] but also through the due process and equal protection clauses of the Fourteenth[23] and the Fifth Amendments. Even prior to the

Court's extension of a right to jury trials in state courts, it was firmly established that if a state chose to provide juries they must be impartial ones.[24]

In gauging whether a jury is impartial or not the courts have developed some unique methods. One of these is the requirement that the potential jurors be comprised of "a representative cross section of the community."[25] It must be noted that this requirement applies only to jury panels — that group of individuals from which the jury itself will ultimately be drawn — and does not apply to the makeup of the particular jury itself.

In this sense it is conceivable that the larger jury panel (sometimes called a jury pool in some jurisdictions) be a representative group of individuals from the community but the actual jury that hears the case may be a narrowly drawn and selected group of individuals from within the panel. To illustrate how this might occur we will explore the modern practices of jury selection.

Typically, the court maintains a list of eligible members of the community who may be called for jury duty. The more popular means of obtaining this list is from voter registration rolls. A technique becoming widespread is to use a list comprised of citizens who have obtained a driver's license. When the court sets a term for jury trials the clerk of the court is charged with sending notice (also known as a jury summons) to the potential jurors. Depending on the needs of the court, anywhere from a few hundred to several thousand potential jurors will be summoned for service. This large group is known as the jury pool or jury panel.

In most jurisdictions the court will schedule a number of cases all requiring jury trials within the same time frame. This is typically referred as a "jury term." In some courts, the jury term is at specific times during the calendar year. In other courts, the jury term is ongoing.

As each case moves into place for its turn at trial the judge will randomly call, from the jury panel, members that will form the jury. The process of selecting jurors is known as voir dire, which is French for "to speak the truth."

During voir dire both the judge and the parties will have an opportunity to examine the potential jurors. This process is designed to reveal any potential prejudice or impartiality among the jury panel. In some courts the entire process, with some exceptions, is conducted by the judge alone, and the parties may submit proposed questions to be asked of the jury members. In other courts the judge plays only a nominal role in voir dire and the parties and their attorneys conduct the inquiry. Almost any topic that has to do with the search for prejudice or impartiality may be inquired into, and jurors are under an obligation "to speak the truth" when asked.

Great latitude is given to the court and the attorneys during voir dire. For instance, in a case dealing with sexual battery or rape the defendant may have a need to know a potential juror's feelings on premarital sex, especially if the defense intends to show that the sexual conduct was voluntary and mutual rather than forced or coerced.

As the process of selecting the jurors continues the parties will be called upon to make their "challenges" to the jury. This means that the party will be asked if he or she wishes to seek dismissal of a potential juror from the panel. There are two types of challenges. The first is known as the "challenge for cause" and the second is known as a "peremptory challenge."

The challenge for cause, as the name implies, means that the party seeking dismissal of the juror has reason. For example, a prosecutor trying a drug case may seek dismissal of potential jurors who have expressed a personal feeling that the drug laws are too harsh in this country. Such an individual may have a prejudice that would prevent him or her from being impartial. Likewise, a juror who has indicated that he or she will always believe anything a police officer says will likely face a challenge from the defense.

The ultimate discretion on whether a juror should be dismissed for cause rests with the judge. Typically, the parties have an unlimited number of challenges for cause. So long as there is cause then the juror can be removed, and failure to remove a potential juror when cause does exist may create an error for appeal.

Unlike the challenge for cause and its unlimited use, the peremptory challenge has only a limited number of uses. The challenge allows a party to exclude a potential juror for almost any reason, without the necessity of showing cause. The challenge is very powerful, and allows the party to excuse a potential juror where little or no cause exists. Normally reserved until all challenges for cause are exhausted — in other words, the parties have successfully used their challenges for cause — the peremptory challenge can be used to dismiss those jurors who were not excused for cause.

With the idea of challenges in mind one can turn again to the issue of selecting an impartial jury. In order to establish a prima facie violation of the fair–cross-section requirement, the defendant must show (1) that the group alleged to be excluded is a "distinctive" group in the community; (2) that the representation of this group in venires from which juries are selected is not fair and reasonable in relation to the number of such persons in the community; and (3) that this under-representation is due to systematic exclusion of the group in the jury-selection process.[26] Areas where such challenges have been successfully prosecuted include exclusions based on race and sex.

In one such case the Court voided a selection system that excluded women unless they had previously filed a written declaration of a desire to serve as a juror.[27] In such a scheme a representative cross section of the community would be impossible to muster since far fewer women were available than men. Requiring women to affirmatively state their desire to serve the court effectively excluded a large portion of the potential jury pool.

In another case the Court invalidated a state system that automatically granted an exemption from service to women who requested such an exemption. Women were not required to affirmatively state their desire to serve, but instead were automatically dismissed if they stated any objection to service. Men were typically required to show cause for such exclusion, and as such the jury panel consisted of a disproportionate number of men.[28]

In other cases, systems that excluded racial minorities have been struck down. For instance, in *Castaneda v. Partida*[29] a Mexican-American defendant successfully proved a prima facie case of intentional exclusion of persons of his ethnic background by showing a substantial under-representation of Mexican-Americans based on a comparison of the group's proportion in the total population of eligible jurors. In this case a showing of disproportion alone was insufficient to establish a prima facie showing of unlawful exclusion, but where a defendant can show a statistical disparity, combined with a demonstration of the easy manipulability of the selection process, a prima facie case may be established.

Other factors are also weighed when examining the issues of impartiality. Some claim that being a public employee is enough to slant a juror toward the government's case, but the courts have disagreed. The Supreme Court has held that, in the absence of an actual showing of bias, a defendant is not denied an impartial jury when he is tried before a jury composed primarily of government employees.[30]

A violation of a defendant's right to an impartial jury does occur when the jury or any of its members is subjected to pressure or influence which could impair freedom of action. Such a finding was made in *Remmer v. United States*,[31] where a potential juror was approached and offered a bribe. In *Smith v. Phillips*,[32] undue pressure was found when it was disclosed that during the trial one of the jurors had been actively seeking employment in the District Attorney's office.

Exposure of the jury to possibly prejudicial material and disorderly courtroom activities may also deny impartiality and must be probed. In *Murphy v. Florida*[33] the Court held that mere knowledge of a criminal defendant's prior criminal record was not enough to create prejudice, but a court should inquire, when it suspects jurors have been exposed to such knowledge, as to the individual juror's ability to serve impartially. Similarly, the court should control the parties in their actions to avoid such exposure.

Private communications, contact, or tampering with a jury, or the creation of circumstances raising the dangers thereof, may also be grounds for finding the juror is no longer impartial.[34] Even the appearance of such impropriety is to be avoided. In *Turner v. Louisiana*[35] the jurors were placed under the care of two deputy sheriffs who were principal prosecution witnesses. Such action, the Court held, opened the door to allegations of private communication or contact and may lead to creation of a less than impartial jury.

Another factor dealing with impartiality is pretrial publicity. The Court has held that where the locality of the trial has been saturated with publicity about a defendant, so that it is unlikely that the defendant can obtain a disinterested jury, the defendant is constitutionally entitled to a change of venue.[36] The change of venue in effect removes the defendant from the locality of the offense and into a neighboring situs where it is expected media coverage will have been less intense.

It is undeniably a violation of due process to subject a defendant to trial in an atmosphere of mob or threatened mob domination.[37] It is incumbent upon the state to provide a safe environment for trial. Likewise, where actions of the outside public may detrimentally affect the juror's ability to remain impartial — in large part because the juror may feel threatened if he or she should find the defendant not guilty — then there are grounds for change of venue.

Impartiality has taken some unique turns in capital cases. One area deals with jurors who have strong feelings for or against capital murder. In *Witherspoon v. Illinois*[38] the Court held that the exclusion in capital cases of jurors conscientiously scrupled about capital punishment — without inquiring whether they could consider the imposition of the death penalty in the appropriate case — violated a defendant's constitutional right to an impartial jury.

Inasmuch as the jury is given broad discretion whether or not to fix the penalty at death, the Court ruled, the jurors must reflect "the conscience of the community" on the issue, and the automatic exclusion of all scrupled jurors "stacked the deck" and made of the jury a tribunal "organized to return a verdict of death."[39] A court may not refuse a defendant's request to examine potential jurors to determine whether they would vote automatically to impose the death penalty. General questions about fairness and willingness to follow the law are inadequate, and a defendant is entitled to much deeper questioning in such cases.[40]

The proper standard for exclusion is "whether the juror's views would 'prevent or substantially impair the performance of his duties as a juror in accordance with his instructions and his oath.'"[41] Thus the juror need not indicate that he or she would "automatically" vote against the death penalty, and "bias [need not] be proved with 'unmistakable clarity.'"[42]

It is the function of the voir dire to give the defense and the prosecution or their trial judge the opportunity to inquire into possible grounds of bias or prejudice potential jurors may have, and to acquaint the parties with the potential jurors.[43] It is good ground for challenge for cause that a juror has formed an opinion on the issue to be tried, but not every opinion a juror may entertain necessarily disqualifies him or her. The judge must determine whether the nature and strength of the opinion raise a presumption against impartiality.[44]

Although government is not constitutionally obligated to allow peremptory challenges, typically a system of peremptory challenges has existed in criminal trials, in which both prosecution and defense may, without stating any reason, excuse a certain number of prospective jurors.[45] This does not mean, however, that a party may exclude a juror for all reasons. For example, in *Swain v. Alabama*[46] the Supreme Court held that a prosecutor's purposeful exclusion of members of a specific racial group from the jury would violate the Equal Protection Clause.

The *Swain* standard was relaxed in *Batson v. Kentucky*,[47] with the result that a defendant may now establish an equal protection violation resulting from a prosecutor's use of peremptory challenges to systematically exclude blacks from the jury. A violation may also occur whether or not the defendant and the excluded jurors are of the same race.[48] Racially discriminatory use of peremptory challenges does not, however, constitute a violation of the Sixth Amendment, the Court ruled in *Holland v. Illinois*.[49] The Sixth Amendment "no more forbids the prosecutor to strike jurors on the basis of race than it forbids him to strike them on the basis of innumerable other generalized characteristics." To rule otherwise, the Court reasoned, "would cripple the device of peremptory challenge" and thereby undermine the Sixth Amendment goal of "impartiality with respect to both contestants."[50]

As a consequence, a defendant who uses a peremptory challenge to correct the court's error in denying a for-cause challenge may have no Sixth Amendment cause of action. Peremptory challenges "are a means to achieve the end of an impartial jury. So long as the jury that sits is impartial, the fact that the defendant had to use a peremptory challenge to achieve that result does not mean the Sixth Amendment was violated."[51]

Over the years, the restraint on racially discriminatory use of peremptory challenges has turned into a two-way street. The Court ruled in 1992 that a criminal defendant's use of peremptory challenges to exclude jurors on the basis of race constitutes "state action" in violation of the Equal Protection Clause.[52] Disputing the contention that this limitation would undermine "the contribution of the peremptory challenge to the administration of justice," the Court nonetheless asserted that such a result would in any event be "too high" a price to pay. "It is an affront to justice to argue that a fair trial includes the right to discriminate against a group of citizens based upon their race."[53]

It followed, therefore, that the limitation on peremptory challenges does not violate a defendant's right to an impartial jury. While a defendant has "the right to an impartial jury that can view him without racial animus," this means that "there should be a mechanism for removing those [jurors] who would be incapable of confronting and suppressing their racism," not that the defendant may remove jurors on the basis of race or racial stereotypes.[54]

V. PLACE OF TRIAL: SELECTING A JURY OF THE VICINAGE

Article III, Section 2 of the Constitution requires that federal criminal cases be tried by a jury in the state and district in which the offense was committed. There has been, however, much debate over the question of whether the jury must be drawn from the "vicinage" or neighborhood of the crime. In the broadest sense the word "vicinage" means neighborhood, and "vicinage of the jury" means jury of the neighborhood or, as it was held in medieval England, jury of the county where the act occurred.[55]

Madison offered an early provision to the amendment that provided and protected the vicinage principle. In this sense a jury would have been chosen only from the county or similar "neighborhood" from which the crime was committed. The language was rebuffed by the Senate, and the present language was adopted as a compromise. From a legal standpoint, the provisions limit the federal government only, and require that the jury be chosen from the district being served.[56] In modern practice the vicinage has been expanded to mean more than the neighborhood but does not expand so much as to allow jurors from outside the district to be chosen.

ENDNOTES

1. W. Blackstone, Commentaries on the Laws of England 349–350 (T. Cooley 4th ed. 1896).
2. Art. III, Sec. 2.
3. Duncan v. Louisiana, 391 U.S. 145, 153 (1968).
4. Duncan v. Louisiana, 391 U.S. 145, 158–59 (1968).
5. Singer v. United States, 380 U.S. 24 (1965).
6. Patton v. United States, 281 U.S. 276, 288 (1930).
7. Thompson v. Utah, 170 U.S. 343 (1898).
8. Callan v. Wilson, 127 U.S. 540 (1888).
9. 399 U.S. 78 (1970).

10. *Id.* at 99–103.
11. Apodaca v. Oregon, 406 U.S. 404 (1972).
12. Apodaca v. Oregon, 406 U.S. 404, 413–14 (1972).
13. District of Columbia v. Clawans, 300 U.S. 617 (1937); Schick v. United States, 195 U.S. 65 (1904); Callan v. Wilson, 127 U.S. 540 (1888).
14. District of Columbia v. Colts, 282 U.S. 63 (1930).
15. Duncan v. Louisiana, 391 U.S. 145, 159–62 (1968); Dyke v. Taylor Implement Mfg. Co., 391 U.S. 216 (1968).
16. Baldwin v. New York, 399 U.S. 66, 69 (1970).
17. United States v. Zucker, 161 U.S. 475, 481 (1896).
18. Kennedy v. Mendoza-Martinez, 372 U.S. 144 (1963).
19. 391 U.S. 194, 198 (1968).
20. McKeiver v. Pennsylvania, 403 U.S. 528 (1971).
21. Hildwin v. Florida, 490 U.S. 638, 640–41 (1989) (per curiam) ("the Sixth Amendment does not require that the specific findings authorizing the imposition of the sentence of death be made by the jury"); Clemons v. Mississippi, 494 U.S. 738 (1990) (appellate court may reweigh aggravating and mitigating factors and uphold imposition of death penalty even though jury relied on an invalid aggravating factor); Walton v. Arizona, 497 U.S. 639 (1990) (judge may make requisite findings as to existence of aggravating and mitigating circumstances).
22. Irvin v. Dowd, 366 U.S. 717 (1961); Turner v. Louisiana, 379 U.S. 466 (1965); Parker v. Gladden, 385 U.S. 363 (1966).
23. Strauder v. West Virginia, 100 U.S. 303 (1880); Alexander v. Louisiana, 405 U.S. 625 (1972).
24. Turner v. Louisiana, 379 U.S. 466 (1965).
25. Williams v. Florida, 399 U.S. 78, 100 (1970); Brown v. Allen, 344 U.S. 443, 474 (1953).
26. Duren v. Missouri, 439 U.S. 357, 364 (1979).
27. Taylor v. Louisiana, 419 U.S. 522 (1975).
28. Duren v. Missouri, 439 U.S. 357 (1979).
29. 430 U.S. 482 (1977).
30. Frazier v. United States, 335 U.S. 497 (1948); Dennis v. United States, 339 U.S. 162 (1950).
31. 350 U.S. 377 (1956).
32. 455 U.S. 209 (1982).
33. 421 U.S. 794 (1975).
34. Remmer v. United States, 347 U.S. 227 (1954).
35. 379 U.S. 466 (1965).
36. Irvin v. Dowd, 366 U.S. 717 (1961) (felony); Groppi v. Wisconsin, 400 U.S. 505 (1971) (misdemeanor).
37. Frank v. Mangum, 237 U.S. 309 (1915); Irvin v. Dowd, 366 U.S. 717 (1961); Sheppard v. Maxwell, 384 U.S. 333 (1966).
38. 391 U.S. 510 (1968).
39. *Id.* at 519, 521, 523.
40. Morgan v. Illinois, 112 S. Ct. 2222 (1992).
41. Wainwright v. Witt, 469 U.S. 412, 424 (1985), quoting Adams v. Texas, 448 U.S. 38, 45 (1980).
42. Wainwright v. Witt, 469 U.S. at 424.

43. Lewis v. United States, 146 U.S. 370 (1892); Pointer v. United States, 151 U.S. 396 (1894).
44. Reynolds v. United States, 98 U.S. 145 (1879).
45. Stilson v. United States, 250 U.S. 583, 586 (1919).
46. 380 U.S. 202 (1965).
47. 476 U.S. 79 (1986).
48. Powers v. Ohio, 499 U.S. 400 (1991) (defendant has standing to raise equal protection rights of excluded juror of different race).
49. 493 U.S. 474 (1990).
50. *Id.* at 484.
51. Ross v. Oklahoma, 487 U.S. 81, 88 (1987).
52. Georgia v. McCollum, 112 S. Ct. 2348 (1992).
53. *Id.* at 2358.
54. *Id.* at 2358–59.
55. W. Blackstone, Commentaries on the Laws of England 350–351 (T. Cooley 4th ed. 1899).
56. Nashville, C. & St. L. Ry. v. Alabama, 128 U.S. 96, 101 (1888).

23 Right of Notification and Confrontation

I. NOTICE OF ACCUSATION

Today we take for granted that criminal indictments and charges are specific in nature, but that has not always been the case. During the Middle Ages and for some time thereafter it was not a requirement that a criminal allegation be specific as to time, place, and manner of the accused crime. Over the centuries, however, this has changed. Today we enjoy a system that requires, under the Constitution, that all criminal accusations be specific.

The constitutional right to be informed of the nature and cause of the accusation serves many purposes. Most obvious is the ability to accurately track a case as it makes its way through the system. The court and the parties are entitled to the knowledge that this case is proceeding because of certain factual and legal allegations.

The constitutional mandate also entitles the defendant to insist that the indictment apprise him or her of the crime charged with such reasonable certainty that he or she can make a defense. Imagine for a moment what kind of defense one would be able to mount if he or she only knew the charge was a felony-level crime. Without knowledge as to the specifics of the crime, such as the time, location, and specific acts alleged, the defendant would be unable to mount any defense.

Another reason for the constitutional mandate is that it allows a defendant to protect himself or herself after judgment against another prosecution on the same charge.[1] This right closely intertwines with the constitutional prohibition against being held accountable for the same act twice.

No indictment is sufficient if it does not allege all of the ingredients that constitute the crime. The first of these deals with the elements of the crime itself, and the Court has held that an indictment or information is fully descriptive of the offense if it merely follows the statutory phraseology.[2] In this sense an indictment or information will sustain constitutional scrutiny if it alleges those acts which are prohibited by the statute in question.

The facts necessary to bring the case within the statutory definition must also be alleged.[3] To this end the allegations must be such that a reasonable person will be able to ascertain the time, place, and manner of the acts charged. An indictment that does not contain such allegations is defective.[4]

The Constitution does not require the government to furnish a copy of the indictment to an accused, but most jurisdictions do provide that.[5] It is sufficient that the court read the charges to a defendant, and it is practice that all indictments or information be on file — as public record — with the clerk of the court. However, for practical purposes most courts provide the defendant a photocopy of the charges against the defendant so that the defendant may read the allegations. Should the defendant require that they be read to him or her, then a court should comply with such a request.

The right to notice of accusation is so fundamental a part of procedural due process that the states are required to observe it.[6] Failure to follow these provisions will trigger the protections found within the Sixth Amendment and the progeny of cases arising therefrom.

II. CONFRONTATION

One of the stronger provisions of the Sixth Amendment is the right of the accused to confront his or her accuser(s). The primary objective of this constitutional provision is to prevent derogatory ex parte actions.[7] The ex parte action prevents the defendant from presenting mitigating evidence or from cross-examination of the witness.

The right of confrontation is "[o]ne of the fundamental guarantees of life and liberty...long deemed so essential for the due protection of life and liberty that it is guarded against legislative and judicial action by provisions in the Constitution of the United States and in the constitutions of most if not of all the States composing the Union."[8]

One of the factors leading to this right was the need to guard against unreasonable prejudice created when one side is allowed virtually unchallenged opportunity to present material against the other. A primary concern was the control of hearsay testimony.

Hearsay testimony, for our purposes, is the statement made out of court by a potential witness which is then repeated in court, as testimony, by another person who has no personal knowledge of the events. In this sense, a witness to an act may tell a friend or neighbor what he or she saw, and the friend or neighbor is called to testify. By allowing the friend or neighbor to testify there is no reasonable grounds for testing the validity of the statements made or the alleged events testified about.

In a series of decisions beginning in 1965, the Court seemed to equate the Confrontation Clause with the hearsay rule, positing that a major purpose of the clause was "to give the defendant charged with crime an opportunity to cross-examine the witnesses against him," unless one of the hearsay exceptions applies.[9] In *Douglas v. Alabama*[10] the prosecution called as a witness the defendant's alleged accomplice, and when the accomplice refused to testify — pleading his privilege against self-incrimination — the prosecutor read to him to "refresh" his memory a confession in which he implicated the defendant. Because the defendant could not cross-examine the accomplice with regard to the truth of the confession, the Court held the Confrontation Clause had been violated.

In *Bruton v. United States*[11] defendants were tried together in one trial. At the trial the court allowed the use of a confession made by one of the defendants, but such use was held to violate the confrontation rights of the other defendant. The grounds for such ruling was that the second defendant was effectively denied his right of confrontation and the ability to cross-examine the codefendant who refused to take the stand. The Court continues to view as "presumptively unreliable accomplices' confessions that incriminate defendants."[12]

More recently, however, the Court has moved away from these cases. "While...hearsay rules and the Confrontation Clause are generally designed to protect similar values it is quite a different thing to suggest that the overlap is complete and that the Confrontation Clause is nothing more or less than a codification of the rules of hearsay and their exceptions as they existed historically at common law." In further explaining their ruling the Court stated that "Our decisions have never established such a congruence; indeed, we have more than once found a violation of confrontation values even though the statements in issue were admitted under an arguably recognized hearsay exception.... The converse is equally true: merely because evidence is admitted in violation of a long-established hearsay rule does not lead to the automatic conclusion that confrontation rights have been denied."[13]

In *California v. Green*[14] the Supreme Court upheld the use of two prior statements made by a witness who claimed at the trial that he had been under the influence of LSD at the time of the statements. The witness stated that because of his drugged condition he could neither deny nor affirm the truth of his prior statements. In upholding the use of the statements the Court noted that the defendant had given at least one of the statements while under oath at preliminary hearing. The fact that the defendant was present at the hearing, represented by counsel, and able to cross-examine at that time was sufficient to allow the introduction of the statement at later trial. "[T]he Confrontation Clause does not require excluding from evidence the prior statements of a witness who concedes making the statements, and who may be asked to defend or otherwise explain the inconsistency between his prior and his present version of the events in question, thus opening himself to full cross-examination at trial as to both stories."[15]

In the absence of prosecutorial misconduct or negligence and where the evidence is not "crucial" or "devastating," the Confrontation Clause is satisfied if the circumstances of presentation of out-of-court statements are such that "the trier of fact [has] a satisfactory basis for evaluating the truth of the [hearsay] statement," and this is to be ascertained in each case by focusing on the reliability of the proffered hearsay statement. This means that an inquiry into the likelihood that cross-examination of the declarant at trial could successfully call into question the declaration's apparent meaning or the declarant's sincerity, perception, or memory.[16]

In *Ohio v. Roberts*[17] the Court explained that it had construed the clause "in two separate ways to restrict the range of admissible hearsay." First, there is a rule of "necessity," under which, in the usual case, "the prosecution must either produce, or demonstrate the unavailability of, the declarant whose statement it wishes to use against the defendant." Second, "once a witness is shown to be unavailable..., the Clause countenances only hearsay marked with such trustworthiness that 'there is no material departure from the reason of the general rule.'"

In this sense, if the hearsay declarant is not present for cross-examination at trial, the "statement is admissible only if it bears adequate 'indicia of reliability.' Reliability can be inferred without more in a case where the evidence falls within a firmly rooted hearsay exception. In other cases, the evidence must be excluded, at least absent a showing of particularized guarantees of trustworthiness."[18]

This standard has been narrowed over the years, and the Court has held that the rule of "necessity" is confined to use of testimony from a prior judicial proceeding, and is inapplicable to co-conspirators' out-of-court statements.[19] The Court has ruled that a co-conspirator's out-of-court statement, especially one made "while the conspiracy is in progress," have "independent evidentiary significance of [their] own."[20] This means that in-court testimony is not a necessary or valid substitute.

Other exceptions to the hearsay rule may also apply. For example, in the federal courts and many state courts a spontaneous declaration, usually known as an excited utterance, may be admissible as a hearsay exception and is not violative of the Sixth Amendment. Similarly, statements made for medical treatment are not barred from trial by the Confrontation Clause.[21]

Contrasting approaches to the Confrontation Clause were taken by the Court in two cases involving state efforts to protect child sex crime victims from trauma while testifying. In *Coy v. Iowa*[22] the Court held that the right of confrontation is violated by a procedure, authorized by statute, placing a one-way screen between complaining child witnesses and the defendant, thereby sparing the witnesses from viewing the defendant. This conclusion was reached although the witnesses could be viewed by the defendant's counsel and by the judge and jury, and despite the fact that the right of cross-examination was in no way limited.

In this type of case the state asserts a strong interest in protecting the child sex-abuse victim from further trauma. The Court's opinion, written by Justice Scalia, declared that a defendant's right during trial to face-to-face confrontation with his or her accusers derives from "the irreducible literal meaning of the clause," and traces "to the beginnings of Western legal culture."[23]

Coy's interpretation of the clause, but not its result, was rejected in *Maryland v. Craig*.[24] In *Craig* the Court upheld Maryland's use of one-way, closed-circuit television to protect a child witness in a sex crime from viewing the defendant. As in *Coy*, procedural protections other than confrontation were afforded: the child witness must testify under oath, is subject to cross-examination, and is viewed by the judge, jury, and defendant.

The critical factual difference between the two cases was that Maryland required a case-specific finding that the child witness would be traumatized by presence of the defendant, while the Iowa procedures struck down in *Coy* rested on a statutory presumption of trauma. But the difference in approach is best explained by the fact that Justice O'Connor's views, expressed in a concurring opinion in *Coy*, became the opinion of the Court in *Craig*.

Beginning with the proposition that the Confrontation Clause does not, as evidenced by hearsay exceptions, grant an absolute right to face-to-face confrontation, the Court in *Craig* described the clause as "reflect[ing] a preference for face-to-face confrontation."[25] This preference can be overcome "only where denial of such confrontation is necessary to further an important public policy and only where the reliability of the testimony is otherwise assured."[26]

Another important distinction is the method used in each case. In *Coy* the defendant was denied the "face to face" confrontation by the partition. In *Craig* the defendant in fact could see the face of the witness/victim as testimony was taken. The use of the closed-circuit television system allowed the defendant the right to see the accuser while still shielding the witness from the potential trauma in facing the alleged attacker.

It must also be pointed out that the Court in *Craig* also relied on the traditional and "transcendent" state interest in protecting the welfare of children, on the significant number of state laws designed to protect child witnesses, and on "the growing body of academic literature documenting the psychological trauma suffered by child abuse victims."[27] These factors continue to be used by the courts in weighing such issues today.

In another case involving child sex crime victims, the Court held that there is no right of face-to-face confrontation at an in-camera (in chambers) hearing to determine the competency of a child victim to testify. In *Kentucky v. Stincer*[28] the Court held that such a hearing does not prevent the "full and effective" opportunity to cross-examine the witness at trial, and as such would not violate the protections of the Sixth Amendment.

III. COMPULSORY PROCESS

The term "compulsory process" describes the ability of a defendant to compel witnesses to appear and testify at trial.[29] The introduction of the provision into the Sixth Amendment also made inapplicable at federal trials the common-law rule that in cases of treason or felony the accused was not allowed to introduce witnesses in his or her defense.[30] "The right to offer the testimony of witnesses, and to compel their attendance, if necessary, is in plain terms the right to present a defense, the right to present the defendant's version of the facts as well as the prosecution's to the jury so it may decide where the truth lies."[31]

Just as an accused has the right to confront the prosecution's witnesses for the purpose of challenging their testimony, the accused has the right to present his or her own witnesses to establish a defense. This right is a fundamental element of due process of law and is applicable to states by way of the Fourteenth Amendment. The right is violated by a state law providing that coparticipants in the same crime could not testify for one another.

This does not mean that the right to present witnesses is absolute. A court may limit the use of witnesses when the defendant has failed to comply with pretrial orders for disclosure of witnesses.[32] Similarly, a court may exclude witnesses whose testimony would be cumulative when added to the testimony of other witnesses.

ENDNOTES

1. United States v. Cruikshank, 92 U.S. 542, 544, 558 (1876); United States v. Simmons, 96 U.S. 360 (1878); Bartell v. United States, 227 U.S. 427 (1913); Burton v. United States, 202 U.S. 344 (1906).
2. Potter v. United States, 155 U.S. 438, 444 (1894).
3. United States v. Carll, 105 U.S. 611 (1882).
4. United States v. Cook, 84 U.S. (17 Wall.) 168, 174 (1872).
5. United States v. Van Duzee, 140 U.S. 169, 173 (1891).

6. In re Oliver, 333 U.S. 257, 273 (1948); Cole v. Arkansas, 333 U.S. 196, 201 (1948); Rabe v. Washington, 405 U.S. 313 (1972).
7. Mattox v. United States, 156 U.S. 237, 242–43 (1895).
8. Kirby v. United States, 174 U.S. 47, 55, 56 (1899). Cf. Pointer v. Texas, 380 U.S. 400, 404–05 (1965). The right may be waived, but it must be a knowing, intelligent waiver uncoerced from defendant. Brookhart v. Janis, 384 U.S. 1 (1966).
9. Pointer v. Texas, 380 U.S. 400, 406–07 (1965).
10. 380 U.S. 415 (1965).
11. 391 U.S. 123 (1968).
12. Lee v. Illinois, 476 U.S. 530, 541 (1986).
13. California v. Green, 399 U.S. 149, 155–56 (1970); Dutton v. Evans, 400 U.S. 74, 80–86 (1970). Compare id. at 93, 94, 95 (Justice Harlan concurring), with id. at 100, 105 n.7 (Justice Marshall dissenting). See also United States v. Inadi, 475 U.S. 387 (1986).
14. 399 U.S. 149 (1970).
15. Id. at 164.
16. Dutton v. Evans, 400 U.S. 74 (1970).
17. 448 U.S. 56 (1980).
18. Id. at 66.
19. United States v. Inadi, 475 U.S. 387 (1986).
20. Id. at 394–95.
21. White v. Illinois, 112 S. Ct. 736, 743 (1992).
22. 487 U.S. 1012 (1988).
23. Id. at 1015, 1021 (1988).
24. 497 U.S. 836 (1990).
25. 497 U.S. at 849.
26. Id. at 850.
27. Id. at 855.
28. 482 U.S. 730, 744 (1987).
29. United States v. Cooper, 4 U.S. (4 Dall.) 341 (C.C. Pa. 1800).
30. See Rosen v. United States, 245 U.S. 467 (1918).
31. Washington v. Texas, 388 U.S. 14, 19–23 (1967).
32. Taylor v. Illinois, 484 U.S. 400 (1988).

24 Assistance of Counsel

I. DEVELOPMENT OF AN ABSOLUTE RIGHT TO COUNSEL AT TRIAL

Exactly where and when the right to counsel developed is not wholly clear. It is known that common law in England did not initially provide for such protection. Surprisingly, the right was denied to anyone charged with a felony but was extended to those charged with a misdemeanor. This practice was later reformed to allow counsel to argue points of law from which the court then generously interpreted the limits of the "legal questions."

The colonial and early state practice in this country varied from jurisdiction to jurisdiction. Many states followed the English model of appointing counsel while others extended the privilege to all cases where counsel could not be retained.

At the same time the Sixth Amendment was being proposed Congress enacted two statutory provisions that recognized the limited need to appoint counsel where the defendant could not afford private counsel.[1] By 1790 this right was extended when Congress enacted new provisions granting to every person indicted for treason or other capital crime an appointed lawyer. In part the statute read "[that] the court before which he is tried, or some judge thereof, shall immediately, upon his request, assign to him such counsel not exceeding two, as he may desire, and they shall have free access to him at all reasonable hours."

Initially the Supreme Court did not address specifically the provisions of counsel under the Sixth Amendment. With the extension of rights through the Congressional mandates the Court found little need to address the amendment in detail. By the early part of the twentieth century, however, the Court found ample cause for expanding the provisions of the amendment, and the ratification of the Fourteenth Amendment following the Civil War prompted application of the amendment to the states.

The real expansion of the amendment began in *Powell v. Alabama*,[2] when the Court set aside the convictions of eight black youths sentenced to death in a hastily carried-out trial without benefit of counsel. Due process, Justice Sutherland said for the Court, always requires the observance of certain fundamental personal rights associated with a hearing, and "the right to the aid of counsel is of this fundamental character."

In addressing the issue, Justice Sutherland wrote: "The right to be heard would be, in many cases, of little avail if it did not comprehend the right to be heard by counsel. Even the intelligent and educated layman has small and sometimes no skill in the science of law."[3]

In addressing the issues of the case the Court noted that the failure to provide the defendants an opportunity to retain counsel violated due process. This was exacerbated by the fact that the Court acknowledged that these defendants, as indigent youths, could not have retained counsel even if given the opportunity. The

Court concluded that, "the necessity of counsel was so vital and imperative that the failure of the trial court to make an effective appointment of counsel was likewise a denial of due process within the meaning of the Fourteenth Amendment."

The Court next addressed the issue in *Johnson v. Zerbst*,[4] when it announced an absolute rule requiring appointment of counsel for federal criminal defendants who could not afford to retain a lawyer. The right to assistance of counsel, Justice Black wrote for the Court, "is necessary to insure fundamental human rights of life and liberty."

The Court distinguished between the right to retain counsel and the right to have counsel provided if the defendant cannot afford to hire a lawyer. The Court stated that "The Sixth Amendment withholds from federal courts, in all criminal proceedings, the power and authority to deprive an accused of his life or liberty unless he has or waives the assistance of counsel."[5]

In addressing the issue of waiver of the right the Court ruled that such waiver must be by the intelligent choice of the defendant, will not be presumed from a silent record, and must be determined by the trial court before proceeding in the absence of counsel.[6] The standards for a valid waiver were tightened in *Walker v. Johnston*,[7] setting aside a guilty plea made without assistance of counsel, by a ruling requiring that a defendant appearing in court be advised of his or her right to counsel and asked whether or not he or she wished to waive the right. The Court strengthened this requirement in later cases.[8]

Early efforts to establish the same rule in the state courts in all criminal proceedings were initially rejected in *Betts v. Brady*.[9] In this case the Court initially held that the Sixth Amendment protections applied in federal court only and that in state courts the due process clause of the Fourteenth Amendment "formulates a concept less rigid and more fluid" than those guarantees embodied in the Bill of Rights. The Court did, however, leave some room for application to the states by suggesting that "special circumstances" surrounding a case may trigger the protections. This standard was not fully examined and was applied on a case-by-case basis rather than in a broad pattern.

Over time the Court abandoned the "special circumstances" language, and in *Hamilton v. Alabama*[10] the Court held that in a capital case a defendant need make no showing of particularized need or of prejudice resulting from absence of counsel; henceforth, assistance of counsel was a constitutional requisite in capital cases. In noncapital cases, developments were such that "the 'special circumstances' rule has continued to exist in form while its substance has been substantially and steadily eroded."[11]

The application of the Sixth Amendment guarantees of counsel were applied to the states through the case of *Gideon v. Wainwright*.[12] In analyzing the protection the Court developed three categories of prejudicial factors, often overlapping in individual cases, which required the furnishing of assistance of counsel. Trial courts were to apply these three categories in determining if the defendant was entitled to appointed counsel.

The first of these categories dealt with the personal characteristics of the defendant.[13] Factors to be considered were the age and maturity of the defendant, the experience of the defendant with the criminal justice system, mental abnormality or competency, and related factors.

The trial courts are also to consider the technical complexity of the charges or of possible defenses to the charges. In this sense the ability of the defendant, or at least the perceived ability of a defendant, to analyze and present complicated defenses is to be considered.[14] This certainly is a valid issue today when we commonly see science take a prominent role in many criminal trials. Issues of DNA, fingerprints, and police procedures may create a unique issue in which the lay defendant is not expected to be knowledgeable.

The final category set forth by the Court examines the events occurring at trial which could raise problems of prejudice.[15] The last characteristic especially had been utilized by the Court to set aside convictions occurring in the absence of counsel.

Against this background, a unanimous Court overruled *Betts v. Brady* and held "that in our adversary system of criminal justice, any person haled into court, who is too poor to hire a lawyer, cannot be assured a fair trial unless counsel is provided for him."[16] In this sense, it appears that any defendant who is without funds to hire an attorney may be appointed counsel provided the Court weighs the particularized issues above.

The Court's opinion in *Gideon* left unanswered the question whether the right to assistance of counsel was claimable by defendants charged with misdemeanors or serious misdemeanors as well as with felonies. Recently that question has been addressed when the Court held that the right applies to any misdemeanor case in which imprisonment is imposed.[17] Like felony cases, the defendant in a misdemeanor may waive his or her right to counsel, but such waiver must also be made in a knowing and voluntary fashion.

The Court has also addressed the issue of court-appointed counsel in juvenile proceedings. The Court held in *In re Gault*[18] and *Specht v. Patterson*[19] that such right exists where the restriction of one's freedom is at jeopardy. While most juvenile proceedings continue to focus on rehabilitation rather than retribution there also remains an opportunity for the courts to deny the youth certain liberty. This interest is strongly protected and warrants the appointment of counsel where the juvenile cannot afford an attorney.

II. PROTECTION OF THE RIGHT TO RETAINED COUNSEL

While the Sixth Amendment provides a guarantee to appointed counsel it also provides protections to the defendant in choosing the counsel he wishes to retain. An early case addressing this issue is *Chandler v. Fretag*,[20] in which a defendant appearing to plead guilty on a low-level felony charge was orally advised, for the first time, that he would also be charged as a "habitual criminal" because of three prior felony convictions. The defendant was informed that if convicted he would be sentenced to life imprisonment. Recognizing the severity of the new charge, the defendant requested a continuance to allow him to retain counsel of his choice. This request was denied by the trial court and the defendant was promptly convicted and sentenced.

In its ruling the Supreme Court held that such action by the trial court was a violation of the defendant's Fourteenth Amendment due process rights. "Regardless of whether [defendant] would have been entitled to the appointment of counsel, his right to be heard through his own counsel was unqualified.... A necessary corollary is that a defendant must be given a reasonable opportunity to employ and consult with counsel; otherwise, the right to be heard by counsel would be of little worth."[21]

III. EFFECTIVE ASSISTANCE OF COUNSEL

The protections of the Sixth Amendment also extend to a right commonly known as the right to "effective assistance of counsel." Almost from the beginning when counsel was appointed to a defendant unable to afford to retain private counsel there have been issues of effective counsel. The major issue is whether the attorney appointed to the defendant was minimally qualified and capable of representing the defendant. This does not mean that the Court will necessarily examine the attorney's abilities as a trial lawyer. Certainly the amendment does not require the government to provide the "best attorney" available to all defendants, but it must provide at least a minimally competent attorney.

One of the primary issues arises when a defendant alleges that his or her counsel was incompetent or not competent enough to provide effective assistance. While the Court touched on the question in earlier cases,[22] it was not until 1984, in *Strickland v. Washington*,[23] that the Court articulated a general test for ineffective assistance of counsel in criminal trials and in capital sentencing proceedings.

The first issue addressed by the test looks at the question of attorney performance. The gauge for measuring the performance of the attorney is an objective standard of reasonableness. From a practical standpoint this standard is relatively low, and even if the attorney appointed does not "specialize" in criminal defense the attorney may still be minimally qualified by virtue of legal education and training.

The reviewing court will also limit its inquiry when it comes to questions of tactics or legal choices. Strategic choices made after thorough investigation of relevant law and facts are "virtually unchallengeable," as are "reasonable" decisions making investigation unnecessary.[24]

In addressing this issue the courts will also look at whether undue prejudice was created by the actions or inaction of the attorney. In order to establish prejudice resulting from attorney error, the defendant "must show that there is a reasonable probability that, but for counsel's unprofessional errors, the result of the proceeding would have been different. A reasonable probability is a probability sufficient to undermine confidence in the outcome."[25] The Court has long held that the appointment must be made in a manner that affords "effective aid in the preparation and trial of the case."[26]

IV. RIGHT TO SELF-REPRESENTATION

The Court has held that the Sixth Amendment, in addition to guaranteeing the right to retained or appointed counsel, also guarantees a defendant the right to represent himself or herself. In some sense this means that a defendant may have a right to defend himself or herself even it means that such representation would be to his or her detriment.

In exercising such right the defendant must waive the right to be represented by counsel knowingly and intelligently. Courts generally go to great lengths to ensure that a defendant is aware of the right to be represented by counsel and that surrendering such right could be detrimental.

Under limited circumstances the trial judge may deny the defendant authority to exercise this right. The most common example arises where the defendant simply lacks the competence to make a knowing or intelligent waiver of counsel. While the defendant may be able to speak the words requesting the right to represent himself or herself, there are instances when such words have no meaning or the defendant truly has no comprehension as to the potential consequences.

Likewise, where a self-represented defendant is so disruptive of orderly procedures, the judge may curtail the right. A defendant who refuses to follow proper court etiquette or rules may be denied the right of self-representation and removed from the courtroom during the trial itself.

The essential elements of self-representation were spelled out in *McKaskle v. Wiggins*.[27] In this case the defendant was allowed to represent himself but was appointed "standby counsel" by the trial court. The Supreme Court held that the core of the right is that the defendant "is entitled to preserve actual control over the case he chooses to present to the jury," and consequently, standby counsel's participation "should not be allowed to destroy the jury's perception that the defendant is representing himself."

In this sense, a trial court may alleviate later appealable issues by allowing a defendant to proceed at trial as a "self-represented" individual, but by appointing "standby" counsel (also known as supplemental counsel and advisory counsel) the court prevents claims of incompetence or denial of counsel. It should be noted that participation of standby counsel, even in the jury's presence and over the defendant's objection, does not violate the defendant's Sixth Amendment rights when serving the basic purpose of aiding the defendant in complying with routine courtroom procedures and protocols. Such acts relieve the trial judge of these tasks and promote effective trials.

V. RIGHT TO ASSISTANCE OF COUNSEL IN NONTRIAL SITUATIONS

A. JUDICIAL PROCEEDINGS BEFORE TRIAL

In earlier sections we established a clear right to counsel for trial proceedings, but what about the pretrial issues and pitfalls that await the criminal defendant? Does the right to assistance of counsel apply at the pretrial stage? And, if so, then at what stage is a defendant entitled to have counsel represent him or her?

The Supreme Court addressed this issue, though in dicta, in the case of *Powell v. Alabama*.[28] In pertinent part the Court stated that: "during perhaps the most critical period of the proceedings... that is to say, from the time of their arraignment until the beginning of their trial, when consultation, thoroughgoing investigation and preparation [are] vitally important, the defendants... [are] as much entitled to such aid [of counsel] during that period as at the trial itself."

This language has gradually been expanded to create a concept commonly referred to as the "a critical stage" requirement. This means that a defendant is entitled to the assistance of counsel at all stages that might be considered critical to the defense. For example, in *Hamilton v. Alabama*[29] the defendant was said to face such a critical stage as early as arraignment where state law required the defense of "insanity" to be pleaded at that stage or potentially be lost.

In *Coleman v. Alabama*[30] the Court held that the preliminary hearing is a "critical stage" necessitating counsel although the only functions of the hearing were to determine probable cause and to review the setting of bail. In *Coleman* the Court recognized that although no defense was required, and that little — if anything — done at that stage would be held against the defendant, a lawyer might, by skilled examination and cross-examination, expose weaknesses in the prosecution's case and thereby save the defendant from being bound over. Thus, a defendant would shed the burden of trial. Likewise, an attorney would arguably be adept at using this stage for discovery or other pretrial maneuvering.

Today, in most jurisdictions, it is recognized that even the earliest stages of a criminal case can represent, under the right conditions, a critical stage to a defendant. As such, many jurisdictions have in place safeguards designed to advise the accused of his or her Sixth Amendment right to counsel as well as to provide counsel when necessary.

B. Pre-Charge Issues: Custodial Interrogation

The Sixth Amendment extends the right to counsel beyond both trial and pretrial matters. One of the areas most affected by this right has to do with custodial interrogation. A custodial interrogation, as we have seen in our discussion of Fifth Amendment material, occurs when the police restrict the freedom of movement of the accused for the purposes of questioning. The most common example is the detention of an accused, transportation to the police station, and subsequent interrogation behind closed doors at the station.

Initially the Court addressed the right to counsel under the rule of "fundamental fairness." This meant that a court would assess whether, under all the circumstances of the case, a defendant was so prejudiced by the denial of access to counsel that his or her subsequent trial was tainted.[31] In some sense the rule held that if there was no injury to defendant because of the denial of counsel then there was no right to counsel. The Court further addressed this issue in later cases.

In *Spano v. New York*[32] the Court addressed the issue in post-indictment interrogations. In *Spano* the defendant, following indictment for criminal acts, was held and interrogated by police. Defendant was denied access to his attorney, and the Court held that under the totality of circumstances a confession obtained in such fashion was involuntary.

The protection was later extended to pre-indictment interrogations in *Escobedo v. Illinois*.[33] Escobedo, a 22-year-old of Mexican extraction, was arrested with his sister and taken to police headquarters for interrogation in connection with the fatal shooting of his brother-in-law about 11 days before. He had been arrested shortly after the shooting, but had made no statement, and he was released after his lawyer obtained a writ of habeas corpus from a state court. Upon his second arrest Escobedo made several requests to see his lawyer, who, although present in the building, and despite persistent efforts, was refused access to his client. Escobedo also was not advised by the police of his right to remain silent and, after persistent questioning by the police, made a damaging statement to an Assistant State's Attorney, which was admitted at the trial.

Escobedo appealed the conviction to the Illinois Supreme Court, but his conviction was affirmed. He then took his appeal to the U.S. Supreme Court, alleging violations of both his Sixth and Fourteenth Amendment rights. The Supreme Court set aside the conviction.

In analyzing the case the Court held that the "interrogation here was conducted before petitioner was formally indicted. But in the context of this case, that fact should make no difference." In this language the Court established language indicating that, under certain circumstances, the Sixth Amendment would apply to pre-indictment custodial interrogations.

The Court also looked at the particular facts of the case for clues to constitutional violations. A significant issue was the fact that Escobedo had been denied his right to an attorney although his attorney was in the building. Likewise, the Court found it significant that the investigation had focused on Escobedo as a suspect rather than a general witness. "Petitioner had become the accused, and the purpose of the interrogation was to 'get him' to confess his guilt despite his constitutional right not to do so."

The Court also analyzed what a holding extending the protections of the Sixth Amendment to pre-indictment confessions might do. "It is argued that if the right to counsel is afforded prior to indictment, the number of confessions obtained by the police will diminish significantly, because most confessions are obtained during the period between arrest and indictment, and 'any lawyer worth his salt will tell the suspect in no uncertain terms to make no statement to police under any circumstances.'"[34]

In overturning Escobedo's conviction the Court effectively set forth specific guidelines for applying the Sixth Amendment to pre-indictment custodial interrogations. First, where an investigation focuses on a particular suspect, rather than being a general investigation, the right to counsel and to remain silent may apply. Second, where a defendant has requested counsel, even at the earliest stages of an investigation, then the Sixth Amendment right to counsel may apply. Third, a confession may not be used where a defendant's Sixth Amendment rights have been violated to gain the confession.

It must be noted that the protections enunciated in *Escobedo* were strengthened in *Miranda v. Arizona*,[35] although the emphasis shifted from the Sixth Amendment to the Fifth Amendment's self-incrimination clause. *Miranda* placed great emphasis upon police warnings with regard to counsel and foreclosure of interrogation in the absence of counsel without a valid waiver by defendant, and established the standard applied to today's police interrogations.

The protections of the Sixth Amendment were expanded again in *Brewer v. Williams*.[36] This case is commonly referred to as the "Christian Burial Confession" and involves police interrogation following an initial criminal arraignment.

On Christmas Eve in 1968, a ten-year-old girl named Pamela Powers went with her family to the YMCA in Des Moines, Iowa, to watch a wrestling tournament in which her brother was participating. At one point the girl went to the restroom by herself and did not return. A search was begun, but it was unsuccessful.

Robert Williams, who had recently escaped from a mental hospital, was a resident of the YMCA. Soon after the girl's disappearance, Williams was seen in the YMCA lobby carrying some clothing and a large bundle wrapped in a blanket. He obtained help from a 14-year-old boy in opening the street door of the YMCA and the door to his automobile parked outside. When Williams placed the bundle in the front seat of his car the boy "saw two legs in it and they were skinny and white." Before anyone else could see what was in the bundle Williams drove away.

His abandoned car was found the following day in Davenport, Iowa, roughly 160 miles east of Des Moines. A warrant was then issued in Des Moines for his arrest on a charge of abduction.

On the morning of December 26, a Des Moines lawyer named Henry McKnight went to the Des Moines police station and informed the officers present that he had just received a long-distance call from Williams, and that he had advised Williams to turn himself in to the Davenport police. Williams did surrender that morning to the police in Davenport, and they booked him on the charge specified in the arrest warrant and gave him the warnings required by *Miranda v. Arizona*.

The Davenport police then telephoned their counterparts in Des Moines to inform them that Williams had surrendered. McKnight, the lawyer, was still at the Des Moines police headquarters, and Williams conversed with McKnight on the telephone. In the presence of the Des Moines chief of police and a police detective named Leaming, McKnight advised Williams that Des Moines police officers would be driving to Davenport to pick him up, that the officers would not interrogate him or mistreat him, and that Williams was not to talk to the officers about Pamela Powers until after consulting with McKnight upon his return to Des Moines.

As a result of these conversations, it was agreed between McKnight and the Des Moines police officials that Detective Leaming and a fellow officer would drive to Davenport to pick up Williams, that they would bring him directly back to Des Moines, and that they would not question him during the trip.

Williams was arraigned and committed to jail in Davenport, Iowa. Detective Leaming and his fellow officer arrived in Davenport about noon to pick up Williams and return him to Des Moines. Soon after their arrival they met with Williams and a Davenport lawyer who, they understood, was acting as Williams' attorney in Davenport. Detective Leaming repeated the Miranda warnings, and told Williams: "[W]e both know that you're being represented here by Mr. Kelly and you're being represented by Mr. McKnight in Des Moines, and...I want you to remember this because we'll be visiting between here and Des Moines."

Williams then conferred again with the Davenport lawyer alone, and after this conference the lawyer reiterated to Detective Leaming that Williams was not to be questioned about the disappearance of Pamela Powers until after he had consulted with McKnight back in Des Moines.[37] When Leaming expressed some reservations, the lawyer firmly stated that the agreement with McKnight, the Des Moines lawyer, was to be carried out — that there was to be no interrogation of Williams during the automobile journey to Des Moines. The Davenport lawyer even requested to be allowed to ride along with police, but he was denied permission.

The two detectives, with Williams in their charge, then set out on the 160-mile drive from Davenport to Des Moines. During the trip Detective Leaming made several attempts to engage Williams in conversation and, in each case, turned the topic to the missing girl. Each time, however, Williams refused to converse with the detective, and stated, "[w]hen I get to Des Moines and see Mr. McKnight, I am going to tell you the whole story."

Detective Leaming knew that Williams was a former mental patient, and he also knew that Williams was deeply religious. The detective successfully engaged the captive Williams in a wide-ranging conversation covering a variety of topics, including the subject of religion. Soon, the detective delivered what has been referred to in the briefs and oral arguments as the "Christian burial speech." Addressing Williams as "Reverend," the detective said:

> I want to give you something to think about while we're traveling down the road.... Number one, I want you to observe the weather conditions, it's raining, it's sleeting, it's freezing, driving is very treacherous, visibility is poor, it's going to be dark early this evening. They are predicting several inches of snow for tonight, and I feel that you yourself are the only person that knows where this little girl's body is, that you yourself have only been there once, and if you get a snow on top of it you yourself may be unable to find it. And, since we will be going right past the area on the way into Des Moines, I feel that we could stop and locate the body, that the parents of this little girl should be entitled to a Christian burial for the little girl who was snatched away from them on Christmas [E]ve and murdered. And I feel we should stop and locate it on the way in rather than waiting until morning and trying to come back out after a snow storm and possibly not being able to find it at all.[38]

Williams asked Detective Leaming why he thought their route to Des Moines would be taking them past the girl's body, and Leaming responded that he knew the body was in the area of Mitchellville — a town they would be passing on the way to Des Moines. Leaming then stated: "I do not want you to answer me. I don't want to discuss it any further. Just think about it as we're riding down the road."

As the car approached Grinnell, a town approximately 100 miles west of Davenport, Williams asked whether the police had found the victim's shoes. When Detective Leaming replied that he was unsure, Williams directed the officers to a service station where he said he had left the shoes; a search for them proved unsuccessful. As they continued toward Des Moines, Williams asked whether the police had found the blanket, and directed the officers to a rest area where he said he had disposed of the blanket. Nothing was found. The car continued toward Des Moines, and as it approached Mitchellville, Williams said that he would show the officers where the body was. He then directed the police to the body of Pamela Powers.

Williams was tried and convicted of murder, over his objections to the admission of evidence relating to or resulting from any statements he made during the automobile ride, and the Iowa Supreme Court affirmed, holding, as did the trial court, that respondent had waived his constitutional right to the assistance of counsel. Williams then petitioned for habeas corpus in Federal District Court, which held that the evidence in question had been wrongly admitted at respondent's trial on the ground, inter alia, that Williams had been denied his constitutional right to the assistance of counsel, and further ruled that he had not waived that right. The Court of Appeals affirmed, and the State appealed.

In affirming the appeals court's actions in overturning Williams' conviction the Supreme Court stated: "The crime of which Williams was convicted was senseless and brutal, calling for swift and energetic action by the police to apprehend the perpetrator and gather evidence with which he could be convicted. No mission of law enforcement officials is more important. Yet '[d]isinterested zeal for the public good does not assure either wisdom or right in the methods it pursues.'"[39]

The Court further stated that, "The pressures on state executive and judicial officers charged with the administration of the criminal law are great, especially when the crime is murder and the victim a small child. But it is precisely the predictability of those pressures that makes imperative a resolute loyalty to the guarantees that the Constitution extends to us all." In this sense the Court clearly acknowledges that some factual situations may encourage law enforcement to cut corners, but it likewise discourages such practice.

The Sixth Amendment protections have also been expanded to protect an accused where the government acts through a non-law enforcement agent. In *United States v. Henry*[40] government agents violated the Sixth Amendment right to counsel when they contacted the cellmate of an indicted defendant and promised him payment under a contingent fee arrangement if he would "pay attention" to incriminating remarks initiated by the defendant and others. The Court concluded that even if the government agents did not intend the informant to take affirmative steps to elicit incriminating statements from the defendant the agents must have known that result would follow.

C. Lineups and Other Identification Situations

The concept of the "critical stage" was expanded to include police lineups in *United States v. Wade*[41] and *Gilbert v. California*.[42] The Court held that an in-court identification of defendants based on out-of-court lineups is inadmissible when a defendant has been denied counsel at the lineup. The Sixth Amendment guarantee, said Justice Brennan in his opinion, was intended to do away with the common-law limitation of assistance of counsel.

When the Bill of Rights was adopted there were no organized police forces as we know them today. The accused confronted the prosecutor and the witnesses against him and the evidence was marshalled, largely at the trial itself. In contrast, today's law enforcement machinery involves critical confrontations of the accused by the prosecution at pretrial proceedings where the results might well settle the accused's fate and reduce the trial itself to a mere formality. In recognition of these realities of modern criminal prosecution, our cases have construed the Sixth Amendment guarantee to apply to "critical" stages of the proceedings.... The plain wording of this guarantee thus encompasses counsel's assistance whenever necessary to assure a meaningful "defence."[43]

Initially it was established that counsel's presence at a lineup is constitutionally necessary because the lineup stage is filled with numerous possibilities for errors, both inadvertent and intentional, which cannot adequately be discovered and remedied at trial.[44] However, because there was less certainty and frequency of possible injustice at this stage, the Court held that the two cases were to be given prospective effect only. The Wade-Gilbert rule is inapplicable to other methods of obtaining identification and other evidentiary material relating to the defendant, such as blood samples, handwriting exemplars, and the like, because there is minimal risk that the absence of counsel might derogate from the defendant's right to a fair trial.[45]

The Court redefined and modified its "critical stage" analysis in subsequent cases. According to the Court, the "core purpose" of the guarantee of counsel is to ensure assistance at trial "when the accused was confronted with both the intricacies of the law and the advocacy of the public prosecutor."[46] But assistance would be almost worthless in modern criminal investigation if restricted to the formal trial itself. For that reason the right to counsel is extended to "pretrial events that might appropriately be considered to be parts of the trial itself."[47] Thus, where the pretrial stage involved the physical presence of the accused at a trial-like confrontation "at which the accused requires the guiding hand of counsel," the Sixth Amendment guarantees the assistance of counsel.

The Court curbed, however, its broad requirement of counsel at pretrial events in *Kirby v. Illinois*[48] when it held that no right to counsel existed with respect to lineups that precede some formal act of charging a suspect. The Sixth Amendment does not become operative, explained Justice Stewart's plurality opinion, until "the initiation of adversary judicial criminal proceedings — whether by way of formal charge, preliminary hearings, indictment, information, or arraignment.... The initiation of judicial criminal proceedings is far from a mere formalism."

Justice Stewart further explained that "...it is only then that the Government has committed itself to prosecute, and only then that the adverse positions of Government and defendant have solidified. It is then that a defendant finds himself faced with the prosecutorial forces of organized society, and immersed in the intricacies of substantive and procedural criminal law. It is this point, therefore, that marks the commencement of the 'criminal prosecutions' to which alone the explicit guarantees of the Sixth Amendment are applicable."[49]

In this sense one might argue that the underlying basis for *Miranda v. Arizona* has been left basically unaffected by *Kirby*, but it appears that *Escobedo v. Illinois* and perhaps other cases have been greatly restricted by limiting the Sixth Amendment protections in pretrial proceedings. As we approach the end of the twentieth century it appears that the Court is on a track to further limit the earlier decisions, primarily those from the Court of the 1960s, which expanded Sixth Amendment protections. Just how far such restrictions will go, however, remains to be seen.

D. POST-CONVICTION PROCEEDINGS

As we conclude this section dealing with the Sixth Amendment we close with a look at the right to counsel in post-conviction proceedings. The most obvious of these proceedings is the sentencing stage. It must be noted that some cases proceed directly from findings of guilt to sentencing. However, many felony-level matters require a formal sentencing phase separate from that of the trial. As such, the question arises whether the defendant is entitled to counsel at the formal sentencing phase.

The Supreme Court held in *Townsend v. Burke*[50] that counsel is required at the sentencing stage. The Court did not require counsel in every case; in fact, those who wish to represent themselves have that right throughout the proceeding and including sentencing. In *Townsend*, however, the Court did establish that where a defendant does require assistance of counsel then such should be allowed.

Likewise, the Court has held that a defendant must be afforded counsel at a hearing on revocation of probation and imposition of the deferred sentence.[51] Beyond this stage, however, it would appear that the issue of counsel at hearings on the granting of parole or probation, the revocation of parole that has been imposed following sentencing, and prison disciplinary hearings will be determined according to due process and equal protection standards rather than by further expansion of the Sixth Amendment.[52]

VI. NONCRIMINAL AND INVESTIGATORY PROCEEDINGS

The Sixth Amendment's guarantees of counsel apply to cases that might be considered noncriminal in nature. For instance, certain state administrative investigations may qualify an accused for assistance of counsel. Likewise, proceedings that lead to commitment, which are essentially criminal punishment, may require counsel as well. This type of application was seen in *Specht v. Patterson*.[53]

Specht was convicted of the crime of indecent liberties under a Colorado statute that provided a maximum sentence of ten years, but he was sentenced under the Sex Offenders Act for an indeterminate term of from one day to life imprisonment. Under the act, an accused could be confined if, after a hearing, the trial court found the person had been convicted of a specified crime and that, "if [left] at large, constitutes a threat of bodily harm to members of the public, or is an habitual offender and mentally ill."

The requisite procedure, a complete psychiatric examination and a report thereof given to the trial judge before sentencing, was complied with in this case, but no hearing was held. The defendant challenged his "incarceration" and the State Supreme Court affirmed the procedure. The defendant sought relief through a habeas corpus proceeding, and the Federal District Court dismissed his action. The Court of Appeals affirmed.

The Supreme Court held that the invocation of the act, which entails the making of a new charge leading to criminal punishment, requires, under the due process clause, that petitioner be present with counsel, have an opportunity to be heard, be confronted with witnesses against him or her, have the right to cross-examine and to offer evidence of his or her own, and that there be findings adequate to make meaningful any appeal that is allowed. Because the act authorized long-term detention of the defendant, which in effect was the same as being sent to prison, the Sixth Amendment would apply.

This case, and those that follow the holding, extend the protections of the Sixth Amendment to non-criminal proceedings. As we see in this case, once the Sixth Amendment protections attach it is also common to see other protections to append as well.

ENDNOTES

1. Section 35 of the Judiciary Act of 1789, Ch.20, 1 Stat. 73.
2. 287 U.S. 45 (1932).
3. *Id.* at 68–69.
4. 304 U.S. 458 (1938).
5. *Id.* at 462, 463.
6. *Id.* at 464–465.
7. 312 U.S. 275 (1941).
8. Von Moltke v. Gillies, 332 U.S. 708 (1948); Carnley v. Cochran, 369 U.S. 506 (1962).
9. 316 U.S. 455 (1942).
10. 368 U.S. 52 (1961).
11. Gideon v. Wainwright, 372 U.S. 335, 350 (1963).
12. *Id.*
13. Youth and immaturity (Moore v. Michigan, 355 U.S. 155 (1957); Pennsylvania *ex rel.* Herman v. Claudy, 350 U.S. 116 (1956); Uveges v. Pennsylvania, 335 U.S. 437 (1948); Wade v. Mayo, 334 U.S. 672 (1948); Marino v. Ragen, 332 U.S. 561 (1947); De Meerleer v. Michigan, 329 U.S. 663 (1947)), inexperience (Moore v. Michigan, *supra* (limited education), Uveges v. Pennsylvania, *supra*), and insanity or mental abnormality (Massey v. Moore, 348 U.S. 105 (1954); Palmer v. Ashe, 342 U.S. 134 (1951)), were commonly cited characteristics of the defendant demonstrating the necessity for assistance of counsel.
14. Technicality of the crime charged (Moore v. Michigan, 355 U.S. 155 (1957); Pennsylvania *ex rel.* Herman v. Claudy, 350 U.S. 116 (1956); Williams v. Kaiser, 323 U.S. 471 (1945)), or the technicality of a possible defense (Rice v. Olson, 324 U.S. 786 (1945); McNeal v. Culver, 365 U.S. 109 (1961)).
15. Gibbs v. Burke, 337 U.S. 772 (1949); Townsend v. Burke, 334 U.S. 736 (1948); Palmer v. Ashe, 342 U.S. 134 (1951); White v. Ragen, 324 U.S. 760 (1945); prejudicial developments during the trial (Cash v. Culver, 358 U.S. 633 (1959).
16. *Id.* at 344.
17. Scott v. Illinois, 440 U.S. 367 (1979).
18. 387 U.S. 1 (1967).
19. 386 U.S. 605 (1967).
20. 348 U.S. 3 (1954).
21. *Id.* at 9, 10.
22. McMann v. Richardson, 397 U.S. 759, 768–71 (1970); Tollett v. Henderson, 411 U.S. 258, 266–69 (1973); United States v. Agurs, 427 U.S. 97, 102 n.5 (1976).
23. 466 U.S. 668 (1984).
24. Georgia v. McCollum, 112 S. Ct. 2348 (1992); Nix v. Whiteside, 475 U.S. 157 (1986).

25. 466 U.S. at 694.
26. Powell v. Alabama, 287 U.S. 45, 71–72 (1932); Glasser v. United States, 315 U.S. 60, 70 (1942).
27. 465 U.S. 168 (1984).
28. 287 U.S. 45, 57 (1932).
29. 368 U.S. 52 (1961).
30. 399 U.S. 1 (1970).
31. Crooker v. California, 357 U.S. 433 (1958) (5–4 decision); Cicenia v. Lagay, 357 U.S. 504 (1958) (5–3).
32. 360 U.S. 315 (1959).
33. 378 U.S. 478 (1964).
34. Watts v. Indiana, 338 U.S. 49, 59.
35. 384 U.S. 436 (1966).
36. 430 U.S. 387 (1977).
37. 430 U.S. 387, 392.
38. 430 U.S. 387, 393.
39. *Id.*, quoting Haley v. Ohio, 332 U.S. 596, 605.
40. 447 U.S. 264 (1980).
41. 388 U.S. 218 (1967).
42. 388 U.S. 263 (1967).
43. *Id.* at 226.
44. *Id.* at 227–39.
45. Gilbert v. California, 388 U.S. 263, 265–67 (1967) (handwriting exemplars); Schmerber v. California, 384 U.S. 757, 765–66 (1966) (blood samples).
46. United States v. Ash, 413 U.S. 300 (1973).
47. *Id.* at 309–10.
48. 406 U.S. 682, 689 (1972).
49. *Id.* at 689–90.
50. 334 U.S. 736 (1948).
51. Mempa v. Rhay, 389 U.S. 128 (1967).
52. Wolff v. McDonnell, 418 U.S. 539, 560–70 (1974); Baxter v. Palmigiano, 425 U.S. 308, 314–15 (1976).
53. 386 U.S. 605 (1967).

Section Seven

Eighth Amendment — Further Guarantees in Criminal Cases

Amendment Text

Excessive bail shall not be required, nor excessive fines imposed, nor cruel and unusual punishments inflicted.

25 Excessive Bail

I. INTRODUCTION

The language of the Eighth Amendment has long been controversial. Some hold that it is clear on its face and that the only matters for interpretation lie in the words "excessive," "cruel," and "unusual." The application of "plain language" or "ordinary use" to these words leads one to the meaning of the amendment — or so many would argue. To others, however, these words are only a portion of what is to be interpreted when dealing with this controversial amendment. What intent did the Framers have when constructing the amendment and how should the amendment be applied are two of the many questions faced in today's courts. As we will see in coming paragraphs, the words may be simple but the concepts are not.

II. STANDARDS OF BAIL

The first area that we will address is bail, an issue that received attention almost immediately after the amendment was ratified. From the beginning one can see a quandary created in addressing Eighth Amendment issues. In *Stack v. Boyle*[1] the Court noted: "This traditional right to freedom before conviction permits the unhampered preparation of a defense, and serves to prevent the infliction of punishment prior to conviction.... Unless this right to bail before trial is preserved, the presumption of innocence, secured only after centuries of struggle, would lose its meaning." This statement emphasizes the primary reason for restrictions on bail; however, it does not clearly indicate what excessive bail may be.

Just a few years later in *Bell v. Wolfish*[2] the Court enunciated a narrower view of the presumption of innocence, describing it as "a doctrine that allocates the burden of proof in criminal trials," and denying that it has any "application to a determination of the rights of a pretrial detainee during confinement before his trial has even begun." In this sense, the Court had effectively restricted the protections that it so clearly set forth in *Stack*. From a practical standpoint, this meant that persons claiming protection under the Eighth Amendment would not have a clear standard from which to apply the amendment. Cases following *Stack* and *Bell* focused first on the historical perspectives in seeking protection under the amendment.

As with many of the provisions within our Constitution one can trace concepts of the bail clause to acts in England. Early protections on the right to bail appear just a few years after the Magna Carta. The Statute of Westminster the First of 1275[3] enumerated those offenses which were bailable and those which were not. Although the right to bail was attacked in the coming years, the statute served for more than five centuries.

One of the significant attacks against the right of bail came in 1628 when the right was infringed upon by the Crown. Upon order of the King a judge was permitted to continue imprisonment of a person without bail. In such cases, those who were alleged to have committed acts against the Crown could be held without the right to bail and an opportunity to adequately prepare a defense. This practice was challenged in *Darnel's Case*,[4] and was one of the moving factors in the enactment of the Petition of Right in 1628.[5] It is also of interest that it was Lord Coke, once again, who led the judicial challenge to the Crown's power. Language of the Petition of Right cited provisions of the Magna Carta as proscribing detention of persons as permitted in *Darnel's Case*.

Although bail was guaranteed by the Magna Carta and its progeny, the right was again assaulted a half century later[6] by various technical subterfuges by which petitions for habeas corpus could not be presented. The habeas corpus action was used to challenge the government's right to keep someone without bail, and by limiting its prosecution the Crown effectively limited the right to bail. Parliament reacted by enacting the Habeas Corpus Act of 1679,[7] which established procedures for accomplishing release from imprisonment. The act also provided penalties for judges who did not comply with the act. Thus, the ability to deny bail on offenses otherwise eligible was taken away even when the order for such denial came from the Crown itself.

Unfortunately, when judges found themselves denied an ability to deny bond they merely turned to the tactic of setting bail so high it could not be met. Parliament once again responded by including in the Bill of Rights of 1689[8] a provision "[t]hat excessive bail ought not to be required." This language, along with essentially the rest of the present Eighth Amendment, was included within the Virginia Declaration of Rights,[9] and was picked up in the Virginia recommendations for inclusion in a federal bill of rights by the state ratifying convention.[10]

From a historical standpoint, the wording of the bail clause is often traced to language contained in the English Bill of Rights Act.[11] The language from that act has carried some controversy, but many commentators hold that the clause has never accorded a right to bail in all cases. Instead, the clause provides that bail shall not be excessive in those cases where it is proper to grant bail. Thus, when this clause was carried over into our Bill of Rights nothing appears to indicate that the Framers intended a different concept.[12]

From this historical perspective we can see that the right to bail generally was conferred by the basic statute of 1275, as supplemented, and the procedure for assuring access to the right was conferred by the Habeas Corpus Act of 1679. Protections against abridgement through the fixing of an excessive bail were conferred by the Bill of Right of 1689. These protections were then introduced by Madison during the Constitutional Convention of 1787, and habeas corpus was thereby strengthened in Article I, Section 9, of the Constitution.

While one can trace the concept of excessive bail there remains some question as to the application thereof. The first question to answer in addressing this issue is whether the First Congress knowingly or inadvertently provided only against abridgement of a right which they did not confer or protect in itself or whether the phrase "excessive bail" was meant to be a shorthand expression of both rights. The only recorded comment of a Member of Congress during debate on adoption of the "excessive bail" provision was that of Mr. Livermore, to wit:

The clause seems to express a great deal of humanity, on which account I have no objection to it; but as it seems to have no meaning in it, I do not think it necessary. What is meant by the terms excessive bail? Who are to be judges?[13]

Compounding the ambiguity is a distinctive trend in the U.S. which had its origin in a provision of the Massachusetts Body of Liberties of 1641.[14] The Massachusetts statement guarantees each man bail except those charged with a capital offense or those held for contempt of court. Similar language appears in other state constitutions, including Pennsylvania and Virginia. This guarantee is also contained in the Northwest Ordinance in 1787[15] along with guarantees of moderate fines and against cruel and unusual punishments. Similar language appears in the Judiciary Act of 1789,[16] which was enacted contemporaneously with the passage of the Bill of Rights through Congress. Based on the presence of such provisions throughout both state and federal legislative acts one could conclude that Congress was aware in 1789 that certain language conveyed a right to bail.

Among the various issues related to bail is the long unresolved question of whether "preventive detention" is constitutionally permissible. Such detentions were often used where the court feared that a defendant may, if released from incarceration, flee from prosecution. Likewise, where a defendant is perceived as a danger to the community the court often denied bail as a means of preventative detention. This issue was not fully addressed until Congress authorized the practice in 1984.

Congress first provided for pretrial detention through statutes applied in the District of Columbia.[17] Certain categories of criminal acts and certain "high risk" individuals were denied bail under the act, and it was held constitutional in *United States v. Edwards*.[18] The law applies, however, only to persons charged with violating statutes applicable exclusively in the District of Columbia.[19]

The practice was extended to other federal courts through the Bail Reform Act of 1966.[20] Amendments contained in the Bail Reform Act of 1984 added general preventive detention authority,[21] and authorized pretrial detention for persons charged with certain serious crimes (e.g., crimes of violence, capital crimes, and crimes punishable by ten or more years imprisonment). To invoke the clause the court or magistrate must find that no conditions for release will reasonably assure both the appearance of the person and the safety of others. Detention can also be ordered in other cases where there is a serious risk that the person will flee or that the person will attempt to obstruct justice.

Preventive detention laws have also been adopted in many of the individual states. For instance, Nebraska instituted such a practice which was upheld in *Parker v. Roth*.[22] The Court first tested and upheld under the due process clause of the Fourteenth Amendment a state statute providing for preventive detention of juveniles in *Schall v. Martin*.[23] Then, in *United States v. Salerno*[24] the Court upheld application of preventive detention provisions of the Bail Reform Act of 1984 against facial challenge under the Eighth Amendment.

The function of bail, the Court explained in *Salerno*, is limited neither to preventing flight of the defendant prior to trial nor to safeguarding a court's role in adjudicating guilt or innocence. "[W]e reject the proposition that the Eighth Amendment categorically prohibits the government from pursuing other admittedly compelling interests through regulation of pretrial release."[25] Instead, "the only arguable substantive limitation of the Bail Clause is that the government's proposed conditions of release or detention not be 'excessive' in light of the perceived evil."[26] Detention pending trial of "arrestees charged with serious felonies who are found after an adversary hearing to pose a threat to the safety of individuals or to the community which no condition of release can dispel" satisfies this requirement, the Court held.[27]

In addressing these issues the Court has held that bail is "excessive" and in violation of the Eighth Amendment when it is set at a figure higher than an amount reasonably calculated to ensure the asserted governmental interest.[28] If the only asserted interest is to guarantee that the accused will stand trial and submit to sentence if found guilty, then "bail must be set by a court at a sum designed to ensure that goal, and no more."[29]

From a procedural standpoint one must first challenge bail at the initial hearing before a magistrate. To challenge bail as excessive, one must first move for a reduction in bail at the lowest applicable level. In many instances, this means that the defendant appears again before the magistrate who initially set bail. If the motion for bail reduction is denied then the defendant must move to the next highest level on appeal.

Where an attempt to challenge excessive bail is denied at the trial level then the defendant may press the matter, by appeal, to the higher level. This often means a defendant will seek an appeal, called an interlocutory appeal, through the Court of Appeals. If unsuccessful at this level a defendant may then seek review at the highest level. From a state court this often means the individual state's highest court such as a state Supreme Court. If denied at this level a defendant may choose to pursue the matter through the federal court.

For the defendant charged in a federal district court the first step in challenging excessive bail is much the same as within the state court system. Once the defendant has exhausted his remedy at the trial court level he or she may seek an appeal at the intermediate appellate court for that jurisdiction. Should a defendant be unsuccessful at the Circuit Court of Appeals level then the matter may be appealed to the United States Supreme Court through a Writ of Certiorari.

It appears that the provisions for bail within the amendment are not applicable to post-conviction release. In other words, where an individual has been tried and convicted there are no constitutional provisions regulating right to bail or the issues on amount. The practice of granting an "appeal bond" has been instituted in many states and has been upheld,[30] but the provisions do not necessarily fall under the Eighth Amendment.

ENDNOTES

1. 342 U.S. 1, 4 (1951).
2. 441 U.S. 520, 533 (1979).
3. 3 Edw. 1, Ch. 12.
4. 3 How. St. Tr. 1 (1627).

5. 3 Charles 1, Ch. 1. Debate on the Petition, as precipitated by Darnel's Case, is reported in 3 How. St. Tr. 59 (1628). Coke especially tied the requirement that imprisonment be pursuant to a lawful cause reportable on habeas corpus to effectuation of the right to bail. *Id.* at 69.
6. Jenkes' Case, 6 How. St. Tr. 1189, 36 Eng. Rep. 518 (1676).
7. 31 Charles 2, Ch. 2.
8. I W. & M. 2, Ch. 2, Clause 10.
9. 7 F. Thorpe, The Federal and State Constitutions, H. R. Doc. No. 357, 59th Cong., 2d sess. 3813 (1909). "Sec. 9. That excessive bail ought not to be required, nor excessive fines imposed, nor cruel and unusual punishments inflicted."
10. 3 J. Elliot, The Debates in the Several State Conventions on the Adoption of the Constitution 658 (2d ed. 1836).
11. See discussion in Carlson v. Landon, 342 U.S. 524, 545 (1952).
12. *Id.*
13. 1 Annals of Congress 754 (1789).
14. The language states that "No mans person shall be restrained or imprisoned by any Authority what so ever, before the law hath sentenced him thereto, If he can put in sufficient securtie, bayle, or mainprise, for his appearance, and good behavior in the meane time, unlesse it be in Crimes Capitall, and Contempts in open Court, and in such cases where some expresse act of Court doth allow it."
15. Art. II, 32 Journals of the Continental Congress 334 (1787), reprinted in 1 Stat. 50.
16. 1 Stat. 91 §33 (1789).
17. D.C. Code §§23–1321 *et seq.*
18. 430 A.2d 1321 (D.C. App. 1981), cert. denied, 455 U.S. 1022 (1982).
19. United States v. Thompson, 452 F.2d 1333 (D.C. Cir. 1971), cert. denied, 405 U.S. 998 (1978).
20. 80 Stat. 214, 18 U.S.C. §§3141-56.
21. 18 U.S.C. §3142(d) and (e).
22. 202 Neb. 850, 278 N.W. 2d 106, cert. denied, 444 U.S. 920 (1979).
23. 467 U.S. 253 (1984).
24. 481 U.S. 739 (1988).
25. *Id.* at 753.
26. *Id.* at 754.
27. *Id.* at 755. The Court also ruled that there was no violation of due process, the governmental objective being legitimate and there being a number of procedural safeguards (detention applies only to serious crimes, the arrestee is entitled to a prompt hearing, the length of detention is limited, and detainees must be housed apart from criminals).
28. Stack v. Boyle, 342 U.S. 1, 4–6 (1951).
29. United States v. Salerno, 481 U.S. at 754.
30. Hudson v. Parker, 156 U.S. 277 (1895).

26 Cruel and Unusual Punishments

I. EXCESSIVE FINES

Although the Eighth Amendment clearly contains language preventing excessive fines the Supreme Court had little to say on the topic for years. In a series of early cases the Court held that it had no appellate jurisdiction to revise the sentence of an inferior court even where the record clearly reflected that the fines were excessive.[1]

Where the Supreme Court has addressed the issue it has typically chosen cases involving indigent persons. From a constitutional standpoint, the Court has elected to deal with the issue of fines levied upon indigents, especially those which resulted in imprisonment upon inability to pay, through application of the equal protection clause.[2] Although these cases address, in part, the issue of excessive fines, they do not fully address the issues arising as an Eighth Amendment claim. This means, in essence, that the Court did not fully develop the meaning of "excessive fines" as applied to the person sentenced.

The Eighth Amendment itself, as were antecedents of the clause in the Virginia Declaration of Rights and in the English Bill of Rights of 1689, "clearly was adopted with the particular intent of placing limits on the powers of the new government."[3] However, the meaning of the phrase as applied to the quantum of punishment for any particular offense, independent of the offender's ability to pay, still awaits litigation.

II. STANDARDS FOR CRUEL AND UNUSUAL PUNISHMENT

The restrictions against cruel and unusual punishment have received somewhat greater attention than the other provisions of the Eighth Amendment. One member of Congress, during debate on the amendment, objected to the provisions by noting that:

> No cruel and unusual punishment is to be inflicted; it is sometimes necessary to hang a man, villains often deserve whipping, and perhaps having their ears cut off; but are we in the future to be prevented from inflicting these punishments because they are cruel? If a more lenient mode of correcting vice and deterring others from the commission of it would be invented, it would be very prudent in the Legislature to adopt it; but until we have some security that this will be done, we ought not to be restrained from making necessary laws by any declaration of this kind.[4]

It is clear that physical punishment was considered as appropriate by at least some members of Congress during the ratification process. We also find, from the debates, complaints that an absence of a bill of rights, including a guarantee against cruel and unusual punishments, would be a mistake.[5] And while it is clear that the question of punishment was much on the minds of the Framers, what is unclear is just how far the government may go in inflicting punishment through corporal or other means before it becomes "cruel and unusual."

III. INTERPRETATION OF THE AMENDMENT

Interpretation of the Eighth Amendment has changed somewhat over time. At first, the Court was inclined to a historical style on interpretation where the Justices often looked at the original intention of the Framers or at the type of punishment in question. In many instances, the Court looked at punishment from a historical perspective, i.e., whether the punishment was something used at the time of ratification and thereby easily considered by the Framers.[6]

The issue of historical perspective is most notably addressed in *Weems v. United States*,[7] which applied a historical consideration when measuring punishment. The Court noted first that the Framers had specifically intended to bar techniques that were condemned in 1789. In measuring this issue the Court concluded that the Framers had intended to prevent the authorization of "a coercive cruelty being exercised through other forms of punishment."[8] The Court later held that when measuring cruel or unusual punishment a court "must draw its meaning from the evolving standards of decency that mark the progress of a maturing society."[9]

IV. DEFINING "CRUEL AND UNUSUAL PUNISHMENTS"

One of the major issues raised in any case dealing with punishment is the clear definition of cruel and unusual punishment. While many may agree that some forms of punishment fall within the range of cruel, the question really is just how much punishment is too much. This issue is a subjective one, and the definition cannot be made with exacting science. For that reason we will first determine types of punishments that clearly may be considered cruel before continuing to the more subtle definitions faced by today's courts.

Over the past centuries man has found hundreds of ways to punish his fellow man. Even within the history of the English common law system we see many forms of punishment that were once accepted but now are considered cruel. For example, the practice of "drawing and quartering" was used to punish prisoners against both the Crown and the church. The act literally required the drawing of the individual limbs of the body apart by using four horses. Other punishments included the disembowelling alive, beheading, public dissecting, and burning alive of the accused. To our modern sensibilities these acts seems atrocious, but in their respective times they were considered appropriate punishments for the crimes committed.

In abolishing these types of punishments the Court noted that "difficulty would attend the effort to define with exactness the extent of the constitutional provision which provides that cruel and unusual punishments shall not be inflicted."[10] The Court also stated that it was "safe to affirm that punishment of torture,...and all others in the same line of unnecessary cruelty, are forbidden."[11]

While the above punishments clearly may be held to be cruel other forms of punishment are not as easily discerned. In many instances the Court looks not only at the historical use of the punishment but also at other factors. For instance, in *Pervear v. Commonwealth*[12] the Court, in upholding capital punishment inflicted by a firing squad, not only looked to traditional practices but also examined the history of executions in the territory concerned, the military practice, and current writings on the death penalty.[13] In this instance, at least, one could hold that punishment might be weighed not by a national standard, but when dealing with a frontier territory, and the hazards of life within such a realm, the Court appeared to say that certain punishments would well be tolerated when they might not be elsewhere.

The Court has also used other amendments in answering the question of punishment. In the case of *In re Kemmler*[14] the Court approved the use of electrocution as a permissible method of administering punishment. In this case the Court applied the Fourteenth Amendment's due process clause rather than the Eighth Amendment.

Many years later, a divided Court, assuming the applicability of the Eighth Amendment to the states, held that a second electrocution was not cruel and unusual punishment when applied after a first electrocution failed.[15] What is unique about this case is that the first attempt at electrocution failed due to a mechanical malfunction. Although the condemned man was electrocuted he did not receive enough voltage to cause death. In weighing the issues Justice Frankfurter tested the issue by due process standards.[16]

The question of cruel and unusual punishment has not been limited to capital punishment. In *Trop v. Dulles*[17] the Court considered the divestiture of the citizenship of a natural-born citizen as cruel or unusual. A divided Court held that such action was to be constitutionally forbidden as a penalty more cruel and "more primitive than torture." Four Justices joined the plurality opinion while Justice Brennan concurred on the ground that the requisite relation between the severity of the penalty and legitimate purpose under the war power was not apparent.[18] Four Justices dissented, denying that denationalization was a punishment and arguing instead that it was merely a means by which Congress regulated discipline in the armed forces.[19]

In holding that such punishment violated the Eighth Amendment the Court held the taking away of one's citizenship entailed statelessness and created "the total destruction of the individual's status in organized society."[20] "The question is whether [a] penalty subjects the individual to a fate forbidden by the principle of civilized treatment guaranteed by the Eighth Amendment." The Court held that a punishment must be examined "in light of the basic prohibition against inhuman treatment," and the Eighth Amendment was intended to preserve the "basic concept...[of] the dignity of man" by assuring that the power to impose punishment is "exercised within the limits of civilized standards."[21]

V. SPECIFIC ISSUES IN CAPITAL PUNISHMENT

In an earlier section we examined a few of the capital punishment cases for determining how far punishment may go. That does not indicate, however, that all forms of capital punishment are allowed, nor that there will not be some issues when dealing with capital punishment. In this section we will explore various issues that arise in death penalty cases.

In early cases the Court refused to consider "the death penalty as an index of the constitutional limit on punishment. Whatever the arguments may be against capital punishment...the death penalty has been employed throughout our history, and, in a day when it is still widely accepted, it cannot be said to violate the constitutional concept of cruelty."[22] A coalition of civil rights and civil liberties organizations mounted a campaign against the death penalty in the 1960s, and the Court eventually confronted the issues involved. While these decisions do provide some insight into the issues raised in death penalty cases it is obvious that no clear line has been drawn against which future capital cases may be measured.

Following a series of cases that attacked the means by which the death penalty was imposed[23] the Court entered what appeared to be a decisive rejection of the attacks in *McGautha v. California.*[24] The issues raised in *McGautha* were based on alleged due process violations. The attack focused on the absence of legislative guidance to the sentencing authority and proposed that without such standards the defendant was denied due process. Justice Harlan, writing for the majority, held that standards were not required because, ultimately, it was impossible to define with any degree of specificity which defendant should live and which should die. The Justice added that while bifurcated proceedings might be desirable, they were not required by due process.[25]

Following these procedural attacks opponents turned to Eighth Amendment claims as a means of confronting capital punishment. In a series of cases the Court heard attacks directly raising the question of the validity of capital punishment under the cruel and unusual punishments clause. To the considerable surprise of many, the Court held in *Furman v. Georgia*[26] that the death penalty, at least as administered, did violate the Eighth Amendment, but there was no unifying opinion which would lay down a bright line rule.

In separate concurring opinions, each of the five Justices in the majority approached the matter from a different angle. Two Justices concluded that the death penalty per se was "cruel and unusual" because the imposition of capital punishment "does not comport with human dignity"[27] or because it is "morally unacceptable" and "excessive."[28] One Justice concluded that because death is a penalty inflicted on the poor and hapless defendant but not the affluent and socially better defendant, it violates the implicit requirement of equality of treatment found within the Eighth Amendment.[29] Justices Stewart and White concluded that capital punishment was both "cruel" and "unusual" because it was applied in an arbitrary, "wanton," and "freakish" manner[30] and so infrequently that it served no justifying end.[31]

On the other side of the argument the four Justices who dissented wrote in their opinions that capital punishment was in fact constitutional. In separate opinions the dissenters argued that the Constitution itself recognized capital punishment in the

Fifth and Fourteenth Amendments. They further argued that the death penalty was not "cruel and unusual" when the Eighth and Fourteenth Amendments were proposed and ratified; thus, execution itself did not constitute cruel and unusual punishment. The dissenters also argued that the Court was engaging in a legislative act when it moved to strike down capital punishment, and that even under modern standards it could not be considered "cruel and unusual."[32]

While capital punishment in this particular case was found to be unconstitutional it is clear that it was not altogether struck down. Only two of the *Furman* Justices thought the death penalty was invalid in all circumstances, and legislative bodies seeking to reinstate the practice immediately set about drafting statutes that would correct the faults identified in the other three majority opinions. Enactment of death penalty statutes by 35 states following *Furman* led to renewed litigation.

Once again, however, the Court failed to establish a clear standard for measuring an act under the Constitution. In a series of cases the Court danced with the issue of capital punishment, and even acknowledged that its opinions were often less than clear in providing guidance. Justice Frankfurter once wrote of the development of the law through "the process of litigating elucidation."[33] Yet, the Court failed time and again to elucidate those standards which were to be applied.

In *Lockett v. Ohio*[34] Chief Justice Burger wrote "The signals from this Court have not...always been easy to decipher." Justice White, in the same case, added: "The Court has now completed its about-face since Furman."[35]

In his dissenting opinion Justice Rehnquist wrote: "The Court has gone from pillar to post, with the result that the sort of reasonable predictability upon which legislatures, trial courts, and appellate courts must of necessity rely has been all but completely sacrificed."[36] He further stated, "I am frank to say that I am uncertain whether today's opinion represents the seminal case in the exposition by this Court of the Eighth and Fourteenth Amendments as they apply to capital punishment, or whether instead it represents the third false start in this direction within the past six years."[37]

From this series of cases, however, we can garner a few rules. The Court determined that the penalty of death for deliberate murder is not per se cruel and unusual.[38] The Court also determined that mandatory death statutes leaving the jury or trial judge no discretion to consider the individual defendant and his crime are cruel and unusual. Likewise, the Court established that standards and procedures may be established for the imposition of death that would remove or mitigate the arbitrariness and irrationality found so significant in *Furman*.[39]

While these decisions lay a foundation for building a constitutional death penalty statute they by no means cleared a perfect path. Divisions among the Justices made it difficult to ascertain the form permissible statutory schemes may take.[40] Three of the Justices in *Furman* found that particular practice unconstitutional but did not altogether reject the death penalty. Problems within the system revolved about discriminatory and arbitrary imposition of the death penalty,[41] and legislatures turned to enactment of statutes that purported to do away with these difficulties.

One of the schemes that seemed destined for attack was statutes providing for automatic imposition of the death penalty upon conviction for certain forms of murder. The statutes commonly provided specified aggravating and mitigating factors that the sentencing authority should consider in imposing sentence. In many instances the statutory scheme established special procedures to follow in capital cases. Beginning in 1976 five cases came before the Court to test such schemes. The Court rejected automatic sentencing but approved other statutes specifying factors for jury consideration.

In Georgia a statute provided for a bifurcated trial wherein guilt would be addressed in the first stage and punishment (if found guilty) was reserved for a second stage. This scheme was challenged in *Gregg v. Georgia*.[42] The statute also required that the jury find at least one of ten statutory aggravating factors before imposing death. Review of death sentences by the Georgia Supreme Court also were included in the statute. Each of these provisions was sustained by the Court on appeal.

Statutes of two other states were similarly upheld. In *Proffitt v. Florida*[43] the Court weighed a statute similar to Georgia's, with the exception that the trial judge, rather than the jury, was directed to weigh statutory aggravating factors against statutory mitigating factors. In *Jurek v. Texas*[44] the Court examined a statute that narrowed the death-eligible class and lumped mitigating factors into the pot for measuring likelihood of future danger to others by the defendant.

During this same time the statues of two other states were invalidated. In *Woodson v. North Carolina*[45] and *Roberts v. Louisiana*[46] the Court overturned statutes that mandated the death penalty for first-degree murder. Several important issues come from these cases and warrant further examination.

First, the Court concluded that the death penalty as a punishment for murder does not itself constitute cruel and unusual punishment. In reaching the conclusion the Court concluded that reenactment of capital punishment statutes by 35 states precluded the Court from finding that this form of penalty was no longer acceptable to a majority of the American people. Neither is it possible, the Court continued, for it to decide that the death penalty does not comport with the basic concept of human dignity at the core of the Eighth Amendment.[47]

From these decisions we can also see that courts are not free to substitute their own judgments for the people and their elected representatives. A death penalty statute, just as all other statutes, comes before the courts bearing a presumption of validity which can only be overcome upon a strong showing by those who attack its constitutionality. The courts are not to determine whether the death penalty validly serves the permissible functions of retribution and deterrence — that judgment is reserved to the state legislatures — but instead to determine only if the proposed scheme meets constitutional requirements.

From these cases one must also conclude that in order for a court to make its determination on the application of a death penalty the court must look to history and traditional usage, to legislative enactment, and to jury determinations. Because death is a unique punishment, the sentencing process must provide an opportunity for individual consideration of the character and record of each convicted defendant and crime along with mitigating and aggravating circumstances.[48]

While the imposition of death is constitutional per se, the procedure by which sentence is passed must be so structured as to reduce arbitrariness and capriciousness as much as possible.[49] What emerged from the prevailing plurality opinions are requirements that the sentencing authority, either jury or judge, be given standards to govern its exercise of discretion and be given the opportunity to evaluate both the circumstances of the offense and the character and propensities of the accused. Similarly, to prevent jury prejudice on the issue of guilt there will be a separate proceeding after conviction at which evidence relevant to the sentence — mitigating and aggravating — will be presented. This scheme is commonly referred to as a bifurcated trial.

The cases also establish that special forms of appellate review be provided not only of the conviction but also of the sentence, to ascertain that the sentence was in fact fairly imposed both on the facts of the individual case and in comparison with the penalties imposed in similar cases.[50]

Following these decisions many states set about restructuring their statutes to comply with the new standards for capital cases. One of the first issues addressed was the requirement that the sentencing authority be given standards narrowing discretion to impose the death penalty. Many states enacted statutes spelling out "aggravating" circumstances which must be present before a sentence of death could be handed out. In many instances, at least one of these must be found before the death penalty may be imposed. It was immediately recognized that the standards must be relatively precise and instructive in providing guidance that minimizes the risk of arbitrary and capricious action by the sentencing authority.

These statutes were also quickly attacked, and the Court invalidated a capital sentence based upon a jury finding that the murder was "outrageously or wantonly vile, horrible, and inhuman," reasoning that "a person of ordinary sensibility could fairly [so] characterize almost every murder" with such terms.[51] Similarly, statutes relying on language that described acts as "especially heinous, atrocious or cruel" for the purposes of determining aggravating circumstance were held to be unconstitutionally vague.[52] The "especially heinous, cruel or depraved" standard is cured, however, by a narrowing interpretation requiring a finding of infliction of mental anguish or physical abuse before the victim's death.[53]

The far-reaching principles of *Furman* and of the *Gregg* series of cases was that the jury should not be "without guidance or direction" in deciding whether a convicted defendant should live or die. The jury's attention was statutorily "directed to the specific circumstances of the crime...and on the characteristics of the person who committed the crime."[54] Discretion was to be channeled and rationalized, but not too much.

In *Lockett v. Ohio*[55] a Court plurality determined that a state law was invalid because it prevented the sentencing authority from giving weight to any mitigating factors other than those specified in the law. "[W]e conclude that the Eighth and Fourteenth Amendments require that the sentencer, in all but the rarest kind of capital case, not be precluded from considering as a mitigating factor, any aspect of a defendant's character or record and any of the circumstances of the offense that the defendant proffers as a basis for a sentence less than death."[56] In other words, the statutes should be sufficiently narrow as to prevent arbitrary and capricious actions against a defendant but not so overly narrow as to preclude a defendant from presenting otherwise mitigating evidence.

While holding fast to the *Lockett* requirement that sentencers be allowed to consider all mitigating evidence, the Court has upheld state statutes that control the relative weight that the sentencer may accord to aggravating and mitigating evidence.[57] Likewise, there is no additional requirement that the jury be allowed to weigh the severity of an aggravating circumstance in the absence of any mitigating factor.[58] The legislature may also specify the consequences of the jury's finding an aggravating circumstance and it may mandate that a death sentence be imposed if the jury unanimously finds at least one aggravating circumstance and no mitigating circumstance. Similarly, if the jury finds that aggravating circumstances outweigh mitigating circumstances it may impose the death penalty.[59] A court also may instruct that the jury "must not be swayed by mere sentiment, conjecture, sympathy, passion, prejudice, public opinion, or public feeling," since in essence the instruction merely cautions the jury not to base its decision "on factors not presented at the trial."[60]

The courts have also weighed the issues of whether to allow character evidence of the victim into evidence when considering the death penalty. Some statutory schemes provided that a victim's family, friends, or others knowing of the victim's character could testify as an aggravating factor when measuring punishment. The Supreme Court initially held that introduction of evidence about the character of the victim or the amount of emotional distress caused to the victim's family or community was inappropriate because it "creates an impermissible risk that the capital sentencing decision will be made in an arbitrary manner."[61] And culpability, the Court added, "depends not on fortuitous circumstances such as the composition [or articulateness] of [the] victim's family, but on circumstances over which [the defendant] has control."[62]

In *South Carolina v. Gathers*[63] the Court addressed a similar issue. In this case the prosecutor provided extensive comments extolling the personal characteristics of a murder victim during the trial. The Court held that such actions can invalidate a death sentence when the victim's character is unrelated to the circumstances of the crime.

The decisions limiting introduction of such evidence have been narrowed recently. In the past decade the membership on the Court has changed, resulting in decisions that in effect overrule the earlier decisions. In one such case the Court held that "victim impact statements" are not barred from evidence by the Eighth Amendment.[64] "A State may legitimately conclude that evidence about the victim and about the impact of the murder on the victim's family is relevant to the jury's decision as to whether or not the death penalty should be imposed."[65]

Many commentators have suggested that the Court's recent move to support the admissibility of victim impact evidence was necessary in order to restore balance to capital sentencing. Exclusion of such evidence tipped the scales in a capital trial by allowing almost limitless introduction of relevant mitigating evidence but restricting otherwise relevant evidence concerning a victim. For example, at one point a state was barred from either offering "'a glimpse of the life' which a defendant 'chose to extinguish,' or demonstrating the loss to the victim's family and to society which have resulted from the defendant's homicide."[66]

A. CAPITAL PUNISHMENT FOR OTHER OFFENSES: RAPE AND NON-MURDER CASES

Other issues arising under death penalty cases deal with the penalty when a murder has not been committed. In *Coker v. Georgia*[67] the Court held that the state may not impose a death sentence upon a rapist who does not take a human life. Although the Court stated the issue in the context of the rape of an adult woman,[68] the opinion at no point sought to distinguish between adults and children. Justice Powell's concurrence expressed the view that death is ordinarily disproportionate for the rape of an adult woman, but that some rapes might be so brutal or heinous as to justify it.[69]

The Court announced that the standard under the Eighth Amendment was that punishments are barred when they are "excessive" in relation to the crime committed. A punishment is "excessive" and unconstitutional if it:

> (1) Makes no measurable contribution to acceptable goals of punishment and hence is nothing more than the purposeless and needless imposition of pain and suffering; or (2) Is grossly out of proportion to the severity of the crime.[70]

The Court went on to say that in order that judgment not be or appear to be the subjective conclusion of individual Justices, attention must be given to objective factors, predominantly "to the public attitudes concerning a particular sentence history and precedent, legislative attitudes, and the response of juries reflected in their sentencing decisions...."[71] While the Court thought that the death penalty for rape passed the first test, it felt it failed the second. Georgia was the sole state providing for death for the rape of an adult woman, and juries in at least nine out of ten cases refused to impose death for rape. Aside from this view of public perception, the Court independently concluded that death is an excessive penalty for an offender who rapes but does not kill. As the Court stated, rape cannot compare with murder "in terms of moral depravity and of injury to the person and the public."[72]

B. FELONY MURDER

Applying the *Coker* analysis, the Court ruled in *Enmund v. Florida*[73] that death is an unconstitutional penalty for felony murder. Felony murder, in most jurisdictions, arises when a person dies while the defendant commits an unrelated felony. In jurisdictions that apply the felony murder doctrine the defendant may be liable for the homicide of the unintended victim. In striking down capital convictions in such cases the Court held that the imposition of capital punishment would be unconstitutional if the defendant did not himself kill, attempt to take life, or intend that anyone be killed.

In addressing this issue the Court determined that death was a disproportionate sentence for one who neither directly took life nor intended to do so. Because the death penalty is a likely deterrent only when murder is the result of premeditation and deliberation, and because the justification of retribution depends upon the degree of the defendant's culpability, the imposition of death upon one who participates in a crime in which a victim is murdered by one of his confederates and not as a result of his own intention serves neither of the purposes underlying the penalty.[74]

In *Tison v. Arizona*,[75] however, the Court eased the "intent to kill" requirement, holding that, in keeping with an "apparent consensus" among the states, "major participation in the felony committed, combined with reckless indifference to human life, is sufficient to satisfy the *Enmund* culpability requirement."[76] A few years earlier,

Enmund had also been weakened by the Court's holding that the factual finding of requisite intent to kill need not be made by the guilt/innocence factfinder, whether judge or jury, but may be made by a state appellate court.[77]

C. RACE

The issue of race of both defendant and victim also has arisen in capital punishment cases. Initially, a measure of protection against jury bias was added by the Court's holding that "a capital defendant accused of an interracial crime is entitled to have prospective jurors informed of the race of the victim and questioned on the issue of racial bias."[78] A year later, however, the Court ruled in *McCleskey v. Kemp*[79] that a strong statistical showing of racial disparity in capital sentencing cases is insufficient to establish an Eighth Amendment violation. Statistics alone do not establish racial discrimination in any particular case, the Court concluded, but "at most show only a likelihood that a particular factor entered into some decisions."[80]

D. EXECUTION OF THE INSANE

Among the recent decisions of note in the area of death penalty cases are those involving the issue of "diminished capacity." In these cases the Court has weighed the question of whether the death penalty can be applied to someone with a limited mental capability or understanding. The issues are not limited to mere capacity, though, but extend to questions surrounding the defendant's competency at the time of the offense, at trial, and at the sentencing phase. Likewise, a defendant's capacity at the time a capital sentence is carried out may be worthy of examination.

One of the more interesting cases involves a defendant who was competent at the time of his offense, at trial, and at sentencing, but who subsequently developed a mental disorder. The Court held in *Ford v. Wainwright*[81] that the Eighth Amendment prohibits the state from carrying out the death penalty on an individual who is insane at the time of execution. The Court held that issues of competency properly raised at execution time must be determined in a proceeding satisfying the minimum requirements of due process.[82] In essence, the Court's opinion meant that a defendant has a right to be sane at the time of his execution.

In reaching their decision, the Justices acknowledged that execution of an insane person has long been held to be cruel and unusual punishment. The issues they addressed in this case focused not on the question of sanity or its definition, but instead on the procedural requirements for reaching conclusions of sanity at the state level. In this case the State of Florida left to the governor the final decision on the issue of sanity. The governor, having been provided reports from three qualified mental health workers, was in fact the final arbiter of sanity, but there were no provisions allowing the defendant to be heard on the issue.

Justice Marshall, joined by Justices Brennan, Blackmun, and Stevens, wrote that "the ascertainment of a prisoner's sanity...calls for no less stringent standards than those demanded in any other aspect of a capital proceeding."[83] Concurring, Justice Powell added that due process might be met by a proceeding "far less formal than a trial," that the state "should provide an impartial officer or board that can receive evidence and argument from the prisoner's counsel."[84]

Justice O'Connor and Justice White concurred, emphasizing Florida's denial of the opportunity to be heard, and did not express an opinion on whether the state could designate the governor as decision maker. Justice Powell's opinion, requiring the opportunity to be heard before an impartial officer or board, thus sets forth the Court's holding.

E. MENTALLY RETARDED

Not surprisingly, in contrast, in a 1989 case the Court found "insufficient evidence of a national consensus against executing mentally retarded people."[85] While the Court conceded that "it may indeed be 'cruel and unusual' punishment to execute persons who are profoundly or severely retarded and wholly lacking the capacity to appreciate the wrongfulness of their actions," retarded persons who have been found competent to stand trial, and who have failed to establish an insanity defense, fall into a different category.

In measuring the ability of a state to execute a retarded person the Court held that there be an individualized consideration of culpability. In other words, each defendant may be measured on his or her own merits and actions. Although not extending the protections against capital punishment seen for the insane the Court has held that a retarded defendant must be offered the benefit of an instruction that the jury may consider and give mitigating effect to evidence of retardation or abused background.[86] In this sense, a jury may consider the degree of retardation or other individual factors when considering the penalty for the crime.

F. JUVENILES

Just as execution of the insane or mentally retarded has seen recent court intervention, so too has the execution of minors. While there is no categorical prohibition on execution of juveniles there have been some issues that arise in those cases. In addressing the issues the Court has often looked at the particular statutory scheme under which such an execution may be carried forth.

A hotly contested area is at what age an execution may be properly applied. Early on the issue arose as to whether a state could execute a juvenile and at what age would such action be considered cruel and unusual punishment. An attack on this issue came in *Thompson v. Oklahoma*.[87]

In Oklahoma no minimum age had been set for capital punishment, and in most instances the act was reserved for adults. However, a provision of the Oklahoma juvenile code allowed some minors to be treated as adults where certain crimes had been committed. Where a minor had committed an act that carried the penalty of death for an adult the minor, once certified to stand trial as an adult, could also face the same penalty.

The Court's ruling of unconstitutionality was divided, and once again no clear rule emerged to guide the states. In reaching their decision four of the Justices favored a flat ruling that execution of anyone younger than 16 at the time of his or her offense is barred by the Eighth Amendment. This, however, was not enough to establish such a rule. Thus, while the Court found neutral ground upon which to strike down this single statutory scheme there was not enough to establish a bright line for future measurement.

The following year the Court again addressed the issue of age for purposes of capital punishment. In *Stanford v. Kentucky*[88] the Court held that the Eighth Amendment does not categorically prohibit imposition of the death penalty for individuals who commit crimes at age 16 or 17. Like Oklahoma, Kentucky had not directly specified a minimum age for the death penalty. The difference, however, was that where Oklahoma sought to execute a 15-year-old, Kentucky intended execution of a 16-year-old. Just as in *Thompson*, Justice O'Connor was the deciding vote.

To Justice O'Connor, the critical difference that led to a vote against Oklahoma's law but not Kentucky's was that there clearly was no national consensus forbidding imposition of capital punishment on 16- or 17-year-old murderers. In her opinion Justice O'Connor noted that two thirds of all state legislatures had concluded that no one should be executed for a crime committed at age 15, and no state had "unequivocally endorsed" a lower age limit.[89] It may also be noted that 15 of 37 states permitting capital punishment decline to impose it on 16-year-old offenders and that 12 decline to impose it on 17-year-old offenders.

From these opinions one can see that the issue of capital punishment as it relates to youthful offenders is not very well defined. On the one hand, Justice Scalia would look exclusively on an assessment of what the state legislatures and Congress have done in setting an age limit for application of capital punishment. Justice Scalia wrote: "A revised national consensus so broad, so clear and so enduring as to justify a permanent prohibition upon all units of democratic government must appear in the operative acts (laws and the application of laws) that the people have approved."[90]

Other Justices proposed a "proportionality review" which would broaden the inquiry and question of the defendant's culpability as one aspect of the gravity of the offense. Such a review would consider age as one indicator of culpability. Similarly, the review would consider other statutory age classifications to arrive at a conclusion about the level of maturity and responsibility that society expects of juveniles.[91] In her opinion, Justice O'Connor disagreed with such an analysis. While recognizing the Court's "constitutional obligation to conduct proportionality analysis," she also indicated that such an analysis could not resolve the underlying issue of the constitutionally required minimum age.[92]

VI. PROCEDURAL DELAY

Since the 1980s and early 1990s the Court has taken a number of steps in an attempt to reduce the many procedural and substantive opportunities for delay in the carrying out of death sentences. The Court has also endeavored to give the states more leeway in administering capital sentencing. The early post-*Furman* stage involving creation of procedural protections for capital defendants gave way to increasing impatience with the delays made possible through procedural protections, especially those associated with federal habeas corpus review.

In *Barefoot v. Estelle*[93] the Court states that "unlike a term of years, a death sentence cannot begin to be carried out by the State while substantial legal issues remain outstanding. Accordingly, federal courts must isolate the exceptional cases where constitutional error requires retrial or resentencing as certainly and swiftly as orderly procedures will permit."

VII. PROPORTIONALITY

In the previous section we concentrated on a review of capital punishment under the Eighth Amendment proscriptions of cruel and unusual punishment. In the following section we will focus on the issue of "proportionality" when measuring punishment under the Eighth Amendment. In essence, we will focus on the primary issue of whether the punishment fits the crime.

The issues of proportionality extend to the earliest days of the Constitution. In addition to prohibiting punishments deemed barbarous and inhumane the Eighth Amendment also condemned "all punishments which by their excessive length or severity are greatly disproportionate to the offenses charged."[94]

This view was adopted by the Court in *Weems v. United States*,[95] where a sentence of 15 years incarceration at hard labor with chains on the ankles, loss of all civil rights, and perpetual surveillance — for the offense of falsifying public documents — was struck down. In addressing the issue of proportionality the Court compared the sentence with those meted out for other offenses. The Court wrote: "This contrast shows more than different exercises of legislative judgment. It is greater than that. It condemns the sentence in this case as cruel and unusual. It exhibits a difference between unrestrained power and that which is exercised under the spirit of constitutional limitations formed to establish justice."[96]

In such an instance the Court used the punishment from other offenses as a measuring stick against the punishment in *Weems*. The Court held that the punishment must be proportional and that at least one way of measuring that proportionality was to compare punishments for different offenses.

The Court has gone back and forth in its acceptance of proportionality analysis in other non-capital cases. One area where we have seen this is in the application of "recidivist statutes." These statutes tend to punish a person convicted of a crime at a higher level than others based on a past record of convictions. An example of such statute would be the increase of punishment upon subsequent convictions for driving under the influence of alcohol.

In *Rummel v. Estelle*[97] the defendant was convicted and then punished under the state's recidivist statute. The defendant had three prior non-violent convictions and he had netted less than $230 from those acts. While opponents of the statute argued that the defendant's punishment was being enhanced because of his status as a three-time convicted felon, rather than the severity of his crimes, the Court upheld a mandatory life sentence.

In reaching its decision the Court dismissed as unavailing the factors relied on by the defendant. The Court held that the nature of the offense as nonviolent was not necessarily relevant to the seriousness of a crime, and the determination of what is a "small" amount of money, being so subjective, was a legislative task. The Court also held that the state's focus on the recidivism, and not the specific acts, was more compelling.[98]

Although the *Rummel* case initially appeared to set a standard for punishment based on recidivism, the Court later modified that rule in *Solem v. Helm*.[99] In *Solem* the Court unequivocally stated that the cruel and unusual punishments clause "prohibits not only barbaric punishments, but also sentences that are disproportionate to the crime committed," and that "[t]here is no basis for the State's assertion that the general principle of proportionality does not apply to felony prison sentences."[100]

Helm, like Rummel, had been sentenced under a recidivist statute following conviction for a nonviolent felony involving a small amount of money.[101] The difference was that Helm's sentence of life imprisonment without possibility of parole was viewed as "far more severe than the life sentence we described in Rummel."[102] The Court pointed out that Rummel had been eligible for parole after 12 years' imprisonment, while Helm had only the possibility of executive clemency, characterized by the Court as "nothing more than a hope for an ad hoc exercise of clemency."[103]

In *Helm* the Court also spelled out the "objective criteria" by which proportionality issues should be judged, to wit:

(i) the gravity of the offense and the harshness of the penalty;
(ii) the sentences imposed on other criminals in the same jurisdiction; and
(iii) the sentences imposed for commission of the same crime in other jurisdictions.[104]

Measured by these criteria Helm's sentence was cruel and unusual. His crime was relatively minor, yet life imprisonment without possibility for parole was the harshest penalty possible in South Dakota, reserved for such other offenses as murder, manslaughter, kidnapping, and arson. In only one other state could he have received so harsh a sentence, and in no other state was it mandated.

It should be noted that the Court was closely divided in rendering these important decisions. The division remained close in later cases as well. In *Harmelin v. Michigan*[105] the Court held that a mandatory term of life imprisonment without possibility of parole was not cruel and unusual as applied to the crime of possession of more than 650 grams of cocaine. This opinion, however, appears to be limited only to those issues of the mandatory nature of the penalty and not the overall severity itself. The Court rejected an argument that sentencing judges in noncapital cases must be allowed to hear mitigating evidence as to the length of sentence.

Justice Scalia wrote: "Severe, mandatory penalties may be cruel, but they are not unusual in the constitutional sense."[106] The Court's opinion, written by Justice Scalia, then elaborated an understanding of "unusual" — set forth elsewhere in a part of his opinion subscribed to only by Chief Justice Rehnquist — that denies the possibility of proportionality review altogether. The Court held that mandatory penalties are not unusual in the constitutional sense because they have "been employed in various form throughout our Nation's history." This is an application of Justice Scalia's belief that cruelty and unusualness are to be determined solely by reference to the punishment at issue, and without reference to the crime for which it is imposed.[107]

A majority of other Justices indicated in the same case that they do recognize at least a narrow proportionality principle.[108] The three-Justice plurality opinion asserted that because of the "serious nature" of the crime there was no need to apply the remaining factors from *Solem*. In this sense the Justices compared the sentence to sentences imposed for other crimes in Michigan, and to sentences imposed for the same crime in other jurisdictions.[109] Dissenting Justices White, Blackmun, and Stevens asserted that Justice Kennedy's approach would "eviscerate" *Solem*.[110]

ENDNOTES

1. See Parsons v. Bedford, 3 Pet. 433, 447 (1830); Ex parte Watkins, 32 U.S. (7 Pet.) 568, 574 (1833); Barton v. Barbour, 104 U.S. 126, 133 (1881).
2. Tate v. Short, 401 U.S. 395 (1971); Williams v. Illinois, 399 U.S. 235 (1970).
3. Browning-Ferris Industries v. Kelco Disposal, Inc., 492 U.S. 257, 266 (1989).
4. 1 Annals of Congress 754 (1789).
5. 2 J. Elliot, The Debates in the Several State Conventions on the Adoption of the Constitution 111 (2d ed. 1836); 3 *id*. at 447–52.
6. Wilkerson v. Utah, 99 U.S. 130 (1878); In re Kemmler, 136 U.S. 436 (1890); cf. Weems v. United States, 217 U.S. 349, 368–72 (1910). On the present Court, Chief Justice Rehnquist subscribes to this view (see, e.g., Woodson v. North Carolina, 428 U.S. 280, 208 (dissenting)), and the views of Justices Scalia and Thomas appear to be similar. See, e.g., Harmelin v. Michigan, 501 U.S. 957, 966–90 (1991) (Justice Scalia announcing judgment of Court) (relying on original understanding of Amendment and of English practice to argue that there is no proportionality principle in noncapital cases); and Hudson v. McMillian, 112 S. Ct. 995, 1010 (1992) (Justice Thomas dissenting) (objecting to Court's extension of the Amendment "beyond all bounds of history and precedent" in holding that "significant injury" need not be established for sadistic and malicious beating of shackled prisoner to constitute cruel and unusual punishment).
7. 217 U.S. 349 (1910).
8. *Id*.
9. Trop v. Dulles, 356 U.S. 86, 100–01 (1958) (plurality opinion).
10. Wilkerson v. Utah, 99 U.S. 130, 135 (1878).
11. *Id*.
12. 72 U.S. (5 Wall.) 475 (1867).
13. *Id*. at 479–80.
14. 136 U.S. 436 (1890).
15. Louisiana *ex rel*. Francis v. Resweber, 329 U.S. 459 (1947).
16. *Id*. at 470.
17. 356 U.S. 86 (1958).
18. *Id*. at 114.
19. *Id*. at 121, 124–27.
20. *Id*. at 99–100.
21. *Id*. at 99–100.
22. Trop v. Dulles, 356 U.S. 86 (1958).
23. See, e.g., Witherspoon v. Illinois, 391 U.S. 510 (1968) (exclusion of death-scrupled jurors). See also Davis v. Georgia, 429 U.S. 122 (1976), and Adams v. Texas, 448 U.S. 38 (1980) (explicating Witherspoon). The Eighth Amendment was the basis for grant of review in Boykin v. Alabama, 395 U.S. 238 (1969) and Maxwell v. Bishop, 398 U.S. 262 (1970), but membership changes on the Court resulted in decisions on other grounds.
24. 402 U.S. 183 (1971).

25. *Id.*
26. 408 U.S. 238 (1972).
27. *Id.* at 257 (Justice Brennan).
28. *Id.* at 314 (Justice Marshall).
29. *Id.* at 240 (Justice Douglas).
30. *Id.* at 306 (Justice Stewart).
31. *Id.* at 310 (Justice White).
32. *Id.* at 375 (Chief Justice Burger), 405 (Justice Blackmun), 414 (Justice Powell), 465 (Justice Rehnquist). Each of the dissenters joined each of the opinions of the others.
33. International Ass'n of Machinists v. Gonzales, 356 U.S. 617, 619 (1958).
34. 438 U.S. 586, 602 (plurality opinion).
35. *Id.* at 622.
36. *Id.* at 629 (dissenting).
37. *Id.* at 633.
38. Coker v. Georgia, 433 U.S. 584, 600 (1977).
39. See Coker v. Georgia, 433 U.S. 584, 600 (1977); Lockett v. Ohio, 438 U.S. 586, 619 (1978); Enmund v. Florida, 458 U.S. 782, 801 (1982).
40. Justices Brennan and Marshall adhered to the view that the death penalty is per se unconstitutional.
41. Justice Douglas thought the penalty had been applied discriminatorily, Furman v. Georgia, 408 U.S. 238 (1972); Justice Stewart thought it had been applied in an arbitrary, "wanton," and "freakish" manner, *id.* at 310; and Justice White thought it had been applied so infrequently that it served no justifying end, *id.* at 313.
42. 428 U.S. 153 (1976).
43. 428 U.S. 242 (1976).
44. 428 U.S. 262 (1976).
45. 428 U.S. 280 (1976).
46. 428 U.S. 325 (1976).
47. *Id.*
48. Woodson v. North Carolina, 428 U.S. 280 (1976); Roberts v. Louisiana, 428 U.S. 325 (1976).
49. Marks v. United States, 430 U.S. 188, 192–94 (1977).
50. Gregg v. Georgia, 428 U.S. 153, 195, 198 (1976) (plurality); Proffitt v. Florida, 428 U.S. 242, 250–51, 253 (1976) (plurality); Jurek v. Texas, 428 U.S. 262, 276 (1976) (plurality).
51. Godfrey v. Georgia, 446 U.S. 420, 428–29 (1980) (plurality opinion).
52. Maynard v. Cartwright, 486 U.S. 356 (1988).
53. Walton v. Arizona, 497 U.S. 639 (1990).
54. Gregg v. Georgia, 428 U.S. 153, 197–98 (1976).
55. 438 U.S. 586 (1978).
56. 438 U.S. at 604.
57. Barclay v. Florida, 463 U.S. 939.
58. *Id.*
59. Boyde v. California, 494 U.S. 370 (1990).
60. California v. Brown, 479 U.S. 538, 543 (1987).
61. Booth v. Maryland, 482 U.S. 496, 503 (1987).
62. *Id.* at 504 n.7. The decision was 5–4 with Justice Powell delivering the opinion of the majority. He was joined by Justices Brennan, Marshall, Blackmun, and Stevens. Chief Justice Rehnquist and Justices White, O'Connor, and Scalia dissented.
63. 490 U.S. 805 (1989).
64. Payne v. Tennessee, 501 U.S. 808 (1991).

65. *Id.* at 827.
66. Payne v. Tennessee, 501 U.S. 808, 822 (1991).
67. 433 U.S. 584 (1977).
68. *Id.* at 592.
69. *Id.* at 601.
70. 433 U.S. 584, 592 (1977).
71. *Id.*
72. *Id.* at 598.
73. 458 U.S. 782 (1982).
74. *Id.*
75. 481 U.S. 137, 158 (1987).
76. *Id.*
77. Cabana v. Bullock, 474 U.S. 376 (1986).
78. Turner v. Murray, 476 U.S. 28, 36–37 (1986).
79. 481 U.S. 279 (1987).
80. 481 U.S. at 308.
81. 477 U.S. 399 (1986).
82. *Id.* at 422.
83. 477 U.S. at 411–12.
84. *Id.* at 427.
85. Penry v. Lynaugh, 492 U.S. 302, 335 (1989).
86. *Id.* at 328.
87. 487 U.S. 815 (1988).
88. 492 U.S. 361 (1989).
89. *Id.* at 370.
90. 492 U.S. at 377.
91. *Id.* at 394–96.
92. *Id.* at 382.
93. 463 U.S. 880, 888 (1983).
94. O'Neil v. Vermont, 144 U.S. 323, 339–40 (1892).
95. 217 U.S. 349 (1910).
96. *Id.* at 381.
97. 445 U.S. 263 (1980).
98. 445 U.S. at 275–82.
99. 463 U.S. 277 (1983).
100. 463 U.S. at 284, 288.
101. The final conviction was for uttering a no-account check in the amount of $100; previous felony convictions were also for nonviolent crimes described by the Court as "relatively minor." 463 U.S. at 296–97.
102. *Id.* at 297.
103. *Id.* at 303.
104. *Id.* at 292.
105. 501 U.S. 957 (1991).
106. *Id.* at 994.
107. *Id.* at 975–78.
108. See *id.* at 996 (Justices Kennedy, O'Connor, and Souter concurring); *id.* at 1009 (Justices White, Blackmun, and Stevens dissenting); *id.* at 1027 (Justice Marshall dissenting).
109. *Id.* at 1004.
110. *Id.* at 1018.

27 Other Issues under the Eighth Amendment

I. CONVICTIONS BASED ON STATUS

The Eighth Amendment proscriptions against punishment have also been extended to prevent convictions for social status. Most notable are those convictions arising from the status of an addict: one who is addicted to a narcotic or alcohol.

In *Robinson v. California*[1] the defendant was convicted of being "addicted to the use of narcotics." In overturning the statute the Court held that it was unconstitutional because it punished the "mere status" of being an addict without any requirement of a showing that a defendant had ever used narcotics within the jurisdiction of the state. In this sense, the Court held that the state could not convict a person for being an addict; instead, there must be a physical act that has been proscribed. In this case the state failed to show that the defendant had committed any act proscribed by law, such as the use of an illegal narcotic, and therefore no illegal act had been committed.

Similar rulings have addressed the status issue as it relates to the use of alcohol. In *Powell v. Texas*[2] the defendant was convicted based on his "status" as an alcoholic. In this instance, the defendant was a well-known "drunk" in the community, and when the police saw him on the street they routinely confronted and often arrested him for public drunkeness. In this case, however, the Court addressed also the issue of whether a person could be convicted of the act even when they may not be able to control the impulse leading to the act.

Justice Marshall, joined by Justices Black and Harlan and Chief Justice Warren, relied in part on the prior decision in *Robinson*. The Court held that the Eighth Amendment proscribed only punishment of "status," and not punishment for "acts." As such, an alcoholic could not be arrested and convicted based on the fact that he was an alcoholic. On the other hand, an alcoholic who is intoxicated may be arrested and convicted without violating *Robinson*.

The Justices expressed a fear that a contrary holding would impel the Court into constitutional definitions of such matters as actus reus, mens rea, insanity, mistake, justification, and duress.[3] In this sense the majority somewhat restricted the holding of *Robinson* by opening the door for convictions based on known status (i.e., being an alcoholic) when coupled, in a limited sense, with the illegal act. Thus, a police officer who knows an individual is an alcoholic may use that information to raise a reasonable suspicion, one needed to make an inquiry of sobriety, and if the person is in fact inebriated then the officer may make a valid arrest.

Justice White concurred, but his opinion showed a reservation to follow the majority fully. Justice White reasoned that if addiction as a status may not be punished neither can the yielding to the compulsion of that addiction, whether to narcotics or to alcohol.[4] However, for Justice White the question came down to an issue of whether an individual could refrain from going into public. In other words, if the disease of alcoholism enticed the person to drink the person should not be punished for the status created by the disease; however, if that person drank but could not remain in private then the act itself became not the alcoholism but being in a public place while intoxicated.

Dissenting Justices Fortas, Douglas, Brennan, and Stewart wished to adopt a rule that "[c]riminal penalties may not be inflicted upon a person for being in a condition he is powerless to change." In other words, one under an irresistible compulsion to drink or to take narcotics may not be punished for those acts.[5] In this sense, one who was an alcoholic could be in a public place and be intoxicated while the person who is not an alcoholic could face arrest and conviction if he were drunk in public.

II. PRISONS AND PUNISHMENT

When it comes to issues of punishment it is hard not to address the cases focusing on prisons. From a legal standpoint it is unquestioned that " '[c]onfinement' in a prison...is a form of punishment subject to scrutiny under the Eighth Amendment standards."[6] In the following section we shall address the conditions within prison which remain constitutional and those that are not.

The Court has long held that "conditions in prison must not involve the wanton and unnecessary infliction of pain, nor may they be grossly disproportionate to the severity of the crime warranting imprisonment...."[7] To be constitutional the conditions within the prison must be such that they not "deprive inmates of the minimal civilized measure of life's necessities."[8] These principles apply both to the treatment of individuals and to the creation or maintenance of prison conditions that are inhumane to inmates generally.[9]

Ordinarily there is both a subjective and an objective inquiry when measuring constitutional violations at the prison level. The first issue is one of intent on behalf of the prison official. Before prison conditions can be deemed unconstitutional, based on cruel and unusual punishment standards, there must be a culpable, "wanton" state of mind on the part of prison officials.[10] In the context of general prison conditions, this culpable state of mind amounts to a "deliberate indifference" standard.[11]

In applying this standard one can see that there is a two-stage process. In the first stage one must look to the statutory language requiring punishment for the particular crime. For example, certain crimes may warrant treatment or incarceration under restricted conditions such as maximum confinement. A person convicted of the highest level of murder, punishable by the death penalty, may be housed in facilities different from other prisoners convicted of lesser crimes. As such, the issue of cruel and unusual punishment will first be weighed based on the statutory requirement, the appropriate conditions as they relate to the punishment intent, and the conditions of similar facilities.

In the second instance, the issue is measured based on the actions and intent of the given prison official. In this sense, before a prison official can be said to be violating Eighth Amendment principles the conditions of the prison must be outside those required by statute, if any applies, and the official must fail to take actions to correct the conditions.

The issues may also vary according to the conditions at the time of the alleged deprivation. In the context of emergency actions, e.g., actions required to suppress a disturbance by inmates, only a malicious and sadistic state of mind is culpable.[12] Thus, where prison officials vary conditions due to an alleged emergency condition the standards for Eighth Amendment violations may vary as well.

The foregoing passages should not lead one to believe that the most extreme conditions within the prisons shall be tolerated. In fact, for some the opposite appears to be true. Beginning with *Holt v. Sarver*,[13] the federal courts found prisons or entire prison systems violative of the cruel and unusual punishments clause. The courts entered broad remedial orders directed to improving prison conditions and ameliorating prison life which were imposed in more than two dozen states.[14] In may also be said that Congress encouraged the bringing of such litigation by enacting the Civil Rights of Institutionalized Persons Act.[15]

While the lower courts took a proactive approach to prison management issues which arose under Eighth Amendment claims, the Supreme Court, in two separate cases, cautioned the courts to proceed with deference to the decisions of state legislatures and prison administrators.[16] In both cases, the prisons involved were of fairly recent vintage and the conditions, while harsh, did not approach the conditions described in many of the lower court decisions that had been left undisturbed.[17] Concerns of federalism and of judicial restraint apparently actuated the Court to begin to curb the lower federal courts from ordering remedial action for systems in which the prevailing circumstances, given the resources states choose to devote to them, "cannot be said to be cruel and unusual under contemporary standards."[18]

III. LIMITATION OF THE CLAUSE
TO CRIMINAL PUNISHMENTS

The Eighth Amendment deals only with criminal punishment; it has no application to civil processes. In holding the amendment inapplicable to the infliction of corporal punishment upon schoolchildren for disciplinary purposes, the Court explained that the cruel and unusual punishments clause "circumscribes the criminal process in three ways: First, it limits the kinds of punishment that can be imposed on those convicted of crimes; second, it proscribes punishment grossly disproportionate to the severity of the crime; and third, it imposes substantive limits on what can be made criminal and punished as such."[19] These limitations, the Court thought, should not be extended outside the criminal process.

ENDNOTES

1. 370 U.S. 660 (1962).
2. 392 U.S. 514 (1968).
3. *Id.* at 532–37.
4. *Id.* at 548.

5. *Id.* at 554, 567.
6. Rhodes v. Chapman, 452 U.S. 337, 345 (1981) (quoting Hutto v. Finney, 437 U.S. 678, 685 (1978)).
7. Rhodes v. Chapman, 452 U.S. 337, 347 (1981).
8. *Id.*
9. Estelle v. Gamble, 429 U.S. 97 (1976).
10. Wilson v. Seiter, 501 U.S. 294 (1991).
11. *Id.* at 303.
12. Whitley v. Albers, 475 U.S. 312 (1986).
13. 309 F. Supp. 362 (E.D. Ark. 1970), aff'd, 442 F.2d 304 (8th Cir. 1971), district court ordered to retain jurisdiction until unconstitutional conditions corrected, 505 F.2d 194 (8th Cir. 1974). The Supreme Court ultimately sustained the decisions of the lower courts in Hutto v. Finney, 437 U.S. 678 (1978).
14. Rhodes v. Chapman, 452 U.S. 337, 353–54 n.1 (1981) (Justice Brennan concurring) (collecting cases).
15. Pub. L. No. 96-247, 94 Stat. 349, 42 U.S.C. §§1997 *et seq.*
16. Bell v. Wolfish, 441 U.S. 520 (1979); Rhodes v. Chapman, 452 U.S. 337 (1981).
17. See, e.g., Pugh v. Locke, 406 F. Supp. 318 (M.D. Ala. 1976) (describing conditions of "horrendous overcrowding," inadequate sanitation, infested food, and "rampant violence"); Ramos v. Lamm, 639 F.2d 559 (10th Cir. 1981) (describing conditions "unfit for human habitation"). The primary issue in both Wolfish and Chapman was that of "double-celling," the confinement of two or more prisoners in a cell designed for one. In both cases, the Court found the record did not support orders ending the practice.
18. Rhodes v. Chapman, 452 U.S. 337, 347 (1981). See also Rufo v. Inmates of Suffolk County Jail, 112 S. Ct. 748 (1991) (allowing modification, based on a significant change in law or facts, of a 1979 consent decree that had ordered construction of a new jail with single-occupancy cells; modification was to depend upon whether the upsurge in jail population was anticipated when the decree was entered, and whether the decree was premised on the mistaken belief that single-celling is constitutionally mandated).
19. Ingraham v. Wright, 430 U.S. 651, 667 (1977).

Section Eight

Fourteenth Amendment — Due Process and Equal Protection

Amendment Text

Section 1. All persons born or naturalized in the United States and subject to the jurisdiction thereof, are citizens of the United States and of the State wherein they reside. No State shall make or enforce any law which shall abridge the privileges or immunities of citizens of the United States; nor shall any State deprive any person of life, liberty, or property, without due process of law; nor deny to any person within its jurisdiction the equal protection of the laws.

Section 2. Representatives shall be apportioned among the several States according to their respective numbers, counting the whole number of persons in each State, excluding Indians not taxed. But when the right to vote at any election for the choice of electors for President and Vice President of the United States, Representatives in Congress, the Executive and Judicial officers of a State, or the members of the Legislature thereof, is denied to any of the male inhabitants of such State, being twenty-one years of age, and citizens of the United States, or in any way abridged, except for participation in rebellion, or other crime, the basis of representation therein shall be reduced in the proportion which the number of such male citizens shall bear to the whole number of male citizens twenty-one years of age in such State.

Section 3. No person shall be a Senator or Representative in Congress, or elector of President and Vice President, or hold any office, civil or military, under the United States, or under any State, who, having previously taken an oath, as a member of Congress, or as an officer of the United States, or as a member of any State legislature, or as an executive or judicial officer of any State, to support the Constitution of the United States, shall have engaged in insurrection or rebellion against the same, or given aid or comfort to the enemies thereof. But Congress may by a vote of two-thirds of each House, remove such disability.

Section 4. The validity of the public debt of the United States, authorized by law, including debts incurred for payment of pensions and bounties for services in suppressing insurrection or rebellion, shall not be questioned. But neither the United States nor any State shall assume or pay any debt or obligation incurred in aid of insurrection or rebellion against the United States, or any claim for the loss or emancipation of any slave; but all such debts, obligations and claims shall be held illegal and void.

Section 5. The Congress shall have power to enforce, by appropriate legislation, the provisions of this article.

28 Due Process of Law

I. THE DEVELOPMENT OF SUBSTANTIVE DUE PROCESS

As we have discussed in earlier chapters, the Fourteenth Amendment was ratified after the Civil War as a means of controlling the states. The protections of the amendment, however, were not immediately applied or accepted by the Court. The significance of the due process clause as a restraint on state action appears to have been grossly underestimated by litigants and courts alike.

In the years immediately following its adoption due process remained primarily a function of the Fifth Amendment and was essentially recognized as a restraint on the federal government. Protections in the state courts came primarily through state statutes, state constitution, or not at all. Eventually, litigants began pushing the courts on the issue of protections under the amendment.

Early cases seeking to apply the protections of the amendment attacked state statutes which gave to one group or entity special standing under the law not enjoyed by others. An example of this type of statutory scheme can be seen in the *Slaughter-House Cases*,[1] in which a group of butchers used the clause to challenge the validity of a Louisiana statute. The statute in question conferred upon one corporation the exclusive privilege of butchering cattle in New Orleans, and in effect excluded any other butcher or corporation from operating.

The Court declared that the prohibition against a deprivation of property "has been in the Constitution since the adoption of the Fifth Amendment, as a restraint upon the Federal power. It is also to be found in some forms of expression in the constitution of nearly all the States, as a restraint upon the power of the States...."

Having set forth this basic principle the Court continued, "We are not without judicial interpretation... of the meaning of this clause. And it is sufficient to say that under no construction of that provision that we have ever seen, or any that we deem admissible, can the restraint imposed by the State of Louisiana upon the exercise of their trade by the butchers of New Orleans be held to be a deprivation of property within the meaning of that provision."[2]

With this language the Court established a precedent that the Fourteenth Amendment will not protect property rights violations except for those by the federal government. For deprivations by the individual states the litigant would have to look to the particular state constitution or state statute. In other words, the Fourteenth Amendment would not be applied to the states for such due process claims.

Four years later, in *Munn v. Illinois*[3] the Court again refused to interpret the due process clause as invalidating state legislation. In *Munn* the primary issue was a statute that regulated the rates charged for the transportation and warehousing of grain. The Court rejected arguments that the legislation effected an unconstitutional deprivation of property by preventing the owner from earning a reasonable compensation for its use and by transferring to the public an interest in a private enterprise.

Writing for the Court, Chief Justice Waite emphasized that "the great office of statutes is to remedy defects in the common law as they are developed.... We know that this power [of rate regulation] may be abused; but that is no argument against its existence. For protection against abuses by legislatures the people must resort to the polls, not to the courts."

The Court continued this trend into the last decade of the nineteenth century. In later cases, however, the Justices gave fair warning that there may be a modification of their views. After noting that the due process clause, by reason of its operation upon "all the powers of government, legislative as well as executive and judicial," could not be appraised solely in terms of the "sanction of settled usage," Justice Mathews, speaking for the Court in *Hurtado v. California*,[4] declared that:

> [a]rbitrary power, enforcing its edicts to the injury of the persons and property of its subjects, is not law, whether manifested as the decree of a personal monarch or of an impersonal multitude. And the limitations imposed by our constitutional law upon the action of the governments, both state and national, are essential to the preservation of public and private rights, notwithstanding the representative character of our political institutions. The enforcement of these limitations by judicial process is the device of self-governing communities to protect the rights of individuals and minorities, as well against the power of numbers, as against the violence of public agents transcending the limits of lawful authority, even when acting in the name and wielding the force of the government.

This declaration effectively put the states on notice that every species of state legislation, whether dealing with procedural or substantive rights, was subject to the scrutiny of the Court when the question of its essential justice was raised.

Industrial expansion, and the remedial social legislation created by states in its wake, led to an increasing number of cases being filed which sought application of the Fourteenth Amendment protections. At the same time, the added emphasis on the due process clause afforded the Court an opportunity to compensate for its earlier virtual nullification of the privileges and immunities clause of the Fourteenth Amendment.

As the Court moved toward an expansion of the protections there was first a need to justify such actions. Theories concerning the relation of government to private rights were available to demonstrate the impropriety of leaving to the state legislatures the same ample range of police power they had enjoyed prior to the Civil War. As these theories were accepted and expanded in the early days of the new growth era the Court turned to the task of overruling the *Slaughter-House Cases* and *Munn v. Illinois*.

The task of overturning these cases took almost 20 years to complete. The first task was to modify the restricted view of the police power advanced by Justice Field in his dissent in *Munn v. Illinois*.[5] This occurred in *Mugler v. Kansas*,[6] where the power was defined as embracing no more than the power to promote public health, morals, and safety. During the same interval, ideas embodying the social compact and natural rights, which had been espoused by Justice Bradley in his dissent in the

Slaughter-House Cases, had been transformed tentatively into constitutionally enforceable limitations upon government.[7]

Notwithstanding the historical controversy that has surrounded the amendment, the Court did extend the protections to individuals as well as corporations as "persons" under the amendment. Many argue that the term "persons" was used as a replacement for citizens and therefore does not include legal entities such as corporations. Others, however, argue that the wording was chosen specifically because it would include the legal fictions we know today as corporations. In either case, it appears today that corporations are equally protected under the amendment.[8]

II. POLICE POWER DEFINED AND LIMITED

The police power of a state today embraces regulations designed to promote the public convenience or the general prosperity as well as those to promote public safety, health, and morals. Police power is not confined to the suppression of what is offensive, disorderly, or unsanitary, but extends to what is for the greatest welfare of the state.[9]

The power of the government to regulate its citizens, both real and corporate, is a fundamental right of government, and is often considered to be one of the least limitable of the exercises of government. While the authority of the government to regulate its citizens through police power is a strong governmental right, it is not omniscient. That is, the power can be limited, and the first method for so doing is the requirement that it cannot be exercised in either an arbitrary nor oppressive manner.

The exercise of police power must bear a real and substantial relation to an end that is public, specifically, the public health, public safety, or public morals, or some other phase of the general welfare.[10] As a general rule, when the exercise of the police power of the government goes too far it is often considered to be a taking of property for which compensation must be paid.[11] This does not mean, however, that the exercise of police power that interferes with property rights, or outright takes property, will always be cause for action.[12] The Court has long held that the exercise of the police power will be upheld when such action is legitimate and serves a greater public good.

III. HEALTH, SAFETY, AND MORALS

Even under the narrowest concept of the police power as limited by substantive due process, it was generally conceded that states could exercise the power to protect the public health, safety, and morals.[13] One of the leading areas where this applies is in safety issues such as fire, occupancy, and building codes.[14] The power has also been upheld when it comes to regulating certain industries such as food preparation, logging, transportation, and alcohol manufacture.

One area in which the power has not been fully applied is the regulation of morality, but there are some exceptions. For example, the Court continues to uphold laws that restrict or exclude the acts of prostitution,[15] gambling, and, in some instances, lotteries.[16] It does appear, however, that lotteries are gaining popularity as a revenue-raising device, and many states are legalizing games of chance.

The Court has also long held the regulation of alcohol consumption as a valid exercise of police power. "[O]n account of their well-known noxious qualities and the extraordinary evils shown by experience to be consequent upon their use, a State...[is competent] to prohibit [absolutely the] manufacture, gift, purchase, sale, or transportation of intoxicating liquors within its borders...."[17]

While one amendment of the Constitution effectively abolishes a national prohibition against alcohol, there is little to prevent a state — or, for that matter, a lesser governmental entity — from prohibiting liquor or tightly controlling it. Several states, including Kansas, still have "dry" counties in which the sale of alcohol is prohibited altogether or limited to specific hours and manners.

Criminal justice professionals are also likely to encounter an exercise of this police power when dealing with motor vehicle laws. It is well established that the highways of a state are public property. While the primary and preferred use of the highways is for private purposes, such as travel by families and transportation of goods between business entities, their uses for purposes of gain generally may be prohibited by the legislature on conditions as it sees fit.[18]

One area where this power is exercised is in the regulation of commercial driver's license. The "commerce clause" of the Constitution allows the federal government to control interstate trucking and transportation, but the states retain the power to regulate intrastate transportation. A state may reasonably regulate licensing and service over certain routes. Likewise, a state may require drivers and operators to meet other standards under their authority through the police power.[19]

ENDNOTES

1. 83 U.S. (16 Wall.) 36 (1873).
2. 83 U.S. (16 Wall.) 36, 80–81 (1873).
3. 94 U.S. 113 (1877).
4. 110 U.S. 516, 528, 532, 536 (1884).
5. 94 U.S. 113, 141–48 (1877).
6. 123 U.S. 623, 661 (1887).
7. Loan Association v. Topeka, 87 U.S. (20 Wall.) 655, 662 (1875).
8. Smyth v. Ames, 169 U.S. 466, 522, 526 (1898); Kentucky Co. v. Paramount Exch., 262 U.S. 544, 550 (1923); Liggett Co. v. Baldridge, 278 U.S. (1928).
9. See Gibbons v. Ogden, 22 U.S. (9 Wheat.) 1, 202 (1824); California Reduction Co. v. Sanitary Works, 199 U.S. 306, 318 (1905); Bacon v. Walker, 204 U.S. 311 (1907); Schmidinger v. Chicago, 226 U.S. 578 (1913); Sligh v. Kirkwood, 237 U.S. 52, 58–59 (1915); Nebbia v. New York, 291 U.S. 502 (1934); Nashville, C. & St. L. Ry. v. Walters, 294 U.S. 405 (1935); Penn Central Transp. Co. v. City of New York, 438 U.S. 104 (1978); City of New Orleans v. Dukes, 427 U.S. 297 (1976); Young v. American Mini Theatres, 427 U.S. 50 (1976).
10. Liggett Co. v. Baldridge, 278 U.S. 105, 111–12 (1928); Treigle v. Acme Homestead Ass'n, 297 U.S. 189, 197 (1936).
11. Penn Central Transp. Co. v. City of New York, 438 U.S. 104 (1978); Agins v. City of Tiburon, 447 U.S. 255 (1980).

12. New Orleans Public Service v. New Orleans, 281 U.S. 682, 687 (1930).
13. Mugler v. Kansas, 123 U.S. 623, 661 (1887).
14. See Pierce Oil Corp. v. Hope, 248 U.S. 498 (1919) (storage of gasoline in improper manner); Standard Oil Co. v. Marysville, 279 U.S. 582 (1929); Barbier v. Connolly, 113 U.S. 27 (1885); Soon Hing v. Crowley, 113 U.S. 703 (1885).
15. Ah Sin v. Wittman, 198 U.S. 500 (1905).
16. Marvin v. Trout, 199 U.S. 212 (1905) (gambling); Stone v. Mississippi, 101 U.S. 814 (1880); Douglas v. Kentucky, 168 U.S. 488 (1897) (lottery).
17. Beer Co. v. Massachusetts, 97 U.S. 25, 33 (1878); Mugler v. Kansas, 123 U.S. 623 (1887); Kidd v. Pearson, 128 U.S. 1 (1888); Purity Extract Co. v. Lynch, 226 U.S. 192 (1912); Clark Distilling Co. v. Western Md. Ry., 242 U.S. 311 (1917); Barbour v. Georgia, 249 U.S. 454 (1919).
18. Stephenson v. Binford, 287 U.S. 251 (1932).
19. Stanley v. Public Utilities Comm'n, 295 U.S. 76 (1935).

29 Procedural Due Process

I. INTRODUCTION

Procedural due process is the means by which an accused exercises his or her rights of confrontation, to present witnesses, to be represented by counsel, and related rights. At its heart is the fundamental right of notice and an opportunity to be heard. Traditionally, these rights were enforced at the federal level through the Bill of Rights or Congressional mandate. At the state level, these rights — prior to the Fourteenth Amendment — were enforced through state constitution or state legislative mandate.

With the ratification of the Fourteenth Amendment and eventual application by the Supreme Court, the rights of an accused gained a new tool for enforcement. From the beginning, however, the Supreme Court was hesitant to establish strict guidelines. Instead, the Court took a case-by-case approach, and in each case asked the principal question of whether the practice in question violated "a fundamental principle of liberty and justice which inheres in the very idea of a free government and is the inalienable right of a citizen of such government."[1]

The Court in recent years has held that practically all the criminal procedural guarantees of the Bill of Rights — the Fourth, Fifth, Sixth, and Eighth Amendments — contain limitations that are fundamental to state criminal justice systems. The Court has also held that the absence of one or the other particular guarantee denies a suspect or a defendant due process of law.[2]

It is also important to remember that the due process clause of the Fourteenth Amendment is not limited to those specific guarantees spelled out in the Bill of Rights, but rather contains protection against practices and policies that may fall short of fundamental fairness without running afoul of a specific provision.[3]

II. THE ELEMENTS OF DUE PROCESS: DEFINITENESS

A fundamental requirement of the due process clause is that statutes establishing crimes or criminal procedure must be clearly written to allow "all citizens" an opportunity to read and understand them. "Legislation may run afoul of the Due Process Clause because it fails to give adequate guidance to those who would be law-abiding, to advise defendants of the nature of the offense with which they are charged, or to guide courts in trying those who are accused."[4]

The Court has held that statutes that establish criminal law must be defined with appropriate definiteness, and there must be ascertainable standards of guilt. "Men of common intelligence cannot be required to guess at the meaning of the enactment.

The vagueness may be from uncertainty in regard to persons within the scope of the act...or in regard to the applicable tests to ascertain guilt."[5]

Statutes which lack the requisite definiteness or specificity are commonly held unconstitutional on "void for vagueness" grounds. Such a statute may be pronounced wholly unconstitutional (unconstitutional "on its face"),[6] or it could be held unconstitutional as applied.[7] Statutes that are unconstitutional as applied are not merely scrapped, but the specific provisions of such a statute are often unavailable.

An example of such statutes arose in *Lanzetta v. New Jersey*,[8] where a New Jersey statute provided that "any person not engaged in any lawful occupation, known to be a member of any gang consisting of two or more persons, who had been convicted at least three times of being a disorderly person, or who had been convicted of any crime in that or any other State, is to be considered a gangster and subject to fine or imprisonment."

In striking down the statute the Court observed that in neither the common law nor any statute are the words "gang" and "gangster" given definite meaning. As such, enforcing agencies and courts were free to construe the terms broadly or narrowly, which meant, in practice, that the term could apply to almost anyone, as long as the officer rendered a broad enough definition.

Likewise, the phrase "known to be a member" was ambiguous, and interpreting officials, along with courts, gave great latitude in determining when someone was a "member" of any proscribed organization. Conceivably, a person who was a mere acquaintance of a known "gangster" could be held to be a gangster as well or could be included as a member of the gang with the slightest proof of membership being sufficient.

Because the statute was overly broad it was held void on its face. This did not mean that another statute, with more definite terms and applications, could not be created, but that this particular statute would not withstand constitutional scrutiny.

Vagrancy laws have been another area where the amendment has been applied. In *Papachristou v. City of Jacksonville*[9] a unanimous Court struck down for vagueness an ordinance that punished:

> dissolute persons who go about begging,...common night walkers,...common railers and brawlers, persons wandering or strolling around from place to place without any lawful purpose or object, habitual loafers,...persons neglecting all lawful business and habitually spending their time by frequenting house of ill fame, gaming houses, or places where alcoholic beverages are sold or served, persons able to work but habitually living upon the earnings of their wives or minor children....

The ordinance was invalid, maintained Justice Douglas for the Court, because it did not give fair notice, did not require specific intent to commit an unlawful act, permitted and encouraged arbitrary and erratic arrests and convictions, committed too much discretion to policemen, and criminalized activities which by modern standards are normally innocent.

Similarly, an ordinance making it a criminal offense for three or more persons to assemble on a sidewalk and conduct themselves in a manner annoying to passers-by was impermissibly vague because it encroached on the freedom of assembly found in the First Amendment.[10]

The Court has upheld other statutes, which on the surface appear to set the same standards. Such was the case in *Colten v. Kentucky*,[11] where a statute authorizing conviction for disorderly conduct of any person who refuses to move along upon police request and who is intent on causing inconvenience, annoyance, or alarm was upheld against facial challenge. The statute was applied to an individual accused of interfering with the police who ticketed a car for valid reasons.

In comparing the findings in *Colten* to those of *Lanzetta* and *Papachristou* we first notice that the three acts differ in the type of conduct they address. In *Colten* the conduct is narrowly defined so that only those dealing with police will be affected. In *Lanzetta* and *Papachristou*, however, the conduct is not well defined and allows police tremendous discretion. The same standards were applied in later cases.

In *Minnesota ex rel. Pearson v. Probate Court* the Court sustained as neither too vague nor indefinite a state law which provided for commitment of a psychopathic personality by probate action akin to a lunacy proceeding. The statute had been construed by the state court as applying to those persons who, by habitual course of misconduct in sexual matters, have evidenced utter lack of power to control their sexual impulses and are likely to inflict injury.[12] While the statute did not specifically define what sexual practices were to fall within the law, the law was clear enough to withstand constitutional scrutiny.

In upholding the statute the Court looked at the underlying conditions — habitual course of misconduct in sexual matters and lack of power to control impulses and likelihood of attack on others — as the means of defining the conduct. In this sense the statute required evidence of past conduct pointing to probable consequences.

When dealing with issues of definiteness the Court will generally focus on the acts being proscribed as well as the means by which they are to be measured. Statutes that create criminal liability for vaguely defined conduct will generally fail constitutional scrutiny.

III. STATUTORY NOTICE

From a legal standpoint the doctrine of notice is conceptually related to the problem of definiteness. The issue focuses on the requisite notice a person must have in order to inform them that an act (or in some cases a failure to act) may create criminal liability.

Most of us have heard the legal maxim, "Ignorantia juris non excusat," or loosely translated, "Ignorance of the law is no excuse." Ordinarily, it can be said that ignorance affords no excuse and that everyone is presumed to know that certain things may not be done. Moreover, the subject matter or conduct may be sufficient to alert one that there are regulatory laws that must be observed.[13] While this principle certainly does apply, there also have been instances where the constitutional requirements for due process have allowed the Court to set aside a statutory scheme where notice is lacking.

In *Lambert v. California*[14] the Court invalidated a municipal code that made it a crime for anyone who had ever been convicted of a felony to remain in the city for more than five days without registering. Emphasizing that the act of being in the city was not itself blameworthy, the Court held that the failure to register was quite "unlike the commission of acts, or the failure to act under circumstances that should alert the doer to the consequences of his deed."

In explaining its decision the Court stated that "Where a person did not know of the duty to register and where there was no proof of the probability of such knowledge, he may not be convicted consistently with due process." The Court likened such an ordinance to the writing of the law in such fine print that no naked eye could read it, or where criminal laws were written in a foreign language so that no natural born citizen could read them.[15]

From a practical standpoint, it is clear that any criminal law must be written in such fashion that a reasonable person will be able to discern from the statute the acts to be avoided. Likewise, under the notice requirements, acts a reasonable person would normally avoid, or those which — by the nature of the acts themselves — would likely be criminal, are not subject to the notice review. Acts which create unique or peculiar criminal liability, however, will be held to the high standard of notice.

IV. ENTRAPMENT

Some criminal acts are difficult to detect or for police to investigate. Prostitution, illegal drug transactions, and fencing of stolen property are among the crimes that fall into this category. Persons conducting these criminal endeavors rarely do so in the light of day or conduct their actions under public scrutiny. Secrecy is a valued commodity, and as such creates a barrier to effective police investigation and action.

Some of that difficulty may be alleviated through electronic and other surveillance techniques, which are covered by the search and seizure provisions of the Fourth Amendment. Police informants and agents may also help police investigate crimes. Sometimes, however, police agents may "encourage" persons to engage in criminal behavior in order to move an investigation along to the arrest and prosecution phase. Where such conduct, either by police or their agents, pushes a person into committing an act they may not normally do then the police may be guilty of entrapment.

The defense of entrapment is not a new defense, nor is it used only in the legal sense. As most parents know, the "he made me do it" defense is quite common among siblings. This defense becomes a concern for the criminal justice professional when it reaches the level where an otherwise "innocent" person may be convicted.

To understand entrapment, it is important that we first establish that there are few clear-cut guidelines for determining when entrapment has occurred. There are no bright line methods for measuring when conduct has gone too far. The Court has long recognized, however, that legislatures do not intend to punish conduct induced by police.[16]

The most common judicial method for determing when entrapment has occured, known as the "subjective approach," requires a two-pronged analysis. First, the question is asked whether the offense was induced by a government agent. Second, if the government has induced the defendant to break the law, "the prosecution must prove beyond reasonable doubt that the defendant was disposed to commit the criminal act prior to first being approached by Government agents."[17]

If the defendant can be shown to have been ready and willing to commit the crime whenever the opportunity presented itself, the defense of entrapment is unavailing, no matter the degree of inducement.[18] On the other hand, "[w]hen the Government's quest for conviction leads to the apprehension of an otherwise law-abiding citizen who, if left to his own devices, likely would never run afoul of the law, the courts should intervene."[19]

A different approach advocated in the past, known as the "objective approach," was traditionally rejected by the Supreme Court — but not all state courts. The objective approach disregards the defendant's predisposition and looks to the inducements used by government agents. The central issue focuses on whether the government employed means of persuasion or inducement creating a substantial risk that the person tempted will engage in the conduct. The higher the inducements needed to create the act the more likely the defense will apply.[20]

Supporters of the "objective approach" argue that by setting clear standards there will be little need for continuing appeals based on entrapment defenses. Proponents have proposed statutes to Congress and many of the individual state courts. The idea is that the government may inquire about a criminal act without invoking the defense of entrapment, and when their efforts reach a high enough level then the defense would come into play. By giving law enforcement a clear guideline on what conduct will be accepted we can cut down on potential abuses and long-term appeals that fill the courts.

Entrapment defenses are most commonly found in narcotics cases where a police officer, or an agent working for police, sets up a drug buy or delivery. The defense has also been used in "sting" operations where stolen property, state secrets, and other valuables are exchanged. Public corruption cases are also popular cases for this defense. Government officials who take bribes or other forms of corruption often claim that it was only the entrapment of overzealous government agents that led to their eventual criminal conduct.[21]

V. CRIMINAL IDENTIFICATION PROCESS

In the earlier sections examining the Fourth and Fifth Amendments we discussed the use of various identification processes used to identify perpetrators of crimes. Tactics such as police lineups, showups, photographic displays, and the like raise not only questions under those amendments but may also raise due process problems. In most of these cases the primary emphasis is on what right the defendant has to be present or to control the process. Other questions focus on admissibility of the "evidence" obtained in these procedures.

The Court addressed the question of the admissibility of an in-court identification or of testimony about an out-of-court identification in *Neil v. Biggers*[22] and *Manson v. Brathwaite*.[23] The Court said that the question is whether there is "a very substantial likelihood of misidentification," and that the issue must be determined "on the totality of the circumstances."

The factors to be considered in evaluating the likelihood of misidentification include the opportunity of the witness to view the suspect at the time of the crime, the witness' degree of attention, the accuracy of the witness' prior description of the suspect, the level of certainty demonstrated by the witness at the confrontation, and the length of time between the crime and the confrontation.[24]

"Suggestive confrontations are disapproved because they increase the likelihood of misidentification, and unnecessarily suggestive ones are condemned for the further reason that the increased chance of misidentification is gratuitous."[25]

The central issue is overall fairness to both the government and the accused. On the one hand the Court recognizes that police must rely on out-of-court identifications to solve many crimes. These identifications, while often questionable by their nature, are an integral part of the overall system, and to exclude them would effectively bind the hands of police. To protect the basic due process rights of an accused, however, the Court has struggled to balance the due process protections with the needs of society.

VI. INITIATION OF THE PROSECUTION

We saw in Section Five on the Fifth Amendment that an indictment is the preferred method of presenting criminal charges against an accused. This does not mean that it is the only method by which charges can be brought.

Simply stated, indictment by a grand jury is not a requirement of due process. A State may proceed instead by what we commonly refer to as "information."[26] Due process only requires that a defendant be given adequate notice of the offense charged against him or her and for which he or she is to be tried.[27] Where, of course, a grand jury is utilized, it must be fairly constituted and free from prejudicial influences.[28]

VII. FAIR TRIAL

The Fourteenth Amendment makes the provisions of the Bill of Rights applicable to the States. This means that the most basic protections of the first eight amendments — fair trial, right to counsel, right to speedy and public trial, right to be free from use of unlawfully seized evidence and unlawfully obtained confessions, etc. — now apply equally to the federal government as well as all states, but this does not exhaust the requirements of fairness.

"Due process of law requires that the proceedings shall be fair, but fairness is a relative, not an absolute concept.... What is fair in one set of circumstances may be an act of tyranny in others."[29] Conversely, "as applied to a criminal trial, denial of due process is the failure to observe that fundamental fairness essential to the very concept of justice. In order to declare a denial of it...[the Court] must find that the absence of that fairness fatally infected the trial; the acts complained of must be of such quality as necessarily prevents a fair trial."[30]

The Fourteenth Amendment means that bias or prejudice either inherent in the structure of the trial system or as imposed by external events will deny one's right to a fair trial. Such bias may include the payment of a judge from the proceeds collected as fines[31] or by other external influences that may taint the trial itself.

Due process is also violated by the participation of a biased or otherwise partial juror. Jurors who are exposed to undue influence by the parties, relatives, or even external sources may taint a trial so as to deny the accused of the basic right of fairness. This may include the exposure of potential jurors to biased or critical media coverage of an event, and may even extend to local "gossip" or innuendo within a particular community.

Some of the more interesting cases involving such outside influences include cases where "mob domination" of a trial or matters surrounding a trial swayed jurors. Such action will "rob the jury" of its judgment on the evidence presented, and is a classic due process violation.[32]

VIII. GUILTY PLEAS

Due process considerations also extend to the act of pleading guilty. Part of the reason for this is to ensure that the government will not create a system that encourages guilty pleas at the risk of losing the right to a fair trial. In understanding this we must first understand the many reasons a person may wish to plead guilty rather than face trial.

The most obvious reason a person may plead guilty is the desire to "do what's right." In our system, however, the confession of one's guilt is only a small part of the overall process in criminal justice. Once one is convicted, either by trial or by confession, there remains an issue of punishment. Punishment in this country can be as mild as a small monetary fine but it may also be the ultimate in retribution by way of the death penalty. The government thus bears a strong burden to provide not only a means for detecting and prosecuting the guilty, but also to provide for only the punishment that fits the crime.

There are a number of different reasons why a defendant may be willing to plead guilty. The most common is the case where the prosecution has an overwhelming amount of evidence against the defendant, but this is not the only reason. It may be because the evidence leaves the outcome in doubt. In other words, there may not be an overwhelming amount of evidence pointing to guilt, but there may be enough that a defendant simply does not wish to take a chance at being convicted of a higher crime.

Likewise, a criminal defendant may wish to secure some tactical or legal advantage offered only through a plea of guilty. The most common of these is the case which is "plea bargained." In this sense the defendant, usually through his or her attorney, agrees to plead guilty if promised the chance to plead to a lesser offense or to control the severity of punishment to be imposed.

The most fundamental of the due process rights affects this ability to plea bargain. It is the principle that the government may not structure its system so as to coerce a guilty plea.[33] A guilty plea must be entered voluntarily, knowingly, and understandingly, even to obtain an advantage, and is sufficient to overcome constitutional objections only when it meets these guildelines.[34]

It is not impermissible for a prosecutor during plea bargains to structure the bargain so that it is advantageous to the state. Remember, the prosecutor must represent the interest of the people, and it is the defendant and the defendant's attorney who must worry about the defendant's best interest. In this sense, a prosecutor is not required to plea bargain — i.e., failure to plea bargain is not a violation of due process. As such, a prosecutor may put a defendant to a hard choice, requiring the defendant to forego the right to go to trial in return for escaping what is likely to be a much more severe penalty if he or she does elect to go to trial.[35]

The court must inquire whether the defendant is pleading voluntarily, knowingly, and understandingly,[36] and "the adjudicative element inherent in accepting a plea of guilty must be attended by safeguards to ensure the defendant what is reasonably due in the circumstances."[37] Those circumstances will vary, but a constant factor is that when a plea rests in any significant degree on a promise or agreement of the prosecutor, so that it can be said to be part of the inducement or consideration, such promise must be fulfilled.

IX. PROSECUTORIAL MISCONDUCT

The concept of due process extends beyond the written law or procedure of a given court. An underlying principle of due process is the expectation that the government will act in a proper manner. When the government, normally represented by a prosecutor, acts outside established guidelines, such actions may constitute a denial of due process.

An example of this can be found when a prosecutor presents testimony which the prosecutor knows to be biased or to have been perjured.[38]

The Court extended this principle in *Miller v. Pate*,[39] when the prosecution represented to the jury that a pair of men's shorts found near the scene of a sex attack belonged to the defendant and that they were stained with blood. The defendant showed in a habeas corpus proceeding that no evidence connected him with the shorts and furthermore that the shorts were not in fact bloodstained. The defendant further showed that the prosecution had known these facts but had apparently misrepresented the evidence to the jury.

Due process is also denied by prosecutor misconduct when evidence is suppressed that may be favorable to the defendant. In *Brady v. Maryland*[40] the Court held "that the suppression by the prosecution of evidence favorable to an accused upon request violates due process where the evidence is material either to guilt or to punishment, irrespective of the good faith or bad faith of the prosecution."

In *Brady* the prosecution suppressed an extrajudicial confession of defendant's accomplice that he had actually committed the murder. While the accomplice's confession likely would not have affected the jury's decision on guilt, it might have affected it as to the question of punishment. Because some part of the trial, if not a greater part, was tainted by the conduct of the prosecutor the whole conviction was overturned.

Today, many states have "discovery" statutes in place that allow a defendant access to material in the possession of the government. Even where such statutes do not require submission of this type of material, however, the Court has held the state to a standard of disclosure where a failure to disclose would result in some deprivation of due process.

In *United States v. Agurs*[41] the Court summarized and somewhat expanded the prosecutor's obligation to disclose to the defense exculpatory evidence in his possession, even in the absence of a request, or upon a general request, by defendant. The obligation is expressed in a tripartite test of materiality of the exculpatory evidence in the context of the trial record. First, if the prosecutor knew or should have known that testimony given to the trial was perjured, the conviction must be set aside if there is any reasonable likelihood that the false testimony could have affected the judgment of the jury.

Second, if the defense specifically requested certain evidence and the prosecutor withheld it, the conviction must be set aside. There has been some debate as to whether the evidence withheld had to be material or even effective, but in most instances it is agreed that if the suppressed evidence might have affected the outcome of the trial then the act of suppressing it was improper.

Third, if the defense did not make a request at all, or simply asked for "all *Brady* material" or for "anything exculpatory," a duty resides in the prosecution to reveal to the defense obviously exculpatory evidence. The *Agurs* holding provides that if the prosecutor does not reveal such material then a reversal of conviction may be required.

Later cases suggest that dismissal is not required and should be considered only if the undisclosed evidence creates a reasonable doubt as to the defendant's guilt. The *Agurs* materiality standard is met only by evidence that "possess[es] an exculpatory value... apparent before [it] was destroyed, and also [is] of such a nature that the defendant would be unable to obtain comparable evidence by other reasonably available means."[42]

One tactic employed by prosecutors — which has been attacked vehemently but found to be proper — is the use of "threats" to seek a higher penalty upon conviction in order to obtain a guilty plea or some other action that will lessen the trial burden. For example, a prosecutor may agree to recommend a lighter sentence if the defendant is convicted provided the defendant surrender his right to a jury trial. If the defendant refuses to surrender such right the prosecutor is not required to recommend the lesser punishment, but may instead argue for — and successfully implement — the maximum punishment allowed under the law.[43]

On the other hand, a prosecutor does deny due process if he penalizes the assertion of a right or privilege by the defendant exercised outside the plea negotiation. The distinction lies in whether the acts of the prosecutor come in conjunction with the plea bargain or whether the acts are made to punish the offender for merely exercising a right. For many, this distinction is too fine a line, but it appears to be one to which the Court is committed.

X. SENTENCING

Due process also protects those who have pleaded guilty or been found guilty after trial and during a sentencing phase. Judicial misconduct mistakes may trigger the protections of the Fourteenth Amendment. For example, in *Townsend v. Burke*[44] the defendant was unrepresented and during sentencing the judge made several mistakes as to the defendant's prior criminal record. These items were used by the judge in handing down a sentence.

In correcting the matter the Supreme Court said that the defendant was denied due process. "[W]hile disadvantaged by lack of counsel, this prisoner was sentenced on the basis of assumptions concerning his criminal record which were materially untrue. Such a result, whether caused by carelessness or design, is inconsistent with due process of law, and such a conviction cannot stand."

In another case, *Williams v. New York*,[45] the Court upheld the imposition of the death penalty although the jury in convicting had recommended mercy. The judge chose to disregard the recommendation of the jury because he was privy to a presentence investigation report concerning the defendant and his past record, which the jury did not see.

The Court viewed as highly undesirable the restriction of judicial discretion in sentencing by requiring adherence to rules of evidence which would exclude highly relevant and informative material; similarly, disclosure of such information to the defense could well dry up sources that feared retribution or embarrassment. Hearsay and rumors would thus be considered and there would be no opportunity for rebuttal.

In *Specht v. Patterson*[46] the Court specifically reaffirmed Williams, but declined to apply it, finding that due process had been denied under circumstances significantly different from those of *Williams*. Specht had been convicted of taking indecent liberties, which carried a maximum sentence of ten years, but was sentenced under a sex offender statute to an indefinite term of one day to life.

The sex offender law, the Court observed, did not make the commission of the particular offense the basis for sentencing. Instead, by triggering a new hearing to determine whether the convicted person was a public threat, a habitual offender, or mentally ill, the law in effect constituted a new charge that must be accompanied by procedural safeguards.

Due process also requires that if counsel is to be provided a defendant it must be provided at all stages, even those "formal" stages that occur some time after conviction. For instance, where the defendant is convicted or pleads guilty, and sentencing is deferred until a later date, then the defendant must be provided an opportunity to be represented by counsel even at the later phase.[47]

ENDNOTES

1. Twining v. New Jersey, 211 U.S. 78, 106 (1908).
2. Duncan v. Louisiana, 391 U.S. 145, 149 n.14 (1968).
3. In re Winship, 397 U.S. 358 (1970).
4. Musser v. Utah, 333 U.S. 95, 97 (1948).
5. Winters v. New York, 333 U.S. 507, 515–16 (1948).
6. Papachristou v. City of Jacksonville, 405 U.S. 156 (1972).
7. Village of Hoffman Estates v. The Flipside, 455 U.S. 489, 494–95 (1982).
8. 306 U.S. 451 (1939).
9. 405 U.S. 156 (1972).
10. Coates v. City of Cincinnati, 402 U.S. 611 (1971).
11. 407 U.S. 104 (1972).
12. Minnesota *ex rel.* Pearson v. Probate Court, 309 U.S. 270 (1940).
13. United States v. Freed, 401 U.S. 601 (1971).
14. 355 U.S. 225 (1957).
15. *Id.* at 228, 229–30.
16. Sorrells v. United States, 287 U.S. 435, 446–49 (1932).

17. Jacobson v. United States, 112 S. Ct. 1535, 1540 (1992).
18. Sherman v. United States, 356 U.S. 369, 376–78 (1958); Masciale v. United States, 356 U.S. 386, 388 (1958); United States v. Russell, 411 U.S. 423, 432–36 (1973); Hampton v. United States, 425 U.S. 484, 488–489 (1976).
19. Jacobson v. United States, 112 S. Ct. 1535, 1543 (1992).
20. Sorrells v. United States, 287 U.S. 435, 458–59 (1932) (separate opinion of Justice Roberts); Sherman v. United States, 356 U.S. 369, 383 (1958) (Justice Frankfurter concurring); United States v. Russell, 411 U.S. 423, 441 (1973) (Justice Stewart dissenting); Hampton v. United States, 425 U.S. 484, 496–97 (1976) (Justice Brennan dissenting).
21. See United States v. Kelly, 707 F.2d 1460 (D.C. Cir. 1983); United States v. Williams, 705 F.2d 603 (2d Cir. 1983); United States v. Jannotti, 673 F.2d 578 (3d Cir.), cert. denied, 457 U.S. 1106 (1982).
22. 409 U.S. 188, 196–201 (1972).
23. 432 U.S. 98, 114–17 (1977).
24. See Stovall v. Denno, 388 U.S. 293 (1967); Simmons v. United States, 390 U.S. 377 (1968); Foster v. California, 394 U.S. 440 (1969); Coleman v. Alabama, 399 U.S. 1 (1970).
25. Neil v. Biggers, 409 U.S. 188, 198 (1972).
26. Hurtado v. California, 110 U.S. 516 (1884).
27. Smith v. O'Grady, 312 U.S. 329 (1941).
28. Norris v. Alabama, 294 U.S. 587 (1935); Cassell v. Texas, 339 U.S. 282 (1950); Eubanks v. Louisiana, 356 U.S. 584 (1958); Hernandez v. Texas, 347 U.S. 475 (1954); Pierre v. Louisiana, 306 U.S. 354 (1939).
29. Snyder v. Massachusetts, 291 U.S. 97, 116, 117 (1934).
30. Lisenba v. California, 314 U.S. 219, 236 (1941).
31. Tumey v. Ohio, 273 U.S. 510 (1927).
32. Frank v. Mangum, 237 U.S. 309 (1915); Moore v. Dempsey, 261 U.S. 86 (1923).
33. United States v. Jackson, 390 U.S. 570 (1968).
34. North Carolina v. Alford, 400 U.S. 25 (1971); Parker v. North Carolina, 397 U.S. 790 (1970).
35. Bordenkircher v. Hayes, 434 U.S. 357 (1978).
36. Boykin v. Alabama, 395 U.S. 238 (1969).
37. Santobello v. New York, 404 U.S. 257, 262 (1971).
38. Mooney v. Holahan, 294 U.S. 103, 112 (1935).
39. 386 U.S. 1 (1967).
40. 373 U.S. 83, 87 (1963).
41. 427 U.S. 97 (1976).
42. California v. Trombetta, 467 U.S. 479, 489 (1984). See also Arizona v. Youngblood, 488 U.S. 51 (1988).
43. Bordenkircher v. Hayes, 434 U.S. 357 (1978); United States v. Goodwin, 457 U.S. 368 (1982).
44. 334 U.S. 736, 740–41 (1948).
45. 337 U.S. 241 (1949).
46. 386 U.S. 605 (1967).
47. Mempa v. Rhay, 389 U.S. 128 (1967).

Appendix A

The Constitution of the United States of America

We the People of the United States, in Order to form a more perfect Union, establish Justice, insure domestic Tranquillity, provide for the common defence, promote the general Welfare, and secure the Blessings of Liberty to ourselves and our Posterity, do ordain and establish this Constitution for the United States of America.

Article I

Section 1

All legislative Powers herein granted shall be vested in a Congress of the United States, which shall consist of a Senate and House of Representatives.

Section 2

The House of Representatives shall be composed of Members chosen every second Year by the People of the several States, and the Electors in each State shall have the Qualifications requisite for Electors of the most numerous Branch of the State Legislature.

No Person shall be a Representative who shall not have attained to the age of twenty five Years, and been seven Years a Citizen of the United States, and who shall not, when elected, be an Inhabitant of that State in which he shall be chosen.

Representatives and direct Taxes shall be apportioned among the several States which may be included within this Union, according to their respective Numbers, which shall be determined by adding to the whole Number of free Persons, including those bound to Service for a Term of Years, and excluding Indians not taxed, three fifths of all other Persons.

The actual Enumeration shall be made within three Years after the first Meeting of the Congress of the United States, and within every subsequent Term of ten Years, in such Manner as they shall by Law direct. The Number of Representatives shall not exceed one for every thirty Thousand, but each State shall have at Least one Representative; and until such enumeration shall be made, the State of New Hampshire shall be entitled to chuse three, Massachusetts eight, Rhode-Island and Providence Plantations one, Connecticut five, New-York six, New Jersey four, Pennsylvania eight, Delaware one, Maryland six, Virginia ten, North Carolina five, South Carolina five, and Georgia three.

When vacancies happen in the Representation from any State, the Executive Authority thereof shall issue Writs of Election to fill such Vacancies.

The House of Representatives shall chuse their Speaker and other Officers; and shall have the sole Power of Impeachment.

Section 3

The Senate of the United States shall be composed of two Senators from each State, chosen by the Legislature thereof, for six Years; and each Senator shall have one Vote.

Immediately after they shall be assembled in Consequence of the first Election, they shall be divided as equally as may be into three Classes. The Seats of the Senators of the first Class shall be vacated at the Expiration of the second Year, of the second Class at the Expiration of the fourth Year, and of the third Class at the Expiration of the sixth Year, so that one third may be chosen every second Year; and if Vacancies happen by Resignation, or otherwise, during the Recess of the Legislature of any State, the Executive thereof may make temporary Appointments until the next Meeting of the Legislature, which shall then fill such Vacancies.

No Person shall be a Senator who shall not have attained to the Age of thirty Years, and been nine Years a Citizen of the United States, and who shall not, when elected, be an Inhabitant of that State for which he shall be chosen.

The Vice President of the United States shall be President of the Senate but shall have no Vote, unless they be equally divided.

The Senate shall chuse their other Officers, and also a President pro tempore, in the Absence of the Vice President, or when he shall exercise the Office of President of the United States.

The Senate shall have the sole Power to try all Impeachments. When sitting for that Purpose, they shall be on Oath or Affirmation. When the President of the United States is tried the Chief Justice shall preside: And no Person shall be convicted without the Concurrence of two thirds of the Members present.

Judgment in Cases of Impeachment shall not extend further than to removal from Office, and disqualification to hold and enjoy any Office of honor, Trust or Profit under the United States: but the Party convicted shall nevertheless be liable and subject to Indictment, Trial, Judgment and Punishment, according to Law.

Section 4

The Times, Places and Manner of holding Elections for Senators and Representatives, shall be prescribed in each State by the Legislature thereof; but the Congress may at any time by Law make or alter such Regulations, except as to the Places of chusing Senators.

The Congress shall assemble at least once in every Year, and such Meeting shall be on the first Monday in December, unless they shall by Law appoint a different Day.

Section 5

Each House shall be the Judge of the Elections, Returns and Qualifications of its own Members, and a Majority of each shall constitute a Quorum to do Business; but a smaller Number may adjourn from day to day, and may be authorized to compel the Attendance of absent Members, in such Manner, and under such Penalties as each House may provide.

Each House may determine the Rules of its Proceedings, punish its Members for disorderly Behaviour, and, with the Concurrence of two thirds, expel a Member.

Each House shall keep a Journal of its Proceedings, and from time to time publish the same, excepting such Parts as may in their Judgment require Secrecy; and the Yeas and Nays of the Members of either House on any question shall, at the Desire of one fifth of those Present, be entered on the Journal.

Neither House, during the Session of Congress, shall, without the Consent of the other, adjourn for more than three days, nor to any other Place than that in which the two Houses shall be sitting.

Section 6

The Senators and Representatives shall receive a Compensation for their Services, to be ascertained by Law, and paid out of the Treasury of the United States. They shall in all Cases, except Treason, Felony and Breach of the Peace, be privileged from Arrest during their Attendance at the Session of their respective Houses, and in going to and returning from the same; and for any Speech or Debate in either House, they shall not be questioned in any other Place.

No Senator or Representative shall, during the Time for which he was elected, be appointed to any civil Office under the Authority of the United States, which shall have been created, or the Emoluments whereof shall have been encreased during such time; and no Person holding any Office under the United States, shall be a Member of either House during his Continuance in Office.

Section 7

All Bills for raising Revenue shall originate in the House of Representatives; but the Senate may propose or concur with amendments as on other Bills.

Every Bill which shall have passed the House of Representatives and the Senate, shall, before it become a law, be presented to the President of the United States: If he approve he shall sign it, but if not he shall return it, with his Objections to that House in which it shall have originated, who shall enter the Objections at large on their Journal, and proceed to reconsider it. If after such Reconsideration two thirds of that House shall agree to pass the Bill, it shall be sent, together with the Objections, to the other House, by which it shall likewise be reconsidered, and if approved by two thirds of that House, it shall become a Law. But in all such Cases the Votes of both Houses shall be determined by Yeas and Nays, and the Names of the Persons voting for and against the Bill shall be entered on the Journal of each House respectively. If any Bill shall not be returned by the President within ten Days (Sundays excepted) after it shall have been presented to him, the Same shall be a Law, in like Manner as if he had signed it, unless the Congress by their Adjournment prevent its Return, in which Case it shall not be a Law.

Every Order, Resolution, or Vote to which the Concurrence of the Senate and House of Representatives may be necessary (except on a question of Adjournment) shall be presented to the President of the United States; and before the Same shall take Effect, shall be approved by him, or being disapproved by him, shall be repassed by two thirds of the Senate and House of Representatives, according to the Rules and Limitations prescribed in the Case of a Bill.

Section 8

The Congress shall have Power To lay and collect Taxes, Duties, Imposts and Excises, to pay the Debts and provide for the common Defence and general Welfare of the United States; but all Duties, Imposts and Excises shall be uniform throughout the United States;

To borrow Money on the credit of the United States;

To regulate Commerce with foreign Nations, and among the several States, and with the Indian Tribes;

To establish an uniform Rule of Naturalization, and uniform Laws on the subject of Bankruptcies throughout the United States;

To coin Money, regulate the Value thereof, and of foreign Coin, and fix the Standard of Weights and Measures;

To provide for the Punishment of counterfeiting the Securities and current Coin of the United States;

To establish Post Offices and post Roads;

To promote the Progress of Science and useful Arts, by securing for limited Times to Authors and Inventors the exclusive Right to their respective Writings and Discoveries;

To constitute Tribunals inferior to the supreme Court;

To define and punish Piracies and Felonies committed on the high Seas, and Offences against the Law of Nations;

To declare War, grant Letters of Marque and Reprisal, and make Rules concerning Captures on Land and Water;

To raise and support Armies, but no Appropriation of Money to that Use shall be for a longer Term than two Years;

To provide and maintain a Navy;

To make Rules for the Government and Regulation of the land and naval Forces;

To provide for calling forth the Militia to execute the Laws of the Union, suppress Insurrections and repeal Invasions;

To provide for organizing, arming, and disciplining, the Militia, and for governing such Part of them as may be employed in the Service of the United States, reserving to the States respectively, the Appointment of the Officers, and the Authority of training the Militia according to the discipline prescribed by Congress;

To exercise exclusive Legislation in all Cases whatsoever, over such District (not exceeding ten Miles square) as may, by Cession of Particular States, and the Acceptance of Congress, become the Seat of the Government of the United States, and to exercise like Authority over all Places purchased by the Consent of the Legislature of the State in which the Same shall be, for the Erection of Forts, Magazines, Arsenals, dock-Yards and other needful Buildings; — And

To make all Laws which shall be necessary and proper for carrying into Execution the foregoing Powers and all other Powers vested by this Constitution in the Government of the United States, or in any Department or Officer thereof.

Section 9

The Migration or Importation of such Persons as any of the States now existing shall think proper to admit, shall not be prohibited by the Congress prior to the Year one thousand eight hundred and eight, but a Tax or duty may be imposed on such Importation, not exceeding ten dollars for each Person.

The Privilege of the Writ of Habeas Corpus shall not be suspended, unless when in Cases or Rebellion or Invasion the public Safety may require it.

No Bill of Attainder or ex post facto Law shall be passed.

No Capitation, or other direct, Tax shall be laid, unless in Proportion to the Census of Enumeration herein before directed to be taken.

No Tax or Duty shall be laid on Articles exported from any State.

No Preference shall be given by any Regulation of Commerce or Revenue to the Ports of one State over those of another: nor shall Vessels bound to, or from, one State, be obliged to enter, clear or pay Duties in another.

No Money shall be drawn from the Treasury, but in Consequence of Appropriations made by Law; and a regular Statement and Account of the Receipts and Expenditures of all public Money shall be published from time to time.

No Title of Nobility shall be granted by the United States: And no Person holding any Office of Profit or Trust under them, shall, without the Consent of the Congress, accept of any present, Emolument, Office, or Title, of any kind whatever, from any King, Prince or foreign State.

Section 10

No State shall enter into any Treaty, Alliance, or Confederation; grant Letters of Marque and Reprisal; coin Money; emit Bills of Credit; make any Thing but gold and silver Coin a Tender in Payment of Debts; pass any Bill of Attainder, ex post facto Law, or Law impairing the Obligation of Contracts, or grant any Title of Nobility.

No State shall, without the Consent of the Congress, lay any Imposts or Duties on Imports or Exports, except what may be absolutely necessary for executing it's inspection Laws: and the net Produce of all Duties and Imposts, laid by any State on Imports or Exports, shall be for the Use of the Treasury of the United States; and all such Laws shall be subject to the Revision and Controul of the Congress.

No State shall, without the Consent of Congress, lay any Duty of Tonnage, keep Troops, or Ships of War in time of Peace, enter into any Agreement or Compact with another State, or with a foreign Power, or engage in War, unless actually invaded, or in such imminent Danger as will not admit of delay.

Article II

Section 1

The executive Power shall be vested in a President of the United States of America. He shall hold his Office during the Term of four Years, and, together with the Vice President, chosen for the same Term, be elected, as follows:

Each State shall appoint, in such Manner as the Legislature thereof may direct, a Number of Electors, equal to the whole Number of Senators and Representatives to which the State may be entitled in the Congress: but no Senator or Representative, or Person holding an Office of Trust or Profit under the United States, shall be appointed an Elector.

The Electors shall meet in their respective States, and vote by Ballot for two Persons, of whom one at least shall not be an Inhabitant of the same State with themselves. And they shall make a List of all the Persons voted for, and of the Number of Votes for each; which List they shall sign and certify, and transmit sealed to the Seat of the Government of the United States, directed to the President of the Senate. The President of the Senate shall, in the Presence of the Senate and House of Representatives, open all the Certificates, and the Votes shall then be counted. The Person having the greatest Number of Votes shall be the President, if such Number be a Majority of the whole Number of Electors appointed; and if there be more than one who have such Majority, and have an equal Number of Votes, then the House of Representatives shall immediately chuse by Ballot one of them for President; and if no Person have a Majority, then from the five highest on the List the said House shall in like Manner chuse the President. But in chusing the President, the Votes shall be taken by States, the Representatives from each State having one Vote; a quorum for this Purpose shall consist of a Member or Members from two thirds of the States, and a Majority of all the States shall be necessary to a Choice. In every Case, after the Choice of the President, the Person having the greatest Number of Votes of the Electors shall be the Vice President. But if there should remain two or more who have equal Votes, the Senate shall chuse from them by Ballot the Vice President.

The Congress may determine the Time of chusing the Electors, and the Day on which they shall give their Votes; which Day shall be the same throughout the United States.

No Person except a natural born Citizen, or a Citizen of the United States, at the time of the Adoption of this Constitution, shall be eligible to the Office of President; neither shall any person be eligible to that Office who shall not have attained to the Age of thirty five Years, and been fourteen Years a Resident within the United States.

In Case of the Removal of the President from Office, or of his Death, Resignation, or Inability to discharge the Powers and Duties of the said Office, the Same shall devolve on the Vice President, and the Congress may by Law provide for the Case of Removal, Death, Resignation or Inability, both of the President and Vice President, declaring what Officer shall then act as President, and such Officer shall act accordingly, until the Disability be removed, or a President shall be elected.

The President shall, at stated Times, receive for his Services, a Compensation, which shall neither be encreased nor diminished during the Period for which he shall have been elected, and he shall not receive within that Period any other Emolument from the United States, or any of them.

Before he enter on the Execution of his Office, he shall take the following Oath or Affirmation: — "I do solemnly swear (or affirm) that I will faithfully execute the Office of President of the United States, and will to the best of my Ability, preserve, protect and defend the Constitution of the United States."

Section 2

The President shall be Commander in Chief of the Army and Navy of the United States, and of the Militia of the several States, when called into the actual Service of the United States; he may require the Opinion, in writing, of the principal Officer in each of the executive Departments, upon any Subject relating to the Duties of their respective Offices, and he shall have Power to Grant Reprieves and Pardons for Offences against the United States, except in Cases of Impeachment.

He shall have Power, by and with the Advice and Consent of the Senate, to make Treaties, provided two thirds of the Senators present concur; and he shall nominate, and by and with the Advice and Consent of the Senate, shall appoint Ambassadors, other public Ministers and Consuls, Judges of the supreme Court, and all other Officers of the United States, whose Appointments are not herein otherwise provided for, and which shall be established by Law: but the Congress may by Law vest the Appointment of such inferior Officers, as they think proper, in the President alone, in the Courts of Law, or in the Heads of Departments.

The President shall have Power to fill up all Vacancies that may happen during the Recess of the Senate, by granting Commissions which shall expire at the End of their next Session.

Section 3

He shall from time to time give to the Congress Information on the State of the Union, and recommend to their Consideration such Measures as he shall judge necessary and expedient; he may, on extraordinary Occasions, convene both Houses, or either of them, and in Case of Disagreement between them, with Respect to the Time of Adjournment, he may adjourn them to such Time as he shall think proper; he shall receive Ambassadors and other public Ministers; he shall take Care that the Laws be faithfully executed, and shall Commission all the Officers of the United States.

Section 4

The President, Vice President and all Civil Officers of the United States, shall be removed from Office on Impeachment for and Conviction of, Treason, Bribery, or other high Crimes and Misdemeanors.

Article III

Section 1

The judicial Power of the United States, shall be vested in one supreme Court, and in such inferior Courts as the Congress may from time to time ordain and establish. The Judges, both of the supreme and inferior Courts, shall hold their Offices during good Behaviour, and shall, at stated Times, receive for their Services, a Compensation, which shall not be diminished during their Continuance in Office.

Section 2

The judicial Power shall extend to all Cases, in Law and Equity, arising under this Constitution, the Laws of the United States, and Treaties made, or which shall be made, under their Authority; — to all Cases affecting Ambassadors, other public ministers and Consuls; — to all Cases of admiralty and maritime Jurisdiction; — to Controversies to which the United States shall be a Party; — to Controversies between two or more States; — between a State and Citizens of another State; — between Citizens of different States; — between Citizens of the same State claiming Lands under Grants of different States, and between a State, or the Citizens thereof, and foreign States, Citizens or Subjects.

In all Cases affecting Ambassadors, other public Ministers and Consuls, and those in which a State shall be Party, the supreme Court shall have original Jurisdiction. In all the other Cases before mentioned, the supreme Court shall have appellate Jurisdiction, both as to Law and Fact, with such Exceptions, and under such Regulations as the Congress shall make.

The Trial of all Crimes, except in Cases of Impeachment, shall be by Jury; and such Trial shall be held in the State where the said Crimes shall have been committed; but when not committed within any State, the Trial shall be at such Place or Places as the Congress may by Law have directed.

Section 3

Treason against the United States, shall consist only in levying War against them, or in adhering to their Enemies, giving them Aid and Comfort. No Person shall be convicted of Treason unless on the Testimony of two Witnesses to the same overt Act, or on Confession in open Court.

The Congress shall have Power to declare the Punishment of Treason, but no Attainder of Treason shall work Corruption of Blood, or Forfeiture except during the Life of the Person attainted.

Article IV

Section 1

Full Faith and Credit shall be given in each State to the public Acts, Records, and judicial Proceedings of every other State. And the Congress may by general Laws prescribe the Manner in which such Acts, Records and Proceedings shall be proved, and the Effect thereof.

Section 2

The Citizens of each State shall be entitled to all Privileges and Immunities of Citizens in the several States.

A Person charged in any State with Treason, Felony, or other Crime, who shall flee from Justice, and be found in another State, shall on Demand of the executive Authority of the State from which he fled, be delivered up, to be removed to the State having Jurisdiction of the Crime.

No Person held to Service or Labour in one State, under the Laws thereof, escaping into another, shall, in Consequence of any Law or Regulation therein, be discharged from such Service or Labour, but shall be delivered up on Claim of the Party to whom such Service or Labour may be due.

Section 3

New States may be admitted by the Congress into this Union; but no new State shall be formed or erected within the Jurisdiction of any other State; nor any State be formed by the Junction of two or more States, or Parts of States, without the Consent of the Legislatures of the States concerned as well as of the Congress.

The Congress shall have Power to dispose of and make all needful Rules and Regulations respecting the Territory or other Property belonging to the United States; and nothing in this Constitution shall be so construed as to Prejudice any Claims of the United States, or of any particular State.

Section 4

The United States shall guarantee to every State in this Union a Republican Form of Government, and shall protect each of them against Invasion; and on Application of the Legislature, or of the Executive (when the Legislature cannot be convened) against domestic Violence.

Article V

The Congress, whenever two thirds of both Houses shall deem it necessary, shall propose Amendments to this Constitution, or, on the Application of the Legislatures of two thirds of the several States, shall call a Convention for proposing Amendments, which, in either Case, shall be valid to all Intents and Purposes, as Part of this Constitution, when ratified by the Legislatures of three fourths of the several States, or by Conventions in three fourths thereof, as the one or the other Mode of Ratification may be proposed by the Congress; Provided that no Amendment which may be made prior to the Year One thousand eight hundred and eight shall in any Manner affect the first and fourth Clauses in the Ninth Section of the first Article; and that no State, without its Consent, shall be deprived of its equal Suffrage in the Senate.

Article VI

All Debts contracted and Engagements entered into, before the Adoption of this Constitution, shall be as valid against the United States under this Constitution, as under the Confederation.

This Constitution, and the Laws of the United States which shall be made in Pursuance thereof; and all Treaties made, or which shall be made, under the Authority of the United States, shall be the supreme Law of the Land; and the Judges in every State shall be bound thereby, any Thing in the Constitution or Laws of any state to the Contrary notwithstanding.

The Senators and Representatives before mentioned, and the Members of the several State Legislatures, and all executive and judicial Officers, both of the United States and of the several States, shall be bound by Oath or Affirmation, to support this Constitution; but no religious Test shall ever be required as a Qualification to any Office or public Trust under the United States.

Article VII

The Ratification of the Conventions of nine States, shall be sufficient for the Establishment of this Constitution between the States so ratifying the same.

Appendix B

Amendments[1] to the Constitution of the United States of America[2]

Amendment I

Congress shall make no law respecting an establishment of religion, or prohibiting the free exercise thereof; or abridging the freedom of speech, or of the press; or the right of the people peaceably to assemble, and to petition the Government for a redress of grievances.

Amendment II

A well regulated Militia, being necessary to the security of a free State, the right of the people to keep and bear Arms, shall not be infringed.

Amendment III

No Soldier shall, in time of peace be quartered in any house, without the consent of the Owner, nor in time of war, but in a manner to be prescribed by law.

Amendment IV

The right of the people to be secure in their persons, houses, papers, and effects, against unreasonable searches and seizures, shall not be violated, and no Warrants shall issue, but upon probable cause, supported by Oath or affirmation, and particularly describing the place to be searched, and the persons or things to be seized.

Amendment V

No person shall be held to answer for a capital, or otherwise infamous crime, unless on a presentment or indictment of a Grand Jury, except in cases arising in the land or naval forces, or in the Militia, when in actual service in time of War or public danger; nor shall any person be subject for the same offence to be twice put in jeopardy of life or limb; nor shall be compelled in any criminal case to be a witness against himself, nor be deprived of life, liberty, or property, without due process of law; nor shall private property be taken for public use, without just compensation.

Amendment VI

In all criminal prosecutions, the accused shall enjoy the right to a speedy and public trial, by an impartial jury of the State and district wherein the crime shall have been committed, which district shall have been previously ascertained by law, and to be informed of the nature and cause of the accusation; to be confronted with the witnesses against him; to have compulsory process for obtaining witnesses in his favor, and to have the Assistance of Counsel for his defence.

Amendment VII

In Suits at common law, where the value in controversy shall exceed twenty dollars, the right of trial by jury shall be preserved, and no fact tried by a jury, shall be otherwise re-examined in any Court of the United States, than according to the rules of the common law.

Amendment VIII

Excessive bail shall not be required, nor excessive fines imposed, nor cruel and unusual punishments inflicted.

Amendment IX

The enumeration in the Constitution, of certain rights, shall not be construed to deny or disparage others retained by the people.

Amendment X

The powers not delegated to the United States by the Constitution, nor prohibited by it to the States, are reserved to the States respectively, or to the people.

Amendment XI

The Judicial power of the United States shall not be construed to extend to any suit in law or equity, commenced or prosecuted against one on the United States by Citizens of another State, or by Citizens or Subjects of any Foreign State.

Amendment XII

The Electors shall meet in their respective states and vote by ballot for President and Vice-President, one of whom, at least, shall not be an inhabitant of the same state with themselves; they shall name in their ballots the person voted for as President, and in distinct ballots the person voted for as Vice-President, and they shall make distinct lists of all persons voted for as President, and of all persons voted for as Vice-President, and of the number of votes for each, which lists they shall sign and certify, and transmit sealed to the seat of the government of the United States, directed to the President of the Senate; — The President of the Senate shall, in the presence of the Senate and House of Representatives, open all the certificates and the votes shall then be counted; — The person having the greatest Number of votes for President, shall be the President, if such number be a majority of the whole number of Electors appointed; and if no person have such majority, then from the persons having the highest numbers not exceeding three on the list of those voted for as President, the House of Representatives shall choose immediately, by ballot, the President. But in choosing the President, the votes shall be taken by states, the representation from each state having one vote; a quorum for this purpose shall consist of a member or members from two-thirds of the states, and a majority of all the states shall be necessary to a choice. And if the House of Representatives shall not choose a President whenever the right of choice shall devolve upon them, before the fourth day of March next following, then the Vice-President shall act as President, as in the case of the death or other constitutional disability of the President — The person having the greatest number of votes as Vice-President, shall be the Vice-President, if such number be a majority of the whole number of Electors appointed, and if no person have a majority, then from the two highest numbers on the list, the Senate shall choose the Vice-President; a quorum for the purpose shall consist of two-thirds of the whole number of Senators, and a majority of the whole number shall be necessary to a choice. But no person constitutionally ineligible to the office of President shall be eligible to that of Vice-President of the United States.

Amendment XIII

Section 1. Neither slavery nor involuntary servitude, except as a punishment for crime whereof the party shall have been duly convicted, shall exist within the United States, or any place subject to their jurisdiction.

Section 2. Congress shall have power to enforce this article by appropriate legislation.

Amendment XIV[3]

Section 1. All persons born or naturalized in the United States and subject to the jurisdiction thereof, are citizens of the United States and of the State wherein they reside. No State shall make or enforce any law which shall abridge the privileges or immunities of citizens of the United States; nor shall any State deprive any person of life, liberty, or property, without due process of law; nor deny to any person within its jurisdiction the equal protection of the laws.

Section 2. Representatives shall be apportioned among the several States according to their respective numbers, counting the whole number of persons in each State, excluding Indians not taxed. But when the right to vote at any election for the choice of electors for President and Vice President of the United States, Representatives in Congress, the Executive and Judicial officers of a State, or the members of the Legislature thereof, is denied to any of the male inhabitants of such State, being twenty-one years of age, and citizens of the United States, or in any way abridged, except for participation in rebellion, or other crime, the basis of representation therein shall be reduced in the proportion which the number of such male citizens shall bear to the whole number of male citizens twenty-one years of age in such State.

Section 3. No person shall be a Senator or Representative in Congress, or elector of President and Vice President, or hold any office, civil or military, under the United States, or under any State, who, having previously taken an oath, as a member of Congress, or as an officer of the United States, or as a member of any State legislature, or as an executive or judicial officer of any State, to support the Constitution of the United States, shall have engaged in insurrection or rebellion against the same, or given aid or comfort to the enemies thereof. But Congress may by a vote of two-thirds of each House, remove such disability.

Section 4. The validity of the public debt of the United States, authorized by law, including debts incurred for payment of pensions and bounties for services in suppressing insurrection or rebellion, shall not be questioned. But neither the United States nor any State shall assume or pay any debt or obligation incurred in aid of insurrection or rebellion against the United States, or any claim for the loss or emancipation of any slave; but all such debts, obligations and claims shall be held illegal and void.

Section 5. The Congress shall have power to enforce, by appropriate legislation, the provisions of this article.

Amendment XV

Section 1. The right of citizens of the United States to vote shall not be denied or abridged by the United States or by any State on account of race, color, or previous condition of servitude.

Section 2. The Congress shall have power to enforce this article by appropriate legislation.

Amendment XVI

The Congress shall have power to lay and collect taxes on incomes, from whatever source derived, without apportionment among the several States, and without regard to any census or enumeration.

Amendment XVII

The Senate of the United States shall be composed of two Senators from each State, elected by the people thereof, for six years; and each Senator shall have one vote. The electors in each State shall have the qualifications requisite for electors of the most numerous branch of the State legislatures.

When vacancies happen in the representation of any State in the Senate, the executive authority of such State shall issue writs of election to fill such vacancies: Provided, That the legislature of any State may empower the executive thereof to make temporary appointments until the people fill the vacancies by election as the legislature may direct.

This amendment shall not be so construed as to affect the election or term of any Senator chosen before it becomes valid as part of the Constitution.

Amendment XVIII

Section 1. After one year from the ratification of this article the manufacture, sale, or transportation of intoxicating liquors within, the importation thereof into, or the exportation thereof from the United States and all territory subject to the jurisdiction thereof for beverage purposes is hereby prohibited.

Section 2. The Congress and the several States shall have concurrent power to enforce this article by appropriate legislation.

Section 3. This article shall be inoperative unless it shall have been ratified as an amendment to the Constitution by the legislatures of the several States, as provided in the Constitution, within seven years from the date of the submission hereof to the States by the Congress.

Amendment XIX

The right of citizens of the United States to vote shall not be denied or abridged by the United States or by any State on account of sex. Congress shall have power to enforce this article by appropriate legislation.

Amendment XX

Section 1. The terms of the President and Vice President shall end at noon on the 20th day of January, and the terms of Senators and Representatives at noon on the 3d day of January, of the years in which such terms would have ended if this article had not been ratified; and the terms of their successors shall then begin.

Section 2. The Congress shall assemble at least once in every year, and such meeting shall begin at noon on the 3d day of January, unless they shall by law appoint a different day.

Section 3. If, at the time fixed for the beginning of the term of the President, the President elect shall have died, the Vice President elect shall become President. If a President shall not have been chosen before the time fixed for the beginning of his term, or if the President elect shall have failed to qualify, then the Vice President elect shall act as President until a President shall have qualified; and the Congress may by law provide for the case wherein neither a President elect nor a Vice President elect shall have qualified, declaring who shall then act as President, or the manner in which one who is to act shall be selected, and such person shall act accordingly until a President or Vice President shall have qualified.

Section 4. The Congress may by law provide for the case of the death of any of the persons from whom the House of Representatives may choose a President whenever the right of choice shall have devolved upon them, and for the case of the death of any of the persons from whom the Senate may choose a Vice President whenever the right of choice shall have devolved upon them.

Section 5. Sections 1 and 2 shall take effect on the 15th day of October following the ratification of this article.

Section 6. This article shall be inoperative unless it shall have been ratified as an amendment to the Constitution by the legislatures of three-fourths of the several States within seven years from the date of its submission.

Amendment XXI

Section 1. The eighteenth article of amendment to the Constitution of the United States is hereby repealed.

Section 2. The transportation or importation into any State, Territory, or possession of the United States for delivery or use therein of intoxicating liquors, in violation of the laws thereof, is hereby prohibited.

Section 3. This article shall be inoperative unless it shall have been ratified as an amendment to the Constitution by conventions in the several States, as provided in the Constitution, within seven years from the date of the submission hereof to the States by the Congress.

Amendment XXII

Section 1. No person shall be elected to the office of the President more than twice, and no person who has held the office of President, or acted as President, for more than two years of a term to which some other person was elected President shall be elected to the office of the President more than once. But this Article shall not apply to any person holding the office of President, when this Article was proposed by the Congress, and shall not prevent any person who may be holding the office of President, or acting as President, during the term within which this Article becomes operative from holding the office of President or acting as President during the remainder of such term.

Section 2. This article shall be inoperative unless it shall have been ratified as an amendment to the Constitution by the legislatures of three-fourths of the several States within seven years from the date of its submission to the States by the Congress.

Amendment XXIII

Section 1. The District constituting the seat of Government of the United States shall appoint in such manner as the Congress may direct: A number of electors of President and Vice President equal to the whole number of Senators and Representatives in Congress to which the District would be entitled if it were a State, but in no event more than the least populous State; they shall be in addition to those appointed by the States, but they shall be considered, for the purposes of the election of President and Vice President, to be electors appointed by a State; and they shall meet in the District and perform such duties as provided by the twelfth article of amendment.

Section 2. The Congress shall have power to enforce this article by appropriate legislation.

Amendment XXIV

Section 1. The right of citizens of the United States to vote in any primary or other election for President or Vice President, for electors for President or Vice President, or for Senator or Representative in Congress, shall not be denied or abridged by the United States or any State by reason of failure to pay any poll tax or other tax.

Section 2. The Congress shall have power to enforce this article by appropriate legislation.

Amendment XXV

Section 1. In case of the removal of the President from office or of his death or resignation, the Vice President shall become President.

Section 2. Whenever there is a vacancy in the office of the Vice President, the President shall nominate a Vice President who shall take office upon confirmation by a majority vote of both Houses of Congress.

Section 3. Whenever the President transmits to the President pro tempore of the Senate and the Speaker of the House of Representatives has written declaration that he is unable to discharge the powers and duties of his office, and until he transmits to them a written declaration to the contrary, such powers and duties shall be discharged by the Vice President as Acting President.

Section 4. Whenever the Vice President and a majority of either the principal officers of the executive departments or of such other body as Congress may by law provide, transmit to the President pro tempore of the Senate and the Speaker of the House of Representatives their written declaration that the President is unable to discharge the powers and duties of his office, the Vice President shall immediately assume the powers and duties of the office as Acting President.

Thereafter, when the President transmits to the President pro tempore of the Senate and the Speaker of the House of Representatives has written declaration that no inability exists, he shall resume the powers and duties of his office unless the Vice President and a majority of either the principal officers of the executive department or of such other body as Congress may by law provide, transmit within four days to the President pro tempore of the Senate and the Speaker of the House of Representatives their written declaration that the President is unable to discharge the powers and duties of his office. Thereupon Congress shall decide the issue, assembling within forty-eight hours for that purpose if not in session. If the Congress, within twenty-one days after receipt of the latter written declaration, or, if Congress is not in session, within twenty-one days after Congress is required to assemble, determines by two-thirds vote of both Houses that the President is unable to discharge the powers and duties of his office, the Vice President shall continue to discharge the same as Acting President; otherwise, the President shall resume the powers and duties of his office.

Amendment XXVI

Section 1. The right of citizens of the United States, who are eighteen years of age or older, to vote shall not be denied or abridged by the United States or by any State on account of age.

Section 2. The Congress shall have power to enforce this article by appropriate legislation.

Amendment XXVII

No law varying the compensation for the services of the Senators and Representatives shall take effect, until an election of Representatives shall have intervened.

ENDNOTES

1. The first ten amendments along with two others that were not ratified were proposed by Congress on September 25, 1789, when they passed the Senate, having previously passed the House on September 24 (1 Annals of Congress 88, 913). They appear officially in 1 Stat. 97. Ratification was completed on December 15, 1791, when the eleventh State (Virginia) approved these amendments, there being then 14 States in the Union.

2. The several state legislatures ratified the first ten amendments to the Constitution on the following dates: New Jersey, November 20, 1789; Maryland, December 19, 1789; North Carolina, December 22, 1789; South Carolina, January 19, 1790; New Hampshire, January 25, 1790; Delaware, January 28, 1790; New York, February 27, 1790; Pennsylvania, March 10, 1790; Rhode Island, June 7, 1790; Vermont, November 3, 1791; Virginia, December 15, 1791. The two amendments that then failed of ratification prescribed the ratio of representation to population in the House, and specified that no law varying the compensation of members of Congress should be effective until after an intervening election of Representatives. The first was ratified by ten States (one short of the requisite number) and the second, by six States; subsequently, this second proposal was taken up by the States in the period 1980–1992 and was proclaimed as ratified as of May 7, 1992. Connecticut, Georgia, and Massachusetts ratified the first ten amendments in 1939.

3. The several state legislatures ratified the Fourteenth Amendment on the following dates: Connecticut, June 30, 1866; New Hampshire, July 7, 1866; Tennessee, July 19, 1866; New Jersey, September 11, 1866 (the New Jersey Legislature on February 20, 1868 "withdrew" its consent to the ratification; the Governor vetoed that bill on March 5, 1868; and it was repassed over his veto on March 24, 1868); Oregon, September 19, 1866 (Oregon "withdrew" its consent on October 15, 1868); Vermont, October 30, 1866; New York, January 10, 1867; Ohio, January 11, 1867 (Ohio "withdrew" its consent on January 15, 1868); Illinois, January 15, 1867; West Virginia, January 16, 1867; Michigan, January 16, 1867; Kansas, January 17, 1867; Minnesota, January 17, 1867; Maine, January 19, 1867; Nevada, January 22, 1867; Indiana, January 23, 1867; Missouri, January 26, 1867 (date on which it was certified by the Missouri secretary of state); Rhode Island, February 7, 1867; Pennsylvania, February 12, 1867; Wisconsin, February 13, 1867 (actually passed February 7, but not signed by legislative officers until February 13); Massachusetts, March 20, 1867; Nebraska, June 15, 1867; Iowa, March 9, 1868; Arkansas, April 6, 1868; Florida, June 9, 1868; North Carolina, July 2, 1868 (after having rejected the amendment on December 13, 1866); Louisiana, July 9, 1868 (after having rejected the amendment on February 6, 1867); South Carolina, July 8, 1868 (after having rejected the amendment on December 20, 1866); Alabama, July 13, 1868 (date on which it was "approved" by the Governor); Georgia, July 21, 1868 (after having rejected the amendment on November 9, 1866 — Georgia ratified again on February 2, 1870); Virginia, October 8, 1869 (after having rejected the amendment on January 9, 1867); Mississippi, January 17, 1870;

Texas, February 18, 1870 (after having rejected the amendment on October 27, 1866); Delaware, February 12, 1901 (after having rejected the amendment on February 7, 1867). The amendment was rejected (and not subsequently ratified) by Kentucky on January 8, 1867. Maryland and California ratified this amendment in 1959.

Case Listing

A

Abington School Dist. v. Schempp, 59
Abrams v. United States, 85
Aguilar v. Texas, 117
Albertson v. SACB, 182
Almeida-Sanchez v. United States, 134
American Communications Ass'n v. Douds, 88
Arizona v. Washington, 167
Arkansas v. Sanders, 132
Ashe v. Swenson, 172

B

Baltimore Dep't of Social Services
    v. Bouknight, 183
Barefoot v. Estelle, 268
Batson v. Kentucky, 225
Bell v. Wolfish, 251
Benton v. Maryland, 164
Berger v. New York, 144
Berkemer v. McCarty, 195
Betts v. Brady, 236
Blockburger v. United States, 171
Boyd v. United States, 149
Boykin v. Alabama, 151
Brady v. Maryland, 294
Brewer v. Williams, 242
Brown v. Mississippi, 184
Brown v. Ohio, 171
Bruton v. United States, 230
Burks v. Unites States, 169

C

California v. Acevedo, 132
California v. Byers, 182
California v. Green, 231
California v. Hodari, 112
Carroll v. United States, 130
Castaneda v. Partida, 223
Chandler v. Fretag, 237
Chimel v. California, 129
Cohens v. Virginia, 47
Coker v. Georgia, 264
Coleman v. Alabama, 158, 240
Colten v. Kentucky, 289
Coolidge v. New Hampshire, 130
Coy v. Iowa, 232

D

De Jonge v. Oregon, 87
Dennis v. United States, 87
Douglas v. Alabama, 230
Draper v. United States, 117

E

Edmund v. Florida, 265
Edwards v. Arizona, 198
Employment Division v. Smith, 70
Entick v. Carrington, 99, 104
Escobedo v. Illinois, 192, 240
Estelle v. Smith, 196
Everson v. Board of Education, 58
Ex parte Andrews, 68
Ex parte Bollman, 42
Ex parte Newman, 68

F

Fiske v. Kansas, 79, 86
Florida v. Riley, 136
Ford v. Wainwright, 266
Furman v. Georgia, 260

G

Gideon v. Wainwright, 236
Gilbert v. California, 244
Gitlow v. New York, 85
Goldman v. United States, 144
Gori v. United States, 167
Grady v. Corbin, 172
Green v. United States, 169
Gregg v. Georgia, 262
Griffin v. Wisconsin, 138

H

Hague v. CIO, 95
Hamilton v. Alabama, 236, 240
Harmelin v. Michigan, 270
Harris v. New York, 199
Harris v. United States, 102
Herndon v. Lowry, 87
Hester v. United States, 135

Index